Monika Otter

The Oxford Book of
Medieval
English Verse

The
Oxford Book of
Medieval
English Verse

Chosen and Edited by
Celia and Kenneth Sisam

Oxford
At the Clarendon Press

Oxford University Press, Ely House, London W. 1

GLASGOW   NEW YORK   TORONTO   MELBOURNE   WELLINGTON
CAPE TOWN   IBADAN   NAIROBI   DAR ES SALAAM   LUSAKA   ADDIS ABABA
DELHI   BOMBAY   CALCUTTA   MADRAS   KARACHI   LAHORE   DACCA
KUALA LUMPUR   SINGAPORE   HONG KONG   TOKYO

ISBN 0 19 812135 0

Printed in Great Britain
at the University Press, Oxford
by Vivian Ridler
Printer to the University

PREFACE

THIS book spans the period from 1150 to 1500, here called 'medieval'. Far-reaching changes—in thought, social conditions, language, literary forms, and themes—distinguish the verse of medieval England from that of the Anglo-Saxons. They are associated with the intellectual movement of the twelfth century which led to the rise of the first European universities, at Paris, Salerno, Bologna, Montpellier, and Oxford. The reconquest of Spain and Sicily from the Saracens about the end of the eleventh century, the opening of trade routes to the Middle East, and the Crusades brought Western Europeans into contact with Islamic culture, and, through it, with the learning of ancient Greece, preserved by the Arabs but long unknown to Western Europe. Arabic books were turned into Latin, chiefly in Spain, where Toledo became a famous centre for translators. So, through Latin translations from Arabic, Western thought was suddenly revitalized by Aristotle's philosophy, Euclid's mathematics, Ptolemaic astronomy, the medical lore of Hippocrates, together with the scientific advances of the Arabs themselves in mathematics, astronomy, medicine, and alchemy (the origin of chemistry). The learning of Greece and Islam nourished scholarly inquiry into antiquity, history, law, philosophy, the natural world, and God who created it. Universities drew students and teachers from many nations. Enthusiasm for learning produced more literate men, more 'clerks', than the Church and administrative service could absorb. This was the age of the 'wandering scholars'. Some joined the ranks of the entertainers who flourished in this period, carrying tunes, songs, satirical verses, parodies, and stories of every kind wherever they could find an audience. New ideas sped from country to country.

The breadth and richness of the culture which the twelfth-century Renaissance spread through Western Europe is seen in the scholars and writers it produced: such as St. Bernard, Abelard, and St. Thomas Aquinas. From Britain itself came men of wide learning, like Bishop Grosseteste, student of philosophy, theology, and science; the philosophers Roger Bacon (noted for his scientific and mathematical studies), Duns Scotus, and William Ockham; John of Salisbury, a classical scholar, distinguished for his latinity; historians such as William of Malmesbury and Matthew Paris; the topographer Gerald of Wales and the lawyer Bracton. All these were ecclesiastics, writing in the language of the Church—Latin. It is against this intellectual background that the vernacular poetry of the period must be set. Chaucer, for instance, busy civil servant as he was for most of his life, shows a range of tastes and interests, scientific and literary, learned as well as popular, typical of the best medieval minds. Like all educated Englishmen he was at home with French literature, the *Roman de la Rose*, the romances, the fabliaux, and the lyric poetry. But he was also familiar with Latin and Italian writers, notably Ovid, Virgil, Statius, Boethius, Dante, Petrarch, Boccaccio. His debt to these and his command of learned and literary allusion show an acquaintance with books old and new which would, in any age, be remarkable. It is a measure of the freedom with which poetry and works of learning circulated among men of letters in fourteenth-century Europe.

From the earliest part of our period hardly any English verse survives. If anything of poetic value was composed between 1000 and 1150, it has been lost. Norman domination did not favour the transmission of English poetry, since until about the middle of the thirteenth century French, or rather the Anglo-Norman dialect which developed in England, was the preferred vernacular language of the literate classes. When English verse is again recorded, it is at first scanty—scraps like 'Canute at Ely' (no. 264) and St. Godrich's Hymn (no. 265). It is also changed.

Anglo-Saxon poets had worked in an isolated and archaic tradition which prescribed metre, mood, and subject. But medieval poets were free to avail themselves of the many different modes which came crowding in with the twelfth-century Renaissance. In place of the long, balanced alliterative line of Anglo-Saxon verse, they could choose from a diversity of metres: various forms of alliterative line—halting, perhaps, and irregular, like Layamon's (no. 1), but capable of impressive poetic power; rhymed couplets, short and long; and a great variety of stanzaic forms, some intended to be sung, others which were literary developments of song patterns. The Anglo-Saxon minstrel had told of death and desolation and grim revenge, of feuds in which, for the Christian, each fresh calamity underlined God's purpose to devastate the world till total destruction should end the millennium. The medieval poet did not share this belief in a dying world: his wider world was quickened by the traditions of many civilizations as they met and fertilized each other and sprang up new. History and legend—Celtic, English, French, Oriental, biblical, and classical—were recast and developed in medieval terms. King Arthur's barely

recorded historical acts grew in the hands of Geoffrey of
Monmouth into the greatest of medieval legends: Merlin,
Guinevere, the fairy land of Avalon, the Round Table and
the deeds of its famous knights all took literary shape in the
twelfth century. Charlemagne became the centre of another
famous cycle of romances. Alexander's campaigns opened
the way to the marvels of the East. Medieval accretions and
local colouring affected biblical and classical story: Pilate
could be turned into a 'riche Jew' and Judas's sister be
blamed for his betrayal (no. 30); St. Stephen was a 'clerk'
who carried the boar's head in King Herod's hall (no. 31).
Britain was linked to the Troy story by an eponymous
founder Brutus (descended from Aeneas), and his name, in
its Welsh form 'Brut', was given to chronicles of British
history. Orpheus became a British king, with faithful
steward, knights, and parliament; by his music he regained
Eurydice, stolen by King Pluto of Fairyland, and reigned
happily afterwards. A hero was expected to prosper in war
and in love, to live and enjoy his success. Zest for life and
an awareness of everything pleasurable around them lends
the poets of medieval England their freshness. The theme
of love, left almost unexplored in extant Anglo-Saxon
poetry, informs romance and lyric, divine as well as secular.
The God of vengeance whom the Anglo-Saxons followed
gives place to the Lover of the Song of Songs.

Form, subject, and spirit of medieval verse were changed.
But, as in earlier times, much of it still reached its public
orally. Manuscripts were scarce, often capriciously spelt,
carelessly copied, and ill punctuated; Middle English dia-
lects differed widely, and there was no standard literary
dialect such as West Saxon had been in the tenth and eleventh

centuries. Few could read. In all ranks of society, whether literate or not, it was customary for books to be read aloud. Criseyde, though she knew how to read, had 'The Siege of Thebes' read to her by a maid, presumably one with special skill. At Havelok's coronation professional entertainers regaled the public by 'romance-reding on the book'. Verse, courtly and popular, was written to be heard. Because it was easier to remember, it was the natural vehicle for matters to which prose now seems more appropriate: short and long stories, saints' lives, chronicles, meditations, and instruction of all kinds. Its diversity was immense, its quality uneven.

We have tried to show the range of interest offered by medieval verse rather than to select for poetic quality alone. Had Chaucer, Langland, Gower, and the *Pearl* poet been allotted their due space, they would have squeezed out nearly all the rest; besides they are accessible in good editions. From the Celtic-speaking parts of the British Isles comes curious verse: an Irishman adorns his satire (no. 62) with mocking inconsequences and self-congratulation; a Welshman's tavern song (no. 241) has English words cast in a Welsh metre. Scotland's most distinctive school of poets arose towards the end of our period and is more fully represented in *The Oxford Book of Scottish Verse*; but in earlier times the wars with England produced some pungent battle songs, not all of them from the English side (nos. 32a, 282). More space has been given to secular than to religious verse because, though less survives, the variety of secular verse is greater: here we find schoolboy, chorister, student, ploughman, farmer, servant-girl, juggler, friar, priest, knight, pilgrim, drunkard, the Man in the Moon, and Reynard the

Fox—most of them in trouble or in love. It is the practice of the series to exclude dramatic verse; but a fragmentary secular interlude (no. 27) has been admitted because of its kinship to lyrics like no. 52.

At the end of the main selection is a group of short 'snatches', mostly proverbs and scraps of lost songs, preserved because, in their day, they were memorable. Some were used to clinch an argument in debate or sermon; others were scribbled on a fly-leaf or margin by a reader whose mind was drifting or a scribe who needed to try his pen. A few short but apparently complete poems are included in this section, and occasional brief excerpts from longer poems. The snatches are numbered like the rest, but their titles are printed only in the Contents.

It is usual to arrange the pieces of an Oxford book of verse in the chronological order of their authors. In the medieval period this method will not serve: much of the poetry is anonymous, and the dates of author, work, and surviving manuscript are rarely known. Often the handwriting of the scribe responsible for the earliest extant manuscript is the surest evidence of date we possess; and handwriting cannot be dated closely. Even if the exact date of a manuscript is known, there may be no means of determining the interval between the original composition and the copy that survives: it could not be guessed from the dates of the two remaining manuscripts (1487 and 1489) that Barbour was writing *The Bruce* in 1375. Pieces known to be early will be found near the beginning of the main collection, late ones near its end. We have arranged them somewhat haphazardly, much as a medieval anthologist might have done. Poems from a single source—one author or one manuscript—will usually be found together. Beyond this no attempt has been made to group them. The juxtaposition of themes, profane and religious, trivial and profound, comic and grave, was natural to medieval minds.

A glance at the Textual Notes will show how much we owe to earlier collectors, especially Carleton Brown, R. L. Greene, and R. H. Robbins. Use has also been made of anthologies which, because they give texts in a partly normalized spelling, are not cited in the Textual Notes: particularly E. K. Chambers and F. Sidgwick, *Early English Lyrics* (London, 1907) and R. T. Davies, *Medieval English Lyrics* (London, 1963).

We are grateful for the help of librarians and their staff, especially those of the British Museum, the Bodleian, Cambridge University Library, the National Libraries of Scotland and Wales; and for permission to consult manuscripts in Lambeth Palace, Lincoln's Inn, the Guildhall, London, Chetham's Library, Manchester; the Cambridge college libraries of Clare, Corpus Christi, Gonville and Caius, Jesus, St. John's, Trinity; the Muniments of King's, the Pepys Library, Magdalene; the Oxford college libraries of Balliol, Merton, St. John's; the libraries of York Minster and the cathedrals of Canterbury, Durham, Lincoln, St. Paul's, and Worcester. The Provost and Fellows of Eton College kindly allowed a manuscript to be deposited in the Bodleian for our use. For photographs and permission to make use of them we are indebted to Trinity College, Dublin, the John Rylands Library, Manchester, Göttingen University Library, and Stiftung Preussischer Kulturbesitz, Staatsbibliothek, Berlin-Dahlem.

PREFACE

For help of various kinds we thank Mrs. D. M. Davin, Miss Anne Elliott, Professor I. Ll. Foster, Mrs. J. E. Heseltine, Dr. R. W. Hunt, Mr. N. R. Ker, Mr. H. L. Pink, Miss Joy Russell-Smith, Dr. F. W. Sternfeld, Mr. D. Wulstan. Professor E. J. Dobson has kindly allowed us to see in manuscript the texts of the songs he and Dr. F. Ll. Harrison are publishing in *Medieval English Songs*, i, and to make use of his commentary on them. To Professor Norman Davis, who has most generously advised us at all stages and who read our work in proof, we are grateful for many corrections, suggestions, and improvements.

C. S.

K. S.

CONTENTS

CONTENTS

CONTENTS

CONTENTS

CONTENTS

CONTENTS

CONTENTS

CONTENTS

CONTENTS

SNATCHES

264 Canute at Ely   265 Godrich's Hymn   266 Fowles in the Frith
267 (i) A Patient Lover (ii) Regret for the Past (iii) Godith and Godrun
(iv) Alfled Spinning   268 Lord, Thy Passion   269 Sunset

    270 A Shield of Red   271 Three Sad Thoughts   272 Parted by Water
273 Fragments of Love-songs   274 At the Wrestling   275 Laundering
276 Lament for Robert de Neville   277 The Ape   278 The Wolf   279
The Wren

    280 The Cat   281 Nature   282 Bannockburn   283 Five Evils   284
Earth to Earth   285 Beware, Annot!   286 The Reluctant Bride   287 A
Love Untrue   288 Fortune's Wheel   289 Three Allegorical Beasts

    290 Thou art so Lovely   291 Drunkenness   292 Hope and Hap   293
Mary, thou Queen   294 To Margaret   295 A Prophecy   296 Go, Penny,
Go!   297 Tax, *anno* 1381   298 John the Miller   299 The Year 1381

    300 When Adam Delved   301–11 Proverbial   312 A Gentleman
313 Three Executors   314 The Bald Man   315 The Shepherd of Ashell
Down   316 Walter Pollard   317 Book Inscriptions   318 At the end of a
Book of Prayers   319 The Ale-House

    320 A Tale of Right Nought   321 Wives Old and Young   322 Against
Hasty Marriage   323 Choosing a Wife   324 Woman's Treachery   325
How to win Respect   326 Advice to a Young Man   327 A Maxim   328
Reason and Faith   329 Richard III's Reign

    330 Football   331 Peace   332 Name Riddles   333 The Nightingale
Sings

THE TEXTS

TITLES, metrical arrangement, paragraphing, capitalization, word-division, punctuation, and spelling are editorial. For vocabulary and syntax the texts may be relied on. They have been checked against the manuscript authority or early print, and substantial changes of reading are recorded in the Textual Notes, pp. 568 ff. They should not be used for the study of Middle English spelling, forms, or dialects. Easier spellings of the medieval period have often been substituted for those of the manuscript; but in some pieces which have a continuous gloss or a spelling system that is distinctive and characteristic (e.g. the works of the *Pearl* poet or Barbour's *Bruce*), more manuscript spellings have been allowed to stand. Pieces composed by the same author or copied by the same scribe are treated, as far as possible, alike. No claim is laid to consistency.

Regular deviations from manuscript spelling are:

(i) Scribal abbreviations are silently expanded.

(ii) The five obsolete Middle English letters are replaced by their modern equivalents: *þ* and *ð* by *th*; *ƿ* by *w*; *ȝ* by *y, i, gh*, and, where it represents *z*, by *s*; *æ* by *a* or *e*. The Middle English letters are kept only in manuscript readings cited in the Textual Notes.

(iii) Some common Middle English verbal contractions have been expanded: e.g. *arttow, wilttou* are printed *art thou, wilt thou*; others are indicated by an apostrophe: e.g. *ich'ot* (ich wot), *ich'il* (ich wil), *th'art* (thou art), *n'is* (ne is), *n'as* (ne was), *n'ere* (ne were), *n'ille* (ne wille), *n'olde* (ne wolde), *n'ite* (ne wite), *n'ot* (ne wot), *n'iste* (ne wiste) *n'abbe* (ne habbe), *n'afde, n'avede, n'adde* (ne hafde etc.), *th'ilke* (the ilke), *e'r* (ever), *ne'r* (never), *de'l* (devel).

(iv) Omitted letters, whether scribal tricks, slips, or genuine phonetic forms, are silently restored when the word intended by the scribe is not in doubt: e.g. *w[u]rse; he[r], the[r], a[l], wo[l]de, y[e]den; wor[l]d, heve[n]riche, an[d]*. Such letters are printed without brackets in the text.

(v) Diacritics are used to show some pronunciations:

(a) An *e* which has now become silent is printed '*ĕ*' when the metre requires it to be pronounced as a syllable: e.g. *sonĕ, lovĕd*. It is often doubtful whether such an *e* is to be pronounced or not, especially at the end of a line and where the scansion is uncertain. In a few songs the music is a guide. Generally *e* is left unmarked at line-ends and in many doubtful cases.

(b) An acute accent denotes an *e* pronounced like Modern French *é* or English final *y*: e.g. *bléaunt, cité* 'city', *meré* 'merry'.

(c) Accentuation unfamiliar in modern English is marked: e.g. *natùre, àpparence*; an abnormal metrical stress is also occasionally so marked: e.g. *Yèt hadde he but litel gold in cofre.*

GLOSSING. As a reader may dip anywhere in the book, every piece is glossed as a separate unit; but in any one piece a word or phrase is seldom glossed after its first occurrence. Words given in *The Concise Oxford Dictionary* in the required sense have not normally been glossed. Where part of a line is glossed, the first and last words of the Middle English are given: e.g. '83.46 f. the . . . hous: those ahead came to a deserted farmhouse'; but when the whole of the latter part of a line is glossed, the first word only of the Middle English is given: e.g. '259.5 make . . . : entertain me in any way.' Line numbers alone are given when a complete line is glossed or an unmistakable word, such as a proper name. If the meaning is doubtful, '?' precedes the gloss. Some hard pieces have a continuous gloss.

PRONUNCIATION. No simple rules which cover all dialects and periods can be given. In general, vowels have their Latin rather than their modern English value; *i* in such words as *pacience, precious, mansioun, special* is pronounced as a syllable. All consonants are sounded: e.g. the *k* in *know* and the *l* in *walk*; *gh* in words like *right* is pronounced like German *ch* in *nicht*.

LAYAMON

The Death of Arthur

MODRED wes i Cornwale and somnede cnihtes feole:
To Irlonde he sende aneouste his sonde;
To Sexlonde he sende aneouste his sonde;
To Scotlonde he sende aneouste his sonde.
He hehten heom to cume alle anan that wolde lond habben— 5
Other seolver other gold other ahte other lond.
On elchere wisen he warnede hine seolven,
Swa deth elc witer mon tha neode cumeth uvenan.
   Arthur that y-herde, wrathest kinge,
That Modred wes i Cornwale mid muchele mon-weorede, 10
And ther wolde abiden that Arthur come riden.
Arthur sende sonde yeond al his kinelonde,
And to cumen alle hehte that quic wes on londe,
Tha to vihte oht weoren, wepnen to beren;
And whaswa hit forsete that the King hete,   15
The King hine wolde a folden quic al forbernen.
Hit lec toward hirede folc unimete,
Ridinde and ganninde swa the rein falleth adune.

Modred was in Cornwall and assembled many knights: straightway he sent his messengers to Ireland; straightway he sent his messengers to the Saxons' land; straightway he sent his messengers to Scotland. He bade come atonce all those who would have land—silver or gold or goods or land. In every way he secured himself, as each wise man does when trouble comes upon him.
   King Arthur, greatly angered, heard that Modred was in Cornwall with a huge host, and that he intended to stay there until Arthur came riding (against him). Arthur sent messengers throughout all his kingdom, and summoned every living man in the land who was fit for war, fit to bear weapons; and whoever disobeyed what the King commanded, the King would burn him alive everywhere in the land. An immense host hastened towards his court, riding and walking, as thick as the rain falls down.

Arthur for to Cornwale mid unimete ferde.
Modred that y-herde and him toyeines heolde   20
Mid unimete folke; ther weore monie veie.
Uppen there Tambre heo tuhten togadere—
The stude hatte Camelford; evermare y-last that ilke worde!
And at Camelforde wes y-somned sixti thusend
And ma thusend therto; Modred wes heore elder.   25
Tha thiderward gon ride Arthur the riche
Mid unimete folke, veie thah hit weore.
Uppe there Tambre heo tuhte tosomne,
Heven here-marken, halden togadere;
Luken sweord longe, leiden o the helmen;   30
Fur ut sprengen; speren brastlien,
Sheldes gonnen shanen, shaftes tobreken.
Ther faht al tosomne folc unimete:
Tambre wes on flode mid unimete blode.
Mon i than fihte non ther ne mihte y-kenne nenne kempe, 35
No wha dude wurse no wha bet, swa that wither wes y-menged;
For elc sloh adunriht, weore he swein, weore he cniht.
Ther wes Modred ofslawe and y-don of lif-dawe,
And alle his cnihtes y-slawe in than fihte.
Ther weoren ofslawe alle tha snelle   40

Arthur marched to Cornwall with an immense army. Modred heard of
it and opposed him with an immense force; there many were doomed.
On the Camel they drew together—the place was called Camelford:
evermore shall that name last! And at Camelford were assembled sixty
thousand men and thousands more besides: Modred was their leader.
Then the mighty Arthur rode thither with an immense force, doomed
though it was. On the Camel they drew together, raised up standards,
closed together; drew long swords, smote on helmets; sparks flew out;
spears clashed, shields broke, shafts shattered. There immense forces
fought all together: Camel was in flood with untold blood. In that
battle nobody could distinguish any fighter, nor who did worse nor who
better, so confused was the conflict; for each man struck mortally, whether
he were peasant or knight. There Modred was slain and the days of his life
ended; and all his knights were slain in the fight. There were slain all the

Arthures hered-men, heye and lowe,
And tha Bruttes alle of Arthures borde,
And alle his fosterlinges of feole kineriches;
And Arthur forwunded mid wal-spere brade:
Fiftene he hafde feondliche wunden—   45
Mon mihte i thare laste twa gloven y-thraste.
Tha n'as ther na mare i than fehte to lave,
Of twa hundred thusend monnen that ther leien to-hauwen,
Buten Arthur the King ane and of his cnihtes tweien.

Arthur wes forwunded wunder ane swithe.   50
Ther to him com a cnave the wes of his cunne:
He wes Cadores sune, the Eorles of Cornwaile;
Constantin hehte the cnave; he wes than kinge deore.
Arthur him lokede on, ther he lay on folden,
And thas word seide mid sorhfulle heorte: 55
'Constantin, thu art wilcume! Thu weore Cadores sone.
Ich the bitache here mine kineriche,
And wite mine Bruttes a to thines lifes,
And hald heom alle tha lawen tha habbeth y-stonden a mine
        dawen,
And alle tha lawen gode that bi Utheres dawen stode.   60
And ich wulle varen to Avalun, to vairest alre maidene,

brave men of Arthur's household, the high and the low, and all the Britons
of Arthur's table, and all his fosterlings from many kingdoms; and Arthur
was mortally wounded with the broad deadly spear: he had fifteen ghastly
wounds—one could thrust two gloves into the smallest of them. Then no
more were left in the fight, of two hundred thousand men who lay there
hacked to pieces, but King Arthur only and two of his knights.

Arthur was most grievously wounded. There came to him a young
man who was of his kin: he was the son of Cador, Earl of Cornwall; the youth
was called Constantine; he was dear to the King. Arthur, as he lay on the
ground, looked on him and said these words with sorrowful heart:
'Constantine, you are welcome! You were Cador's son. I entrust you here
with my kingdom. Guard my Britons always as long as you live, and
maintain for them all the laws that stood in my days, and all the good
laws that stood in Uther's days. And I will go to Avalon, to the fairest of

To Argante there quene, alven swithe shene;
And heo shal mine wunden makien alle y-sunde,
Al hal me makien mid haleweiye drenchen.
And seothe ich cumen wulle to mine kineriche   65
And wunien mid Brutten mid muchelere wunne.'
    Efne than worden ther com of se wenden
That wes an short bat lithen, shoven mid uthen;
And twa wimmen therinne, wunderliche y-dihte.
And heo nomen Arthur anan and aneouste hine vereden,   70
And softe hine adun leiden, and forth heo gunnen lithen.
Tha wes hit y-wurthen that Merlin seide whilen:
That weore unimete care of Arthures forthfare.
    Bruttes y-leveth yete that he beon on live,
And wunnien in Avalun mid fairest alre alven;   75
And lokieth evere Bruttes yete whan Arthur cumen lithe.
N'is never the mon y-boren of never nane burde y-coren
The cunne of than sothe of Arthure suggen mare.
Bute while wes an witeye Merlin y-hate:
He bodede mid worde—his quides weoren sothe—   80
That an Arthur shulde yete cum Anglen to fulste.

all maidens, to the Queen Argante, that very beautiful fairy; and she shall
make my wounds all sound, make me whole with healing drinks. And
afterwards I will come to my kingdom and dwell with the Britons in
great happiness.'
    At these words there came moving in from the sea a small boat, driven
by the waves; and two women in it, wondrously arrayed. And straightway
they took Arthur up and swiftly carried him, and softly laid him down, and
sailed away. Then was fulfilled what Merlin once prophesied: that there
should be boundless grief at Arthur's going hence.
    The Britons still believe that he is alive and dwells in Avalon with the
most beautiful of all the fairies; and the Britons still look forward always
to the time when Arthur shall return. There is no man born of woman
however good that can tell more of the truth about Arthur. But there was
once a prophet named Merlin: he prophesied in words—the things he said
were true—that an Arthur should yet come to be a help to the people of
England.

2 *Charm against Wens*

WENNE, wenne, wenchichenne,
    Her ne scealt thu timbrien, ne nenne tun habben;
Ac thu scealt north heonene to than nihgan berhge,
Ther thu havest, ermig, enne brother.
He the sceal legge leaf et heafde.   5
Under fot-volmes, under vether earnes,
Under earnes clea, a thu geweornie!
Clinge thu alswa col on heorthe,
Scring thu alswa scerne a wage,
And weorne alswa weter on anbre!   10
Swa litel thu gewurthe alswa linset-corn,
And miccli lesse alswa anes hand-wurmes hupe-ban;
And alswa litel thu gewurthe thet thu nawiht gewurthe!

3 *Winterfall*

MERY it is while sumer y-last
    With fugheles song;
Oc now negheth windes blast
    And weder strong.

2. Wen, wen, wen-chicken (*i.e.* little wen), you shall not build here, nor have a dwelling; but you must go north from here to the nearby hill where, wretch, you have a brother. He shall lay a leaf at your head. Under the soles of (the eagle's) feet, under the eagle's wing, under the eagle's claw, ever may you wither! May you waste away like a coal in the hearth, may you rot away like dung on the wall, and dry up like water in a pitcher! May you become as little as a grain of linseed, and much littler than a handworm's hip-bone; and may you become so little that you become nothing!

3. 1 y-last: lasts   2 fugheles: birds'   3 Oc: but   negheth: approaches   4 strong: rough

Ey! ey! what this night is long!   5
And ich with wel michel wrong
Sorow and murne and fast.

4   *White was His Naked Breast*

WHIT was His nakede brest
    And red of blod His side,
Bleik was His fair andlèd,
    His woundè deep and wide;

And His armès y-streight   5
    Hy upon the rode;
On fif stedès on His body
    The stremès ran o blode.

5   *Owl against Nightingale*

ICH was in onè sumere dale,
  In onè swithè diyèle hale;
Y-herde ich holdè gretè tale
An ule and onè nightègale.
That plaid was stif and starc and strong,   5
Sum whilè softe and lud among;
And either ayein other swal
And let that uvelè mod ut al;

3. 5 what: how   6 and I most unjustly

4. 2 of: with   3 Bleik: pale   andled: face   4 wounde: wounds
5 y-streight: stretched   7 stedes: places   8 the streams of blood
ran

5. I was in a summery valley, in a very secluded corner; I heard an owl and
a nightingale having a great debate. The argument was fierce and hard-
hitting and heated—sometimes quiet, sometimes noisy; each swelled with

And either seide of othres custe
That alrè-wursté that hi wuste;   10
And hure and hure of othres songe
Hi holdé plaiding swithé stronge.

    The nightègale bigan tho speche
In one hurne of oné breche,
And sat up oné fairé bowe   15
Ther were abuté blostme ynowe,
In oré fasté thikké hegge
Y-meind mid spire and grené segge.
Heo was the gladder for the rise,
And sang a felé cunné wise;   20
Bet thughte the drem that he were
Of harpe and pipé than he n'ere;
Bet thughté that he were y-shote
Of harpe and pipé than of throte.

    Tho stod an old stok ther biside,   25
Ther the ulé sang hire tide,
And was mid ivy al bi-growe:
It was thare ulé erdingstowe.

    The nightègalé hi y-seigh
And hi biheld and overseigh,   30
And thughté wel ful of thare ule—

anger against the other, and they vented all their ill-feeling; and each said of the other's character the very worst that she knew; and in particular they had a most heated argument about each other's song.

The nightingale opened the debate in the corner of a cleared strip of woodland; she sat on a lovely bough, smothered with blossom, in an impenetrable thick hedge with reeds and green sedge growing through it. She was the happier for the branch, and sang in strains of many kinds; the sound seemed rather as if it came from harp and pipe than anything else; it seemed as if it were emitted from harp and pipe rather than from throat.

Now there stood an old stump nearby, where the owl sang her hours, and it was all overgrown with ivy: it was the owl's home.

The nightingale observed her and gazed at her and studied her, and she

For me hi halt lodlich and fule.
'Unwight', heo seide, 'awey thu flee!
Me is the wurs that ich thee see.
Y-wis, for thinė fulė lete   35
Wel ofte ich my song forlete;
Min herte atflighth and falt my tunge
Whenne thu art to me y-thrunge;
Me lustė bet speten thane singe
Of thinė fulė yowėlinge!'   40
    Thes ule abod fort it was eve—
Heo ne mighte no leng bileve:
For hirė hertė was so gret
That wel neigh hirė fnast atshet—
And warp a word ther-after longe: 45
'Hu think thee nu by minė songe?
Wenest thu that ich ne cunnė singe,
Thei ich ne cunne of writelinge?
Y-lomė thu dest me grame
And seist me bothė teene and shame.   50
If ich thee helde on minė fote
(So it bitidė that ich mote!)
And thu were ut of thinė rise,
Thu sholdest singe on other wise!'

had a very low opinion of the owl—for she is considered loathsome and
disgusting. 'Vile creature', she said, 'fly off! I feel the worse for seeing you.
In fact, because of your disgusting appearance I very often leave off my
singing; my heart fails and my tongue is silenced when you force your
company upon me; I would rather spit than sing at your horrible wailing!'
    The owl waited till evening—she could contain herself no longer: for
her heart was so swollen with rage that her breath almost failed her—and
after that long time she spoke up: 'How does my song strike you now?
Do you suppose I don't know how to sing, even if I don't know about
warbling? You're always annoying me, abusing me and insulting me.
If I held you in my claw (if only I had the chance!) and you were out of
your branch, you'd sing another tune!'

8

The nightėgalė yaf answàre: 55
'If ich me loki with the bare
And me shildė with the blete,
Ne reche ich nought of thinė threte;
If ich me holde in minė hegge,
Ne reche ich never what thu segge!   60
Ich wot that thu art unmilde
With hem that ne muwe from thee shilde;
And thu tukest wrothe and uvele
Wher thu might over smale fuwele.
For-thy thu art loth al fowel-kenne,   65
And allė hi thee driveth henne
And thee bi-shricheth and bi-gredeth
And wel narewe thee bi-ledeth;
And ek for-thy the sulvė mose,
Hire thankės, woldė thee to-tose.   70
Thu art lodlich to biholde,
And thu art loth in manye folde:
Thy body is short, thy swere is smal,
Gretture is thyn heved ne thu al;
Thyn eyėn beeth col-blake and brode,   75
Right so hi weren y-peint mid wode;
Thu starest so thu wille a-biten
Al that thu might mid clivrė smiten;

The nightingale answered: 'As long as I avoid the open and guard myself against lack of cover, I don't care at all about your threatening; if I keep to my hedge, I don't care in the least what you say! I know that you are far from kind to those that can't protect themselves against you; and that, wherever you have power over small birds, you maul them cruelly and viciously. That's why you're hated by all the bird tribes, and they all drive you off, screeching and screaming at you, and mob you; and that's also why even the tit would willingly tear you to pieces. You're horrible to look at, and you're loathsome in lots of ways: your body's squat, your neck's small, and your head is bigger than all the rest of you; your eyes are coal-black and staring, just as if they were painted with woad; and you glare as if you'd like to crunch up everything you could strike with your

Thy bile is stif and sharp and hoked
Right as an ewel that is croked;   80
Ther-mid thu clechest ever among,
And that is on of thinė song!
Ac thu thretest to mine fleisse,
Mid thinė clevres woldest me meisse.
Thee were y-cundere to one frogge   85
That sit at mulnė under cogge;
Snailės, mus, and fulė wighte
Beeth thinė cunde and thinė righte.
Thu sittest a-day and flighst a-night:
Thu cuthest that thu art on unwight.   90
Thu art lodlich and unclene—
By thinė neste ich it mene,
And ek by thinė fulė brode:
Thu fedest on hem a wel ful fode!'

6   *Wealth and Wisdom*

THUS queth Alfred:
        Withute wisdome
Is wele wel unwurth;
For thei o man aghte

5. claws. Your bill is strong and sharp and hooked just like a bent meat-hook;
you're always snapping with it, and that's the sort of song you sing! But
you threaten violence to my person, and would like to crush me with your
talons. A frog sitting under the mill-wheel would be fitter for you; snails
and mice and disgusting creatures are your natural and proper diet. You
roost by day and fly by night: you show you're a wicked creature. You're
foul and dirty—I'm referring to your nest and also to your squalid young:
in them you are rearing a filthy brood!'

6. 1 queth: said   3 wealth is quite worthless   4 f. for though a
man possessed seventy acres

Huntseventy acres, 5
And he hi hadde y-sowen
Alle mid rede golde,
And that gold grewe
So gres doth on erthe:
N'ere he for his wele 10
Never the wurthere,
Bute he him of frumthe
Frend y-wurche.
For what is gold bute ston
But if it haveth wis man? 15

7   *Going to Hell*

ALLE bakbiteres hi wendeth to helle,
Robberes and reveres and the manquelle;
Lechers and horlings thider shulleth wende,
And ther hi shulle wunie ever buten ende.
Alle thees false chapmen the feend hem wille habbe, 5
Bakeres and breweres for alle men hi gabbe:
Lowe hi holdeth here galun, mid berme hi hine fulleth,
And ever of the purse that selver hi tulleth;
Bothe hi maketh feble here bred and here ale;
Habbe hi that selver, ne telleth hi never tale. 10

---

6. 6 hi: them   7 mid: with   9 So gres: as grass   10–13 he
would not be any the better off for his wealth, unless from the beginning
he make himself friends   15 unless a wise man has it

7. 1 hi wendeth: they go   2 reveres: pillagers   manquelle: murderers
3 horlings: fornicators   shulleth: shall   4 wunie: dwell   buten:
without   5 chapmen: traders   hem: them   habbe: have   6 for
. . . : they lie more than all men   7 they keep their gallon low, they
fill it with froth   8 tulleth: draw out   9 feble: poor   10 as
long as they have the money, they never care

Goode men, for Godes luve, bileveth suche sinne,
For at then ende it binimeth hevenriche winne.
 Alle preestes wives, ich wot hi beeth forlore;
Thees persones, ich wene, ne beeth hi nought forbore,
Ne thees prude yonge men that luvieth Malekin,   15
And thees prude maidenes that luvieth Janekin.
At chirche and at cheping whenne hi togedere cume,
Hi runeth togederes and speketh of derne luve;
Whenne hi to chirche cometh to then holy day,
Everich wille his leef y-see ther, if he may: 20
Heo beholdeth Watekin mid swithe glad eye;
At hom is hire *Pater Noster*, biloken in hire teye;
Masses and matines ne kepeth heo nought,
For Wilekin and Watekin beeth in hire thought.
Robin wille Gilot leden to then ale,   25
And sitten ther togederes and tellen here tale;
He may quiten hire ale and sithe don that game;
An eve to go mid him ne thincheth hire no shame.
Hire sire and hire dame threteth hire,to bete;
N'ille heo forgo Robin for al here threte.   30
Ever heo wille hire skere, ne com hire no man nigh,
Fort that hire wombe up arise on high.
 Goode men, for Godes luve, bileveth youre sinne,
For at then ende it binimeth hevenriche winne.

---

11 bileveth: leave off 12 for in the end it will take away the joy of
the kingdom of heaven 13 ich . . . : I know they will be damned
14 these parsons, I think, will not be spared 17 cheping: market
18 runeth: whisper derne: secret 19 to then: on the
20 Everich . . . y-see: each wants to see his sweetheart 21 Heo: she
mid swithe: with a very 22 biloken . . . : shut up in her box
23 ne . . . : she cares nothing for 26 tellen . . . : talk (of love)
27 quiten: pay for sithe: afterwards 28 in the evening to go with
him seems to her no shame 30 N'ille heo: she will not 31 hire
skere: deny her guilt com: has come 32 Fort that: until
wombe: belly

fl. c. 1250

8

Where is Paris and Helene?

WHER is Paris and Heleine,
    That weren so bright and faire on bleo,
Amadas and Ideine,
    Tristram, Iseude, and allė theo,
Ector, with his sharpė meine,   5
    And Cesar, riche of worldės feo?
Hi beeth y-gliden ut of the reine
    So the shef is of the cleo.

It is of hem also it n'ere;
    Of hem me haveth wonder y-told.   10
N'ere it reuthė for to here
    How hi were with pine aquold,
And what hi tholeden alive here?
    Al is here hot y-turnde to cold.
Thus is this world of falsė fere: 15
    Fol he is the on hire is bold.

2 bleo: appearance   3 Idoine   4 Isolde   theo: those   5
sharpe meine: impetuous strength   6 riche . . .: mighty in worldly
possessions   7 f. They have disappeared from the (earthly) kingdom
like the sheaf from the hill-side   9–12 It is as if they had not been;
terrible things have been told of them. Would it not be piteous to hear
how cruelly they were killed   13 tholeden: suffered   14 here:
their   15 fere: appearance   16 he is foolish who trusts to it

13

9   *A Prisoner's Prayer*

AR ne couthe ich sorwė none,
   Now ich mot manen myn mone;
Carful, wel sore ich sichė:
Giltless ich tholyė muchele shamė.
Help, God, for thyn swetė namė,   5
   King of hevenė-richė!

Jesu Crist, sooth God, sooth man,
   Loverd, thou rew ùpon me!
Of prisùn ther ich in am
   Bring me out and makyė free.   10
Ich and minė feren sumė—
   God wot ich ne lyė noght—
For othrė habbeth misnumė
   Been in this prisùn y-broght.
Almighty,   15
That wel lightly
   Of bale is hale and botė,
Hevene-King,
Of this woning
   Out us bringė motė!   20
Foryef hem,
The wikkė men,
   God, if it is thy willė,
For whos gilt

1 f. Before I knew no sorrow, now I must make my lament   3
Carful: wretched   siche: sigh   4 tholye: suffer   5 name: sake
6 hevene-riche: the kingdom of heaven   8 Lord, have pity on me
9 ther . . .: in which I am   11 I and some of my companions
13 because others have done wrong   15–22 Almighty King of
Heaven, who very easily curest and relievest distress, mayst thou bring
us out of this misery! Forgive them, the wicked men

We beeth y-pilt   25
  In this prisun illė.

Ne hopė none to this livė:
Here ne may he bilivė;
Highė thegh he stighė
  Deth him felleth to groundė.   30
Now hath man wele and blissė,
Rathe he shal ther-of missė;
Worldės welė, mid y-wissė,
  Ne lasteth bute an stoundė.
Maiden that bare the Heven-King,   35
Bisech thyn Sone, that swetė thing,
That He habbe of us rewsing
And bring us of this woning,
  For His muchelė milsė.
He bring us out of this wo   40
And us techė werchen so
In this life, go how s'it go,
That we moten ay and o
  Habben the echė blissė.

10   *Sumer is y-cumen in*

S UMER is y-cumen in,
   Ludė sing, cuccu!
Groweth sed and bloweth med
And springth the wudė nu.

9. 25 y-pilt: thrust   27 Let no man trust to this life   28 bilive: remain   29 high though he climb   31 wele: prosperity 32–4 quickly he must forfeit it; worldly prosperity, indeed, lasts but a little while   37 that He have pity on us   39 milse: mercy   40 He bring: May He bring   41 werchen so: so to act   42 go...: however it may go   43 f. that we may for ever and ever have eternal bliss **10.** 2 lude: loudly   3 f. Seed grows and meadow flowers and the wood comes into leaf now

15

Sing, cuccu! 5
Awė bleteth after lamb,
Lowth after calvė cu;
Bulluc sterteth, buckė ferteth.
Meriė sing, cuccu!
Cuccu, cuccu, 10
Wel singės thu, cuccu;
Ne swik thu never nu!

Sing, cuccu, nu! Sing, cuccu!
Sing, cuccu! Sing, cuccu, nu!

11　　　　　　　*A Bidding Prayer*

BIDDE we with milde stevene
　　Til ure Fader, the King of hevene,
In the mununge of Cristes pine,
For the laverd of this hus and al lele hine;
For alle Cristen folk that is in goode life, 5
That God shilde hem today fro sinne and fro sithe;
For alle tho men that are in sinne bunden,
That Jesus Crist hem leyse for His haly wunden;
For quike and for deade and al mankinde,
And that us here good don, in hevene mot they it finde; 10
And for alle that on erthe us feden and foster,
Saye we nu alle the haly *Pater Noster.*

---

10. 6 Awe: ewe　　　7 cow lows for calf　　　8 sterteth: leaps
ferteth: breaks wind　　12 do not ever stop now

11. 1 Let us pray with humble voice　　2 Til: to　　3 mununge:
remembrance　　pine: torment　　4 for the master of this house and
all faithful servants　　6 shilde hem: shield them　　sithe: mischance
7 tho: those　　bunden: bound　　8 leyse: release　　haly wunden:
holy wounds　　10 and may those who do us good here find good in
heaven　　11 foster: maintain　　12 nu: now

An Easter Song

S UMER is comen and winter gon,
   This day beginnès to longe,
And thes fowlès everichon
   Joye hem with songe.
So strongè care me bint,   5
Al with joyè that me fint
   In londe,
Al for a child
That is so mild
   Of honde.   10

That child, that is so mild and wlank
   And eke of gretè mounde,
Bothe in boskès and in bank
   Y-sought me haves a stounde.
Y-founde He havedè me,   15
For an appel of a tree
   Y-bounde;
He brak the bond
That was so strong
   With wounde.   20

That child that was so milde and hold
   To me aluttè lowe.
From me to Giwès He was sold:
   Ne couthen he Him nought knowe.

2 longe: lengthen   3 everichon: every one   4 Joye hem:
rejoice   5 f. so strongly sorrow grips me, despite the joy that is felt
everywhere   9 f. mild . . .: gracious with His hand   11 wlank:
noble   12 mounde: power   13 boskès: bushes   14 a
stounde: a while   15 havede: had   21 hold: gracious   22
alutte: bowed   23 Giwes: Jews   24 they could not recognize Him

'Do wey', saiden he,   25
'Naile we him upon a tree
   A lowe;
Ac arst we shullen
Shamy him
   A throwe.'   30

Jesu is the childès name,
   King of allè lande;
Of the King he maden game
   And smiten Him with hande.
To fonden Him upon a tree   35
He yeven Him woundès two and three
   Mid hande;
Of bitter drink
He senden Him
   A sande.   40

Deth He nam o roodè-tree,
   The lif of us alle;
Ne mighte it nought other be
   Bute we sholden falle;
And wallen in hellè dep   45
N'erè neverè so swet
   Withalle;
Ne mighte us savy
Castel, towr,
   Ne halle. . . .   50

25 'Have done', they said   27–30 on the hill; but first we must
shame him for a time   33 they mocked the King   35 fonden:
test   36 He yeven: they gave   37 Mid: with   39 f. they
sent Him a present   41 nam o: received on   43 f. otherwise
we were bound to have fallen   45 wallen: to boil

18

Deth He nam, the swete mon,
  Wel heye upon the roode.
He wesh our sinnes everichon
  Mid His swete bloode.
Mid floode He lighte adown   55
And brak the yates of that prisoùn
  That stoode,
  And ches here
  Out that there
    Were goode.   60

He ros Him ene the thridde day
  And sette Him on His trone.
He wille come a Domèsday
  To deme us everichone.
Grone he may and wepen ay,   65
The man that deyeth withoute lay
  Alone.
  Grante us, Crist,
  With thyn uprist
    To gone.   70

13   *Of One that is so Fair and Bright*

O F one that is so fair and bright,
  Velud maris stella,
Brighter than the dayes light,
  Parens et puella,

12. 53 wesh: washed away   everichon: each one   55 floode: *i.e.*?
Christ's blood, which washed away Adam's sin (see Rev. 1:5)   lighte . . .:
descended   56 yates: gates   57 which were standing   58–60
and chose out of them those that were good there   61 Him ene: by
His own power   63 a: on   66 lay: faith   69 f. to go with
you in your resurrection

Ich crie to thee; thou see to me!   5
Levedy, pray thy Sone for me,
   Tam pia,
That ich moté come to thee,
   Maria.

Levedy, flowr of allé thing,   10
   Rosa sine spina,
Thou beré Jesu, Hevené-King,
   Gratia divina.
Of allé thou berst the pris,
Levedy, quene of Paraÿs   15
   Electa.
Maidé mildé moder is
   Effecta.

Of caré conseil thou art best,
   Felix fecundata;   20
Of allé wery thou art rest,
   Mater honorata.
Bisek Him with mildé mood
That for us allé shad His blood
   In cruce   25
That we moten comen til Him
   In luce.

Al this woreld war forlore
   Eva peccatrice,
Til our Loverd was y-bore   30
   De te genitrice.

5 see to: look upon   6 Levedy: lady   8 mote: may
12 bere: bore   14 You are the best of all   15 Parays: Paradise
19 In distress you are the best counsellor   23 Beseech Him with
gentle heart   24 shad: shed   26 til: to   28 war forlore: had
been lost   30 Loverd: Lord

With '*ave*' it went away
Thuster night, and comth the day
   Salutis;
The wellé springeth out of thee   35
   Virtutis.

Wel He wot He is thy Sone
   Ventre quem portasti;
He wil nought werné thee thy bone,
   Parvum quem lactasti.   40
So hende and so good He is,
He haveth brought us to blis
   Superni,
That haves y-dit the foulé pit
   Inferni.   45

14   *Ubi Sunt?*

WHERE beeth they biforen us weren,
   Houndés ladden and havekés beren,
And hadden feeld and wode?
The riché levedies in here bour,
That weréden gold in here tressour,   5
   With here brighté rode,

Eten and drunken and maden hem glad;
Here lif was al with gamen y-lad;
   Men kneléden hem biforen.
They beren hem wel swithé heye,   10

13. 33 Thuster: dark   39 werne: deny   bone: request   41
hende: gracious   44 y-dit: shut

14. 1 they: they (who)   2 who led hounds and carried hawks
4 levedies: ladies   here: their   5 wereden: wore   tressour: head-
dress   6 rode: complexion   7 hem: them(selves)   8 gamen:
pleasure   y-lad: led   10 wel swithe heye: very proudly

And in a twinkling of an eye
  Here soulės weren forloren.

Where is that lawing and that song,
That trailing and that proudė yong,
  Tho havekes and tho houndes?   15
Al that joy is went away;
That wele is comen to waylaway,
  To manye hardė stoundes.

Here paradis hy nomen here,
And now they lien in helie y-fere;   20
  That fire it brennės evere.
Long is ay and long is o,
Long is way and long is wo;
  Thennes ne cometh they nevere.

Dreghy here, man, then, if thou wilt,   25
A litel pine that me thee bit;
  Withdraw thine eises ofte.
Thegh thy pinė be unrede,
And thou thenke on thy mede,
  It shal thee thinken softe.   30

If that feend, that foulė thing,
Through wikkė roun, through fals egging,
  Nethere thee haveth y-cast,

---

12 forloren: lost   13 lawing: laughing   14 trailing: trailing of robes   yong: gait   15 Tho: those   16 went: gone 17 wele: happiness   waylaway: lamentation   18 stoundes: times of trial   19 hy nomen: they took   20 y-fere: together   21 brennes: burns   22 ay: always   o: ever   23 way: misery 24 Thennes: thence   25 Dreghy: endure   26 a littl esuffering that is imposed on you   27 forgo your comforts often   28 Though your pain be severe   29 And: if   30 it shall seem mild to you 32 roun: counsel egging: incitement   33 Nethere: down

Up! and be good chaunpioun;
Stand, ne fall na more adown   35
  For a litel blast.

Thou tak the roodė to thy staf,
And thenk on Him that there-on yaf
  His lif that was so leef.
He it yaf for thee; thou yeeld it Him;   40
Ayein His fo that staf thou nim,
  And wrek Him of that theef. . . .

Maiden moder, hevene-queen,
Thou might and canst and owest to been
  Oure sheeld ayein the fende.   45
Help us sinnė for to fleen,
That we moten thy Sone y-seen
  In joye withouten ende.

15   *Sweet Jesu*

S WETĖ Jesu, King of blisse,
  Myn hertė love, myn hertė lisse,
Thou art swetė mid y-wisse:
Wo is him that thee shal misse.

  Swetė Jesu, myn hertė light,   5
  Thou art day withouten night;
  Thou yive me strengthe and ekė might
  For to lovien thee al right.

14. 37 to: as   38 yaf: gave   39 leef: dear   40 yeeld: repay
41 Ayein: against   nim: take   42 wrek of: avenge on   44 might:
have the power   owest: ought   46 fleen: shun   47 moten: may
15. 2 hertė: heart's   lisse: joy   3 mid y-wisse: indeed   4 that
. . .: who must be without you

Swetė Jesu, my soulė bote,
In myn herte thou sette a rote   10
Of thy love that is so swote,
And wite it that it springė mote.

16   *The Fox and the Wolf*

A FOX gan out of the wodė go,
  Afingret so that him was wo—
He n'as nevere in nonė wise
Afingret erer half so swithe.
He ne held nouther way ne strete,   5
For him was loth men to mete:
Him were levere meten one hen
Than half an hundred wimmèn!
He strok swithė overal,
So that he ofsey ane wal;   10
Withinne the wallė was an hous;
The fox was thider swithė fous;
For he thoughte his hunger aquenche
Other mid mete other mid drenche.
Abouten he biheld wel yerne.   15
Tho erest bigan the fox to erne
Al fort he com to anė walle;
And som therof was a-falle,

15. 9 soule bote: soul's salvation   10 thou sette: may you plant
11 swote: sweet   12 and tend it so that it may grow

16. 1 gan go: went   2 Afingret: famished   3 f. he had never in
any way been half so terribly famished before   5 He followed
neither path nor road   6 as he did not care to meet people   7 he
had rather meet one hen   9 f. He went quickly all about till he caught
sight of a wall   12 the fox was very keen to be there   13 aquenche:
satisfy   14 either with food or drink   15 yerne: eagerly
16 Then for the first time the fox began to run   17 fort: till   com:
came

And was the wal overal to-broke,
And an yat ther was y-loke.   20
At the formeste bruchè that he fond
He lep in, and over he wond.
Tho he was innè, smere he low,
And therof he hadde game ynow:
For he com in withouten leve   25
Bothen of haiward and of reve.

An hous ther was, the dore was ope,
Hennen weren therinne y-crope
Five—that maketh annè flok—
And mid hem sat an kok.   30
The kok him was flowen on hey
And two hennen him seten ney.
'Fox,' quod the kok, 'what dest thou thare?
Go hom! Crist thee yevè care!
Oure hennen thou dest oftè shame.'   35
'Be stille, ich hote, a Godès name!'
Quath the fox; 'Sire Chauntecler,
Thou flee adown and com me ner.
I n'abbè don here nought bute good:
I have leten thine hennen blood.   40
Hy weren seke under the ribbe
That hy ne mighte non lenger libbe
Bute here eddre were y-take—

19 overal...: everywhere broken down   20 and there was a shut
gate   21 At the first opening that he found   22 lep: leapt
wond: went   23 f. When he was in, he laughed merrily, and he was
very well pleased with himself   25 com: had come   26 haiward:
hedge-keeper   reve: land-steward   28 hens had crept in there
30 mid: with   31 The cock himself had flown up high   32 seten
ney: sat near   33 quod: said   dest: do   34 yeve: give   care:
sorrow   36 Be quiet, I tell you, in God's name   38 flee: fly
ner: nearer   39 n'abbe: haven't   41 Hy: They   seke: sick
42 non...: live no longer   43 Bute: unless   eddre: blood from a vein

That I do for almès sake.
Ich have hem letten eddre-blood,   45
And thee, Chauntecler, it wolde don good:
Thou havest that ilke under the splen;
Thou nestès nevere dayès ten!
For thine lif-dayes beeth al a-go
Bute thou by minè redè do.   50
I do thee lete blood under the brest,
Other sone axe after the prest.'
'Go way!' quod the kok, 'wo thee bi-go!
Thou havest don oure kinnè wo.
Go mid than that thou havest nouthe—   55
Acursed be thou of Godès mouthe!
For were I adown, by Godès name,
Ich mighte been siker of othre shame.
Ac wiste it ourè cellerère
That thou were y-comen here,   60
He wolde soone after thee yonge
Mid pikes and stones and stavès stronge.
Alle thine bones he wolde to-breke:
Thenne we weren wel a-wreke!'
    He was stille, ne spak na more;   65
Ac he werth a-thurst wel sore:
The thurst him didè morè wo
Than havede rather his hunger do.
Overal he ede and soughte.

48 you won't nest (live) ten days   49 a-go: passed   50 unless
you act on my advice   51 do . . . blood: shall cause you to be let
blood   52 or else ask for the priest at once   53 wo . . .: may
harm befall you   55 Go with what you've now got   56 of: from
58 siker: sure   59 But if our cellarer knew it   61 yonge: go
63 to-breke: break to pieces   64 then we would be well avenged
66 Ac he werth: but he (the fox) was   68 than his hunger had done
earlier   69 He went searching everywhere

On aventure his wit him broughte   70
To ane pitte was water inne,
That was y-makėd mid grete ginne.
Two boketes ther he founde:
That other wendė to the grounde,
That when me shulde that one upwinde,   75
That other wolde adown winde.
He ne understood nought of the ginne;
He nom that boket and lep therinne,
For he hopede ynow to drinke.
This boket biginneth to sinke: 80
To late the fox was bethought!
Tho he was in the ginne y-brought
Ynow he gan him bethenche,
Ac it ne halp mid nonė wrenche:
Adown he moste, he was therinne;   85
Y-caught he was mid swikele ginne.
It mighte han y-been wel his wille
To lete that boket hangy stille.
What mid sorewe and mid drede,
Al his thurst him over-ede.   90
Al thus he com to the grounde,
And water ynow ther he founde!
Tho he fond water, yerne he drank:
Him thoughte that water therė stank,

---

70 On aventure: by chance   71 to a well in which there was water
72 ginne: ingenuity   74–6 the second went to the bottom, so that
when one hauled up the one, the other would go down   77 ginne:
device   78 nom: seized   79 hopede: expected   81 was
bethought: took thought   82 Tho: When   83 f. he began to
think hard enough, but no trick was any use   85 moste: must (go)
86 swikele: treacherous   87 It might indeed have been more agreeable
to him   88 stille: undisturbed   90 over-ede: left   91
grounde: bottom   93 yerne: copiously   94 Him thoughte: it
seemed to him

For it was to-yeines his wille.   95
'Wo worthe', quath the fox, 'lust and wille,
That ne can meth to his mete!
If ich n'avede to muchel y-ete,
This ilkė shamė n'add I nouthe,
N'adde lust y-been of minė mouthe.   100
Him is wo in echė lande
That is theef mid his hande.
Ich am y-caught mid swikele ginne,
Other sum devel me broughte her-inne.
I was wonėd to been wis,   105
Ac now of me y-don it is.'
The fox wep and reuliche bigan.

  Ther com a wolf gon after than
Out of the depė wodė blive,
For he was afingret swithe.   110
Nothing he ne found in al the nighte
Wher-mid his hunger aquenchė mighte.
He com to the pitte, thene fox y-herde—
He him knew wel by his rerde,
For it was his neighėbore   115
And his gossip, of children bore.
Adown by the pitte he sat.
Quod the wolf: 'What may been that
That ich in the pitte y-here?
Art thou Cristine other my fere?   120

---

95 to-yeines: against   96 f. 'A curse', said the fox, 'upon appetite and
desire, upon him who knows no moderation in eating'   98 n'avede:
hadn't   99 f. I shouldn't now have had this particular ignominy,
had it not been for the appetite of my mouth   104 Other: or else
105 was woned: used   106 but now I am done for   107 The
fox wept and lamented bitterly   108 A wolf came along after that
109 blive: quickly   113 thene: the   114 rerde: voice   116
and his crony from childhood   120 Are you a Christian or my friend?

Say me sooth, ne gabbe thou me nought,
Who haveth thee in the pitte y-brought?'
The fox hine y-knew wel for his kin,
And tho erest com wit to him;
For he thoughtè mid summe ginne   125
Himself upbringe, thene wolf therinne.
Quod the fox: 'Who is now there?
Ich wene it is Sigrim that ich here.'
'That is sooth', the wolf sede,
'Ac what art thou, so God thee rede?'   130
    'A!' quod the fox, 'ich wille thee telle,
Onalpy word ich liè n'elle.
Ich am Renèward, thy frend;
And if ich thine come havede y-wend,
Ich haddè so y-bede for thee   135
That thou sholdest comen to me.'
'Mid thee?' quod the wolf, 'wher-to?
What shulde ich in the pittè do?'
Quod the fox: 'Thou art unwis:
Her is the blisse of paradis: 140
Her ich may evere wel fare,
Withouten pine, withouten care;
Her is metè, her is drinke,
Her is blisse withouten swinke;
Her n'is hunger nevermo,   145
Ne non other kinnès wo:
Of allè goode her is ynow.'

121 gabbe: lie   123 hine: him   for . . .: as his relative   124
and then for the first time a good idea came to him   125 ginne:
trick   126 thene . . .: (put) the wolf in   129 sede: said   130
so . . .: God help you   132 I won't lie one single word   133
frend: kinsman   134 f. and if I had expected your coming, I would
have prayed for you so   137 Mid: with   wher-to: what for
142 pine: suffering   144 swinke: toil   145 nevermo: nevermore
146 nor misery of any other kind

Mid th'ilkė wordės the wolf low:
'Art thou ded, so God thee rede,
Other of the worlde?' the wolfe sede.   150
Quod the wolf: 'Whenne storvė thou,
And what dest thou therė now?
Ne beeth nought yet three dayes ago
That thou and thy wif alsò
And thinė children, smale and grete,   155
Alle togedere mid me ete.'
'That is sooth', quod the fox,
'Godė thank, now it is thus
That ich am to Cristė wend—
N'ot it none of minė frend.   160
I n'olde, for al the worldės good,
Been in the worlde ther ich hem fond.
What shuld ich in the worldė go
Ther n'is butė care and wo,
And livie in filthe and in sinne?   165
Ac her beeth joyės felė kinne:
Her beeth bothė sheep and get.'
    The wolf haveth hunger swithė gret,
For he n'addė yare y-ete;
And tho he herdė speken of mete   170
He wolde bletheliche been there.
'A!' quod the wolf, 'goode y-fere,
Many good mel thou havest me binome.
Let me adown to thee come

---

148 low: laughed   150 Other: or   151 storve: died
158 Gode thank: thanks be to God   159 wend: gone   160 N'ot:
know not   161 n'olde: would not   162 ther . . .: where I met
them   163 What: Why   164 Ther: where there   166 fele
kinne: of many kinds   167 get: goats   169 because he hadn't
eaten for a long time   170 tho: when   171 bletheliche: gladly
172 y-fere: friend   173 binome: deprived

And al ich willė thee foryive.'   175
'Ye!' quod the fox, 'were thou y-shrive,
And sinnen havedest al forsake
And to clenė lif y-take,
Ich woldė so biddė for thee
Tnat thou sholdest comen to me.'   180
'To whom shold ich', the wolf sede,
'Been y-knowe of mine misdede?
Her n'is nothing alive
That me couthė her now shrive.
Thou havest been ofte myn y-fere;   185
Wilt thou now my shrift y-here,
And al my lif I shal thee telle?'
'Nay', quod the fox, 'I n'elle!'
'N'elt thou?' quod the wolf; 'Thyn ore!
Ich am afingret swithė sore: 190
Ich wot tonight ich worthė ded
Bute thou do me sumnė red.
For Cristės lovė, be my prest!'
The wolf bey adown his brest
And gan to siken harde and stronge.   195
    'Wilt thou', quod the fox, 'shrift underfonge?
Tel thine sinnen one and one,
That ther bilevė never one.'
'Soone,' quod the wolf, 'wel y-faye!
Ich habbe been qued al my lifdaye: 200
Ich habbė widėwenė curs—

---

177 havedest: had you   179 bidde: pray   182 confess
my misdeeds   184 couthe: could   188 n'elle: won't
189 ore: mercy   191 worthe ded: shall be dead   192 unless you
help me   194 bey: bent   195 siken: sigh   196 underfonge:
receive   197 one . . .: one by one   198 bileve: remain   199
Soone: at once   y-faye: gladly   200 qued: evil   201 wide-
wene: widows'

Therfore ich fare the wurs.
A thousend sheep ich habbe a-biten
And mo, if hy weren y-writen—
Ac it me ofthinketh sore!   205
Maister, shal I tellen more?'
'Ye', quod the fox, 'al thou most sugge,
Other elleswher thou most abugge.'
'Gossip', quod the wolf, 'foryef it me!
Ich habbe ofte said qued by thee.   210
Men saide that thou on thinė live
Misferdest mid minė wive;
Ich thee aperseivede onė stounde,
And in bedde togedere ou founde;
Ich was oftė ou ful ney,   215
And in bedde togedere ou sey:
Ich wendė, also othre doth,
That ich y-seyė werė soth,
And therfore thou were me loth—
Goodė gossip, ne be thou nought wroth!'   220
    'Wolf,' quod the fox him tho,
'Al that thou havest her-bifore y-do
In thought, in speche, and in dede,
In eche otheres kinnės quede,
Ich thee foryeve at thissė nede.'   225
'Crist thee foryeldė!' the wolf sede;
'Now ich am in clenė live
Ne reche ich of childė ne of wive.

204 mo: more   y-writen: recorded   205 but I regret it bitterly
207 most sugge: must tell   208 Other: or   abugge: pay   209
foryef: forgive   210 by: about   212 Misferdest: sinned
213 I observed you one time   214 ou: you   215 ney: near
216 sey: saw   217 f. I supposed, as others do, that what I saw was true
221 tho: then   224 in every other kind of wickedness   226
foryelde: reward   227 Now: now that   228 reche of: care about

32

Ac say me what I shal do
And how ich may comen thee to.'   230
'Do?' quod the fox, 'Ich wille thee lere.
Y-sist thou a boket hangy there?
Ther is a bruche of hevene-blisse!
Lep therinne, mid y-wisse,
And thou shalt comen to me sone.'   235
Quod the wolf, 'That is light to done.'

  He lep in, and wey sumdel
(That wiste the fox ful wel):
The wolf gan sinke, the fox arise;
Tho gan the wolf sore agrise.   240
Tho he com amidde the pette
The wolf thene fox upward mette.
'Gossip,' quod the wolf, 'what now?
What havest thou y-munt? Whider wilt thou?'
'Whider ich wille?' the fox sede,   245
'Ich wille up, so God me rede!
And now go down with thy meel:
Thy bi-yete worth wel smal!
Ac ich am therof glad and blithe
That thou art nomen in clene live.   250
Thy soule-knel ich wille do ringe,
And masse for thine soule singe.'
The wreche binethe nothing ne find
Bute cold water, and hunger him bind.

229 But tell me what I am to do   231 lere: instruct   232 Y-sist
thou: do you see   233 bruche: piece   234 mid . . .: to be sure
235 sone: at once   236 light: easy   237 He leapt in, and weighed
a fair amount   240 agrise: be afraid   241 When he came half-
way down the well   242 upward: on his way up   244 What
are you up to? Where are you going?   247 with . . .: for your
meal   248 biyete worth: gain will be   250 nomen: taken
251 do: cause to   253 find: finds   254 bind: pinches

To coldė gistninge he was y-bede;   255
Froggen haveth his dow y-knede!
The wolf in the pittė stood,
Afingret so that he was wood.
Ynow he cursede that thider him broughte;
The fox therof litel roughte!   260
    The pit him was the housė ney
Ther freren woneden swithė sley.
Tho that it com to the time
That hy shulden arisen ine,
For to suggen here oussong,   265
O frerė ther was among
Of here sleep hem shulde aweche,
When hy shulden thidere reche.
He saide: 'Ariseth, one and one,
And cometh to oussong everichone!'   270
This ilkė frerė heyte Ailmer—
He was here maister curtiler.
He was of-thurst swithė stronge
Right amidward here oussonge.
Alonė to the pitte he ede,   275
For he wendė bete his nede.
He com to the pitte and drow,
And the wolf was hevy ynow.
The frere mid al his mainė tey

255 gistninge: banquet   y-bede: bidden   256 dow: dough
258 wood: mad   259 that: him who   260 roughte: cared
261 him was: was   262 where very wise friars lived   263 Tho
that: When   264 That ine: at which   265 to say their matins
266 O: one   among: among them   267 whose duty it was to rouse
them from their sleep   268 reche: go   269 He said: 'Get up,
each one of you   270 everichone: everyone   271 heyte: was
called   272 curtiler: gardener   274 amidward: in the middle of
275 ede: went   276 wende bete: thought to satisfy   277 drow:
drew   279 tey: pulled

So longe that he thene wolf y-sey.   280
For he sey thene wolf ther sitte
He gradde: 'The devel is in the pitte!'
   To the pitte hy gunnen gon
Alle mid pikes and staves and ston,
Ech man mid that he hadde—   285
Wo was him that wepne n'adde!
Hy comen to the pitte, thene wolf up-drowe.
Tho hade the wreche fo-men ynowe
That werèn egre him to slete
Mid grete houndès, and to bete.   290
Wel and wrothe he was y-swunge,
Mid staves and speres he was y-stunge.
The fox bi-charde him, mid y-wisse,
For he ne fond nones kinnès blisse,
Ne of dintes foryevènesse.   295

17   *Love is Weal, Love is Wo*

L OVE is soft, love is swete, love is good sware;
  Love is muchè tene, love is muchel care.
Love is blissenè mest, love is bot yare;
Love is wondred and wo with for to fare.

Love is hap, who it haveth; love is good hele.   5
Love is lecher and lees, and leef for to tele.

16. 280 until at last he caught sight of the wolf   281 For: Because
282 gradde: cried   283 gunnen gon: went   285 mid that: with what
289 egre: eager   slete: bait   291 wrothe: severely   y-swunge:
thrashed   293 bi-charde: duped   294 nones kinnes: of no kind
295 foryevenesse: remission

17. 1 good sware: kind words   2 tene: suffering   care: sorrow
3 Love is greatest of joys, love is a ready cure   4 wondred: misery
5 hap: good luck   who: whoever   hele: fortune   6 lees: false
leef . . .: apt to deceive

LOVE IS WEAL, LOVE IS WO

Love is doughty in the world with for to dele.
Love maketh in the land many unlele.

Love is stalwarde and strong to striden on stede.
Love is loveliche a thing to wommanė nede.   10
Love is hardy and hot as glowindė glede.
Love maketh many may with terės to wede.

Love hath his steward by sty and by strete.
Love maketh many may hire wongės to wete.
Love is hap, who it haveth, on for to hete.   15
Love is wis, love is war, and wilful ansete.

Love is the softeste thing in hertė may slepe.
Love is craft, love is good with carės to kepe.

Love is lees, love is leef, love is longinge.
Love is fol, love is fast, love is frovringe.   20
Love is sellich an thing, whoso shal sooth singe.

Love is wele, love is wo, love is gladhede.
Love is lif, love is deth, love may us fede.

Were love al so londdrey as he is first kene,
It were the wordlokstė thing in worlde were, ich wene.

---

8 unlele: unfaithful   9 striden . . .: mount a horse   10
to . . .: necessary for women   11 Love is fierce and hot as a glowing
coal   12 may: maiden   wede: be frenzied   13 sty: path
14 wonges: cheeks   15 on . . .: to be inflamed with   16 war:
prudent   wilful ansete: strong-willed adversary   18 craft: strength
with . . .: at preserving from cares   20 fol: foolish   fast: steady
frovringe: comfort   21 sellich an: a marvellous   22 gladhede:
gladness   24 al so londdrey: just as long-lasting   kene: intense
25 it would be the most precious thing in the world, I suppose

It is y-said in an song, sooth is y-sene,   26
Love comseth with care and endeth with tene,
Mid lavedy, mid wivė, mid maidė, mid quene.

18   *I Sigh when I Sing*

I SIKE al when I singe
   For sorwė that I see,
When ich with wepinge
   Biholde upon the tree:
I see Jesu, my swete,   5
His hertė-blood forlete
   For the love of me;
His woundės waxen wete.
Marìė, milde and swete,
   Thou haf mercy of me!   10

Hey upon a downe,
   As al folk it see may,
A mile without the towne,
   Aboutė the mid-day,
The roode was up arerde.   15
His frendės weren of-ferde:
   They clungen so the clay.
The roodė stont in ston;
Marỳ herself alon—
   Her song was way-la-way.   20

17. 26 sooth . . .: seen to be true   27 comseth: begins   28 Mid
lavedy: with lady

18. 1 sike: sigh   3 ich: I   6 forlete: shed   **11 Hey: high**
15 arerde: raised   16 of-ferde: afraid   17 they shrank like clay
(*i.e.* with horror)   18 stont: stands   20 way-la-way: lamentation

When ich Him biholde
　　With ey and hertė bo,
I see His body colde;
　　His blee waxeth al blo.
He hangeth al of bloode　　　　　　　　25
So hey upon the roode
　　Bitwixen thevės two.
How shold I singė more?
Marỳ, thou wepė sore,
　　Thou wist al of His wo.　　　　　　30

Wel oftė when I sike,
　　I makė my mon;
Ivel it may me like—
　　And wonder n'is it non—
When I see hangė hey　　　　　　　　35
And bitter painės drey
　　Jesu my lemmòn.
His woundės sorė smerte;
The sper is at His herte
　　And thurgh His sidė gon.　　　　　40

The nailes beeth al to stronge,
　　The smith is al to sleye;
Thou bledės al to longe,
　　The tree is al to heye.
The stonės waxen wete—　　　　　　　45
Allas! Jesu, my swete,
　　Few frendės hafdės neye,

22 bo: both　　23 colde: grow cold　　24 blee: colour　　blo: livid
25 of bloode: bleeding　　29 wepe: wept　　30 wist: knew　　32
mon: lament　　33 it may (indeed) please me ill　　36 drey: suffer
37 lemmon: beloved　　40 gon: (has) gone　　42 sleye: skilful
47 hafdes: you had　　neye: near

But Sein Jon murnind
And Marỳ wepind,
   That al thy sorwè seye.   50

Wel oftè when I slepe
   With sorwe ich am thurgh-soght;
When I wake I wepe,
   I thenkè in my thoght:
Allas! that men beeth woode,   55
Biholdeth on the roode
   And seleth—ich ly noght—
Her soulès into sin
For any worldès win,
   That was so dere y-boght!   60

19   *Hail Mary!*

HAIL Mary!
   Ich am sary;
Haf pité of me and mercy,
   My levedy;
To thee I cry.   5
For my sinnès dred am I,
When I thenk that I shal by
   That I haf mis y-don
In word, in work, in thoght folỳ.
   Levedy, her my bon.   10

18. 48 murnind: mourning   50 seye: saw   52 thurgh-soght:
pierced through   55 woode: mad   56 ff. behold the cross and—I am
not lying—**sell** their souls into sin for any worldly delight, (their souls)
that were bought so dear!

19. 2 I am sorry   4 levedy: lady   7 by: pay for   8 what I
have done wrong   9 foly: foolish, sinful   10 Lady, hear my
prayer

My bon thou her,
Levedy der,
That ich ask with rewful cher.
Thou len me her,
Whil ich am fer,   15
Do penànce in my prayèr;
Ne let me noght ler that thou ber
   At min ending-day;
The warlais thay wil be her
   For to take thair pray.   20

To take thair pray,
As I her say,
Thay ar redy both night and day.
So stronge ar thay
That we ne may   25
Againes thaim stand—so way-la-way!—
But if thou help us, mightful may,
   With thy Sonès grace.
When thou comes, thay flit away,
   Dar thay not see thy face.   30

Thy face to see
Thou grant it me,
Levdy fulfilled of pité;
That I may be
In joy with thee   35
To see thy Son in Trinité,
That suffered pine and ded for me
   And for al man-kin.

14 len: grant   15 fer: in health   17 do not deny me the
countenance you bear   19 warlais: devils   22 her: hear
26 way-la-way: alas   27 But if: unless   may: maid   29 flit: go
33 fulfilled of: filled with   37 pine: torment   ded: death   38
man-kin: mankind

His flesh was spred on roodė-tree
   To leys us al of sin.   40

Of sin and care
He maked us bare,
When He tholėd pinės sare.
To droupe and dare
We aghte wel mare,   45
As for the houndės doth the hare,
When we thenk how we shal fare
   When He shal deem us all;
We shal haf need thare
   Upon Marỳ to call.   50

20

Undo!

ALLAS, allas, wel ivel I sped!
  For sinne Jesu fro me is fled,
   That lively fere.
At my dore he standes alone
And calles 'Undo!' with reuful mone   5
   On this manère:

'Undo, my leef, my douvė dere,
Undo! Why stand I steken out here?
   Ik am thy make.
Lo, my heved and minė lockes   10
Ar al biweved with blody dropes
   For thinė sake.'

19. 40 leys: deliver   42 bare: free   43 tholed: suffered   sare: sore   44 f. we ought much more to cringe and cower   48 deem: judge

20. 1 ivel . . .: I have fared ill   3 that life-giving companion   5 reuful mone: pitiful lament   7 leef: beloved   douve: dove   8 steken: shut   9 Ik: I   make: spouse   10 heved: head   11 biweved: covered

21 *Wait a Little*

LOVERD, thou clepedest me,
    And ich noght ne answàredè thee
Bute wordès slow and slepye:
'Tholè yet! Thole a litel!'
Bute 'yet' and 'yet' was endèlis,   5
And 'thole a litel' a long way is.

22 *Queen of Heaven*

EDY be thou, Hevene-Quenè,
    Folkès frovre and engles blis,
Moder unwemmed and maiden clenè,
    Swich in world non other n'is.
On thee it is wel ethsenè   5
    Of allè wimmen thou havest the pris.
My swetè levedy, heer my benè
    And rew of me, if thy wille is.

Thou asteye so the day-rewè
    The deleth from the derkè night;   10
Of thee sprang a lemè newè
    That al this world haveth y-light.
N'is non maide of thinè hewè,
    So fair, so shene, so rudy, so bright.

21. 1 Lord, you called me   2 ich: I   3 Bute: except
4 Thole: wait

22. 1 Edy: Blessed   2 frovre: comfort   engles: angels'   3 un-
wemmed: unspotted   4 Swich: such   5 ethsene: evident
6 havest . . .: are supreme   7 levedy: lady   bene: prayer   8 rew
of: pity   9 You arose like the dawn   10 The deleth: which parts
11 leme: light   12 y-light: lit   14 shene: beautiful   rudy:
rosy

Swetė levedy, of me thou rewė   15
   And have mercy of thyn knight.

Sprungė blostme of onė rotė,
   The Holy Gost thee rest upon;
That was for mankunnės botė
   And here soule to alesen for on.   20
Levedy mildė, softe and swotė,
   Ich cry thee mercy, ich am thy mon,
Bothe to hande and to fotė,
   On allė wisė that ich con.

Thou art erthe to goodė sedė;   25
   On thee lighte the hevene-dew,
Of thee sprang the edy bledė,
   The Holy Gost hir on thee sew.
Thou bring us out of care, of dredė
   That Evė bitterliche us brew;   30
Thou shalt us into hevene ledė—
   Wel swete is the ilkė dew.

Moder ful of thewės hendė,
   Maidė drey and wel y-taught,
Ich am in thine lovė-bendė,   35
   And to thee is al my draught.
Thou me shild, ye, from the fendė,
   As thou art free and wilt and maught;

17 Blossom sprung from a single root   18 rest: came   19 f. that was for the salvation of mankind, to redeem their souls in exchange for one   21 softe: gentle   swote: sweet   22 Ich: I   mon: servant   23 *i.e.* wholly   24 in every way I know   26 lighte: descended   27 blede: fruit   28 hir . . .: sowed it in you   30 brew: brewed   33 thewes hende: gracious virtues   34 drey: patient   35 love-bende: love-bonds   36 draught: inclination   37 Shield me, indeed, from the devil   38 free: generous   maught: can

Help me to my livès endè,
　　And make me with thyn Sone y-saught. . . .　40

23　　　　　*Of Jesu Christ I Sing*

NOW ich see blostmè springe,
　　Ich herde a fugheles song,
A swetè longinge
　　Myn hertè thurghout sprong,
That is of luvè newe,　　　　　　　　　　5
That is so swete and trewe
　　It gladieth al my song.
Ich wot mid y-wisse
My lif and eke my blisse
　　Is al theron y-long.　　　　　　　　　　10

Of Jesu Crist I singe
　　That is so fair and fre,
Swetest of allè thinge;
　　His owe ich owe wel be.
Ful fer He me soghte,　　　　　　　　　　15
Mid hard He me boghte,
　　With woundè two and three;
Wel sore He was y-swunge
And for me mid spere y-stunge,
　　Y-nailèd to the tree.　　　　　　　　　　20

When ich myselfè stande
　　And mid herte y-see

22. 40 y-saught: reconciled

23. 1 f. Now that I see blossom coming out (and) I have heard a bird's song
4 sprong: has sprung up　　　7 gladieth: makes joyful　　　8 mid . . .:
with certainty　　　10 y-long: dependent　　　12 fre: noble　　　14 I
ought indeed to be His own　　　15 fer: far　　　16 Mid hard: with
suffering　　　18 y-swunge: scourged

Y-therlèd feet and hande
  With gretè nailès three—
Bloody was His heved;   25
Of Him n'as noght by-leved
  That of pine were free—
Wel oghtè myn herte
Al for His luvè smerte,
  Sic and sory be.   30

A way! that I ne can
  To Him turne al my thoght
And makien Him my lefman
  That thus me hath y-boght
With pine and sorewe longe,   35
With woundè depe and stronge:
  Of luve ne can I noght.
His blood fel to the grounde
Out of His swetè wounde,
  That of pine us hath y-broght.   40

Jesu, lefman softe
  Thou yif me strengthe and might,
Longinge sore and ofte
  To servy thee aright;
And leve me pinè drye   45
Al for thee, swete Marìe,
  That art so fair and bright.
Maiden and moder milde,
For love of thinè childe
  Ernde us hevene light.   50

23 **Y-therled**: pierced   25 heved: head   26 no part was left
of Him   27 pine: pain   29 smerte: to feel pain   31 A way:
Alas   33 lefman: beloved   37 I am incapable of love   40 of:
out of   41 softe: kind   42 yif: give   45 and grant that I may
endure pain   50 win heaven's light for us by your intercession

Jesu, lefman swete,
  Ich sendė thee this song,
And wel ofte ich thee grete
  And biddė thee among.
Yif me soonė lete   55
And minė sinnės bete,
  That ich have do thee wrong.
At minė livės ende,
When ich shal hennė wende,
  Jesu, me underfong! Amen.   60

24   *All Too Late*

WHENNE mine eynen misteth
      And mine eren sisseth
And my nose coldeth
And my tunge foldeth
And my rude slaketh   5
And mine lippes blaketh
And my mouth grenneth
And my spotel renneth
And myn her riseth
And myn herte griseth   10
And mine handen bivieth
And mine feet stivieth—
Al to late, al to late,

23. 54 and pray to you constantly   55–7 Grant that I may straight-
way renounce and atone for my sins, for what I have done wrong to
you   59 shal: must   henne: hence   60 underfong:
receive

24. 1 eynen: eyes   2 sisseth: ? sing   4 foldeth: fails   5 and
my colour fades   6 blaketh: grow pale   7 grenneth: gapes
8 and my spittle runs   9 her: hair   riseth: ? stands on end   10
griseth: quakes   11 bivieth: tremble   12 stivieth: stiffen

Whenne the bere is at the gate!
  Thenne I shal flit   15
From bedde to flore,
From flore to here,
From here to bere,
From bere to pit,
And the pit fordit.   20
Thenne lith myn hous uppe myn nese:
Of al this world ne give ich a pese!

25   *If Man him Bethought*

I F man him bithoghte,
  Inderlike and ofte,
Hu harde is the fore
Fro bedde to flore;
Hu rewful is the flitte   5
Fro flore to pitte,
Fro pitte to pine
That nevre shal fine—
I wene non sinne
Shulde his herte winne.   10

26   *The Whale*

C ETHEGRANDE is a fis,
  The moste that in water is,
That thou woldes sayen yet,

24. 14 bere: bier   15 shal flit: must go   17 here: hair-shroud
19 pit: grave   20 fordit: will shut   21 f. Then my house will lie
upon my nose: for all this world I shall not give a pea!

25. 2 Inderlike: earnestly   3 fore: going   5 flitte: passing
6 pitte: grave   7 pine: torment   8 fine: end

26. 1 Cethegrande: great whale   fis: fish   2 moste: largest   3
yet: moreover

If thou it sawe when it flet,
That it were an eiland   5
That sete on the see-sand.
  This fis, that is unride,
Thenne him hungreth he gapeth wide;
Out of his throte it smit an ande,
The sweteste thing that is o lande.   10
Therfore othre fisses to him drawen;
When hie it felen hie aren fawen:
Hie cumen and hoven in his mouth;
Of his swike hie arn uncouth.
This cete thenne his chaveles luketh,   15
These fisses alle in suketh.
The smale he wille thus biswiken,
The grete may he noght bigripen.
  This fis wuneth with the see-ground,
And liveth ther evre hail and sound   20
Til it cumeth the time
That storm stireth al the see.
Thenne sumer and winter winnen
Ne may it wunen therinne:
So drovi is the sees ground,   25
Ne may he wunen ther that stound,
Oc stireth up and hoveth stille,
Whiles that weder is so ille.
The shipes that arn on see fordriven—

  4 flet: was floating   5 eiland: island   6 sete: rested   7
unride: huge   8 when he is hungry he gapes wide   9 it . . .:
there issues a breath   10 o lande: on earth   12 when they
smell it they are delighted   13 hoven: linger   14 swike: treachery
uncouth: ignorant   15 This whale then snaps his jaws   17 bi-
swiken: entrap   18 bigripen: catch   19 This fish dwells by the
sea-bottom   20 hail: safe   23 Thenne: When winnen: contend
25 drovi: disturbed ground: bottom   26 stound: time   27 but
rises up and stays still   29 fordriven: storm-driven

Loth hem is ded and lef to liven— 30
Biloken hem and seen this fis;
An eiland hie wenen it is.
Therof hie aren swithe fawen,
And mid here might therto hie drawen,
Shipes on festen 35
And alle up gangen,
Of ston mid stel in the tunder
Bel to brennen on this wunder;
Warmen hem wel and eten and drinken.
The fir he feleth and doth hem sinken; 40
For soone he diveth down to grounde
He drepeth hem all withouten wounde.

Significacio

This devel is mikel with wile and maght
So witches haven in here craft:
He doth men hungren and haven thrist 45
And many other sinful list;
Tolleth men to him with his ande;
Who-so him folweth, he findeth shande:
Tho arn the little, in leve lawe;
The mikle ne may he to him drawe. 50
The mikle I mene the stedefast
In righte leve mid fles and gast.

30 death is hateful to them and life precious 31 Biloken hem: look about them 33–8 They are very glad of that, and make for it with all their might, moor their ships to it and all disembark, to kindle a fire upon this marvel with stone and steel in the tinder 39 Warmen hem: they warm themselves 40 doth: makes 41 soone: as soon as 42 drepeth: slays 43 f. This devil is strong in such guile and power as witches use in their craft 45 thrist: thirst 46 list: desire 47 Tolleth: entices 48 shande: ruin 49 those are the little ones, feeble in faith 52 in true faith with body and soul

Who-so listneth develes lore, ＼
On lengthe it shal him rewen sore;
Who-so festeth hope on him,   55
He shal him folwen to helle dim.

27   *A Student Courting*

I   *CLERICUS.* Damisel, rest thee wel.
     Puella. Sir, welcum, by Saint Michèl!
     Clericus. Wher is thy sire? Wher is thy dame?
     Puella. By Gode, is nother her at hame.
     Clericus. Wel were swilk a man to life   5
     That swilk a may might have to wife!
     Puella. Do way, by Crist and Leönàrd!
     No wil I love no clerc faillàrd;
     No keep I herberg clerc in house no i flore,
     But his ers ly withouten dore.   10
     Go forth thy way, good sire,
     For here hast thou losit al thy hire.
     Clericus. Now, now, by Crist and by Saint Jhon,
     In al this land ne wist I none,
     Maiden, that I love more than thee,   15
     If me might ever the better be.
     For thee I sorwe night and day;
     I may say ay 'wayleway!'

26. 54 in the end he shall repent it bitterly   55 whoever puts his trust
in him

27. 4 nother her: neither of them   5 f. Any man would be well off
who could have such a girl as his wife   7 Do way: That's enough
8–10 I refuse to love a good-for-nothing student; I've no wish to receive
a student in house or ?hall, unless his backside is outside the door
12 losit . . .: completely wasted your time   14 wist I: I have known
16 ? even if I could ever be better off (*i.e.* by loving another)   18 **ay:**
for ever

I love thee more than my life;
Thou hates me more than gait dos knife: 20
That is nought for misgilt;
Certes, for thy love am I spilt.
A, swete maiden, rew of me
That is thy love, and ay shal be!
For the love of the moder of hevene,   25
Thou mend thy moode and heer my stevene!
Puella. By Crist of hevene and Saint Jon!
Clerc of scole ne keep I non;
For many good wimman have they don shame.
By Crist, thou mightes have been at hame!   30
Clericus. Sin it n'other gat may be
Jesu Crist bitech I thee,
And sende newlich bot therinne,
That I be lesit of al my pine.
Puella, Go now, truan! go now, go!   35
For mikel canst thou of sorwe and wo!

II   *Clericus.* God thee blisse, Mome Helwis.
     Mome Helwis. Son, welcum, by San Denis!
     Clericus. Ich am comen to thee, Mome—
     Thou hel me nought, thou say me sone—   40
     Ich am a clerc that hauntes scole;
     I lede my lif with mikel dole:
     Me were lever to be dede

20 gait: goat   21 misgilt: misconduct   22 spilt: destroyed
26 change your mind and hear my plea   28 I don't want any university student   30 you might have stayed at home   31–4 since it cannot be otherwise, I commit you to Jesu Christ, and may He quickly send a happy outcome in this affair, so that I may be released from all my suffering   35 truan: good-for-nothing   36 a lot you know about sorrow and woe!   37 Mome Helwis: Aunt Heloise   39 Ich: I 40 hide nothing from me, tell me quickly   41 hauntes: goes to 42 dole: sorrow   43 I had rather be dead

Than lede the lif that ich lede,
For a maiden whit and sheen—   45
Fairer o land have I none seen.
Ho hat maiden Malkin, I wene—
Now thou wost whom I mene;
Ho wunes at the townes ende,
That swete lif, so fair and hende.   50
But if ho wil hir mood amende,
Newly Crist my ded me sende!
Men kend me hider, withouten faile,
To have thy help and thy counsaile.
Therfor am I comen here,   55
That thou shalt be my erand-bere,
To make me and that maiden saught;
And I shal give thee of myn aught,
So that ever, al thy lif,
Shalt thou be the better wif;   60
So help me Crist, and I may spede,
Richlich shalt thou have thy mede.
Mome Helwis. A, son, what sayst thou? *Benedicite*!
Lift up thy hand and blisse thee!
For it is both sin and shame   65
That thou on me has laid this blame;
For ich am an old quene and a lame;
I lede my lif with Godes love;
With my roc I me fede;

---

45 sheen: beautiful   46 o: on   47 Ho hat: she is called
48 wost: know   49 wunes: lives   townes: of the village
50 lif: creature   hende: pretty   51–3 Unless she's willing to
change her mind, may Christ quickly send me my death! I was directed
here, in fact   56 erand-bere: go-between   57 saught: reconciled
58 of . . .: something I have   61 and . . .: if I succeed   63 *Bene-
dicite* pronounced 'Bencité'   64 blisse thee: cross yourself   66
blame: imputation   67 quene: woman   lame: infirm   69
with my distaff I earn my living

Can I do none other dede   70
But my *Pater Noster* and my *Crede*
To say Crist for missedede,
And myn *Avy Mary*,
'For my sinnes ich am sary',
And my *De Profundis*   75
For al that in sin lys.
For can I me none other thing;
That wot Crist, of hevene King.
Jesu Crist of hevene high
Give that they may henge high,   80
And give that I may see
That they be hengen on a tree
That this lie has laid me on,
For holy wimman am I on.

28   *Wight in the Broom*

'SAY me, wight in the brom,
 Teche me how I shule don
That min housebonde
Me lovien wolde.'

'Hold thine tunge stille   5
And have al thine wille.'

27. 71 f. but say my *Pater Noster* and my Creed to Christ, for my misdeeds
76 lys: lie (dead)   77 I don't know how to do anything else
78 wot: knows   80 Give: grant   henge: hang   83 f. who
have made this lying charge against me, for I am a holy woman.

28. 2 shule: am to

29   *Lady, I Thank Thee*

LEVEDY, ich thankė thee
⎣   With hertė swithė milde
That good that thou havest y-don me
    With thinė swetė childe.

Thou art good and swete and bright,   5
    Of alle other y-coren;
Of thee was that swetė wight
    That was Jesùs y-boren.

Maidė mildė, bidde I thee
    With thinė swetė childe   10
That thou erndiė me
    To habben Godės milce.

Moder, loke on me
    With thinė swete eye;
Reste and blissė gif thou me,   15
    My levedy, then ich deye.

30   *Judas*

IT was upon a Shere Thorsday that oure Loverd aras;
⎣ Ful mildė were the wordės He spak to Judàs:

'Judas, thou most to Jurselem, oure metė for to bugge;
Thritty platen of selver thou bere upo thy rugge.

29. 1 Levedy: lady   ich: I   2 swithe milde: very humble   3
That: (for) that   6 y-coren: chosen   9 bidde: pray   11
erndie: intercede for   12 to have God's mercy   15 gif: give
16 then: when
30. 1 Shere...: Maundy Thursday that our Lord arose   3 most: must
(go)   bugge: buy   4 thirty pieces of silver you are to carry on your back

54

JUDAS

Thou comest fer i the brode strete, fer i the brode strete; 5
Some of thinè kinèsmen ther thou meight y-mete.'

Y-mettè with his sister, the swikelè wimòn:
'Judas, thou were wurthè me stendè thee with ston,
Judas, thou were wurthè me stendè thee with ston,
For the falsè prophetè that thou bilevest upon.' 10

'Be stillè, levè sister, thyn hertè thee tobreke!
Wistè myn Loverd Crist, ful wel He wolde be wreke.'

'Judas, go thou on the rok, high upon the ston,
Lay thyn hevèd i my barm, sleep thou thee anon.'

Soonè so Judas of slepè was awake, 15
Thritty platen of selver from him weren y-take.

He drow himselvè by the top, that al it lavede a bloode;
The Jewès out of Jurselem awenden he were woode.

Forth him com the richè Jew that heightè Pilatus:
'Wilt thou selle thy Loverd, that heightè Jesus?' 20

'I n'il selle my Loverd for nonès cunnès eighte,
Bute it be for the thritty platen that He me biteighte.'

5 fer: far   6 meight: may   7 Y-mette: (He) met
swikele: treacherous   8 were...thee: deserve to be stoned   11 f.
Be quiet, dear sister, may your heart break within you! If my Lord Christ
knew, He would be properly avenged   14 lay your head in my lap,
go to sleep directly   15 Soone so: as soon as   17 He tore his hair,
so that it all streamed with blood   18 awenden: supposed   woode:
mad   19 him com: came   heighte: was called   21 I will not
sell my Lord for riches of any kind   22 Bute: unless   biteighte:
entrusted

'Wilt thou selle thy Lord Crist for enès cunnès golde?'
'Nay, bute it be for the platen that He habben wolde.'

In Him com our Lord gon, as His postles seten at mete: 25
'How sittè ye, postles, and why n'illè ye ete?
How sittè ye, postles, and why n'illè ye ete?
Ich am y-bought and y-sold today for ourè mete.'

Up stood him Judas: 'Lord, am I that?
I n'as never o the stude ther me thee evel spak.'   30

Up him stood Peter, and spak with al his mighte:
'Though Pilatus him come with ten hundred knighte,
Though Pilatus him come with ten hundred knighte,
Yet ich woldè, Loverd, for thy lovè fighte.'

'Stillè thou be, Peter! Wel I thee y-knowe;   35
Thou wilt forsake me thrièn ar the cok him crowe.'

31   *Saint Stephen*

S AINT Steven was a clerk in King Herowdès halle,
And servèd him of bred and cloth, as every king befalle.

Steven out of kichoun cam with borès hed on hande;
He saw a sterre was fair and bright over Bedlem stande.

30. 23 enes . . .: gold of any kind   24 habben: have   25 Our
Lord came walking in as His apostles were sitting at their meal   26
How: why   28 Ich: I   29 f. am . . .: is it me? I was never in
the place where evil was spoken of you   32 him come: should come
34 for thy love: for love of you   35 Stille: quiet   36 thrien . . .:
thrice before the cock crows

31. 2 of . . . cloth: with food and clothes   befalle: would befit   4
sterre: star (which)   Bedlem Bethlehem

He kest adown the borės hed and went into the halle: 5
'I forsake thee, King Herowdės, and thy werkės alle.

I forsake thee, King Herowdės, and thy werkės alle;
Ther is a child in Bedlem born is beter than we alle.'

'What aileth thee, Steven? What is thee befalle?
Lakketh thee either mete or drink in King Herowdės halle?' 10

'Lakketh me neither mete ne drink in King Herowdės halle;
Ther is a child in Bedlem born is beter than we alle.'

'What aileth thee, Steven? art thou wood, or thou ginnest to
    brede?
Lakketh thee either gold or fee or any richė wede?'

'Lakketh me neither gold ne fee, ne non richė wede; 15
Ther is a child in Bedlem born shal helpe us at our nede.'

'That is al so sooth, Steven, al so sooth, y-wis,
As this capoun crowė shal that lith here in myn dish.'

That word was not so soonė said, that word in that halle,
The capoun crew *Christus natus est* among the lordės alle. 20

'Riseth up, myn tormentòures, by two and al by one,
And ledeth Steven out of this town and stoneth him with
    stone.'

Tooken he Steven and stonėd him in the way;
And therfor is his even on Cristės owėn day.

5 kest: cast   13 wood . . .: mad, or are you beginning to find fault
14 fee: goods   wede: clothes   17 al so: just as   y-wis:
indeed   18 lith: lies   19 not so soone: no sooner   21 Riseth:
rise   by two . . .: *i.e.* every one of you   23 Tooken he: they
took   24 even: eve

32   *(a) The Scots in Berwick (1296)*

WENES King Edward with his longe shankes
    For to win Berwik, al oure unthankes?
Gas, pikes him!
And when he has it,
Gas, dikes him!   5

(b) The English Retort

'PIKES him
    And dikes him',
  In scorn saiden he.
He pikes, he dikes
On lengthe as him likes,   5
  How best may be.
Scatered are the Scottes,
Hodered in their hottes—
  Nevere they ne thee!
Right if I rede,   10
They tumbed in Twede
  That woned by the see.

(*a*). 2 oure . . .: against our will   3 Go, stab him   5 go, ditch him

(*b*). 3 he: they   5 f. wherever he likes, in the best manner
8 f. huddled in their huts—may they never thrive!   10 If I'm not mistaken   11 tumbed: fell   12 woned: lived

33   *The Battle of Dunbar (1296)*

THE foot-folk
   Put the Scottes in the polk
And nackened their nages.
By waye
Herd I never saye   5
   Of prester pages
To pike
The robes of the rike
   That in the feeld felle.
They token ay tulk   10
The rough raggy skulk,
   Rughin in helle . . . .

For Scottes
Telle I for sottes
   And wreches unwar,   15
Unsele
Dintès to dele,
   Them drow to Dumbar!

34   *Havelok at Grimsby and Lincoln*

GRIM was fishere swithè good
   And mikel couthè on the flood.
Many good fish therinne he took

33. 2 polk: mire   3 and stripped naked their backsides   4 any-
where   6–8 of fellows smarter to pillage the clothes of the men of
rank   10 f. They consigned every man to the rough shaggy rascal
12 Rughin: Ruffin (devil's name)   14 I reckon are fools   15 unwar:
imprudent   16 ff. unlucky in dealing blows, they went to Dunbar

34. 1 swithe: very   2 and had great experience of the sea

Bothe with net and with hook:
He took the sturgiun and the whal   5
And the turbut and lax with-al;
He took the sele and the el
(He spedde oftė swithė wel);
Keling he took and tumbėrel,
Hering and the makėrel,   10
The butte, the shulle, the thornėbake.
Goodė paniers dide he make—
One til him, and other thrinne
Til hise sones—to beren fish inne
Up o lande to selle and change.   15
Forbar he neither town ne grange
That he ne to yede with his ware;
Cam he nevere home hand-bare,
That he ne broughtė bred and sowel
In his shirte or in his cowel,   20
In his pokė benes and corn:
His swink ne havede he nought forlorn.
And when he took the grete laumprèy,
Ful wel he couthe the rightė wey
To Lincòlne, the goodė borough: 25
Ofte he yede it thorough and thorough
Til he havėde al wel sold
And ther-fòre the penies told.

---

6 lax: salmon   7 el: eel   9 Keling: cod   tumberel: ?codling   11 ?halibut, plaice, ray   12 f. he had stout creels made—one for him, and three others   15 Up o lande: inland   change: barter   16 f. There was no village or farm that he failed to visit with his wares   18 hand-bare: empty-handed   19 sowel: relish   20 cowel: cloak   21 poke: bag   22 he had not wasted his labour   23 grete laumprey: sea lamprey   24 couthe: knew   righte: direct   26 yede: went   28 and counted the pence (he got) for it

Then he com thenne hy werė blithe,
For home he broughtė felė sithe   30
Wastels, simenels with the horn,
Hise pokės fulle of mele and corn,
Netės flesh, shepes, and swines,
And hemp to maken of goodė lines,
And strongė ropės to hise nettes,   35
In the see-weres he ofte settes.

   Thusgate Grim him fairė ledde:
Him and his gengė wel he fedde
Wel twelf winter other more.
Havelok was war that Grim swank sore   40
For his mete, and he lay at home;
Thought he: 'Ich am now no grome;
Ich am wel waxen and wel may eten
More than evere Grim may geten:
Ich etė more, by God on live,   45
Than Grim and hisė children five!
It ne may nought been thus longe.
Goddot! I wille with thee gonge
For to leren sum good to gete:
Swinken ich woldė for my mete.   50
It is no shamė for to swinken:
The man that may wel eten and drinken
That n'ought ne have but on swink long.

---

29 When he came from there they were glad   30 fele sithe: many
times   31 cakes and horn-shaped simnels   33 Netes: ox's
35 to: for   36 which he often shoots in the sea-weirs (enclosures for
catching fish)   37 In this way Grim managed well   38 genge:
household   39 other: or   40 war: aware   swank: toiled
42 Ich: I   grome: boy   43 waxen: grown   45 God . ..: the
living God   48 f. God knows, I want to go with you to learn to
make some money   50 Swinken: work   53 ought not to have it
(food and drink) except by work

To liggen at home it is ful strong!
God yeldė him, ther I ne may,   55
That haveth me fed to this day!
Gladlike I wille the paniers bere;
Ich wot ne shal it me nought dere
Thegh ther be inne a birthen gret
Al so hevy as a net.   60
Shal ich nevere lengere dwelle:
Tomorwen shal ich forth pelle.'
    On the morwen, when it was day,
He stirt up soone and nought ne lay,
And cast a panier on his bac   65
With fish givèled as a stac.
Al so michel he bar him one
So hy foure, by minė mone!
Wel he it bar and solde it wel:
The silver he broughte home ilkė del,   70
Al that he ther-fòrė took—
Withheld he nought a ferthinges nook.
So yede he forth ilkė day
That he nevere at homė lay,
So wolde he his mester lere.   75
    Bifel it so a strong dere
Bigan to rise of corn of bred,
That Grim ne couthė no good red

---

54 liggen: lie   ful strong: too bad   55 May God reward him, as
I cannot   58 dere: hurt   59 Thegh: though   60 as heavy as
an ox   61 I must not delay any longer   62 pelle: hurry   64
stirt: jumped   soone: at once   66 giveled: piled up   as: like
67 f. He carried as much by himself as they four, in my opinion
70 silver: money   ilke del: every bit   71 ther-fore: for it
72 a . . . : a fraction of a farthing   75 so anxious was he to learn his
trade   76 It so happened that a severe dearth   77 corn . . . :
corn for bread   78 ne . . . : had no idea

How he sholde his meiné fede.
Of Havelok havede he michel drede,   80
For he was strong and wel moughte ete
More than evere moughte he gete;
Ne he ne moughte on the see take
Neither lenge ne thornébake,
Ne none other fish that doughte   85
His meiné feden with he moughte.
Of Havélok he havede care
Whilgat that he mighté fare—
Of his children was him nought;
On Havélok was al his thought—   90
And saidé: 'Havelok, deré sone,
I wené that we deyé mone
For hunger: this dere is so strong,
And ouré mete is outen long.
Betere is that thou henné gonge   95
Than thou heré dwellé longe:
Hethen thou maght gangen to late!
Thou canst ful wel the righté gate
To Lincòlne, the goodé borough—
Thou havest it gon ful ofté thorough;   100
Of me ne is me nought a slo.
Betere is that thou thider go,
For ther is many good man inne;
Ther thou maght thy meté winne.
But wo is me thou art so naked!   105

79 meiné: household   80 For Havelok he had great anxiety
81 moughte: could   84 lenge: ling   85 f. nor any other fish of
value with which he could feed his household   88 Whilgat: how
89 he was not worried about his children   92 mone: must   93
dere: dearth   94 outen: out, exhausted   95 henne gonge: go
from here   97 f. from here you might go too late! You know very
well the direct way   101 I don't care at all (lit. a sloe) about myself
103 for in that place is many a man of substance

Of my sail I woldė thee were maked
A cloth thou mightest innė gonge,
Sone, no cold that thou ne fonge.'
 He took the sherės of the nail
And made him a cowel of the sail,   110
And Havelok dide it soonė on;
Haved he neither hosen ne shon,
Ne none kinnės other wede:
To Lincòlne barfoot he yede.
When he cam ther he was ful wil,   115
Ne havede he no frend to gangen til.
Two dayes ther fastinde he yede,
That none for his werk wolde him fede.
The thriddė day herde he calle:
'Bermen, bermen, hider forth alle!'   120
Povre that on footė yede
Sprongen forth so sparke on glede.
Havelok shof down nine or ten
Right amidėward the fen,
And stirtė forth to the cook,   125
Ther the erlės mete he took
That he boughtė at the brigge;
The bermen let he allė ligge
And bar the metė to the castel,
And gat him there a ferthing wastel.   130

107 a garment you could go about in 108 fonge: catch 109
of: off 110 cowel: cloak 111 dide...: put it on at once 112
shon: shoes 113 nor any other kind of garment 115 wil: at a loss
116 gangen til: go to 117 fastinde: fasting 120 Bermen: porters
hider forth: (come) along here 121 Povre: poor men 122 sprang
forward like a spark from a live coal 123 shof: shoved 124
right in the middle of the mud 125 stirte forth: bounded forward
126 Ther: as 127 brigge: i.e. High Bridge, Lincoln 128 he left
all the porters lying 130 and got for himself a farthing cake
there

That other day kepte he ook
Swithė yerne the erlės cook,
Til that he sagh him on the brigge
And by him many fishes ligge.
The erlės mete havede he bought   135
Of Cornwalìe, and caldė oft:
'Bermen, bermen, hider swithe!'
Havelok it herde and was ful blithe
That he herdė 'Bermen!' calle.
Allė made he hem down falle   140
That in his gatė yeden and stoode—
Wel sixtenė laddės goode;
As he lep the cookė til
He shof hem alle upon an hil,
Astirtė til him with his rippe   145
And bigan the fish to kippe.
He bar up wel a cartė-lode
Of segges, laxes, of playces brode,
Of grete laumprees, and of eles;
Sparede he neither tos ne heles   150
Til that he to the castel cam,
That men fro him his birthen nam.
Then men haveden holpen him down
With the birthen of his crown,
The cook stood and on him low,   155
And thoughte him stalworthe man ynow,
And saidė: 'Wilt thou been with me?

131 f. The next day also he watched out very eagerly for the earl's cook
133 sagh: saw   135 f. He had bought the Earl of Cornwall's pro-
visions and called repeatedly   137 swithe: quickly   140 hem:
them   141 gate: way   143 lep . . .: ran to the cook   144 hil:
heap   145 bounded towards him with his basket   146 kippe:
pick up   148 segges: cuttlefish   150 i.e. he ran as fast as he
could   152 nam: took   153 Then: when   154 of: from
155 low: smiled

Gladlike wille ich feden thee.
Wel is set the mete thou etes
And the hirė that thou getes.'   160
'Goddot!' quoth he, 'levė sire,
Bidde ich you none other hire,
But yeveth me ynow to ete;
Fir and water I wille you fete,
The fir blow and ful wel maken;   165
Stickės can ich breken and craken,
And kindlen ful wel a fir
And maken it to brennen shir;
Ful wel can ich cleven shides,
Eles to-turven of here hides;   170
Ful wel can ich dishes swillen,
And don al that ye evere willen.'
Quoth the cook: 'Wille I no more.
Go thou yonder and sit thore,
And I shal yeve thee ful fair bred,   175
And make thee broÿs in the led.
Sit now down and et ful yerne—
Datheit who thee metė werne!'
    Havelok sette him down anon,
Also stille as a ston,   180
Til he havede ful wel eten—
Tho havede Havelok fairė geten!
When he havede eten ynow,
He cam to the welle, water up-drow,

---

159 set: invested   161 leve: dear   162 Bidde: ask   163
yeveth: give   164 Fir: fuel   fete: fetch   166 can: know how to
168 brennen shir: burn bright   169 cleven . . .: split kindling wood
170 skin eels   173 Wille: want   174 thore: there   176 broys:
broth   led: pot   177 yerne: heartily   178 a curse on anyone
who denies you food   179 anon: at once   180 Also: as
182 then Havelok had done well for himself   184 -drow: drew

And fildė ther a michel so.   185
Bad he non agein him go,
But bitween his handes he bar it in
Al him one to the kichìn.
Bad he none him water to fete,
Ne fro brigge to bere the mete;   190
He bar the turves, he bar the star,
The wodė fro the brigge he bar;
Al that evere shulden hy nitte,
Al he drow and al he kitte:
Wolde he nevere haven rest   195
Morė than he were a best.
Of allė men was he most meke,
Laughinde ay and blithe of speke:
Evere he was glad and blithe—
His sorwe he couthė ful wel mithe.   200
It ne was none so litel knave
For to leiken ne for to plawe
That he ne woldė with him playe;
The children that yeden in the waye
Of him hy diden al her wille   205
And with him leikeden her fille.
Him loveden allė, stille and bolde,
Knightės, children, yunge and olde—
Alle him loveden that him sowe,
Bothen heyė men and lowe.   210

185 so: pail   186 he asked nobody to partner him   188 him
one: by himself   189 him . . .: to fetch him water   191 star:
sedge (for kindling)   193 nitte: use   194 kitte: cut   196 any
more than if he had been a beast   198 speke: speech   200 mithe:
conceal   201–3 there was no boy so small for playing games and sports
that he would not play with him   204 in . . .: in the streets
205 f. did what they liked with him and played with him as much as they
wanted   207 stille: quiet   209 sowe: saw

35 *A Lover's Stratagem*

THE porter thoughtė what to rede:
He let flowres gaderen in the mede
(He wiste it was the maidenes wille),
Two coupen he let of flowrės fille;
That was the rede that he thought tho,   5
Florice in that o coupe do.
Tweyė geggės the coupė bere,
So hevy charged that wroth they were;
They bad God yif him evil fin
That so many flowrės dide therin!   10
   Thider that they weren y-bede
Ne were they nought aright be-rede,
Ac they turned in here left hond
Blaunchėflourės bowr anond:
To Clarice bowr the coupe they bere   15
With the flowres that therinne were.
There the coupe they sette adown
And yaf him herė malisoun
That so fele flowres hem broughte on honde;
They wenten forth and leten the coupe stonde.   20
   Clarice to the coupe com and wolde
The flowrės handlen and beholde.
Floris wende it hadde been his sweet wight,
In the coupe he stood upright;

1 what . . .: what to do   2 he had flowers picked in the meadow
3 wiste: knew   4 coupen: baskets   5 f. rede . . .: plan that he
then devised, to put Floris in one of the baskets   7 Two servants
carried the basket   8 charged: loaded   9 they prayed God to
give a bad end to him   10 dide: put   11–14 They were not
rightly directed to the place they were told to go to, but they turned to
their left into the chamber beside Blaunchflour's   15 Clarice's
18 f. and cursed the man who had loaded them with so many flowers
20 leten . . .: left the basket standing   21 com: came   23 wende:
supposed   sweet wight: sweetheart

And the maiden al for drede   25
Began to shrichen and to grede.
Tho he segh it n'as nought hié
Into the coupe he stirte ayé,
And held him betrayed al clene;
Of his deth he ne yaf nought a bene.   30
   Ther come to Clarice maidenes lepe
By ten, by twenty, in one hepe,
And askedè what hirè were
That hié makede so loude bere.
Clarice hir understood anonright   35
That it was Blaunchèflours swete wight,
For here bowrès neghè were,
And selden that they n'eren y-fere,
And either of other counseil they wiste,
And michel either to other triste.   40
Hié yaf hir maidenes answere anon
That into bowre they sholden gon;
'To this coupe ich cam and wolde
The flowrès handly and beholde,
Ac er ich it ever wiste   45
A boterfleye toyein me fliste.
Ich was so sor a-drad of than,
That schrichen and greden I began.'

26 schrichen . . .: shriek and scream   27 When he saw it was
not her   28 stirte ayé: darted back   29 f. and thought he had
been utterly betrayed: he did not rate his chance of life at a bean   31
come lepe: came running   32–4 in tens and twenties, all together,
and asked what was the matter with her that she made so loud an outcry
35 Clarice realised at once   37 here: their   neghe: close to-
gether   38 f. and it was seldom that they were not together, and
each knew the other's secrets   40 michel: greatly   triste: trusted
41 Hie yaf: She gave   anon: directly   43 ich: I   44 handly:
touch   45 f. but before I knew it a butterfly flew at me   47 a-
drad . . .: frightened of it

The maidenes haddė therof gle,
And turnede ayein and let Clarice be. 50
   So soone so the maidenes weren a-gon
To Blauncheflours bowr Clarice went anon
And saide leyende to Blaunchėflour:
'Wilt thou seen a ful fair flowr?
Swich a flowr that thee shal like, 55
Have thou seën it a lite.'
'Avoy! dameisele,' quath Blaunchėflour,
'Hié that loveth paramour
And hath therof joye may love flowres;
Ac ich libbe in sorewe in these towres. 60
Ich y-here, Clarice, withoutė gabbe,
The Amiral wil me to wivė habbe.
Ac th'ilkė day shal never be
That men shal atwitė me
That I shal been of love untrewe, 65
Ne chaungy lovė for non newe,
For no love ne for non eie;
So doth Floris in his contreie.
Now shal swetė Floris misse
Shal non other of me have blisse.' 70
   Clarice stant and behalt that reuthe
And the treunesse of this treuthe.
Leyende she saide to Blaunchėflour:
'Com now, see that ilchė flowr';

49 hadde . . .: were amused at this   50 turnede ayein: went away
51 So: as   53 leyende: smiling   55 Swich: such   like: please
56 once you have seen it a little   57 Avoy: shame on you   58
she who is deeply in love   60 Ac: but   libbe: live   61 withoute
gabbe: truly   62 Amiral: Emir   to . . .: have as his wife   64
atwite: reproach   66 f. or change my love for a new one, on account
of any love or fear   69 Now that sweet Floris shall not have me
71 Clarice stands and beholds that pitiful sight   72 treuthe: loyalty
74 ilche: same

To the coupe they yeden tho.   75
Wel blisful was Florìssè tho,
For he had y-herd al this;
Out of the coupe he stirte, y-wis.
Blaunchèflour chaungede hewe;
Wel soone either other knewe: 80
Withouten speche togidere they lepe,
They clipte and kiste and eke wepe.
Herè kissing laste a mile,
And that hem thoughtè litel while.

    Claricè behalt al this—   85
Here contenaunce and herè blis—
And leyende saide to Blaunchèflour:
'Felawe, knowest thou ought this flowr?
Litel er n'oldest thou it see,
And now thou ne might it lete fro thee;   90
He moste conne wel muchel of art
That thou woldest yif therof any part!'
Bothe these swetè thinges for bliss
Falleth down hir feet to kiss,
And crieth hir mercy al weping   95
That hiè hem bewreye nought to the king,
To the king that hiè hem nought bewreye,
Wher-thourgh they were siker to deye.

    Tho spak Clarice to Blaunchèflour
Wordès ful of fin amour: 100

75 yeden tho: went then   78 y-wis: indeed   79 hewe: colour
80 immediately each knew the other   81 togidere . . .: they sprang
together   82 clipte: embraced   wepe: wept   83 laste: lasted
a mile: i.e. a very long time   84 hem thoughtè: seemed to them
85 behalt: watches   86 contenaunce: behaviour   88 Felawe:
friend   ought: at all   89 a little earlier you refused to see it
90 it lete: let it go   91 f. anyone would have to be very artful for
you to be willing to give him any part of it   95 crieth hir: cry to
her (for)   96 bewreye: betray   98 through which they would
be sure to die   100 fin amour: pure love

'Ne doutė you namore withalle
Than to myself it hadde befalle;
Witė ye wel witerly
That hele ich wille youre bother drury.'
 To one bedde hié hath hem y-brought,   105
That was of silk and sendal wrought.
They sette hem there wel softe adown,
And Clarice drow the courtin roun. . . .
 Now hadde the Amiral swich a wone
That every day ther sholdė come   110
Two maidenes out of herė bowre
To serven him up in the towre,
That one with towaille and basìn
For to washen his handės in,
That other sholde bringe combe and mirður   115
To serven him with gret honòur;
And thei they servede him never so faire,
A-morewen sholde another paire;
And mest was woned into the towr
Therto Clarìce and Blaunchéflour.   120
So long him servede the maidenes route
That here servìce was come aboute:
On the morewen that thider come Florìce
It fel to Blaunchéflour and to Clarìce.
 Clarice (so wel hir mote betide)   125
Aros up in the morewen-tide

101–4 do not fear any more for yourselves indeed than if it had happened
to me; rest assured that I mean to conceal the love-making of you both
106 sendal: ?fine linen   107 sette hem: settled themselves   108 and
Clarice drew the curtain round   109 wone: habit   117 thei: though
118–20 the next day another pair had to (serve him); and Clarice and
Blauncheflour were most used to (doing) this in the tower   121 route:
company   122 here service: their turn to serve   123 on the
morning after Floris came there   125 so . . .: may she have good
fortune

And clepede after Blauncheflour
To wende with hir into the towr;
Blauncheflour saide: 'Ich am comende',
Ac hir answère was al slepende.   130
Clarice in the way is nome
And wende that Blauncheflour had come;
Soone so Clarice com in the towr
The Amiral asked after Blauncheflour.
'Sire', hié saide anonright,   135
'Hié hath y-wakèd al this night
And y-kneelèd and y-looke
And y-rad upon hir booke,
And bad to God hir orisoun
That He thee yive His benisoun   140
And thee heldè longe alive.
Now she slepeth al so swithe,
Blauncheflour, that maiden swete,
That hié ne may nought comen yete.'
'Certès', said the king,   145
'Now is hié a swetè thing!
Wel aughte ich hir yerne to wive
Whenne hié bit so for my live.'

---

127 clepede: called   128 wende: go   129 comende: coming
130 al . . .: given in her sleep   131 Clarice set out on her way
132 wende: thought   133 Soone so: as soon as   135 anonright:
at once   136 y-waked: stayed awake   137 y-looke: looked
138 y-rad: read   139 bad: prayed   141 helde: keep   142
al . . .: so heavily   145 Certes: certainly   147 I ought indeed to
desire her as my wife   148 bit: prays

36 *Four Wise Men on Edward II's Reign*

*D*ES plu sages de la tere
  Ore escotez un sarmoun,
Of four wise men that ther were,
  Why Engèland is brought adown.

The firstè saide: 'I understande   5
Ne may no king wel been in lande,
  Under God Almighte,
But he kunne himself rede
How he shal in landè lede
  Every man with righte.   10
    For might is right,
    Night is light,
    And fight is flight.
      For might is right, the land is lawèless;
      For night is light, the land is lorèless;   15
      For fight is flight, the land is namèless.'

That other saide a word ful good:
Who-so roweth again the flood,
  Of sorwe he shal drinke;
Also hit fareth by the unsele: 20
A man shal have litel hele
  Ther-again to swinke.
    Now one is two,

1–4 Now listen to a discourse by the wisest in the land, by four wise
men that there were, (telling) why England is brought low   8–10
unless he can think out for himself how he is to govern everyone in the
land justly   14 For: because   15 loreless: without principles
16 nameless: without glory   17 other: second   18 again: against
20–2 the same goes for misfortune: a man shall have little success in
struggling against it

Wele is wo,
And frend is fo.   25
   For one is two, the land is strengthéless;
   For wele is wo, the land is reuthéless;
   For frend is fo, the land is lovéless.'

That thriddé saide: 'It is no wonder
Of these heirés that goth under   30
  When they comen to lande
Proude and stoute, and ginneth yelpe;
Ac of thing that sholdé helpe
  Have they nought on hande.
    Now lust haveth leve,   35
    Theef is reve,
    And pride hath sleve.
      For lust hath leve, the land is thewéless;
      For theef is reve, the land is penyless;
      For pride hath sleve, the land is almésless.'   40

The forthé saide that he is wood
That dwelleth to muchel in the flood
  For gold or for aughte.
For gold or silver or any wele,
Hunger or thirst, hete or chele,   45
  Al shal gon to naughte.
    Now wille is rede,
    Wit is quede,
    And good is dede.

24 Wele: happiness   30–4 about these heirs who do no good when they inherit, proud and haughty, and start boasting; but they do nothing that might help.   35–7 Now desire is given licence, a thief is land-steward, and pride flaunts fine clothes   38 theweless: without virtue   41 wood: mad   43 aughte: possessions   44 wele: riches   45 hete . . .: heat or cold   47–9 Now will is policy, reason is discredited, and goodness is dead

For wille is rede, the land is wrecful;   50
For wit is quede, the land is wrongful;
For good is dede, the land is sinful.

37   *Sir Orfeo*

WE reden ofte and finde y-write,
   As clerkės don us to wite,
The layės that been of harping
Been y-founde of frely thing:
Sum been of wele, and sum of wo,   5
And sum of joy and merthe also;
Sum of bourdes, and sum of ribaudry,
And sum ther been of the faiëry;
Sum of trechery, and sum of gile,
And sum of happes that fallen by while;   10
Of allė thing that men may see
Most to lowe forsoothe they be.
In Britain these layes aren y-write,
First y-founde and forth y-gete,
Of àventures that fillen by dayes,   15
Wherof Britouns made her layes.
When they might owher heren
Of àventurės that ther weren,
They her harpės tooke with game,
Maden layes and yaf it name.   20

36. 50 wrecful: full of misery

37. Orfeo: Orpheus   2 as learned men inform us   3 f. the lays made for harping, which are composed about noble themes   5 wele: happiness   7 bourdes: jests   8 faiery: magic   10 and some about happenings that occur from time to time   12 to lowe: to be praised   13 Britain: Brittany   14 first composed and set forth   15 about happenings that occurred in bygone days   16 Britouns: Bretons   her: their   17 owher: anywhere   19 with game: merrily   20 yaf: gave

Of àventures that han befalle
I can sum tellè, but nought alle.
Herken, lordinges that been trewe,
And I wil you telle of Sir Orphèwe.
   Orfeo was a king,   25
In Ingèlond an heigh lording,
A stalworth man and hardy bo;
Large and curteis he was alsò.
His fader was comen of King Pluto,
And his moder of King Juno,   30
That sum time were as godes y-hold
For àventours that they dide and told.
   Orfeo most of any thing
Lovede the glee of harping;
Siker was every good harpòur   35
Of him to havè muche honòur.
Himself lovèd for to harpe
And layde theron his wittès sharpe.
He lernèd so, ther nothing was
A better harper in no plas;   40
In the world was never man born
That onès Orpheo sat beforn,
And he might of his harping here,
He shuldè thinkè that he were
In one of the joys of Paradis,   45
Suche joy and melody in his harping is.
   This king sojournd in Traciens,
That was a cité of noble defens;

---

21 han: have   23 lordinges: gentlemen   27 a man both
stalwart and brave   28 Large: generous   29 comen of: descended
from   31 y-hold: regarded   34 glee . . .: playing of the harp
35 Siker: sure   36 Of: from   38 and applied his keen intelligence
to it   39 nothing: in no way   42 who once sat before Orfeo
43 And: if   44 He shulde: *i.e.* who would not   47 Traciens: *i.e.*
Thrace

(For Winchester was clepèd tho
Traciens withouten no).⁣   50
The king hadde a queen of pris
That was y-cleped Dame Heurodis,
The fairest levedy, for the nones,
That might gon on body and bones,
Ful of love and of goodnesse;   55
Ac no man may telle her fairnesse.

Befell so in the còmessing of May,
When mery and hot is the day,
And away beeth winter-showrs,
And every feeld is ful of flowrs,   60
And blosmè breme on every bough
Overal waxeth mery enough.
This ichè queen, Dame Heurodis,
Took two maidenès of pris,
And went in an undrentide   65
To playè by an orchard-side,
To see the flowrès sprede and spring,
And to here the fowlès sing.

They sett hem down allè three
Under a fair impè-tree,   70
And wel soone this fairè quene
Fel on slepe upon the grene.
The maidens durst her nought awake,
But lete her ligge and rest take.
So she slepe til afternone,   75

49 cleped tho: called then   50 withouten no: undeniably   51 of pris: excellent   52 Heurodis: Eurydice   53 f. the fairest lady, indeed, in figure and form, that ever walked   56 Ac: but   57 comessing: beginning   61 breme: glorious   62 grow everywhere very beautiful   63 iche: same   65 undrentide: morning   66 playe: amuse themselves   67 sprede: open   69 hem: them(selves) 70 impe-tree: orchard-tree   72 on slepe: asleep   74 ligge: lie 75 slepe: slept

That undertide was al y-done.
Ac as soone as she gan awake
She cried and lothly bere gan make:
She froted her handen and her fete,
And crached her visage—it bled wete;   80
Her richė robe hié al to-ritt,
And was reveysed out of her witt.
The two maidens her beside
No durst with her no leng abide,
But ourn to the palàis ful right,   85
And toldė bothe squier and knight
That her queen awedė wold,
And bad hem go and her athold.
Knightes ourn, and levedis alsò,
Damisels sixty and mo;   90
In the orchard to the queen hye come
And her up in her armės nome,
And brought her to bed attė last,
And held her there finė fast;
Ac ever she held in o cry,   95
And wolde up and owỳ.
    When Orfeo herdė that tiding,
Never him n'as wers for no thing.
He come with knightės tene
To chaumber right befor the quene,   100
And beheld, and said with grete pité:

76 That: until   77 gan awake: awoke   78 bere: uproar
79 froted: tore at   80 crached: scratched   bled wete: was wet with
blood   81 hie: she   to-ritt: ripped to pieces   82 and became
demented   84 leng: longer   85 ourn: ran   right: straight
87 awede wold: was going mad   88 athold: restrain   90 mo:
more   91 hye come: they came   92 nome: took   94 fine
fast: very tight   95 f. but always she cried in the same strain, and
wanted to get up and go   98 he was never so distressed at anything
99 come: came   tene: ten

'O leef lif, what is thee,
That ever yete hast been so stille,
And now gredest wonder shille?
Thy body, that was so white y-core,   105
With thine nailes is al to-tore.
Allas! thy rode, that was so red,
Is al wan, as thou were ded;
And also thine fingres smale
Beeth al blody and al pale.   110
Allas! thy lovesom eyèn two
Looketh so man doth on his fo.
A! dame, ich beseche mercỳ,
Lete been al this reweful cry,
And tel me what thee is, and how,   115
And what thing may thee helpè now.'

   Tho lay she stille attè last,
And gan to wepè swithè fast,
And saidè thus the kingè to:
'Allas! my lord, Sir Orfeo,   120
Sithen we first togider were,
Onès wroth never we n'ere,
But ever ich have y-lovèd thee
As my lif, and so thou me.
Ac now we motè delen a-two: 125
Do thy best, for I mot go.'
   'Allas!' quath he, 'forlorn ich am.
Whider wilt thou go, and to wham?

---

102 O my dear one, what troubles you   103 stille: quiet   104
and now shriek amazingly loud   105 white y-core: exquisitely white
106 to-tore: torn to pieces   107 rode: face   108 as: as if   109
smale: slender   112 so: as   113 ich: I   114 Lete been: stop
115 what . . .: what troubles you, and why   117 Tho: then   118
swithe: very   121 Sithen: since   122 Ones: once   125 but
now we must part   127 forlorn: desolated

Whider thou gost, ich'il with thee,
And whider I go, thou shalt with me.'　　　130
'Nay, nay, sir, that nought n'is;
Ich'il thee telle al how it is:
As ich lay this undertide
And slepe under our orchard-side,
Ther come to me two fair knightes　　　135
Wel y-armèd al to rightes,
And bad me comen an heighing
And spekè with her lord the king.
And ich answèrd at wordès bold,
I no durst nought, no I n'old.　　　140
They prikèd ayain as they might drive;
Tho com her king also blive,
With an hundred knightes and mo,
And damisels an hundred alsò,
Al on snowè-whitè stedes;　　　145
As white as milke were her wedes:
I no seigh never yete before
So fairè creàtours y-core.
The king hadde a crown on hed:
It n'as of silver no of gold red,　　　150
Ac it was of a precious ston—
As bright as the sunne it shon.
And as soon as he to me cam,
Wold ich, n'old ich, he me nam,
And madè me with him ride　　　155
Upon a palfray, by his side,
And broughtè me to his palàys,

129 ich'il: I will (go)　　　131 nought n'is: cannot be　　　136 al . . . :
in proper style　　　137 an heighing: in haste　　　139 at: with
140 no I n'old: nor was I willing　　　141 they rode away as fast as they
could　　　142 also blive: immediately　　　147 seigh: saw　　　148
such exquisitely fair creatures　　　154 he seized me willy-nilly

Wel atird in ichė ways,
And shewėd me castels and towrs,
Rivers, forestes, frith with flowrs,   160
And his richė stedes ichone;
And sithen me brought ayain home
Into our owėn orchard,
And said to me thus afterward:
"Looke, dame, to-morwe that thou be   165
Right here under this impė-tree,
And then thou shalt with us go,
And livė with us evermo;
And if thou makės us ylet,
Wher thou be, thou worst y-fet,   170
And to-tore thine limės al,
That nothing helpė thee no shal;
And thei thou beest so to-torn,
Yete thou worst with us y-born." '

    When King Orfeo herd this cas,   175
'O we!' quath he, 'allas, allas!
Lever me were to lete my lif
Than thus to lese the queen my wif!'
He askėd conseil at ich man,
Ac no man him help no can.   180
    Amorwe the undertide is come,
And Orfeo hath his armes y-nome,
And wel ten hundred knightes with him
Ich y-armėd stout and grim;

---

158 well furnished in every way   160 frith: woodland   161
stedes: estates   ichone: each one   162 sithen: afterwards   165
Looke: see   168 -mo: -more   169 ylet: resistance   170
wherever you are, you shall be fetched   172 so that nothing shall save
you   173 thei: though   174 worst: shall be   175 this cas:
what had happened   176 we: woe   177 I had rather lose my life
178 lese: lose   179 ich: each   180 can: knows how to   181
Amorwe: on the morrow   182 y-nome: taken up   183 wel: fully

And with the queen wenten he   185
Right unto that impé-tree.
They made sheltrom in ich a side,
And said they woldé there abide,
And dié ther everichon
Er the queen shuld from hem gon.   190
Ac yete amiddés hem ful right
The queen was away y-twight,
With faiëry forth y-nome;
Men wist never wher she was become.

    Tho was ther crying, wepe and wo!   195
The king into his chaumber is go,
And oft swooned upon the stone,
And made swiche dole and swiche mone
That neighe his lif was y-spent:
Ther was non amendément.   200

    He cleped togider his baròuns,
Erlés, lordés of renouns;
And when they al y-comen were,
'Lordinges', he said, 'befor you here
Ich ordainy myn highe stewàrd   205
To wite my kingdom afterward;
In my stedé been he shal,
To kepe my landés overal.
For, now ich have my queen y-lore,
The fairest levedy that ever was bore,   210
Never eft I n'il no woman see.

185 he: they   187 sheltrom: rank of armed men   189
everichon: every one   191 amiddes: in the middle of   192
y-twight: snatched   193 carried off by magic   194 become:
gone   195 Tho: then   197 stone: stone floor   198 and
grieved and lamented so much   200 amendement: cure   201
cleped: called   202 renouns: renown   206 wite: look after
208 **kepe: rule**   overal: everywhere   209 y-lore: lost   211 eft:
again

Into wilderness ich'il tee,
And livè ther evermore
With wildè bestes in holtès hore.
And when ye understand that I be spent,   215
Make you then a parlèment,
And chesè you a newè king.
Now doth your best with al my thing.'
   Tho was ther weeping in the halle,
And gretè cry among hem alle;   220
Unnethè might old or yong
For weeping speke a word with tong.
They kneelèd adown al y-fere,
And prayd him, if his willè were,
That he no shuld nought from hem go.   225
'Do way!' quath he, 'it shal be so.'
   Al his kingdom he forsook;
But a sclavin on him he took;
He no haddè kirtel no hood,
Shert, no non other good.   230
But his harp he took algate,
And dide him barfoot out at the yate;
No man mostè with him go.
   O way! what ther was wepe and wo
When he, that hadde been king with crown,   235
Went so poverlich out of town!
Thurgh wode and over heth
Into the wilderness he geth.

---

212 tee: go   214 holtes hore: grey woods   215 spent: dead
217 chese you: choose for yourselves   218 doth: do   thing:
affairs   221 Unnethe: scarcely   223 y-fere: together   226 Do
way: enough!   228 sclavin: pilgrim's mantle   229 kirtel:
tunic   231 algate: anyway   232 and went barefoot out of the
gate   233 moste: might   234 alas! what weeping and grief there
was   236 poverlich: wretchedly   238 geth: goes

Nothing he fint that him is ais,
But ever he liveth in gret malais.   240
He that hadde y-werd the fowe and gris,
And on bed the purper bis,
Now on hard hethe he lith,
With leves and gresse he him writh.
He that hadde had castels and towrs,   245
River, forest, frith with flowrs,
Now, thei it comenci to snewe and frese,
This king mot make his bed in mese.
He that had y-had knightes of pris
Befor him kneeland, and levedis,   250
Now seeth he nothing that him liketh
But wildė wormės by him striketh.
He that had y-had plenté
Of mete and drink, of ich deinté,
Now may he al day digge and wroote   255
Er he finde his fille of roote.
In sumer he liveth by wild frut
And berien but goodė lite;
In winter may he nothing finde
But rootė, grases, and the rinde.   260
Al his body was away dwine
For missais, and al to-chine.
Lord! who may telle the sore
This king sufferd ten yere and more?

239 he finds nothing that gives him comfort   241 He who had
worn striped and grey fur   242 purper bis: dark red cloth   244
writh: covers   247 thei: though   snewe: snow   248 mot: must
mese: moss   250 kneeland: kneeling   251 liketh: pleases
252 (nothing) but fearsome snakes which glide past him   254 deinté:
delicacy   255 wroote: root, grub   256 roote: roots   258 and
berries of but little worth   260 rinde: bark   261 dwine: wasted
262 missais: hardship   to-chine: scarred   263 sore: distress

His here of his berd, blac and rowe,   265
To his girdelstede was growe.
His harp, whereon was al his glee,
He hidde in an holwė tree;
And when the weder was clere and bright,
He took his harp to him wel right   270
And harpėd at his owėn wille.
Into alle the wode the soun gan shille,
That alle the wilde bestes that ther beeth
For joye abouten him they teeth;
And alle the fowlės that ther were   275
Come and sete on ich a brere,
To here his harping afine,
So michė melody was therin;
And when he his harping letė wold,
No best by him abidė n'old.   280
    He might see him besides
Oft in hot undertides
The king o fairy with his rout
Com to hunt him al about,
With dim cry and blowing;   285
And houndes also with him berking;
Ac no best they no nome,
No never he n'ist whider they become.
And other while he might him see
As a gret host by him tee,   290
Wel atourned ten hundred knightes,

265 rowe: rough   266 girdelstede: waist   267 glee: pleasure
272 soun . . .: sound rang out   274 teeth: come   276 sete: sat
brere: briar   277 afine: to the end   278 miche: much   279
lete: cease   280 n'old: would (not)   281 him besides: near him
283 rout: company   284 him . . .: all round him   287 nome:
took   288–90 nor did he ever know what became of them. And at
other times he could see a great host passing by him   291 atourned:
equipped

Ich y-armėd to his rightes,
Of cuntenauncė stout and fers,
With many desplaid banėrs,
And ich his swerd y-drawė hold—   295
Ac never he n'ist whider they wold.
And other while he seigh other thing:
Knightes and levedis com dauncing
In queint atirė, gisėly,
Queintė pas and softly;   300
Tabours and trumpės yede hem by,
And al maner minstralcy.

   And on a day he seigh him beside
Sixty levedis on hors ride,
Gentil and jolif as brid on ris—   305
Nought o man amonges hem ther n'is—
And ich a faucoun on hand bere,
And riden on haukin by o rivère.
Of game they foundė wel goode haunt,
Maulardes, hairoun, and cormeraunt;   310
The fowlės of the water ariseth,
The faucouns hem wel deviseth;
Ich faucoun his prey slough.
That seigh Orfeo, and lough:
'Parfay!' quath he, 'ther is fair game,   315
Thider ich'il, by Godės name!

292 to . . .: in proper style   293 fers: fierce   295 f. and each
holding his drawn sword—but he never knew where they were going
297 seigh: saw   299 in elegant dress, expertly   300 Queinte pas:
with intricate steps   301 yede . . .: went with them   302 maner:
manner of   305 graceful and gay as a bird on the bough   306 o:
one   307 bere: carrying   308 riding a-hawking by a river-bank
309 wel . . .: great plenty   310 mallards, heron, and cormorant
311 of: from   312 deviseth: mark   313 slough: killed   314
ough: laughed   315 Parfay: by my faith   game: sport   316
Thider ich'il: I mean to go there

Ich was y-won swich werk to see.'
He aros, and thider gan tee.
To a levedy he was y-come,
Beheld, and hath wel undernome,   320
And seeth by al thing that it is
His owèn queen, Dam Heurodis.
Yern he beheld her, and she him eke,
Ac nother to other a word no speke.
For missais that she on him seigh,   325
That had been so riche and so heigh,
The terès fel out of her eighe.
The other levedis this y-seighe,
And makèd her away to ride—
She most with him no lenger abide.   330
   'Allas!' quath he, 'now me is wo.
Why n'il deth now me slo?
Allas! wreche, that I no might
Diè now after this sight!
Allas! to longè last my lif,   335
When I no dar nought with my wif,
No hiè to me, o word speke.
Allas! why n'il myn hertè breke?
Parfay!' quath he, 'tide what betide,
Whider so these levedis ride,   340
The selvè way ich'il streche;
Of lif no deth me no reche.'
   His sclavin he dide on also spac,

317 y-won: used   swich: such   318 gan tee: went   320
undernome: observed   321 by al thing: by every sign   323 Yern:
eagerly   324 nother: neither   325 because of the signs of
privation she saw in him   327 eighe: eyes   330 most: might
lenger: longer   332 slo: slay   335 to: too   last: lasts   337
hie: she   339 tide . . .: come what may   341 selve: same
streche: go   342 I do not care about life or death   343 he put
on his mantle straightaway

And heng his harp upon his bac,
And had wel goode wil to gon—   345
He no spard nother stub no ston.
In at a roche the levedis rideth,
And he after, and nought abideth.

  When he was in the roche y-go
Wel three milė other mo,   350
He com into a fair cuntrày,
As bright so sunne on sumers day,
Smoothe and plain and al greene—
Hille no dale n'as ther none y-seene.
Amidde the land a castel he seigh,   355
Riche and real, and wonder heigh.
Al the utėmastė wal
Was clere and shine as cristàl;
An hundred towrs ther were about,
Degisėlich, and bataild stout;   360
The butras com out of the diche,
Of redė gold y-archėd riche;
The vousour was anowrnėd al
Of ich maner divers aumal.
Within ther wer widė wones   365
Al of precious stones.
The werst piler on to beholde
Was al of burnist gold.
Al that land was ever light;
For when it shuld be therk and night   370

344 heng: hung   345 f. and he was very eager to go—he stopped
for nothing (*lit.* neither stump nor stone)   347 roche: rock   348
abideth: lingers   350 other mo: or more   356 real: royal
357 utemaste: outermost   358 shine: bright   360-4 wonderful,
and strongly embattled; the buttress rose out of the moat, arch-shaped, and
made of rich red gold; the vaulting was all decorated with every different
kind of enamel-work   365 wones: halls   370 therk: dark

The richė stonės lightė gunne
As bright as doth at noone the sunne.
No man may telle, no thenche in thought,
The richė werk that ther was wrought:
By al thing him think that it is   375
The proudė court of Paradis.
  In this castel the levedis alight;
He wold in after, if he might.
Orfeo knokketh at the gate,
The porter was redi therate,   380
And asked what he wold have y-do.
'Parfay!' (quath he) 'ich am a minstrel, lo!
To solas thy lord with my glee,
If his swetė willė be.'
The porter undide the gate anon,   385
And lete him into the castel gon.
  Then he gan behold about al,
And seigh liggeand within the wal
Of folk that were thider y-brought,
And thought dede, and n'arė nought.   390
Sum stoodė withouten hade,
And sum non armės n'ade,
And sum thurgh the body haddė wounde,
And sum lay wode, y-bounde,
And sum armėd on hors sete,   395
And sum astrangled as they ete,
And sum were in water adreint,

---

371 lighte gunne: shone   373 thenche: conceive   375 from all
the signs it seems to him that it is   378 wold: wanted (to go)
381 wold . . .: wanted   383 glee: music   385 anon: at once
388 liggeand: lying   389 Of folk: people   390 and seemed dead,
and were not   391 hade: head   392 n'ade: had not   394
wode: mad   395 sete: sat   396 astrangled: choked   397
adreint: drowned

And sum with fire al forshreint;
Wives ther lay on childbedde
Sum ded, and sum awedde;   400
And wonder fele ther lay besides
Right as they slepe her undertides.
Eche was thus in this world y-nome,
With faiëry thider y-come.
Ther he seigh his owèn wif,   405
Dame Heurodis, his leef lif,
Slepe under an impè-tree:
By her clothes he knewe that it was he.

   And when he hadde behold these merveils alle,
He went into the kingès halle.   410
Then seigh he ther a seemly sight,
A tabernacle blisseful and bright;
Therin her maister king sete,
And her queen fair and swete.
Her crownes, her clothès, shine so bright   415
That unnethe behold he hem might.

   When he hadde beholden al that thing,
He kneeled adown befor the king.
'O lord' (he said) 'if it thy willè were,
My minstralcy thou shust y-here.'   420
The king answèrd: 'What man art thou,
That art hider y-comen now?
Ich, no non that is with me,
No sent never after thee.
Sithen that ich here regny gan   425

398 forshreint: scorched to death   400 awedde: gone mad   401
wonder fele: very many   402 just as they were taking their forenoon
sleep   403 y-nome: taken   404 faiery: magic   406 leef: dear
408 *second* he: she   412 tabernacle: canopied throne   413 maister:
lord   415 shine: shone   416 unnethe: scarcely   420 shust:
shouldst   425 Since I began to reign here

I no fond never so folehardy man
That hider to us durstè wende,
But that ich him wold ofsende.'
'Lord,' quath he, 'trowe ful wel,
I n'am but a pover minstrel;   430
And, sir, it is the maner of ous
To sechè many a lordès hous;
Thei we nought welcòm no be,
Yete we mot profery forth our glee.'

   Befor the king he sat adown,   435
And took his harp so mery of soun,
And tempreth his harp, as he wel can,
And blisseful notès he ther gan,
That al that in the palais were
Com to him for to here,   440
And liggeth adown to his fete,
Hem thinketh his melody so swete.
The king herkneth and sit ful stille;
To here his glee he hath goode wille;
Goode bourde he hadde of his glee;   445
The riche queen also hadde he.

   When he hadde stint his harping,
Then saidè to him the king:
'Minstrel, me liketh wel thy glee.
Now aske of me what it be,   450
Largèlich ich'il thee pay:

---

426 fond: found   428 unless I chose to send for him   430
pover: poor   431 ous: us   432 seche: visit   433 Thei:
though   434 glee: music   436 soun: sound   437 tempreth:
tunes   can: knows how   438 gan: began (to make)   441 and
lie down at his feet   442 Hem thinketh: seems to them   443 sit . . . :
sits very quiet   444 wille: pleasure   445 bourde: entertainment
446 and so had the noble queen   447 stint: stopped   449 liketh:
pleases   450 what it be: whatever it may be   451 I am willing
to reward you generously

Now speke, and thou might assay.'
'Sir,' he said, 'ich besechė thee
That thou woldest yivė me
That ich levedy, bright on blee,   455
That slepeth under the impė-tree.'
'Nay,' quath the king, 'that nought n'ere!
A sory couple of you it were,
For thou art lenė, rowe, and blac,
And she is lovesom, withouten lac;   460
A lothlich thing it were for-thy
To seen her in thy compainy.'

    'O sir,' he said, 'gentil king,
Yete were it a wel fouler thing
To here a lesing of thy mouthe: 465
So, sir, as ye saidė nowthe,
What ich wold asky have I shold,
And nedės thou most thy word hold.'
The king said: 'Sithen it is so,
Take her by the hand and go;   470
Of her ich'il that thou be blithe.'

    He kneeled adown, and thanked him swithe;
His wif he took by the hand,
And dide him swithe out of that land,
And went him out of that thede—   475
Right as he com the way he yede.

452 assay: put it to the test   455 that same lady, fair of face
457 that . . .: that would be impossible   458 an ill-matched couple
you two would make   459 rowe: rough   460 lovesom: lovely
lac: fault   461 for-thy: therefore   465 lesing: lie   466
nowthe: just now   467 I was to have whatever I liked to ask
468 nedes: necessarily   most: must   469 Sithen: since   471
I wish you happiness with her   472 swithe: very much   474
and made his way quickly out of that land   475 thede: country
476 he went exactly the same way as he had come

So long he hath the way y-nome
To Winchester he is y-come,
That was his owėn cité;
Ac no man knewe that it was he.   480
No forther than the townės ende
For knoweleche he no durstė wende;
But with a begger y-bilt ful narwe,
Ther he took his herbarwe,
To him and to his owėn wif,   485
As a minstrel of pover lif,
And askėd tidinges of that land,
And who the kingdom held in hand.
The pover begger in his cot
Told him everich a grot: 490
How her queen was stole awy
Ten yere gon with faiëry;
And how her king en exile yede,
But no man n'ist in whichė thede;
And how the steward the land gan hold;   495
And other many thinges him told.
    Amorwė, ayain noonėtide,
He maked his wif ther abide;
The beggers clothes he borwed anon,
And heng his harp his rigge upon,   500
And went him into that cité,
That men might him behold and see.
Erlės and baròunės bold,

---

477 he has travelled on his way so far (that)   482 knoweleche:
fear of recognition   483 y-bilt: housed   narwe: meanly   484
herbarwe: lodging   485 To: for   488 held . . .: ruled   490
told him every detail   491 her: their   awy: away   492 gon:
ago   faiery: magic   493 en: into   494 n'ist: knew   496
other many: many other   497 ayain: towards   500 rigge:
back

Burjais and levedis him gun behold.
'Lo,' they said, 'swiche a man!   505
How long the here hangeth him upan!
Lo, how his berd hangeth to his knee!
He is y-clungen also a tree!'

   And as he yede in the strete,
With his steward he gan mete,   510
And loude he sett on him a cry:
'Sir stewàrd,' he said, 'mercỳ!
Ich am an harpour of hethènesse;
Help me now in this distresse!'
The steward said: 'Come with me, come;   515
Of that ich have thou shalt have some.
Everich goode harpour is welcom me to
For my lordès love Sir Orfeo.'

   In the castel the steward sat atte mete,
And many lording was by him sete.   520
Ther were trumpours and tabourers,
Harpours fele, and crouders;
Miche melody they makèd alle;
And Orfeo sat stille in the halle,
And herkneth. When they been al stille   525
He took his harp and tempred shille;
The blissfulest notes he harpèd there
That ever any man y-herd with ere;
Ich man likèd wel his glee.

    The steward beheld and gan y-see,   530

504 citizens and ladies looked at him   505 swiche: what   506
him upan: upon him   508 y-clungen also: wrinkled like   510 gan
mete: met   511 and he appealed to him loudly   513 hethenesse:
heathen lands   516 that: what   518 for the sake of my lord Sir
Orfeo   520 sete: seated   521 f. there were trumpeters and
tabour-players, many harpers and fiddlers   524 stille: quiet   526
tempred shille: tuned it clearly   530 beheld . . .: watched and
observed

And knewe the harp also blive.
'Minstrel,' he said, 'so mot thou thrive,
Where hadest thou this harp, and how?
I pray that thou me tellé now.'
'Lord,' quath he, 'in uncouthe thede,   535
Thurgh a wilderness as I yede,
Ther I founde in a dale
With liouns a man to-torén smale,
And wolves him frete with teeth so sharp.
By him I fond this ichė harp;   540
Wel ten yere it is y-go.'
'O,' quath the steward, 'now me is wo!
That was my lord Sir Orfeo.
Allas! wreche, what shal I do,
That have swiche a lord y-lore?   545
A way! that ich was y-bore!
That him was so hard grace y-yarked
And so vilé deth y-marked!'
Adown he fel a-swoon to grounde.
His barouns him took up in that stounde,   550
And telleth him how it geth—
It n'is no bot of manés deth.
  King Orfeo knew wel by than
His steward was a trewé man
And loved him as he aught to do,   555
And stant up and said thus: 'Lo,
Steward, herknė now this thing:

531 also blive: immediately   532 so . . .: so may you prosper
535 uncouthe thede: a strange land   539 frete: devoured   540
iche: same   541 y-go: ago   545 y-lore: lost   546 A
way: alas   547 that so cruel a fate was ordained for him   548 y-
marked: destined   549 a-swoon: in a swoon   550 in . . .: at
once   551 it geth: it (i.e. life) goes   552 there is no remedy for
man's death   553 than: that   556 stant: stands

96

If ich were Orfeo the king,
And hadde y-suffred ful yore
In wildernesse miche sore,   560
And hadde y-won my queen awy
Out of the land of faïery,
And hadde y-brought the levedy hende
Right here to the townes ende,
And with a begger her in y-nome,   565
And were myself hider y-come
Poverlich to thee, thus stille,
For to assay thy goode wille,
And ich founde thee thus trewe,
Thou no shust it never rewe: 570
Sikerlich, for love or ay,
Thou shust be king after my day.
And if thou of my deth hadest been blithe
Thou shust have voided also swithe.'
     Tho al tho that therin sete   575
That it was King Orfeo underyete,
And the steward him wel knewe:
Over and over the bord he threwe,
And fel adown to his fete;
So dide everich lord that ther sete;   580
And al they said at o crying:
'Ye beeth our lord, sir, and our king!'
Glad they were of his live.
To chaumber they ledde him als bilive,

559 ful yore: a very long while   560 sore: distress   561 awy:
away   563 hende: gracious   565 and lodged her with a beggar
567 stille: secretly   571 certainly, for love or fear (i.e. in any event)
574 you would have lost your office at once   575 Then all those
who were sitting in there   576 underyete: realized   578 he
leapt clean over the table   581 and they all cried with one voice
583 of . . .: that he was alive   584 als bilive: immediately

And bathèd him, and shaved his berd, 585
And tirèd him as a king apert.
And sithen with gret processioun
They brought the queen into the town
With al maner minstralcy.
Lord! ther was grete melody! 590
For joye they wepè with her eighe
That hem so sounde y-comen seighe.

　Now King Orfeo newe coround is,
And his queen Dame Heurodis,
And livèd long afterward; 595
And sithen was king the stewàrd.

　Harpours in Bretaine after than
Herd how this mervàile began,
And made herof a lay of goode liking,
And nempned it after the king; 600
That lay 'Orfeo' is y-hote;
Goode is the lay, swete is the note.

　Thus com Sir Orfeo out of his care.
God graunt us allè wel to fare.
　　　　　Amen.

38　　　　　*Now Springs the Spray*

N　OW springès the spray,
　　All for love ich am so seek
That slepen I ne may.

---

37. 586 and dressed him as a king for all to see　　587 sithen: afterwards
591 f. they wept for joy with their eyes because they saw them come back
so safe and sound　　　593 coround: crowned　　　597 than: that
599 of . . .: well-pleasing　　　600 nempned: named　　　601 y-hote:
called　　602 note: tune

38. 1 Now that the spray comes into leaf　　2 ich: I　　seek: sick

NOW SPRINGS THE SPRAY

As I me rode this endrè day
  O my playinge,   5
Seigh ich wher a litel may
  Bigan to singe:
    'The clot him clinge!
    Wai is him i love-longinge
Shal libben ay!'   10
      Now springès, etc.

Soon ich herde that mirie note
  Thider I drough;
I fonde hire in an erber swote
  Under a bough,   15
  With joy enough.
    Soon I asked: 'Thou mirie may,
    Why singest thou ay?'
    Now springès, etc.

Then answèrde that maiden swote   20
  Mid wordès fewe:
'My lemmàn me haves bihote
  Of lovè trewe:
  He chaunges anewe.
    If I may, it shal him rewe,   25
    By this day!'
    Now springès, etc.

4 f. As I was riding the other day for pleasure   6 Seigh: saw
may: maid   8 may the clod (of the grave) shrivel him   9 f.
Wretched is he who must always live in love-longing   12–14 As
soon as I heard that delightful song I went there; I found her in a lovely
arbour   17 Soon: at once   21 Mid: with   22 My sweetheart
has made me a vow   25 I shall make him rue it, if I can   26 i.e.
indeed

39 *The Annunciation*

GABRIEL, from Hevene-King
    Sent to the maidè swetè,
Broughtè thire blisful tidìng
  And faire he gan hir gretè:
    'Hail be thou, ful of grace aright!   5
    For Godès Sone, this hevene-light,
      For mannès love
      Wil man become,
      And taken
    Fles of thee, maiden bright,   10
      Mankin free for to maken
  Of sinne and devles might.'

Mildèliche him gan andswèren
  The mildè maiden thannè:
    'Whichè wisè shold ich beren   15
    Child withouten mannè?'
      Th'angel saide: 'Ne dred thee nought;
      Thurgh th'Holy Gost shal been y-wrought
      This ilchè thing
      Wherof tiding   20
      Ich bringè;
    Al mankin worth y-bought
      Thurgh thy swete childingè
  And out of pine y-brought.'

3 thire: these   tiding: tidings   4 gan . . .: greeted her   5
aright: truly   9 f. taken Fles: become incarnate   11 Mankin:
mankind   13 Mildèliche: gently   14 thanne: then   15 how
should I bear   19 ilche: same   22 worth . . .: shall be redeemed
23 childinge: child-bearing   24 pine: torment

When the maiden understood   25
  And th'angels wordės herdė,
Mildėliche with mildė mood
  To th'angel hie andswėrdė:
    'Our Lordės thew-maiden y-wis
    Ich am, that her-aboven is.   30
      Anentis me
      Fulforthėd be
      Thy sawė:
    That ich, sithen His wil is,
      Maiden, withouten lawė,   35
    Of moder have the blis.'

Th'angel wente away mid than
  Al out of hirė sightė;
Hirė womb arisė gan
  Thurgh th'Holy Gostės mightė.   40
    In hir was Crist biloken anon,
    Sooth God, sooth man in fles and bon,
      And of hir fles
      Y-borėn wes
      At timė.   45
    Wher-thurgh us cam good won:
      He bought us out of pinė
    And let Him for us slon.

Maiden-moder makėles,
  Of milcė ful y-boundė,   50

25 understood: received   27 mood: heart   28 hie: she
29–36 Truly I am the handmaid of Our Lord, who is above. Let your saying
about me be fulfilled: that, since it is His will, I, a maiden, against the law
of nature, may have the joy of a mother   37 mid than: at that
41 biloken anon: enclosed forthwith   42 Sooth: true   44 f. was
born at the due time   46 won: fortune   48 and allowed Him-
self to be slain for us   49 makeles: matchless   50 *i.e.* abounding
in mercy

Bid for us Him that thee ches,
  At whom thou gracė foundė,
    That He forgive us sinne and wrake
    And clene of every gilt us make,
      And hevene-blis,   55
      When our time is
        To sterven,
    Us give, for thinė sake,
      Him so here for to serven
    That He us to Him take.   60

40   *World's Bliss, Have Good Day!*

WORLDÈS blissė, have good day!
  Now from myn hertė wend away.
Him for to loven myn hert is went
That thurgh His sidė sperė rent;
His hertė-blood shed He for me,   5
Nailėd to the hardė tree;
That swetė body was y-tent,
Prenėd with nailės three.

Ha Jesù! thyn holy heved
With sharpė thornės was bi-weved;   10
Thy feirė neb was al bi-spet,
With spot and blood meind al bi-wet;

39. 51 f. pray for us to Him who chose you, from whom you received grace
53 wrake: injury   55–60 and grant us the bliss of heaven, when our
time to die comes, for your sake, (and grant us) so to serve Him here that
He take us to Himself

40. 2 wend: turn   3 went: turned   4 through whose side spear
tore   7 y-tent: stretched   8 Prened: pierced   9 heved: head
10 bi-weved: encircled   11 neb: face   bi-spet: spat upon
12 all drenched with spittle mingled with blood

Fro the crunė to the to
Thy body was ful of pine and wo,
And wan and red.   15

Ha Jesù! thy smartė ded
Be my sheld and my red
From develes lorė.
Ha! swetė Jesù, thyn orė!
For thinė pinės sorė,   20
Tech hertė myn right lovė thee
Whos hertė-blood was shed for me.

41   *The Song of Lewes*

SITTETH allė stille and herkneth to me:
The King of Alėmaigne, by my leauté,
Thritty thousend pound askėde he
For to make the pees in the countré,
        And so he didė more.   5
Richard, though thou be ever trichard,
        Trichen shalt thou nevermore!

Richard of Alėmaigne, whil that he was king,
He spende al his tresour upon swiving;
Haveth he nought of Walingford o ferling.   10
Let him habbe as he brew—balė to dring—
        Maugré Windėsore!
Richard, though thou be ever trichard, *etc.*

40. 14 pine: pain   15 wan: discoloured   16 smarte ded: painful
death   17 red: help   19 ore: mercy   21 right . . .: to love
thee aright

41. 1 Sitteth stille: sit quiet   2 leauté: faith   5 and he asked for
more too   6 trichard: deceiver   7 Trichen: deceive   9 swiving: lechery   10 o . . .: one farthing   11 Let him have as he's
brewed—sorrow to drink   12 Maugré: in spite of

The King of Alêmaigne wendê do ful wel:
He seisede the milne for a castèl;   15
With here sharpê swerdês he groundê the stel!
He wendê that the sailês were mangonel
    To helpê Windêsore!
  Richard, *etc.*

The King of Alêmaigne gaderêde his host,   20
Makêde him a castel of a milnê-post!
Wendê with his pride and his muchelê bost,
Broughtê from Alêmaigne many sory gost
    To storê Windêsore.
  Richard, *etc.*   25

By God that is aboven us, he didê muchê sinne
That lette passen over see the Erl of Warinne!
He hath robbêd Engêland, the morês and the fenne,
The gold and the selver, and y-borên henne,
    For love of Windêsore,   30
  Richard, *etc.*

Sire Simond de Mountfort hath swore by his chin,
Havede he now here the Erl of Warin,
Shulde he never morê come to his in,
Ne with sheeld ne with spere ne with other gin   35
    To helpê Windêsore.
  Richard, *etc.*

Sire Simond de Montfort hath swore by his top,
Havede he now here Sir Hue de Bigot,

14 wende: thought to   15 milne: mill   16 he ground the
steel of their sharp swords (*i.e.* took the mill-stones for grindstones)
17 mangonel: catapults   20 gaderede: gathered   21 milne-post:
post supporting mill   22 wende: went   23 gost: soul
24 store: supply   29 y-boren henne: carried (them) off   33
Havede: had   34 in: lodging   35 gin: device   38 top:
crown (of his head)   39 Hugh Bigod

Al he shuldė quite here twelfmonėth scot;   40
Shulde he nevermorė with his foot pot
    To helpė Windėsore.
    Richard, *etc.*

Be thee leef, be thee loth, Sire Edward,
Thou shalt ridė sporėless o thy lyard   45
Al the rightė way to Doverė-ward;
Shalt thou nevermorė brekė forėward—
    And that reweth sore.
Edward, thou didest as a shreward,
    Forsoke thyn emės lore.   50
    Richard, *etc.*

42   *Annot and John*

ICH'OT a burde in a bowr as beryl so bright,
  As saphyr in silver seemly on sight,
As jaspė the gentil that lemeth with light,
As gernet in golde and ruby wel right;
As onycle heo is on y-holden on hight,   5
As diamaund the dere, in day when heo is dight.
Heo is coral y-cud with cayser and knight;
As emeraude amorewen this may haveth might;

41. 40 he would have to pay in full for their twelve months' entertainment
41 pot: push forward   44 Be . . . loth: whether you like it or not
45 sporeless . . .: without spurs on your grey horse   46 to . . .:
to Dover   47 foreward: agreement   48 reweth: grieves (you)
49 shreward: scoundrel   50 emes lore: uncle's (Simon de Mont-
fort's) counsel

42. I know a maiden in a chamber as bright as beryl, a*s* beautiful to look at
as sapphire (set) in silver, as the noble jasper that sparkles with light, as
garnet well (set) in gold and ruby; as an onyx she is highly regarded, as the
precious diamond, when she is dressed by day. She is coral famous with
emperor and knight; as an emerald in the morning this maiden has power;

The might of the margarite haveth this may mere;
For charbocle ich hire ches by chin and by chere.　　10

Hire rode is as rose that red is on ris,
With lilye-white lerès lofsum heo is;
The primerole heo passeth, the pervenke of pris,
With alisaundre thereto, ache and anìs.
Cointe as columbine—such hire cunde is—　　15
Glad under gore in gro and in gris,
Heo is blosme upon blee brightest under bis,
With celydoyne and sauge, as thou thyself sis.
　That sight upon that seemly, to blis he is brought;
　Heo is solsecle to sauve is forsought.　　20

Heo is papejay in pyn that beteth me my bale,
The trewe tortle in a towr—I telle thee my tale;
Heo is thrustle thriven and thro that singeth in sale,
The wilde laveroc on wolkne and the wodèwale;
Heo is faucoun in frith, dernest in dale,　　25
And with everich a gomè gladest in gale.
From Weye heo is wisest into Wirhàle;
Hire name is in a note of the nightègale:

the power of the pearl has this noble maid; I prize her as a carbuncle-stone in cheek and countenance.

　Her colour is like the red rose on the spray, with lily-white complexion she is lovely; she surpasses the primrose, the prized periwinkle, and alexander also, parsley and anise. Delicately made as the columbine—such is her nature—delightful in clothing of grey furs, she appears in fine linen as the brightest blossom, like celandine and sage, as you yourself see. He who looks upon that lovely lady is brought to bliss; she is a sunflower which is sought out for healing.

　She is a (gay) parrot (when I am) in torment who soothes my anguish, the true turtle-dove in a tower—I tell you my opinion; she is a thrush, fine and excellent, which sings in the hall, the wild lark in the sky and the golden oriole; she is a falcon in the forest, deepest hidden in the dale, and most pleasing in her song to every man. She is the wisest from the Wye to the Wirral; her name is in a note of the nightingale:

In annote is hire namė— nempneth it non!
Whoso right redeth roune to Johon.   30

Alysoun

B ETWENĖ March and Averil,
       When spray biginneth to springe,
The litel fowl hath hirė wil
     On hirė lud to singe.
Ich libbe in love-longinge   5
For semlokest of allė thinge;
Heo may me blissė bringe—
     Ich am in hire baundòun.
          An hendy hap ich habbe y-hent;
          Ich'ot from hevene it is me sent;   10
          From allė wimmen my love is lent,
               And light on Alysoun.

On hew hire her is fair ynough,
     Hire browė browne, hire eyė blake;
With lofsom chere heo on me lough,   15
     With middel smal and wel y-make.
Bute heo me willė to hire take

---

42. in a note is her name—do not any of you mention it! Let whoever interprets it correctly whisper to John.

43. 2 when the twig begins to shoot   3 f. hath . . .: delights to sing in her (own) language   5 Ich libbe: I live   6 for the fairest of all creatures   7 Heo may: she can   8 baundoun: power   9 I have had rare good fortune   10 Ich'ot: I know   11 lent: departed   12 light: has fallen   13 her: hair   14 browe: eyebrows   15 with lovable looks she smiled on me   16 middel smal: slim waist   y-make: shaped   17 Bute: unless

For to been hire owèn make,
Longe to liven ich'ille forsake,
    And feyè fallen adown.   20
        An hendy hap, *etc.*

Nightès when I wende and wake—
    Forthy myn wongès waxeth won—
Levedy, al for thinè sake
    Longing is y-lent me on.   25
    In world n'is non so witer mon
    That al hire bounté tellè con:
    Hire swire is whitere than the swon,
        And fairest may in town.
            An hendy hap, *etc.*   30

Ich am for wowing al forwake,
    Wery so water in wore,
Lest any revè me my make
    Ich habbe y-yirned yore.
    Betere is tholièn whilè sore   35
    Than mournen evermore.
Gainest under gore,
    Herknè to my roun.
        An hendy hap, *etc.*

---

18 make: mate   19 ich'ille forsake: I will refuse   20 feye:
doomed to die   22 f. At night when I toss and lie awake—which is
why my cheeks grow pale   24 Levedy: lady   25 y-lent: come
26 witer: wise   27 that he knows how to describe all her excellence
28 swire: neck   29 may: maid   31-5 Through wooing I am
quite worn out by lack of sleep, weary as the waters in ?a troubled pool,
lest anyone rob me of my mate whom I have long desired. It is better to
suffer pain for a time   37 Most gracious woman under gown (*i.e.*
alive)   38 roun: song

44   *A Maid Mars Me*

WITH longing I am lad,
  On molde I waxė mad:
A maidė marreth me.
I grede, I grone unglad;
For selden I am sad   5
   That seemly for to see.
  Levedy, thou rewė me!
To routhe thou havest me rad;
Be bote of that I bad;
   My lif is long on thee.   10

Levedy of allė londe,
Les me out of bonde;
  Brought ich am in wo.
Have resting on honde
And send thou me thy sonde   15
   Soone, er thou me slo;
  My rest is with the ro.
Though men to me han onde,
To love n'il I nought wonde
   Ne lete for non of tho.   20

1 am lad: go (*lit.* am led)   2 molde: earth   4 grede: wail   5 selden: seldom   am sad: have the satisfaction   6 seemly: fair one   7 Levedy: lady   rewe: pity   8 routhe: sorrow   rad: brought   9 f. be the cure of it (as) I have begged; my life depends on you   11 londe: lands   12 Les: free   13 ich: I   14 Consider (my) peace of mind   15 sonde: message   16 Soone: at once   slo: slay   17 *i.e.* I am restless as the roe   18 to . . .: bear me ill will   19 wonde: cease   20 nor desist for any of them

Levedy, with al my might
My love is on thee light,
  To menskė when I may.
Thou rew and reed me right.
To dethe thou havest me dight: 25
  I deye longe er my day—
  Thou levė upon my lay.
Treuthe ich have thee plight
To don that ich have hight
    Whil my lif lastė may.   30

Lilie-whit heo is,
Hir rode so rose on ris,
  That reveth me my rest.
Womman war and wis,
Of pride heo bereth the pris,   35
  Burde one of the best.
  This womman woneth by west,
Brightest under bis;
Heven I tolde al his
    That o night were hir gest.   40

22 light: lighted   23 menske: worship (you)   24 reed: guide
25 dight: consigned   27 leve upon: believe   28 Treuthe: troth
29 to do what I have promised   31 heo: she   32 f. her com-
plexion like the rose on the spray, she who robs me of my rest   34
war: prudent   35 in splendour she is pre-eminent   36 Burde: lady
37 woneth by: dwells in the   38 bis: fine linen   39 f. I should
reckon he would have all heaven who for one night might be her guest

45 *The Farmer's Complaint*

ICH herde men upon mold make muche mone
How he beeth y-tened of here tilyinge:
Goode yeres and corn bothe beeth a-gone;
    Ne kepeth here no sawe ne no song singe.
Now we mote worche—n'is ther non other wone;   5
    May ich no lengere live with my lesinge.
Yet ther is a bitterer bit to the bone,
    For ever the forthe peny mot to the Kinge.

Thus we carpeth for the King and carieth ful colde,
    And weneth for to kevere and ever beeth a-cast;   10
Whoso hath any good hopeth he nought to holde,
    Bute ever the levest we leseth alast.

Lither is to lesen ther-as litel is,
    And haveth manye hinen that hopieth ther-to:
The hayward heteth us harm to habben of his;   15
    The bailif bockneth us bale and weneth wel do;
The wodeward waiteth us wo that loketh under ris—
    Ne may us rise no rest, riches, ne ro.

I heard men on earth complain greatly how they are harassed in their
farming: good years and good corn-crops are both gone: they do not care
to hear any yarns or sing any songs. Now we must work—there is no other
course; I can no longer live with my losses. There is a still more bitter cut
to the bone, for always every fourth penny must go to the King.

So we complain because of the King and are sorely distressed, and expect
to recover and are always cast down; whoever has anything of value does
not expect to keep it, but always what we most value we lose in the end.

It is bad to lose where there is little, and we have many petty officials
who expect a rake-off: the hayward promises us penalties so as to get
his share; the bailiff ?threatens trouble for us and expects to do well; the
wood-keeper does us harm when we look under the trees—no rest,

Thus me pileth the pore that is of lite pris:
    Nede in swot and in swink swinde mot swo.   20

Nede he mot swinde, though he had swore,
    That n'ath nought an hood his hed for to hide.
Thus wil walketh in land and lawe is forlore,
    And al is piked of the pore the prikyares pride.

Thus me pileth the pore and piketh ful clene;   25
    The riche men raimeth withouten any right;
Her landes and her ledes liggeth ful lene
    Thurgh bidding of bailifs such harm hem hath hight.
Men of religioun me halt hem ful hene,
    Baroun and bonde, the clerc and the knight.   30
Thus wil walketh in land and wondred is wene,
    Falsshipe fatteth and marreth with might.

Stant stille i the stede and halt him ful sturne
    That maketh beggres go with burden and bagges.
Thus we beeth hunted from hale to hurne;   35
    That er werede robes now wereth ragges.

prosperity, or peace can be our lot. Thus the poor man who is of small account is robbed: so in sweat and toil he needs must perish.

He needs must perish, though he had sworn the contrary (*i.e.* in spite of himself), he who has not a hood to cover his head. So will walks the land and law is abandoned, and all the horseman's (*i.e.* rich man's) proud array is stolen from the poor.

Thus the poor are robbed and stripped clean; powerful men take at will without any right; their lands and their people are starved through the demands of bailiffs who have threatened them with such penalties. Men in religious orders are looked down upon by baron and peasant, cleric and knight. So will walks the land and misery is to be expected, deceit grows fat and brings ruin by his power.

He stands there unmoved and behaves quite mercilessly, he who makes men beggars with burdens and bags. Thus we are hunted from corner to corner; we who wore robes before now wear rags.

Yet cometh budeles with ful muche bost:
  'Greithe me silver to the grene wax;
Thou art writen i my writ—that thou wel wost!'—
  Mo than ten sithen told I my tax.   40
'Thenne mot ich habbe hennen arost,
  Fair on fish-day launprey and lax;
Forth to the chepen!'—geineth no chost,
  Though I selle my bil and my borstax.

Ich mot legge my wed wel if I wille,   45
  Other selle my corn on gras that is grene.
Yet I shal be foul cherl, though he han the fille;
  That ich alle yer spare thenne I mot spene.

Nede I mot spene that I spared yore;
  Ayain thes cachereles come thus I mot care.   50
Cometh the maister budel brust as a bore,
  Saith he wille my bigging bringe ful bare.
Mede I mot minten—a mark other more—
  Though ich at the set day selle my mare.
Thus the grene wax us greveth under gore,   55
  That me us hunteth as hound doth the hare.

Moreover tax-collectors come with great threats: 'Get me money to pay
your tax-demand; you are down in my writ—that you well know!'—
more than ten times over I paid my tax. 'Then I must have roast hens, on
fish-day fine lamprey and salmon. Be off to the market!'—no argument is
any use, even though I have to sell my bill and my ?pick-axe.

I must give good security if I am willing, or sell my corn green. Yet I
shall be a wretched beggar, though they have plenty; what I save all year
I must spend then.

I needs must spend what I saved long ago; thus I have to worry about the
coming of these catchpolls. The chief tax-collector comes bristling like
a boar, says he means to strip my home quite bare. I must try a bribe—a
mark or more—even though on the set day I have to sell my mare. Thus
tax-collection distresses us deeply (*lit.* under clothing), in that they hunt
us as hound hunts the hare.

He us hunteth as hound hare doth on hille;
   Sithe I took to the land such tene me was taught.
N'abbeth ne'r budeles boded her fille,
   For he may scape and we aren ever caught.   60

Thus I kippe and cache cares ful colde,
   Sithe I counte and cot hade to kepe.
To seche silver to the King I my seed solde:
   Forthy my land leye lith and lerneth to slepe.
Sithe he my faire fegh fette i my folde,   65
   When I thenk o my wele wel nigh I wepe.
Thus bredeth manye beggares bolde,
   And our rye is roted and ruls er we repe.

Ruls is our rye and roted in the stree,
   For wickede wederes, by brokes and by brinke.   70
Ther wakeneth in the world wondred and wee—
   As good is swinden anon as so for to swinke!

They hunt us as hound hunts hare on the hill; since I took to farming I have experienced such trouble. Tax-collectors have never declared their full takings, for they can escape and we are always caught.

So I get and gather most cruel troubles, since I have had accounts to keep and a small holding. To procure money for the King I sold my seed; for that reason my land lies fallow and learns to sleep. Since they fetched away my fine cattle in my fold, when I think of my possessions I very nearly weep. Thus many bold beggars multiply, and our rye is rotted and ?blighted before we reap it.

Blighted is our rye and rotted in the straw, because of disastrous storms, by streams and bank (*i.e.* through flooding). Misery and woe are rife in the world—it is as well to die at once as so to toil.

46   *The Lady in the Wood*

IN a frith as I can fare fremede
   I founde a wel fair fenge to fere:
Heo glistnede as gold when it glemede;
   N'as ne'r gome so gladly on gere.
I wolde wite in world who hir kenede,   5
   This burde bright, if hire wil were.
Heo me bad go my gates lest hir gremede;
   Ne kepte heo non hening here.

'Y-here thou me now, hendest in helde;
   N'ave I thee none harmes to hethe;   10
Casten I wil thee from cares and kelde;
   Comelich I wil thee now clethe.'

'Clothes I have on for to caste
   Such as I may were with winne.
Betere is were thinne boute laste   15
   Than side robes and sinke into sinne.
Have ye yor wil, ye waxeth unwraste;
   Afterward yor thank beeth thinne.

1 As I was going in a wood, a stranger   2 fenge: prize   to fere: as a companion   3 Heo: she   4 f. there was never anyone so beautiful in her appearance. I wished to know who in the world bore her   6 burde: lady   7 f. She bade me go my way lest she became angry; she did not care to hear any dishonourable suggestion   9 f. hendest . . .: most gracious in kindness; I have no insults to mock you with   11 Casten I wil: I wish to free   kelde: cold, misery   12 Comelich: becomingly   clethe: clothe   14 winne: pleasure   15 It is better to wear threadbare clothes without reproach   16 side: flowing   17 If you have your will, you will become unfaithful   18 thank . . .: gratitude will be small

Betere is make forewardes faste
    Than afterward to menen and minne.'   20

'Of minning ne minte thou na more;
    Of menske thou were wurthe, by my might.
I take on hand to holde, that I hore,
    Of al that I thee have behight.
Why is thee loth to leven on my lore   25
    Lengere than my love were on thee light?
An other mighte yerne thee so yore
    That n'olde thee nought rede so right.'

'Such reed me mighte spacliche rewe
    When al my ro were me atraght;   30
Soone thou woldest sechen an newe
    And take another withinne niye naght.
Thenne might I hungren on hewe,
    In ech an hird been hated and forhaght,
And been y-caired from alle that I knewe,   35
    And bede clevien ther I hade claght.

'Betere is taken a comeliche i clothe
    In armes to kisse and to clippe

---

19 forewardes faste: firm agreements   20 menen: complain
minne: remember   21–8 Do not think any more about remembering;
you deserve honourable treatment, to the extent of my power. I undertake
to keep, till I grow old, all the promises I have made to you. Why are you
unwilling to trust to my guidance longer than (the short time) I have been
in love with you? Another might have courted you a long time who would
not guide you so well.   29 f. I might quickly regret such advice
when all my peace of mind was taken from me   31 sechen: seek
32 niye naght: nine nights   33 on hewe: among (my) family
34 in every household be hated and despised   35 y-caired: driven
36 and bidden to stick to the man I had embraced   37 (Yet) it is
better to take (a man) handsomely dressed   38 clippe: embrace

Than a wreche I wedded so wrothe—
   Though he me slowe ne might I him aslippe.'   40
'The beste reed that I can to us bothe:
   That thou me take and I thee toward hippe.
Though I swore by treuthe and othe,
   That God hath shaped may non atlippe.'

'Mid shupping ne may it me ashunche: 45
   N'as I never wiche ne wile.
Ich am a maide—that me ofthunche!
   Leef me were gome boute gile.'

47   *The White Beauty*

A WALĖ whyt as whallės bon,
  A grain in gold that goodly shon,
A tortle that myn herte is on,
   In townė trewe.
Hir gladshipė n'is never gon   5
  Whil I may glewe.

When heo is glad,
Of al this world namore I bad

46. 39 f. than that I wedded some wretch so unhappily—though he should
kill me I could not escape him   41 reed: course   can: know
42 hippe: jump   43 f. Though I swore (the contrary) by pledge
and oath, what God has ordained nobody can avoid   45 ?it (God's
decree) cannot be deflected by ?shape-shifting   46–8 I never was
witch or sorceress. I am a maiden—that I may regret! An honest man
would be welcome to me

47. A beauty white as ivory, a pearl set in gold that shone gloriously, a
turtle-dove that I have set my heart on, always true. The joy of her is
never gone while I can sing.

    When she is joyful, in all this world I asked nothing else than to be set

Than be with hir myn one bistad
    Withoutė strif.   10
The care that ich am in y-brad
    I wite a wif.

A wif n'is non so worly wrought.
When heo is blithe to bedde y-brought
Wel were him that wiste hir thought,   15
    That thriven and thro!
Wel I wot heo n'il me nought—
    Myn herte is wo!

How shal of that lefly sing
That thus is marrėd in mourning?   20
Heo me wil to dethė bring
    Longe er my day.
Greet hir wel, that swetė thing
    With eynen gray.

Hir eye haveth wounded me y-wisse,   25
Hir bendė browen that bringeth blisse.
Hir comely mouth that mightė kisse
    In muchė mirthe he were.
I woldė chaungė myn for his
    That is hir fere.   30

alone beside her without discord. The misery in which I am (?)burning I
blame on a woman.

There is no woman so exquisitely made. When she is laid happily in bed
lucky would be the man who knew her thoughts, that excellent and noble
lady! Well I know that she will not have me—my heart is sad!

How shall he who is thus desolated by grief celebrate that lovely creature?
She will drive me to death long before my time. Greet her well, that sweet
thing with grey eyes.

Her eyes have wounded me indeed, her arched eye-brows that give
delight. Anyone who could kiss her lovely mouth would be in great joy.
I wish I could exchange my (lot) for that of the man who is her companion.

Wolde hir feré be so free
And wurdés were that so mighte be,
Al for one I wolde yeve three
   Withouté cheep.
From helle to hevene and sonne to see   35
   N'is non so yeep
Ne half so free.
Whoso wile of love be trewe, do listné me.

Herkneth me, I ou telle—
In such wondring for wo I welle: 40
N'is no fyr so hot in helle
   As to mon
That loveth derne and dar nought telle
   What him is on.

Ich unne hir wel and heo me wo;   45
Ich am hir frend and heo my fo.
Me thincheth myn herte wil breke a-two
   For sorewe and site.
In Godés greeting mote heo go,
   That wale white!   50

If her companion would be so generous and fortune befell that it might be so, I should be willing to give three (kisses) in exchange for one, without bargaining. Between hell and heaven, sun and sea, there is no one so wise nor half so lovely. Whoever wishes to be true in love, let him listen to me.

Listen to me, I tell you—in such ?distress I am burning for grief: there is no fire in hell so hot as the fire in him who loves secretly and dare not tell what his trouble is.

I wish her well and she wishes me sorrow; I am her friend and she my foe. It seems to me my heart will break in two for sorrow and grief. May she go with God's blessing, that white beauty!

Ich wolde ich were a threstelcok,
A bounting other a lavercok,
 Swetė brid!
Bitwene hir curtel and hir smok
I wolde been hid.   55

48   *Spring*

L ENTEN is come with love to towne,
 With blosmen and with briddės rowne,
  That al this blissė bringeth:
Dayėsėyės in thes dales,
Notės swete of nightėgales—   5
  Ech fowl song singeth.
The threstelcok him threteth o,
Away is herė winter wo,
  When wodėrovė springeth.
Thes fowlės singeth ferly fele,   10
And wliteth on here winnė wele,
  That al the wodė ringeth.

The rosė raileth hirė rode,
The levės on the lightė wode
  Waxen al with wille.   15
The moonė mandeth hirė blee,

47. I wish I were a thrush, a bunting or a lark, sweet bird! Between her gown and her petticoat I wish I were hidden.

48. 1 Lenten: spring to towne: to the world 2 with blossoms and with birds' song 4 Dayeseyes: daisies 7 The cock-thrush chides continually 8 here: their 9 woderove: woodruff 10 ferly fele: wonderfully many   11 ?And warble about their wealth of joys 13 The rose displays her redness   14 lighte: bright 15 grow joyously 16 The moon sheds her radiance

The lilie is lofsom to see,
    The fenil and the fille.
Wowès thesè wildè drakès;
Milès murgeth herè makès,   20
    As strem that striketh stille.
Mody meneth, so doth mo—
Ich'ot ich am one of tho
    For love that likès ille.

The moonè mandeth hirè light;   25
So doth the seemly sunnè bright,
    When briddès singeth breme.
Dewès donketh the downes;
Deerès with here dernè rownes,
    Domès for to deme;   30
Wormès woweth under cloude;
Wimmen waxeth wonder proude—
    So wel it wil hem seme.
If me shal wantè wille of on,
This winnè wele I wil forgon,   35
    And wight in wode be fleme.

17 lofsom: lovely   18 fille: thyme   19 Wowes: woo
20 Miles: *unexplained*   murgeth . . .: gladden their mates   21 striketh
stille: glides silently   22–4 The passionate man complains, and so do
more—I know I am one of those that are wretched because of love
26 seemly: beautiful   27 breme: gloriously   28 donketh: moisten
29 f. animals with their secret calls by which they communicate   31
under cloude: under ground   32 proude: elated   33 so well will
it suit them   34 ff. If I do not have my will of one, I intend to forgo
this wealth of joys, and straightway become a fugitive in the wood.

49 *Blow, Northern Wind*

B LOW, northerne wind,
   Send thou me my sweeting.
Blow, northerne wind,
Blow, blow, blow!

Ich'ot a burde in bowrè bright   5
That sully seemly is on sight,
Menskful maiden of might,
   Fair and free to fonde.
In all this worthlichè won
A burde of blood and of bon   10
Never yete I n'ustè non
   Lufsomere in londe.
     Blow, etc.

With lokkès lefliche and longe,
With frount and facè fair to fonde,   15
With mirthès manye mote heo monge,
   That brid so breme in bowre.
With lufsom eyè, grete and goode,
With browèn blisful under hoode.
He that reste Him on the roode   20
   That lefliche lif honòure!
     Blow, etc.

2 sweeting: sweetheart   5–12 I know a lady beautiful in bower
who is wonderfully lovely to look at, a gracious maiden of virtue, fair
and excellent to see. In all this glorious dwelling-place a lady of flesh and
blood I never yet knew lovelier on earth   14 lefliche: beautiful
15 frount: forehead   16 she may give delight to many people
17 brid: lady breme: excellent   19 browen: eye-brows 20 f. May
He who hung upon the cross honour that beautiful lady!

Hirè lerè lemès light
Asè a launtèrne a-night,
Hirè blee blikieth so bright,   25
    So fair heo is and fin.
A sweetly swire heo hath to holde,
With armès, shuldrè, as mon wolde,
And fingres fairè for to folde—
    God wolde heo wer myn!   30
        Blow, *etc.*

Middel heo hath menskful smal,
Hire lovelich chere as cristàl,
Thighès, leggès, feet, and al
    Y-wrought wes of the beste.   35
A lufsom lady lastèles
That sweeting is and ever wes;
A betere burdè never n'es,
    Y-heried with the heste.
        Blow, *etc.*   40

Heo is derèworthe in day,
Graciouse, stout and gay,
Gentil, jolyf so the jay,
    Worthlich when heo waketh;
Maiden miriest of mouth,   45
By est, by west, by north and south;

23 Her face glows radiant   25 her countenance shines so bright
26 fin: exquisite   27 She has a lovely neck to embrace   28 mon
wolde: one would wish   29 folde: clasp   30 Would God she
were mine!   32 She has an elegantly slender waist   33 chere:
complexion   35 was formed in the finest way   36 lasteles:
faultless   38 never n'es: never was   39 honoured among the
highest   41 dereworthe: lovable   42 stout: dignified   43
jolyf: vivacious   44 delightful during her waking hours

Ther n'is fiélé ne crouth
    That such mirthés maketh.
      Blow, *etc.*

Heo is coral of goodnesse,   50
Heo is ruby of rightfulnesse,
Heo is cristal of clennesse
    And baner of bealté;
Heo is lilie of largesse,
Heo is parvenke of prowesse,   55
Heo is solsecle of sweetnesse
    And lady of lealté.
      Blow, *etc.*

To Love, that leflich is in londe,
I tolde him, as ich understonde,   60
How this hende hath hent in honde
    An herté that myn wes;
And hire knightes me han so sought—
Syking, Sorèwing and Thought:
Tho three me han in balé brought   65
    Ayain the powr of Pees.
      Blow, *etc.*

To Love I putté plaintès mo:
How Syking me hath siwèd so,

47 f. there is neither viol nor fiddle that gives such entertainment
52 clennesse: purity   53 and banner of beauty   54 largesse:
liberality   55 periwinkle of perfection   56 solsecle: sunflower
57 and queen of faithfulness   59 that . . .: who is dear everywhere
61 f. how this fair (lady) has taken possession of a heart that was mine
63 han: have   sought: assailed   64 Syking: Sighing   Thought:
Anxiety   65 f. those three have reduced me to misery, destroying
the power of Peace   68 plaintes mo: further complaints   69
siwed: pursued

And ekė Thought me thrat to slo   70
  With maistry, if he mighte;
And Sorewe swore in balful bende
That he woldė for this hende
Me ledė to my livės ende
  Unlawfulliche in lighte.   75
    Blow, *etc.*

Love me listnede ech word
And begh him to me over bord
And bad me hentė that hord
  Of myn hertė hele;   80
'And biseche that swete and swote,
Er than thou falle as fen of fote,
That heo with thee wille of bote
  Dereworthlichė dele.'
    Blow, *etc.*   85

For hirė love I carke and care,
For hirė love I droupne and dare,
For hirė love my blisse is bare,
  And all ich waxė won;
For hirė love in sleep I slake,   90
For hirė love al night ich wake,
For hirė love mourning I make,
  More than any mon.
    Blow, *etc.*

70–5 and also Anxiety threatened to slay me by his power, if he could; and Sorrow swore that he would, for this fair (lady's) sake, keep me in cruel bonds to the end of my life unlawfully ?in the world   78–80 and bowed to me across the table and bade me recover that treasure of my heart's well-being   81 swote: dear one   82–4 before you drop like mud from the foot, that she will graciously grant you your cure   86 For love of her I fret and grieve   87 droupne . . .: droop and despair   88 bare: gone   89 and I grow all pale   90 in . . .: I lose my sleep   91 wake: lie awake

50   *Winter Wakens All My Care*

WINTER wakeneth al my care,
   Now thes levės waxeth bare;
Ofte I sike and mournė sare
   When it cometh in my thought
   Of this wórldės joye, how it geth al to nought.   5

Now it is, and now it n'is
Al so it ne'r n'ere, y-wis;
That many man saith, sooth it is:
   'Al goth butė Godės wille.
   Alle we shulė deyė, though us like ille.'   10

Al that grevė groweth grene,
Now it faleweth al bidene.
Jesu, help that it be sene,
   And shild us from helle!
   For I n'ot whider I shal, ne how longe her dwelle.   15

51   *Now Shrinketh Rose and Lily-Flower*

NOW shrinketh rose and lilie-flour,
   That whilen ber that swete savòur
   In sumer, that swete tide;

50. 2 Now: now that   3 sike: sigh   sare: grievously   5 geth: goes   7 as if it had never been, indeed   8 That: what   9 bute: except   10 We must all die, though it displeases us   11 All the grove grows green   12 f. now it withers all at once. Jesu, help to make this plain   14 shild: preserve   15 n'ot . . . shal: know not where I must go

51. 1 shrinketh: withers   2 whilen ber: once bore

Ne is no quene so stark ne stour,
No no levedy so bright in bour   5
   That ded ne shal by-glide.
    Whoso wil flesh-lust forgon
And hevene-blis abide,
   On Jesu be his thought anon,
That therlèd was His side.   10

From Petresbourgh in o morwening,
As I me wende o my playing,
   On my folìe I thoughte;
Menen I gan my mourning
To hir that ber the Hevene-King,   15
   Of mercy hir besoughte:
    'Lady, pray thy Sone for ous,
That us deerè boughte,
   And shild us from the lothè hous
That to the feend is wroughte.'   20

Myn herte of dedès was for-dred,
Of sinne that I have my flesh fed
   And folewed al my time,
That I n'ot whider I shal be led
When I ligge on dethès bed—   25
   In joye or into pine.
    On a lady myn hope is,

4 stark . . .: strong and stern   5 f. nor any lady so beautiful in bower that death shall not steal upon her   8 abide: await   9 anon: constantly   10 whose side was pierced   11 in . . .: one morning   12 as I went for pleasure   14 I made my lament   15 ber: bore   16 Of: for   19 shild: preserve   lothe: hateful   20 to: for   wroughte: made   21 f. My heart was terrified at my deeds, at the sins with which I have indulged my flesh   24 so that I do not know where I am to be taken   25 ligge: lie   26 pine: torment

Moder and virgìne;
  We shulen into hevene-blis
  Thourgh hirė medicine.   30

Betere is hirė medicine
Than any mede or any wine;
  Hir herbės smelleth swete.
From Catenas into Diveline
N'is ther no leche so fine   35
  Oure sorėwės to bete.
    Man that feleth any sor
  And his folìe wil lete,
    Withoutė gold other any tresòr
  He may be sound and sete.   40

Of penaunce is hir plaster al;
And ever serven hir I shal
  Now and al my live.
Now is free that er was thral
Al thourgh that levedy gent and smal—   45
  Heried be hir joyės five!
    Wher-so any sek is,
  Thider hiė blive;
    Thourgh hire beeth y-brought to blis
  Bo maiden and wive.   50

For He, that dide His body on tree,
Of ourė sinnės have pité,
  That weldės hevene-bowres,

29 shulen: must (go)   32 mede: mead   34 From Caithness
to Dublin   35 leche: physician   fine: skilled   36 bete: cure
38 lete: abandon   39 other: or   40 sete: content   45
gent . . .: graceful and slender   46 Heried: praised   47 sek: sick
48 let him hasten there (*i.e.* to her) quickly   50 Bo: both   51–3
In order that He, who put His body on the cross, may have pity on our
sins, (He) who rules heaven's bowers

Wimman with thy jolité,
   Thou thench on Godès showres;   55
Though thou be whit and bright on blee,
   Falewen shule thy flowres.
Jesu, have mercỳ of me,
   That al this world honòures!

52   *De Clerico et Puella*

'MY deth I love, my lif ich hate, for a levedy shene;
   Heo is bright so dayès light—that is on me wel sene:
Al I falewe so doth the lef in sumer when it is grene.
If my thought helpeth me nought, to whom shal I me mene?

'Sorewe and sike and drery mood bindeth me so faste   5
That I wene to walkè wood if it me lengere laste.
My sorewe, my care, al with a word heo mighte away caste.
What helpeth thee, my swete lemmàn, my lif thus for to gaste?'

'Do way, thou clerk! Thou art a fool; with thee bidde I nought
   chide;
Shalt thou never live that day my love that thou shalt bide.   10
If thou in my bowr art take, shame thee may betide:
Thee is bettere on footè gon than wicked hors to ride.'

51. 54 jolité: gaiety   55 thench: think   showres: pains   56
whit: fair   blee: face   57 Falewen: fade   59 That: (Jesu) whom
52. 1 ich: I   levedy: lady   shene: beautiful   2 Heo: she
so: as   that . . .: that (my state) is apparent in me   3 falewe: fade
4 me mene: complain   5 sike: sighing   mood: mind   6
walke wood: rage in madness   lengere: longer   8 How does it
help you, my dear sweetheart, so to ruin my life   9 Stop it, student!
You are a fool; I don't want to argue with you   10 bide: experience
12 It's better for you to go on foot than to ride a sorry horse (*i.e.* to
execution)

DE CLERICO ET PUELLA

'Waylaway! Why sayst thou so? Thou rew on me, thy man!
Thou art ever in my thought in landè wher ich am.
If I deyè for thy love, it is thee mikel sham;   15
Thou lete me live and be thy leef, and thou my swete lemmàn.'

'Be stille, thou fool!—I calle thee right—canst thou never
    blinne?
Thou art waited day and night with fader and al my kinne.
Be thou in my bowr y-take, lete they for no sinne
Me to holde and thee to slon; the deth so thou might winne.' 20

'Swete lady, thou wend thy mood; sorewe thou wilt me kithe;
Ich am al so sory man so ich was whilen blithe.
In a window ther we stood we kiste us fifty sithe—
Fair beheste maketh many man al his sorewes mithe.'

'Waylaway! Why sayst thou so? My sorewe thou makest newe.
I lovede a clerk al par amours; of love he was ful trewe;   26
He n'as nought blithè never a day bute he me sonè seye.
Ich lovede him betere than my lif—what bote is it to leye?'

'Whil I was a clerk in scole wel muchel I couthe of lore.
Ich have tholèd for thy love woundès felè sore,   30
Fer from thee and eke from men, under the wodè-gore.
Swete lady, thou rew of me! Now may I no more.'

13 Waylaway: Alas   rew: have pity   14 wher: wherever
15 mikel: great   16 leef: lover   17 blinne: stop   18 waited:
watched for   with: by   19 f. If you are caught in my room, they
will have no compunction (*lit.* desist for no pity) in confining me and
killing you; you can bring about your death that way   21 wend . . .:
change your mind; you wish to give me sorrow   22 al so: just as
whilen: once   23 ther: where   sithe: times   24 beheste:
promise   mithe: hide   26 par amours: secretly   27 bute:
unless   seye: saw   28 bote: good   leye: lie   29 couthe
. . .: knew about learning   30 tholed: suffered   fele: many
31 Fer: far   under . . .: under? cover of the wood   32 may I:
I can (do)

130

'Thou semest wel to been a clerk, for thou spekest so stille.
Shalt thou never for my love woundės tholė grille.
Fader, moder, and al my kin ne shal me holde so stille   35
That I n'am thyn, and thou art myn, to don al thy wille.'

53 *When the Nightingale Sings*

WHEN the nightėgalė singes, the wodės waxen grene;
Lef and gras and blosmė springes in Avėril, I wene,
And love is to myn hertė gon with onė spere so kene:
Night and day my blood it drinkes, myn hertė deth me tene.

Ich have lovėd al this yer, that I may love na more;   5
Ich have sikėd many sik, lemman, for thyn ore;
Me n'is lovė never the ner, and that me reweth sore:
Swetė lemman, thench on me! Ich have loved thee yore.

Swetė lemman, I praye thee of love onė speche;
Whil I live in world so wide other n'ille I seche.   10
With thy love, my swetė leef, my blis thou mightės eche;
A swetė coss of thy mouth mightė be my leche.

Swetė lemman, I praye thee of a lovė-bene:
If thou me lovest as men says, lemman, as I wene,
And if it thy willė be, thou loke that it be sene;   15
So muchel I thenke upon thee that al I waxė grene.

52. 33 stille: ? persistently   34 grille: cruel

53. 3 one: a   4 deth . . .: causes me pain   5 Ich: I   that . . .: in
such a way that I cannot love more   6 I have sighed many a sigh,
sweetheart, for your mercy   7 ner: nearer   me reweth: grieves me
8 thench on: think of   yore: long   9 I . . .: I beg you for one
word of love   10 other . . .: I will not seek another   11 leef:
dear   eche: increase   12 coss: kiss   leche: physician   13 of . . .:
for a love-favour   15 thou . . .: see that it is apparent

Betweně Lincolne and Lindesèye, Northamptoun and Lounde,
Ne wot I non so fair a may as I go fore y-bounde.
Swetě lemman, I praye thee, thou lovie me a stounde!
    I wile mone my song   20
    On whom that it is on y-long.

54   *The Man in the Moon*

MAN in the mooně stand and strit;
    On his bot-forke his burthen he bereth.
It is muche wonder that he n'adown slit:
    For doute leste he falle, he shoddreth and shereth.
When the forst freseth muche chele he bit;   5
    The thornes beeth kene his hattren to-tereth.
N'is no wight in the world that wot when he sit,
    Ne, bute it be the hegge, what wedes he wereth.

Whider trowe we this man ha the way take?
    He hath set his o foot his other to-foren.   10
For non highte that he hath ne seeth me him ne'r shake:
    He is the sloweste man that ever was y-boren!

53. 17 Lound (Lincolnshire)   18 I know no maid so fair as she for
whom I go enchained   19 stounde: while   20 f. I will declare
my song to her whom it concerns

54. The man in the moon stands in full stride; on his hay-fork he carries his
load. It is great wonder that he does not fall down: for fear of falling he
shudders and ? swerves. When frost freezes he endures great cold; the
thorns which tear his clothes are sharp. There is nobody in the world who
knows when he sits down, nor, unless it be the hedge, what garments he
wears.
    Where do we suppose this man is going? He has set one foot before the
other. Whatever need to hurry he has, one never sees him move: he is the
slowest man that was ever born! Has he been in the field driving stakes,

Wher he were o the feeld pichinde stake,
  For hope of his thornes to dutten his doren?
He mot mid his twi-bil other trous make   15
  Other al his dayes werk ther were y-loren.

This ilke man upon high whene'r he were—
  Wher he were i the moonė boren and y-fed?—
He leneth on his forke as a grey frere.
  This crokede caynard sore he is a-dred.   20
It is many day go that he was here;
  Ich'ot of his ernde he n'ath nout y-sped:
He hath hewe sumwher a burthen of brere;
  Therefore sum hayward hath taken his wed.

'If thy wed is y-take, bring hom the trous;   25
  Sete forth thyn other foot, strid over sty!
We shule praye the hayward hom to our hous
  And maken him at eise for the maistrỳ;
Drinke to him deerly of ful good bous,
  And our Dame Douse shal sitten him by.   30
When that he is drunke as a dreint mous,
  Thenne we shule borewe the wed at the bailỳ.'

with the object of stopping his gaps with his thorns? He must either make a bundle of thorns with his two-edged axe or else his whole days work there would be wasted.

Whenever this same man is on high—was he born and reared in the moon?—he leans on his fork like a grey friar. This hunched sluggard is greatly afraid. It is many days past that he was here; I know he has not succeeded in his errand: he has cut somewhere a load of briars; some hayward has taken his pledge (to pay) for it.

'If your pledge has been taken, bring home the bundle; put your other foot forward, stride along the way! We shall invite the hayward home to our house and make him perfectly at ease; give him plenty to drink of very good liquor, and our Dame Douce shall sit beside him. When he is as drunk as a drowned mouse, then we shall recover the pledge from the bailiff.'

This man hereth me nought, though ich to him crye;
  Ich'ot the cherl is def—the de'l him to-drawe!
Though ich yeye upon high, n'ille he nought hye: 35
  The lostlesse ladde can nought o lawe.
    'Hupé forth, Hubert, hosédé pye!
    Ich'ot th'art amarscled into the mawe!'
Though me teene with him that myn teeth mye,
  The cherl n'il nought adown er the day dawe. 40

55   *An Unfortunate Lover*

L ITEL wot it any mon
        How derné love may stonde,
Bute it were a free wimmòn
    That muche of love had fonde.
The love of hir ne lasteth no wight longe: 5
Heo haveth me plight, and witeth me with wronge.
    Ever and oo for my leef ich am in greté thoghte:
    I thenche on hir that I ne see nought ofte.

I woldé nemné hir to-day
And I dorste hir minne. 10

54. This man does not hear me, though I shout to him; I reckon the fellow is deaf—the devil rend him! Though I shout at the top of my voice, he refuses to hurry; the listless lout knows nothing about ? law (? proper conduct). 'Hop along, Hubert, stockinged magpie! I reckon you are ? paralysed to the belly!' Though I rage against him so that my teeth grind, the fellow refuses to come down before day dawns.

55. 1 f. Little does anyone know what a secret love can be like   3 unless he love a beautiful woman   4 fonde: experienced   5 love of hir: her love   no wight: not at all   6 She has promised (it) to me, and blames me unjustly   7 Ever and ay for my dear I am in great distress   8 thenche on: think about   9 nemne: name   10 if I dared mention her

Heo is that fairestė may
  Of ech ende of hir kinne.
  Bute heo me love, of me heo havės sinne—
  Wo is him that loveth the love that he ne
    may ne'r y-winne.
    Ever and oo, *etc.*   15

Adown I fel to hir anon
  And cried: 'Lady, thyn ore!
Lady, ha mercy of thy mon!
  Lef thou no false lore.
  If thou dost, it wil me rewė sore: 20
  Love drecheth me that I ne may live na more.'
    Ever and oo, *etc.*

Miry it is in hirė towr
  With hatheles and with hewe;
So it is in hirė bowr   25
  With gomenes and with glewe.
  Bute heo me lovye, sore it wil me rewe—
  Wo is him that loveth the love that ne'**r** n'il
    be trewe.
    Ever and oo, *etc.*

'Fairest fode upo loft,   30
  My goode leef, I thee greete

11 may: maid   12 of all the members of her race   13 unless
she loves me, she does me wrong   14 ne'r: never   16 anon:
straightway   17 ore: mercy   18 ha: have   mon: man
19 Believe no false tale   20 rewe: distress   21 drecheth: torments
23 Miry: delightful   24 with noblemen and servants   26 with
amusements and entertainment   27 Bute: unless   28 ne'r n'il:
never will   30 fode . . .: child in chamber

As felė sithe and oft
　As dewės dropes beeth weete,
　As sterrės beeth in welkne, and grases sour
　　and sweete'—
Whoso loveth untrewe, his herte is seldė seete.　35
Ever and oo, *etc.*

56　　　　　*At the Crucifixion*

'STAND wel, moder, under roodė,
　Behold thy child with gladė moodė;
　Blithė moder might thou be.'
'Sone, how may I blithė standė?
I see thyn feet, I see thyn handė,　　　　　5
　Nailėd to the hardė tree.'

'Moder, do way thy wepingė;
I thole this ded for mannės thingė;
　For owėn giltė thole I non.'
'Sone, I fele the dedė-stoundė;　　　　　10
The sword is at myn hertė-groundė
　That me behightė Simeon.'

'Moder, rew upon they berėn!
Thou washe away tho bloody terėn;
　It don me wersė than my ded.'　　　　　15

55. 32 fele sithe: many times　　　33 as there are wet drops of dew
34 sterres: stars　　welkne: sky　　grases: herbs　　　35 untrewe:
someone unfaithful　　selde seete: seldom content

56. 2 moode: heart　　　3 might: may　　　7 do way: cease　　　8 I
suffer this death for man's sake　　　9 owen: my own　　　10 dede-
stounde: death-pangs　　11 myn . . .: the bottom of my heart　　　12
which Simeon promised me　　　13 beren: son　　　14 tho: those
teren: tears　　　15 they affect me worse than my death

AT THE CRUCIFIXION

'Sone, how might I terès wernè?
I see tho bloody floodès ernè
 Out of thyn hertè to myn fet.' . . .

'Moder, if I dare thee tellè,
If I ne die, thou gost to hellè: 20
 I thole this ded for thinè sake.'
'Sonè, thou beest me so mindè,
Wit me nought; it is my kindè
 That I for thee sorwè make.'

' Moder, mercy! let me dyè,   25
For Adam out of hellè byè,
 And al mankin that is forloren.'
'Sonè, what shal me to redè?
Thy pinè pineth me to dedè;
 Let me dyèn thee beforen.'   30

'Moder, nutarst thou might lerè
What pinè tholen that childrè berè,
 What sorwè haven that child forgon.'
'Sone, I wot, I can thee tellè:
Bute it be the pine of hellè,   35
 Morè sorwe ne wot I non.'

'Moder, rew of moder carè,
Now thou wost of moder farè,
 Though thou be clenè maidenman.'

16 werne: restrain   17 erne: run   22 Son, you are so much in
my thought   23 Wit: blame   kinde: nature   26 For: so as to
27 mankin: mankind   forloren: lost   28 Son, what am I to do?
29 pine: torment   dede: death   31 Mother, now for the first
time you can learn   32, 33 that: those who   33 forgon: lose
35 Bute: unless   37 f. Mother, have pity on a mother's grief, now
that you know about a mother's lot   39 maidenman: virgin

'Sonĕ, help at allĕ nedĕ,   40
Allĕ tho that to me gredĕ—
  Maiden, wif, and fol wimmàn.'

'Moder, I may no lenger dwellĕ;
The time is cume I fare to hellĕ;
  The thriddĕ day I rise upon.'   45
'Sone, I willĕ with thee foundĕ,
I dye y-wis of thinĕ woundĕ;
  So rewful ded was nevere non.' . . .

57   *On the Passion*

WHENNE ich see on roode
       Jesu my lemmàn,
And beside Him standen
Marie and Johàn,
And His rig y-swungen   5
And His side y-stungen
For the love of man:
Wel ow ich to wepen
And sinnĕs forleten,
If ich of lovĕ can,   10
If ich of lovĕ can,
If ich of lovĕ can.

56. 41 tho: those   grede: cry   42 fol: wanton   43 no . . .: stay
no longer   45 I shall rise on the third day   46 founde: go
47 y-wis: indeed   wounde: wounds

57. 1 ich: I   2 lemman: sweetheart   5 and His back scourged
6 y-stungen: pierced   8 ow: ought   9 and give up sins
10 can: am capable

The Pound of Flesh

THEN sent the King Constantine
    Sendmen til his moder Elìne,
For to do seke withouten hon
The cros that Crist was on don,
To find that haly tree sumquar,   5
And do a kirc be raisèd thar.
Benciras and Ansièrs,
Thir twa men war messagers;
Thay war sent to the queen fra Rome—
But herkens hider how thay gave dome.   10
   This levedy had that day hir with
A Cristen man was good goldsmith:
Quat thing that sho wald him mouth
At mak til hir ful wel he couth.
But pour he was, of littel aght,   15
And til a Jew he mikel aght—
A summe of monee for to amount—
That askèd him ful hard acount.
It was wel sene that it was hard,
For he him asked with slik forward,   20
If he his monee mought not get,
That he suld yeild him for his det

---

2 f. messengers to his mother Helena, to cause a search to be made without delay for   4 on don: put on   5 haly . . .: holy tree somewhere   6 do: cause to   thar: there   8 Thir: these   war: were   10 but listen to this, how they gave judgement   11 levedy: lady   day: time   12 was: (who) was   13 f. whatever she liked to mention to him, he knew well how to make it for her   15 aght: property   16 and to a Jew he owed much   17 for . . .: at interest   18 who required of him very hard terms of settlement 20 with . . .: on such terms   21 mought: might   22 suld: should   yield: pay

That ilk weght that thar was less
—He suld yeild—of his awn fless.
   The day is gan, the det unquit,   25
The body most beleve for it.
The Cristen dred ful sar the pine,
But the Jew wald never fine.
Bath to the queenès court thay come,
The Jew thraly bad give him dome;   30
Sharp grounden knif in hand he bar,
The Cristen man stood naked thar.
Thay wald have all again him bought,
But grant of Jew then gat thay nought
Of ransun, namar than a ress: 35
Wald he of her but of his fless.
   Said Benciras and Ansièrs:
'Thou sal have, brother, al that thee fers;
The queen has biden us to deme
To thee al that to right is queme.   40
Say me then that thou wil him dight,
If he be dempt to thee with right.'
'How?' said the Jew, 'but, by my lay,
The werst that ever I can or may!
His eyèn first put out I sal,   45
And his hend he werkes withal,
Tung and nese, and sithen the lave,

23 less: wanting   24 fless: flesh   25 gan: past   26 most...
must be left (to pay) for it   27 sar: sorely pine: pain   28 wald:
would fine: desist   29 Bath: both come: came   30 thraly:
angrily dome: judgement   31 bar: carried   33 they were
all willing to redeem him   34 grant: consent gat: got
35 for ransome, no more than a rush (*i.e.* not a bit)   36 her: *i.e.*
the queen   38 sal: shall thee fers: is your due   39 deme:
adjudge   40 to . . .: is consonant with justice   41 that . . .:
what you will do to him   42 dempt: adjudged   43 How: what
lay: faith   46 hend . . .: hands which he works with   47 tongue
and nose, and then the rest

Til that I al my covenand have.'
The messagers him gave answàre:
'Then semes it nought thou wil him spare: 50
Tak then thy fless, that grantes he thee,
Swa that the blood may savèd be;
A drope of blood if that he tine
We give for dome the wrang is thine.
Quatsum his fless was sald and bought,   55
His blood to sell he never it thought.
Yeild thee thyn fless he is wel on-knawn;
Save him the blood, that is his awn.'

Then said that Jew: 'By saint Drightìne,
Me think the wers part is mine;   60
For-don ye have me with your dome
That ye Romaìns has brought fro Rome.
Maugré thar-for mot thay have,
All that swilk a dome me gave!'
Benciras then said: 'Parfay!   65
Al has this court herd thy missay;
Me and my laverd Sir Ansìre,
Thou has missaid us in thyn ire.
But we will missay thee na wight,
But elles of thee we will ha right.   70
The levedy sent us hider to
This court for rightwisnes to do,
And sothfastnes ha we thee said:
Thar-for has thou us missaid.'

52 Swa: in such a way   53 tine: lose   54 we give judgement
that you are in the wrong   55 Quatsum: even though   57 ? He
fully admits that he must pay you your flesh   58 awn: own   59
saint Drightine: holy God   61 For-don: ruined   63 may they
have misfortune because of it   64 swilk: such   65 Parfay: by my
faith   66 missay: abuse   67 laverd: lord   69 na wight: not
at all   70 but otherwise we mean to do justice on you   71 hider:
here   72 rightwisnes: justice   73 sothfastnes: truth   ha: have

The levedy bad withouten lite   75
Thay suld the jugement give it tite;
For siker was sho then of site,
That the Cristen man was quite.
The Jew was dempt swa that the quene
Suld all his catel have bidene,   80
In hir mercy his tung to tak
That in hir court slik missay spak.
The Jew him thought selcouthly tene
At this dome that was swa kene,
And said on hight, that all mought here;   85
'Me war lever you for to lere
Quar lis your laverd rodè-tree
Than dempt swa smertly for to be.'
'God wat, my freind', then said Elìne,
'Thou sal be quit of al thy pine   90
If thou will do as we thee bid,
To shew us quar that cros is hid.'

'ROBERT OF GLOUCESTER'

c. 1325

59   *Town against Gown at Oxford*

SIR EDWARD, that was by este tho mid power gret ynow,
Soonè, toward Lentè, toward the March he drow.

58. 75 lite: delay   **76** tite: promptly   **77** for she was then secure
from anxiety   **78** That: because   quite: free   **79** dempt swa: so
sentenced   **80** catel: property   bidene: entirely   **81** and to put
his tongue at her mercy.   **82** slik: such   **83** It seemed to the Jew
he was extraordinarily ill used   **84** kene: harsh   **85** on hight: aloud
mought: might   **86** f. I had rather show you where your Lord's cross lies
88 smertly: severely   **90** pine: punishment   **92** quar: where
59. 1 The Lord Edward, who was then (1264) in the east with a con-
siderable force   **2** March: Welsh border   drow: moved

His way he nom by Oxenford, ac the burgeis anon
The gates made faste ayen him of the town echon.
He wende and lay withouté town atté Kingés Halle,   5
And wendé forth a-morwé mid his men alle.
The gatés, tho he was y-wend, were alle up y-brought
Sooné, buté Smithé gate, ac that n'as undo nought.
The clerkes hadde ther-thoru muche solàs y-lore
To playé toward Beumond: anuid hi were ther-fore.   10
The bailifs hi bede ofté to graunty her solàs
To playe, and undo that gate; ac for nought it was.
So that an fewe wilde hinen a light reed therof nome,
And à day after meté with axes thider come
And that gate to-hewe and to-dashté there,   15
And sithé thoru Beumond to Harèwelle it bere,
And *subvenite sancti* fasté gunné singe,
As me deth when a ded man me wille to pitté bringe.
Willam the Spicer and Geffray of Henksey, that tho were
Portreven, and Nicole of Kingestone, that was mere,   20
Nome of thes clerkés and in prison caste,
And n'olde hem nought delivery, yet the Chaunceler bed
    faste.

---

3 nom: took   ac . . .: but the citizens at once   4–10 made every
gate of the town fast against him. He turned and stayed outside the town at
the King's Hall (of Beaumont), and on the next day marched on with all
his men. When he was gone, the gates were all opened immediately, except
the Smiths' gate, but that was not opened. The students had thereby lost
a great amenity in their recreations around Beaumont: they were annoyed
about that   11 hi bede: they asked   12 ac . . .: but it was of
no avail   13 hinen . . .: lads decided on a reckless course   14 a:
one   come: came   15 to-hewe: cut to pieces   to-dashte: smashed
16 sithe: then   Harewelle: *unidentified*   bere: carried   17 *subvenite
sancti*: funeral antiphon sung as a corpse was carried to church   faste . . .:
stoutly sang   18 as is done when a dead man is being carried to his
grave   19 that tho: who then   20 Portreven: bailiffs   mere:
mayor   21 Nome of: seized some of   22 and refused to release
them, pressingly though the Chancellor of the University demanded (it)

The clerkès were tho wrothè, the burgeis were tho bolde
And thretnede to nimè mo, and of her wrathe lite tolde.
  The ferste Thorsday in Lentè the burgeis were wel fers 25
And, the while men were atte mete, arerdè tweie banèrs,
And wende hem forth y-armèd mid al her power there
To defouly alle the clerkès ar hi y-war were.
As hi come ayen Alle Halwen mid power so strong,
At Saintè Marie churche a clerk the commun bellè rong. 30
Thes clerkes up from her mete, and to Godès gracè
    truste,
And seyè that hi were y-shend bute hi the bet hem wuste.
Hi mettè with thes burgeis and bigunne to shetè faste;
Y-wounded ther was many one; ac the burgeis attè laste
Hi bigunnè to flee faste—hem thoughtè longe er— 35
So that the clerkès hadde the stretès soone y-ler.
The bowyeres shoppe hi breke and the bowès nome
    echon,
Sithè the porterevès house hi sette a-fire anon
In the south-half of the towne, and sithe the spicerie
Hi breke from ende to other, and dide al to robberie. 40
For the mere was viniter, hi breke the viniterie,
And alle othere in the town, and that was lite maistrie.
Hi caste away the dosils that win orn abrod so

24 nime . . .: seize more, and took little notice of their anger   25
fers: in fighting mood   26 arerde tweie: raised two   27 wende
hem: marched   28 defouly: crush   ar . . .: before they realized
29 come ayen: came past   Halwen: Saints   30 rong: rang   31 up:
got up   32 and saw that they would be killed unless they defended
themselves more actively   33 shete: shoot   35 hem . . .: it
seemed to them (too) long before (they could get away)   36 y-ler:
empty   37 breke: broke into   bowes . . .: seized every bow
39 spicerie: spice-shop   40 they wrecked from end to end, and looted
everything   41 For: because   viniter: vintner   viniterie: wine-
store   42 alle othere: everything else   lite maistrie: little credit
43 dosils: barrel-plugs   orn . . .: ran about so freely

That it was pité gret of so muche harm y-do.
Therfore, tho the king com and wisté swich trespàs,   45
Alle the clerkes out of the town he drof for that cas,
Ne fort after Michelmasse hi ne come namore ther.

ROBERT MANNYNG OF BOURNE

fl. c. 1325

60   *The Dancers of Colbek*

IT was upon a Cristemesse night
  That twelve fooles a carolle dight,
In wodehed, as it were in cuntek;
They come to a town men calle Colbek.
The cherche of the town that they to come   5
Is of Saint Magne, that suffred martyrdome;
Of Saint Bukcestre it is alsò,
Saint Magnes sister, that they come to.
Here names of alle thus fond I write,
And as I wot now shul ye wite: 10
Here lodèsman, that made hem glew,
Thus is write, he hight Gerlèw.
Twey maidens were in here covìne,
Maiden Merswinde and Wibèssine.

59. 44 that it was a great shame so much damage was done   45
tho . . .: when the king came and learnt the extent of the offence   46
for . . .: because of this incident   47 fort: until

60. 1 night: eve   2 carolle: dance accompanied with song   dight:
made   3 wodehed: madness   cuntek: lawlessness   4 come:
came   Kölbigk (Saxony)   5 to come: came to   6 Magnus
8 that: (the church) which   9–11 The names of all of them I found
written thus, and you shall now know them as I do: their leader, who
directed their singing   12 hight: was called   13 Twey: two
covine: band

ROBERT MANNYNG

Alle these come thider for that ènchesoun   15
Of the preestès doughter of the toun.

The preest hight Robert, as I can ame;
Azone hight his sone by name;
His doughter, that these men wulde have,
Thus is write, that she hight Ave.   20
Echone consented to o wil
Who shuld go Ave out to til;
They graunted echone out to sende
Bothe Wibèssine and Merswinde.

These wommen yede and tolled her out   25
With hem to carolle the cherche about.
Bevune ordeined here carolling;
Gerlew endited what they shuld sing.
This is the carolle that they sunge,
As telleth the Latin tunge: 30
'*Equitabat Bevo per silvam frondosam,*
Ducebat secum Merswindam formosam.
Quid stamus? cur non imus?'
'By the levèd wode rode Bevoline,
With him he leddè fair Merswine.   35
Why standè we? why go we nought?'
This is the carolle that Grisly wrought.
This song sunge they in the cherchèyerd—
Of foly were they nothing afèrd—
Unto the matines were allè done,   40
And the messè shuld biginnè sone.

---

15 f. for . . .: on account of the daughter of the priest of the town
17 can ame: think   21 everyone agreed unanimously   22 til:
entice   25 yede: went   tolled: lured   26 hem: them   34
levèd: leafy   37 Grisly: Gerlew   39 nothing aferd: in no way
afraid   40 Unto: until   41 messe: mass

The preest him revèst to beginnè messe,
And they ne left ther-fore never the lesse,
But daunsèd forth as they bigan—
For all the messè they ne blan.   45

The preest, that stood at the autère
And herd here noise and herè bere,
Fro the auter down he nam
And to the cherchè porche he cam
And said: 'On Goddes behalve, I you forbede   50
That ye no lenger do swich dede;
But cometh in on fair manère
Goddès servise for to here,
And doth at Cristin mennès lawe:
Carolleth no more, for Cristès awe!   55
Worshippeth Him with alle your might
That of the Virgine was bore this night.'

For alle his bidding lefte they nought,
But daunsèd forth as they thought.
The preest there-for was sore agreved: 60
He prayd God, that he on beleved,
And for Saint Magne, that He wulde so werche—
In whos worship sette was the cherche—
That swich a venjaunce were on hem sent,
Ar they out of that stede were went,   65

42 him revest: robed himself   43 and they did not desist on that
account at all   45 blan: stopped   46 autere: altar   47 bere:
uproar   48 nam: went   51 lenger: longer   swich: such
52 cometh: come   54 doth at: behave according to   55 for . . .:
out of reverence for Christ   58 lefte: desisted   59 thought:
intended   60 there-for: at that   agreved: incensed   61-3 he
prayed God, in whom he trusted, and for the sake of St. Magnus—in
whose honour the church was built—that He (God) would bring it about
65 Ar: before   stede: place

That they might ever right so wende
Unto that timė twelvemonth ende
(In the Latine that I fond thore
He saith not 'twelvemonth' but 'evermore');
He cursėd hem there allė same   70
As they carolėd on here game.
 As soone as the preest hadde so spoke
Every hand in other so fast was loke
That no man might with no wunder
That twelvemonthe parte hem asunder. 75
 The preest yede in when this was done
And commaunded his sone Azòne
That he shulde go swithe after Ave,
Oute of that carolle algate to have.
But al to late that word was said,   80
For on hem alle was the venjaunce laid.
 Azone wende wel for to spede;
Unto the carolle as swithe he yede;
His sister by the arm he hente,
And the arm fro the body wente;   85
Men wundred allė that there wore,
And merveile mowe ye herė more,
For sethen he had the arm in hand,
The body yede forth caroland,

---

66 right . . .: go on like that 67 *i.e.* for twelve months' time 68
fond thore: found there 70 same: together 71 on . . .: for their
amusement 73 loke: locked 74 wunder: miraculous power
78 swithe: quickly 79 algate . . .: to get (her) by any means
82 Azo expected to succeed 83 as swithe: at once 84 hente:
seized 86 that . . .: who were there 87 and you may hear a
greater marvel 88 sethen: after 89 caroland: dancing

And nother the body ne the arm   90
Bledde never bloode, cold ne warm,
But was as drye, with al the haunche,
As of a stok were rive a braunche.
  Azone to his fader went
And brought him a sory presènt: 95
'Looke, fader,' he said, 'and have it here,
The arm of thy doughter dere
That was myn ownè sister Ave,
That I wende I might a save.
Thy cursing now sene it es   100
With venjaunce on thy ownè fles.
Felliche thou cursedest, and over-soone;
Thou askedest venjaunce: thou hast thy boone!'
  You thar not aske if there was wo
With the preest and with many mo.   105
The preest that cursèd for that daunce,
On some of his fil harde chaunce.
He tooke his doughter arm forlorn
And biried it on the morn;
The nextè day the arm of Ave   110
He fond it ligging above the grave.
He biried it another day,
And eft above the grave it lay.
The thriddè time he biried it,

90 nother: neither   ne: nor   92 haunche: shoulder   93 as
if a branch were torn from a trunk   99 a save: have saved
100 es: is   101 fles: flesh   102 Felliche: savagely   103 boone:
request   104 You thar: you need   105 mo: more
107 some: one   fil: fell   108 he took his daughter's torn off arm
109 morn: morrow   111 ligging: lying   113 eft: again

149

ROBERT MANNYNG

And eft was it cast out of the pit.   115
The preest wulde birie it no more:
He dredde the venjaunce ferly sore.
Into the cherche he bare the arme
For drede and doute of morė harme;
He ordeined it for to be   120
That every man might with eye it see.
    These men that yede so carolland
Alle that yerė, hand in hand,
They never out of that stedė yede,
Ne none might hem thennė lede.   125
There the cursing first bigan,
In that place aboute they ran,
That never ne felt they no werynes—
As many bodyes for going dos—
Ne mete ete, ne drank drinke,   130
Ne slepte onely alėpy winke.
Night ne day they wist of none,
When it was come, when it was gone;
Frost ne snow, hail ne raine,
Of colde ne hete, felte they no paine;   135
Heer ne nailės never grewe,
Ne solowed clothes, ne turnėd hewe;
Thunder ne lightning did hem no dere—
Goddes mercy did it fro hem were—
But sunge that song that the wo wrought: 140
'Why standė we? why go we nought?'

---

117 ferly: extremely   119 doute: fear   125 thenne: thence
126 There: where   128 without feeling any weariness   129 for...:
do from activity   131 nor slept even a single wink   132 They
were unaware of night or day   136 Heer: hair   137 nor did
(their) clothes grow dirty, nor (their) complexion change   138 dere:
harm   139 were: ward off

What man shuld ther be in this live
That ne wulde it see and thider drive?
The Emperoure Henry come fro Rome
For to see this hardė dome.   145
When he hem say, he weptė sore
For the mischefe that he say thore.
He did come wrightės for to make
Covering over hem, for tempest sake.
But that they wrought it was in vain,   150
For it come to no certàin;
For that they sette on o day,
On the tother down it lay.
Ones, twyes, thryės, thus they wrought,
And all here making was for nought.   155
Might no covering hile hem fro colde
Til time of mercy that Crist it wolde.
    Time of grace fil thurgh His might
At the twelvemonth ende, on the Yolė night.
The same houre that the preest hem band,   160
The same houre atwinne they wand;
That houre that he cursed hem inne,
The same houre they yede atwinne,
And as in twinkeling of an eye
Into the cherchė gun they flye,   165

142 in . . .: living   143 who would not want to see it and hasten
there   145 dome: punishment   146 say: saw   147 mischefe:
misfortune   thore: there   148 did: caused to   149 for . . .: for
bad weather   150 that: what   151 for it came to nothing
152 f. for what they built one day was lying flat the next day   155
and all their work was in vain   156 hile: protect   157 till the
time of mercy which Christ willed   158 fil: fell, came   159
Yole night: Christmas Eve   160 band: bound   161 atwinne:
apart   wand: went   165 gun . . .: they fled

And on the pavement they fil alle downe
As they had be dede, or fal in a swoune.
   Three days stil they lay echone,
That none stered other flesh or bone;
And at the three dayès ende   170
To life God graunted hem to wende.
They sette hem up and spak apert
To the parishe preest, sire Robèrt:
'Thou art ensample and ènchesoun
Of oure long confusioun;   175
Thou maker art of oure travàile,
That is to many grete mervàile;
And thy travàile shalt thou soone ende,
For to thy long home soone shalt thou wende.'
   Alle they rise that ichè tide   180
But Avè: she lay dede beside.
Grete sorowe had her fader, her brother;
Merveile and drede had alle other:
I trow no drede of soulè dede,
But with pine was brought the body dede.   185
The first man was the fader, the prest,
That deyd after the doughter nest.
This iche arme that was of Ave,
That none mightè leye in grave,
The Emperoure did a vessel werche   190
To do it in and hange in the cherche,

---

167 As: as if   fal: fallen   169 stered: stirred   other: either
171 wende: return   172 They stood up and spoke plainly   174 f.
you are the occasion and cause of our long humiliation   179 long:
eternal   180 They all rose that very hour.   181 beside: beside them
184 f. not, I am sure, fear for the death of her soul, but because her body
died in great pain   187 nest: next   190 did . . .: had a vessel
made   191 do: put

That alle men might see it and knawe,
And thenk on the chaunce when men it sawe.
　These men that hadde go thus carolland
Alle the yere, fast hand in hand,　　　　　　　195
Though that they were then asunder,
Yet alle the worlde spake of hem wunder.
That same hopping that they first yede,
That daunce yede they thurgh land and lede;
And, as they ne might first be unbounde,　　　200
So eft togeder might they never be founde,
Ne might they never come ayain
Togeder to o stede, certàin.
　Foure yedè to the court of Rome,
And ever hopping about they nome;　　　　　　205
Sunderlepès come they theder,
But they come never eft togeder.
Here clothes ne roted, ne nailès grewe,
Ne heer ne wax, ne solowed hewe,
Ne never hadde they amendèment,　　　　　　210
That we herde, at any corseint,
But at the virgine Saint Edight,
There was he botened, Teodright,
On oure Lady day, in lenten tide,
As he slepte her toumbe beside:　　　　　　　215
There he had his medicine
At Saint Edight, the holy virgìne.

193 and remember what had happened when they saw it　　　199
lede: nation　　　201 eft: afterwards　　　203 o . . .: one place, indeed
205 nome: went　　　206 they came there separately　　　209 wax:
grew　　　211 corseint: saint's shrine　　　212 Edith of Wilton
213 botened: cured　　Theodric　　　214 Lady: Lady's　lenten: spring

153

Bruning the bishop of Saint Tolous
Wrote this tale so merveilous;
Sethe was his name of more renoun— 220
Men callèd him the pope Leoun.
This at the court of Rome they wite,
And in the kronikeles it is write
In many stedes beyond the see,
More than is in this cuntré. 225
Therfor men saye—and wel is trod—
'The nerè the cherche, the firther fro God'.

61 *Lollay, Lollay, Little Child!*

LOLLAY, lollay, litel child! Why wepest thou so sore?
Nedès most thou wepe; it was y-yarked thee yore
Ever to lib in sorow and sich, and mourne evermore,
As thyn eldren did er this, whil hi alivès wore.
    Lollay, lollay, litel child! child, lollay, lullow! 5
    In to uncouth world y-comen so art thou.

Bestès and thos fowlès, the fishes in the flood,
And ech shef alivès y-maked of bone and blood,
When hi cometh to the world, hi doth hem self sum
    good—
Al but the wrechè brol that is of Adames blood. 10
    Lollay, lollay, litel child! to care art thou be-mette;
    Thou n'ost nought this worldès wild befor thee is y-
    sette.

60. 218 *i.e.* Bruno bishop of Toul   220 Sethe: afterwards   221
Leo IX   226 trod: believed   227 nere: nearer

61. 2 most: must   y-yarked . . .: ordained for you long ago   3 lib:
live   sich: sighing   4 eldren: forebears   hi: they   wore: were
6 uncouth: unknown   7 thos: these   8 shef: creature
9 hem: them   10 brol: brat   11 be-mette: destined   12 you
do not know the power of this world which is in wait for you

LOLLAY, LOLLAY, LITTLE CHILD

Child, if it betideth that thou shalt thrive and thee,
Thench thou wer y-fostred up thy moder knee;
Ever hab mind in thy hert of thos thingės three: 15
Whan thou comest, whan thou art, and what shal come
    of thee.
    Lollay, lollay, litel child! child, lollay, lollay!
    With sorow thou com into this world, with sorow
        shalt wend away.

Ne trist thou to this worlde: it is thy foulė fo;
The rich he maketh pover, the porė rich alsò;   20
It turneth wo to weel and ek weel to wo—
Ne tristė no man to this world, whil it turneth so.
    Lollay, lollay, litel child! thy foot is in the wheele;
    Thou n'ost wheder turnė to wo other weele.

Child, thou art a pilgrim in wikednes y-born;   25
Thou wandrest in this falsė world, thou lokė thee beforn.
Deth shal comė with a blast out of a wel dim horn,
Adames kin down to cast, himself hath y-don beforn.
    Lollay, lollay, litel child! so wo thee worp Adàm
    In the land of Paradis, through wikednes of Satàn.   30

Child, thou n'art a pilgrim, but an uncouth gest;
Thy dayės beeth y-toldė, thy jurneys beeth y-kest;
Wheder thou shalt wendė north other est,
Deth thee shal betidė with bitter bale in brest.

Lollay, lollay, litel child! this wo Adam thee
    wraughte   35
When he of the appel ete and Eve it him betaughte.

62   *An Irish Satire*

HAIL Saint Michael with thy longe spere!
  Fair beeth thy winges up thy sholdère;
Thou hast a rede kirtil anon to thy fote:
Thou art best angel that ever God maked!
    This vers is ful wel y-wrought;   5
    It is of wel ferre y-brought.

Hail Saint Cristofre with thy longe stake!
Thou ber our Loverd Jesus Crist over the brod lake.
Many grete conger swimmeth aboute thy fete.
How many hering to peny at West Chep in London?
    This vers is of Holy Writte;   11
    It com of noble witte. . . .

Hail Saint Dominic with thy longe staffe!
It is at the over-end croked as a gaffe.
Thou berest a book on thy bak—ich wene it is a bible;
Though thou be a good clerk, be thou not to heigh.   16
    Trie rime, la, God it wot!
    Such an other on erthe I n'ot.

61. 35 wraughte: wrought   36 betaughte: gave

62. 2 up: upon   3 anon to: reaching to   6 of wel ferre: from
very far   8 ber: bore   Loverd: Lord   lake: stream
10 to: for a   12 com: came   14 over-: upper-   gaffe: iron
hook   15 ich: I   16 to heigh: too proud   17 An excellent
rhyme indeed, God knows   18 n'ot: do not know

Hail Saint Franceis with thy many fowles,
Kites and crowes, ravenes and owles,   20
Foure and twenty wild gees and a poucok!
Many bold begger seweth thy route.
    This vers is ful wel y-sette;
    Swithe ferre it was y-fette.

Hail be ye freres with the white copes!   25
Ye habbeth a hous at Drochda wher men maketh ropes.
Ever ye beeth roilend the landes al aboute;
Of the water daissers ye robbeth the churches.
    Maister he was swithe good
    That this sentence understood   30

Hail be ye marchans with your grete packes
Of draperie, avoir-de-peise, and your wol-sackes,
Gold, silver, stones riche, markes and ek poundes!
Litil yive ye therof to the wreche pover.
    Sleigh he was and ful of witte   35
    That this lore put in writte. . . .

Hail be ye bouchers with your bole-ax!
Fair beeth your barmhatres, yelow beeth your fax;
Ye standeth at the shamel, brod ferlich bernes,
Fleyis you foloweth, ye swoloweth ynow!   40

21 poucok: peacock   22 seweth: follows route: train   23 y-sette: composed   24 it was fetched from very far   26 habbeth: have   Drogheda   27 roilend: roaming   28 daissers: ? sprinklers   29 f. He needed to be a very good scholar to understand the meaning of this   31 marchans: merchants   32 avoir-de-peise: goods sold by weight   33 riche: precious   34 wreche pover: miserable poor   35 Sleigh: knowing   36 writte: writing   37 bouchers: butchers bole-ax: pole-axe   38 barmhatres: aprons fax: hair   39 shamel: meat-stall   ferlich . . .: fearsome fellows   40 Fleyis: flies

The best clerk of al this town
Craftfullich maked this bastòun.

Hail be ye bakers with your loves smale
Of white bred and of blake, ful many and fale!
Ye pincheth on the right weight ayens Goddes law: 45
To the faire pillory ich rede ye take hede.
   This vers is y-wrought so welle
   That no tung, y-wis, may telle. . . .

Hail be ye hokesters down by the lake,
With candles and golokes and the pottes blake,   50
Tripes and kine feet and shepen hevedes!
With the hory tromchery hory is youre inne.
   He is sory of his lif
   That is fast to such a wif! . . .

Maketh glad, my frendes; ye sitteth to long stille;   55
Speketh now and gladieth and drinketh al your fille!
Ye habbeth y-herd of men lif that woneth in land;
Drinketh deep and maketh glade, ne hab ye non other
      nede.
   This song is y-said of me;
   Ever y-blessed mot ye be!   60

---

42 bastoun: stanza   44 fale: numerous   45 *i.e.* your loaves are underweight   ayens: contrary to   46 rede: advise   48 y-wis: indeed   49 hokesters: women pedlars   50 golokes: tubs 51 **kine** . . .: cows' feet and sheep's heads   52 hory tromchery: filthy ? rubbish   inne: dwelling   53 He is sorry to be alive   55 stille: silent   56 gladieth: be merry   57 You have heard the way men live who dwell in the land   58 hab: have   59 This song of mine is finished   60 mot: may

63 *The Land of Cockayne*

FER in see by west Spaygne
Is a land y-hote Cokaygne;
Ther n'is land under heven-riche
Of wele, of goodnes it y-liche;
Though Paradis be mery and bright,   5
Cokaygn is of fairer sight.
What is ther in Paradis
But grasse and flowr and grenė ris?
Though ther be joy and grete dute,
Ther n'is metė butė frute;   10
Ther n'is hallė, bowr, no benche,
But water mannės thurst to quenche.
Beeth ther no men butė two—
Ely and Enok alsò:
Elinglichė may hi go   15
Wher ther woneth men no mo.
In Cokaygne is mete and drink,
Withoutė carė, how and swink;
The mete is trie, the drink is clere
To nonė, russin and soppère.   20
I sigge for sooth, boutė were,
Ther n'is land on erthe his pere;
Under heven n'is land, y-wisse,
Of so muchel joy and blisse.

---

1 Far out in the sea west of Spain   2 y-hote: called   3
-riche: kingdom   4 wele: prosperity   it . . .: like it   6 sight:
appearance   8 ris: bough   9 dute: delight   10 bute: except
11 no: nor   14 Ely: Elijah   15 f. desolately may they go where
there are no more men living   18 how . . .: trouble and toil
19 trie: choice   20 To none: at the midday meal   russin:
afternoon snack   21 I say truly, without doubt   22 his pere:
its equal   23 y-wisse: certainly

Ther is many swetė sighte;   25
Al is day, n'is ther no nighte.
Ther n'is baret nother strif,
N'is ther no deth, ac ever lif;
Ther n'is lac of mete no cloth;
Ther n'is man no womman wroth;   30
Ther n'is serpent, wolf no fox,
Hors no capel, cowe no ox;
Ther n'is shepe no swine no gote,
No non horwe, la, God it wote!
Nother harace nother stode;   35
The land is ful of other gode.
N'is ther fley, flee no louse
In cloth, in townė, bed no house;
Ther n'is dunner, slete no haile,
No non vilė worm no snaile,   40
No non storme, rain no winde.
Ther n'is man no womman blinde;
Ok al is gamė, joy and glee:
Wel is him that ther may be!
Ther beeth rivers grete and fine   45
Of oilė, milk, hony and wine;
Water serveth ther to no thing
But to sight and to washing;
Ther is many maner frute,
Al is solas and dedute.   50
    Ther is a wel fair abbėy
Of whitė monkės and of grey.

---

27 baret: fighting   nother: nor   28 ac: but   29 cloth: clothing   32 capel: hack   34 horwe: filth   la: indeed   35 neither breeding stable nor stud   38 towne: village   39 dunner: thunder   43 Ok: but   game: pleasure   44 Wel is him: he is fortunate   47 f. water is used for no purpose there except for appearance and for washing   50 solas . . .: pleasure and delight

Ther beeth cloisters, bowres and halles:
Al of pasteyes beeth the walles,
Of flesh, of fishe and richė mete,   55
The likfullest that man may ete;
Flouren cakes beeth the shingles alle
Of cherchė, cloister, bowr and halle;
The pinnės beeth fat pudinges,
Richė mete to princes and kinges.   60
Man may therof ete ynough,
Al with right and nought with wough.
Al is commùne to yung and old,
To stoute and sternė, meke and bold.

    Ther is a cloister fair and light,   65
Brod and long, of seemly sight.
The pilers of that cloister alle
Beeth y-turnėd of cristàle,
With her bas and capitale
Of grenė jaspe and rede coràle   70
    In the praër is a tree
Swithė likful for to see:
The roote is gingever and galingale,
The siouns beeth al sedėwale;
Triė maces beeth the floure,   75
The rind canèl of swete odòure,
The frute gilofre of goodė smakke;
Of cucubės ther n'is no lakke;
Ther beeth roses of rede blee,
And lilie likful for to see.   80

55 riche mete: sumptuous food   56 likfullest: most delightful
57 Flouren: made of flour   59 pinnes: fastening pegs   60 to: for
61 Man: one   62 wough: wrong   64 sterne: brave   66 of
. . .: of handsome appearance   69 bas: base   71 praer: meadow
72 Swithe: very   73 gingever: ginger   74 siouns: shoots
sedewale: zedoary   76 canel: cinnamon   77 gilofre: clove
smakke: taste   78 cucubes: cubebs   79 blee: colour

They faloweth never day no night—
This oughtė be a swetė sight!
  Ther beeth four welles in the abbèy,
Of triacle and halėwey,
Of baum and ekė piement,   85
Ever ernend to right rent;
Of they stremės al the molde
Stonės preciouse and golde:
Ther is saphir and uniune,
Carbuncle and astiune,   90
Smaragde, lugre and prassiune,
Beril, onix, topasiune,
Ametist and crisolite,
Calcedun and epetite.

  Ther beeth briddės many and fale: 95
Throstil, thruishe and nightingale,
Chalandrė and wodėwale,
And other briddės without tale,
That stinteth never by her might
Mery to sing, day and night.   100
  Yete I do you mo to witte:
The gees y-rosted on the spitte
Fleeth to that abbey, God it wot,
And gredeth: 'Gees! al hot, al hot!'

---

81 faloweth: wither   83 welles: springs   84 triacle: healing mixture   halewey: healing lotion   85 baum: balm   piement: spiced wine   86 f. ?always running to good profit; all the beds of those streams (are)   89 uniune: large pearl   90 astiune: astrion, a star-like precious stone   91 emerald, ligure, and prasine   94 chalcedony and hepatite   95 fale: numerous   97 chalandre: kind of lark   wodewale: golden oriole   98 tale: number   99 which never cease with all their might   101 Yet I would have you know further   103 Fleeth: fly   104 gredeth: cry

Hi bringeth garlek gret plentee,　　　　105
The best y-dight that man may see.
The laverokès, that beeth couth,
Lighteth adown to mannès mouth,
Y-dight in stew ful swithè wel,
Powdred with gilofre and canèl.　　　　110

64　　　　　　　　*Bird on Briar*

B RID onè brerè, brid, brid onè brerè,
　　Kind is come of lovè, lovè to cravè.
Blithful brid on me, on me, thou rewè,
　　Or greith, lef, greith thou me my gravè.

Ich am so blithè, so bright, brid on brerè,　　　5
　　When I see that hendè, hende in hallè;
Hie is whit of limè, lovèly, trewè,
　　Hie is fair and flowr, and flowr of allè.

Mighte ich hire at willè, willè havè,
　　Stedèfast of lovè, lovèly, trewè,　　　　10
Of my sorwe hie may, hie may me savè
　　Joye and blisse were ere, were ere me newè.

---

63. 106 y-dight: prepared　　　107 The larks, which are known for their
excellence　　　109 cooked in a pot most excellently

64. 2 Kind: nature　　of: because of　　　3 Blithful: joyful　　rewe: have
pity　　　4 greith: prepare　　lef: dear　　　6 hende: gracious one
7 Hie: she　　lime: limb　　　9 If I could have her at my will　　　12
were . . .: would ever be renewed for me

fl. c. 1325

65 *Hymn to the Virgin*

MARYE, maidė milde and free,
   Chambre of the Trinité,
Onė whilė list to me,
   As ich thee greete with songe;
Though my fet unclenė be,   5
   My mes thou underfonge.

Thou art quene of Paradis,
Of hevene, of erthe, of al that is;
Thou berė thanė King of blis
   Withoutė sinne and sore.   10
Thou hast y-right that was amis,
   Y-wonne that was y-lore.

Thou art the culvere of Noé
That broughte the braunche of olive tree
In toknė that pais sholdė be   15
   Betwextė God and menne.
Swetė levedy, help thou me
   Whenne ich shal wendė henne.

Thou art the bushe of Sinaÿ,
Thou art the rightė Sarraÿ,   20

1 free: noble   4 ich: I   5 fet: vessel   6 receive my
offering   9 bere: bore   thane: the   10 sore: pain   11 y-
right: righted   that: what   12 y-lore: lost   13 culvere: dove
15 pais: peace   17 levedy: lady   18 shal: must   henne: hence
20 rightė Sarray: legitimate (wife) Sarah

Thou hast y-brought us out of cry,
  Of calenge, of the fende.
Thou art Cristès owne drurỳ,
  And of Davyes kende.

Thou art the slinge, thy Sone the ston,   25
That Davy slang Golye upon;
Thou art the yerd al of Aaròn
  Me dreye y-segh springinge.
Witnesse at hem everichon
  That wiste of thine childinge. . . .   30

Thou art Hester, that swetè thinge,
And Assever, the richè kinge,
Thee hath y-chose to his weddinge
  And quene he hath afonge;
For Mardocheüs, thy derlinge,   35
  Sire Haman was y-honge. . . .

By righte tokninge thou art the hel
Of whan spellede Danyèl;
Thou art Emaus, the riche castèl
  Ther resteth allè werye;   40
In thee restede Emanuel
  Of whan y-speketh Isaÿe.

In thee is God become a child,
In thee is wreche becomè mild;

21 f. out . . . calenge: beyond the call, the claim   23 **drury**: love
24 kende: race   26 which David slung at Goliath   27 **yerd**: rod
28 which, dry, was seen to bud   29 f. Take as witness every one of
them that knew of your child-bearing   31 Hester: Esther   32–4
and Ahasuerus, the mighty king, has chosen you in matrimony and taken
(you) as queen   35 Mordecai   36 y-honge: hanged   37 f.
By true symbolism you are the hill of which Daniel spoke   40 **Ther**:
where   42 whan: whom   44 wreche: vengeance

That unicorn that was so wild   45
　　Alaid is of a cheste:
Thou hast y-taméd and y-stild
　　With milke of thy breste.

In the Apocalyps Saint John
Y-segh ane wimman with sunne be-gon,   50
Thané moone al under hire ton,
　　Y-crownéd with twelve sterre:
Swilk a levedy n'as nevere non
　　With thané feend to werre.

As the sunne taketh hire pas   55
Withouté breche thorghout that glas,
Thy maidenhod unwemmed it was
　　For bere of thiné childe.
Now, sweté levedy of solàs,
　　To us sinfulle be thou milde!   60

Have, levedy, this litel song
That out of sinful herté sprong;
Ayens the feend thou make me strong,
　　And yif me thy wissinge.
And though ich habbe y-do thee wrong,   65
　　Thou graunte me amendinge!

46 is subdued by a virgin   50 saw a woman clothed with the sun
51 ton: toes   52 sterre: stars   53 f. such a lady there never was
to make war upon the fiend   55 f. Just as the sun passes without
interruption through glass   57 unwemmed: unspotted   58
bere: bearing   63 Ayens: against   64 and give me your
guidance   65 habbe y-do: have done

66

The Hawthorn

OF every kinnė tree, of every kinnė tree,
  The hawethorn bloweth swetest
Of every kinnė tree.
My lemman she shal be, my lemman she shal be,
  The fairest of her kinne,   5
My lemman she shal be.

67

The Irish Dancer

ICH am of Irlande,
  And of the holy lande
    Of Irlande.
Goode sire, pray ich thee,
Of saintė charité,   5
Come and daunce with me
  In Irlande.

68

The Maid of the Moor

MAIDEN in the mor lay,
  In the mor lay,
Sevenightė fulle,
Sevenightė fulle,
Maiden in the mor lay,   5
  In the mor lay,
Sevenightė fulle and a day.

66. 1 kinne: kind of   4 lemman: sweetheart   5 kinne: race
67. 1 Ich: I   5 in the name of holy charity
68. 1 lay: dwelt

Well was hirė mete;
   What was hirė mete?
The primėrole and the—   10
The primėrole and the—
Well was hirė mete;
   What was hirė mete?
The primėrole and the violete.

Well was hirė dring;   15
   What was hirė dring?
The cheldė water of the—
The cheldė water of the—
Well was hirė dring;
   What was hirė dring?   20
The cheldė water of the wellė-spring.

Well was hirė bowr;
   What was hirė bowr?
The redė rose and the—
The redė rose and the—   25
Well was hirė bowr;
   What was hirė bowr?
The redė rose and the lilie-flowr.

69   *His Sweetheart Slain*

WERE ther outher in this town
      Ale or wyn,
Ich it woldė buggė
  To lemman myn.

68. 8 mete: food   10 primerole: primrose   15 dring: drink
17 chelde: cold

69. 1 outher: either   3 f. I was glad to buy it for my sweetheart

Welle wo that was so hardy 5
  For to make my leef al blody!
Though he were the Kingės sone
  Of Normaundy,
Yet ich wolde awrekė be
  For lemman myn. 10
Welle wo was me tho,
  Wo was me tho;
The man that leseth that he loveth,
  Him is al so.
No lore I ne lerdė, 15
  Ne no more I n' can;
But Crist ich hire bitechė
  That was my lemmàn.

70   *A Drunkard*

. . . is drunken,
  Drunken, drunken,
Y-drunken is Tabart,
Y-drunken is Tabart
  At the wine. 5

Hay! Robyne, Malkin,
  Suster, Walter, Peter!
Ye drunke al depe,
And ich'ille eke.
Standeth alle stillė, 10
  Stillė, stillė, stillė,

69. 5 woe indeed to him who was so bold (as)   6 leef: dear   9 awreke: avenged   11 I was very wretched then   13 leseth that: loses what   14 so it is with him   15–18 I have not been educated, and I know no more; but to Christ I commend her who was my sweetheart

70. 9 and I will too

Standeth alle stillé,
  Stille as any ston.
Trippe a litel with thy foot,
  And let thy body gon!   1

LAURENCE MINOT

fl. c. 1330

71   *Halidon Hill (1333)*

SCOTTES out of Berwik and of Abirdene,
  At the Bannokburn were ye to kene;
There slogh ye many sakless, as it was sene,
And now has King Edward wroken it, I wene.
    It is wroken, I wene, well wurth the while!   5
    Ware yet with the Scottes, for they ar full of gile!

Where ar ye Scottes of Saint Johnes town?
The boste of youre baner is beten all down.
When ye bosting will bede, Sir Edward is bown
For to kindel you care and crak youre crown.   10
    He has crakked youre crowne, well wurth the while!
    Shame betide the Scottes, for they ar full of gile!

Scottes of Striflin were steren and stout,
Of God ne of gude men had they no dout.
Now have they, the pelers, priked about;   15

---

71. 2 kene: bold   3 slogh: slaughtered   sakless: innocent   4
wroken: avenged   5 well . . .: happy the occasion   6 Ware
yet with: always watch out for   7 Saint . . .: Perth   8 boste:
pride   9 bede: offer   bown: ready   10 kindel: cause   13
Striflin: Stirling   steren: fierce   14 dout: fear   15 Now these
pilferers have done their galloping around

But at the last Sir Edward rifild their rout.
  He has rifild their rout, well wurth the while!
  But ever are they under but gaudes and gile.

Rughfute riveling, now kindels thy care;
Berebag with thy boste, thy biging is bare.   **20**
  Fals wretche and forsworn, whider wilt thou fare?
  Busk thee unto Brig, and abide thare.
    Thare, wretche, shalt thou won, and wery the while;
    Thy dwelling in Dondé is done for thy gile.

The Scot gas in burghes and betes the stretes;   **25**
Al these Inglis men harmes he hetes;
Fast makes he his mone to men that he metes,
But fune frendes he findes that his bale betes.
    Fune betes his bale, well wurth the while!
    He uses al threting with gaudes and gile.   **30**

But many man thretes and spekes ful ill
That sum time were better to be stane-still.
The Scot in his wordes has wind for to spill,
For at the last Edward shall have al his will.
    He had his will at Berwik, well wurth the while!   **35**
    Scottes broght him the keyes—but get for their gile.

---

16 rifild: stripped   18 but underneath they are always but tricks
and deceit   19 Rough-footed clod-hopper, now your troubles start
20 Berebag: pack-carrier   biging: dwelling   22 Hurry off to
Bruges and stay there   23 won: live   wery . . .: curse the time
24 Dundee   done: over   25 gas: goes   burghes:
cities   betes: tramps   26 he promises injuries to all these
Englishmen   27 mone: complaint   28 but he finds few friends
that alleviate his misery   32 stane-still: silent as a stone   33 spill:
waste   36 get: watch

72   *The Newly Born*

T HEN has a man less might than a beste
      When he is born, and is sene leste:
For a best, when it is born, may ga
As-tite after, and rin to and fra;
But a man has na might ther-to,   5
When he is born, swa to do;
For then may he nought stande ne crepe,
But ligge and sprawel and cry and wepe.
For unnethes is a child born fully
That it ne biginnes to goule and cry;   10
And by that cry men may knaw than
Whether it be man or woman;
For when it is born it cryes swa:
If it be man, it says 'a, a',
That the first letter is of the nam   15
Of our formė-fader Adàm.
And if the child a woman be,
When it is born it says 'e, e'.
E is the first letter and the hede
Of the name of Eve that bigan our dede.   20
Therfor a clerk made on this manère
This vers of metre that is writen here:
Dicentes E vel A quotquot nascuntur ab Eva.
'Alle thas', he says, 'that comes of Eve,
That is, al men that here bihoves leve,   25

---

2 sene leste: seen at his smallest   3 f. may . . . rin: can walk
immediately afterwards, and run   5 ther-to: for that   6 swa: so
8 ligge: lie   9 unnethes: scarcely   10 before it begins to yowl
and cry   11 than: then   16 forme-fader: first father   19
hede: beginning   20 dede: death   24 thas: those   25 bihoves
leve: must live

When they ar born, what-swa they be,
They say outher "a, a" or "e, e".'
   Thus is here the biginning
Of our life sorow and greting
Til whilk our wrechednes stirres us;   30
And therfor Innocent says thus:
Omnes nascimur eiulantes, ut naturae nostrae
miseriam exprimamus.
He says: 'Al ar we born gretand
And makand a sorowful sembland,   35
For to shew the grete wrechednes
Of our kind that in us es.'
Thus when the time come of our birthe,
Al made sorow and na mirthe;
Naked we come hider and bare   40
And poore, swa shal we hethen fare.

WILLIAM HEREBERT

d. 1333

73   *My Folk, What Have I Done Thee?*

M Y folk, what habbe I do thee,
   Other in what thing teenèd thee?
Gin nouthe and answère thou me.

For from Egỳpte ich laddè thee
Thou me ledest to roodè-tree   5
   My folk, what habbe I do thee? *etc.*

72. 26 what-swa: whoever   27 outher: either   29 greting:
weeping   30 to which our misery moves us   34 f. gretand . . .:
weeping and looking miserable   37 kind: nature   es: is   38, 40
come: came   41 swa . . .: so must we depart hence

73. 1 habbe: have   2 Other: or   teened: vexed   3 Gin nouthe:
begin now   4 For: because   ich ladde: I led

Through wildernesse ich laddè thee,
And fourty yeer biheddè thee,
And angeles bred ich yaf to thee,
And into reste ich broughtè thee.   10
    My folk, what habbe I do thee? *etc.*

What morè shulde ich haven y-don
That thou ne havest nought underfon?
    My folk, what habbe I do thee? *etc.*

Ich thee fedde and shruddè thee,   15
And thou with eisil drinkst to me,
And with sperè stingest me.
    My folk, what habbe I do thee? *etc.*

Ich Egỳptè beet for thee,
And herè teem I slow for thee,   20
    My folk, what habbe I do thee? *etc.*

Ich delèdè the see for thee,
And dreintè Pharaön for thee,
And thou to princes sellest me.
    My folk, what habbe I do thee? *etc.*   25

In beem of cloude ich laddè thee,
And to Pilàt thou ledest me.
    My folk, what habbe I do thee? *etc.*

With angeles mete ich feddè thee,
And thou bufetest and scourgest me.   30
    My folk, what habbe I do thee? *etc.*

---

8 bihedde: looked after   9 yaf: gave   13 underfon: received
15 shrudde: clothed   16 with . . .: give me vinegar to drink   20
teem: offspring   slow: slew   22 delede: divided   23 dreinte:
drowned   26 beem: pillar

Of the stone ich drank to thee,
And thou with gallė drincst to me.
    My folk, what habbe I do thee? *etc.*

Kinges of Canaan ich for thee beet,   35
And thou betest myn heved with reed.
    My folk, what habbe I do thee? *etc.*

Ich yaf thee crowne of kinėdom,
And thou me yifst a crowne of thorn.
    My folk, what habbe I do thee? *etc.*   40

Ich muchel worship dide to thee,
And thou me hangest on roodė-tree.
    My folk, what habbe I do thee? *etc.*

74   *Who is This that Cometh from Edom?*

'WHAT is he, this lordling, that cometh from the fight
With blood-rede wedė so grisliche y-dight,
So faire y-cointisėd, so seemlich in sight,
So stiflichė gangeth, so doughty a knight?'

'Ich it am, ich it am, that ne speke butė right,   5
Champioun to helen mankinde in fight.'

'Why thenne is thy shroud red, with blood al y-meind,
Ase troddarės in wringė with must al bespreind?'

73. 32 From the rock I gave you drink   36 heved: head   38
kinedom: kingship   41 worship: honour

74. 2 grisliche . . .: terribly arrayed   3 y-cointised: apparelled
seemlich . . .: fair to see   4 So. .. gangeth: who goes so bravely
5 Ich it am: It is I   6 helen: save   7 shroud: clothing   y-
meind: mingled   8 like treaders in the wine-press all spattered with
must

'The wring ich habbe y-trodded al myself one,
And of al mankindè ne was none other wone.   10
Ich hem habbe y-trodded in wrathe and in grame,
And al my wede is bespreind with herè blood y-same,
And al my robe y-foulèd to here gretè shame.
The day of th'ilkè wrechè liveth in my thought;
The yeer of medès yelding ne foryet ich nought.   15
Ich lookèd al aboutè some helping mon;
Ich soughte al the routè, but help n'as ther non.
It was myn ownè strengthè that this bote wroughte,
Myn owè doughtinessè that help ther me broughte.
Ich habbe y-trodded the folk in wrathe and in grame,   20
Adreint al with shennesse, y-drawe down with shame.'

'On Godès milsfulnesse ich wil bethenchè me,
And herien Him in allè thing that He yeldeth me.'

75   *Christ's Coming*

I SAGH Him with flesh al bi-spred: He cam from Est.
I sagh Him with blood al bi-shed: He cam from West.
I sagh that manye He with Him broughte: He cam from
     South.
I sagh that the world of Him ne roughte: He came from
     North.

74. 9 habbe: have   one: alone   10 of: for   wone: hope   11
hem: them   grame: anger   12 here . . .: their blood together
13 y-fouled: defiled   here: their   14 wreche: vengeance   15
medes yelding: reward-giving   foryet: forget   16 some . . .: for
some man who would help   17 soughte: searched   route: crowd
18 bote: salvation   19 owe: own   21 Adreint: drowned   shennesse:
ignominy   22 milsfulnesse: mercifulness   bethenche: bethink
23 herien: praise   yeldeth: grants
75. 1 I . . . bi-spred: I saw Him with body all spread out   2 bi-shed:
drenched   4 roughte of: cared about

'I come from the wedlok as a swete spouse that habbe my
    wif with me y-nume.   5
I come from fight as staleworthe knight that mine fo habbe
    overcume.
I come from the cheping as a riche chapman that mankinde
    habbe y-bought.
I come from an uncouthe lande as a sely pilegrim that ferr
    habbe y-sought.'

76   *Steadfast Cross*

S TEDDEFAST cross, inmong alle other
    Thou art a tree mikel of prise;
In braunche and flowrė swilk another
    I ne wot non in wode no rise.
Swete be the nailes, and swete be the tree,   5
And sweter be the birden that hanges upon thee.

?RICHARD ROLLE

d. 1349

77   *Love Is Life*

L OVE is lif that lasteth ay, ther it in Crist is fest,
    When wele ne wo it chaungė may, as written hath
    men wisest;

75. 5 habbe y-nume: have taken   6 staleworthe: stalwart   7
cheping: market   chapman: merchant   8 uncouthe: unknown
sely: innocent   ferr . . .: have travelled far

76. 1 inmong: among   2 mikel . . .: of great price   3 swilk:
such   4 no rise: nor thicket

77. Love is life that lasts for ever, when it is fixed upon Christ, since neither
prosperity nor adversity can change it, as the wisest men have written; the

The night is turnèd into day, the travail into rest.
If thou wil love as I thee say, thou may be with the best.

Love is thought with gret desire of a fair loving;   5
Love is likened to a fire that quenchen may no thing;
Love us clenseth of our sin, love our bot shal bring;
Love the Kingès hert may win, love of joy may sing.

The sete of love is set ful hegh, for into heven it ran;
Me think that it in erth is slegh, that maketh man pale
    and wan;   10
The bed of blisse it goth ful negh—I tel thee as I can;
Though us think the way be dregh, love coupleth God
    and man.

Love is hotter that the cole; love may non beswike;
The flaume of love who might it thole if it were ever y-
    like?
Love us covereth and maketh in quert and lifteth to heven-
    rike;   15
Love ravisheth Crist into our hert—I wot no lust it like.

night is turned into day, labour into rest. If you are willing to love as I tell you, you can be with the best.

Love is thinking of a fair loved one with great desire; love is likened to a fire which nothing can quench; love cleanses us of our sin, love shall bring our salvation; love can win the King's heart, love can sing for joy.

The throne of love is set on high, for it has mounted up to heaven; it seems to me that on earth it is deceptive, in that it makes one pale and wan; (yet) it goes very near to the bed of bliss (*i.e.* the bridal bed of Christ and the soul)—I speak to you from knowledge; though to us the way seems weary, love unites God and man.

Love is hotter than the live coal; nobody can cheat love; who could endure the flame of love if it were always of the same intensity? Love heals us and restores to health and raises to the kingdom of Heaven; love forcibly carries Christ into our hearts—I know no pleasure like it.

LOVE IS LIFE

Ler to love, if thou wil live when thou shal hethen fare.
Al thy thought to Him thou yive that may it kepe fro
care.
Loke thy hert fro Him not twin, though thou in wand-
ring ware;
So thou may Him weld with win, and love Him ever-
mare.   20

Jesu, that me lif hath lent, into thy love me bring;
Tak to thee al myn entent, that thou be my dèsiring.
Wo fro me away wer went and comen my coveiting,
If that my soul had herd and hent the song of thy praising.

Thy love is ever-lastand fro that we may it fele;   25
Therin me make brenand that no thing may me kele.
My thought take in thy hand and stabil it every dele,
That I be not heldand to love this worldès wele.

If I love an erthly thing that payeth to my will,
And set my joy and my liking when it may cum me till,   30
I may me drede of dèperting, that wil be hote and ill;

Learn to love, if you wish to live when you must go hence. Devote all
your thought to Him who has power to keep it from care. See that your
heart does not part from Him, though you should be in distress; so can
you possess Him with joy, and love Him evermore.

Jesu, who has given me life, bring me to thy love; take to thyself all my
desire, so that thou become the object of my longing. Woe would be gone
from me and my desire would be realized, if my soul had heard and appre-
hended the song of thy praise.

Thy love is everlasting from the time that we are able to feel it; make
me burn in it so that nothing can cool me. Take my thought into thy
power and make it completely steadfast, so that I do not incline to love this
world's prosperity.

If I love an earthly thing that pleases my will, and if I account it my joy
and delight when it should come to me, I may fear separation, which will

179

For al my welth is but weping when pine my soul shal
   spill.

The joy that men hath sene is likened to the hay,
That now is fair and grene and now witing away.
Such is this world, I wene, and shal be to domès day   35
In travail and in tene, for flee no man it may.

If thou love in al thy thought, and hate the filth of sin,
And gif thy hert Him that it bought, that He it weld with
   win,
As thy soul Crist hath sought and therof wold not blin,
So thou shal to blisse be brought and heven won within. 40

The kind of love this es, ther it is trusty and trew:
To stand in stableness and chaungè for no new.
The lif that love might find, or ever in hert it knew—
Fro care turneth that kind, and led in mirth and glew.

For-thy love thou, I rede, Crist, as I thee telle.   45
With aungels take thy stede; that joy looke thou not selle.

be searing and painful; for all my wealth will be but weeping when
torment shall destroy my soul.

The joy that men have perceived is likened to hay, which is now fair
and green and now vanishes away. Such is this world, I believe, and
shall till Doomsday be in toil and tribulation, for no man can escape it.

If you love with all your thought, and hate the filth of sin, and give
your heart to Him who bought it, so that He may possess it with joy, as
Christ has sought your soul and would not cease from seeking it, so you
shall be brought to bliss, and dwell in heaven.

The characteristic of love, when it is faithful and true, is this: to remain
constant and not to change for any new love. The person who has been
able to find love, or who ever knew it in his heart—(him) that charac-
teristic (of love) turns from care, and leads to joy and happiness.

Therefore, I advise (you), love Christ, as I tell you. Take your place
among angels; see that you do not barter away that joy. Hate no adversity

In erthe thou hate no quede but that thy love might felle;
For love is stalwarth as dede, love is hard as helle.

Love is a light birthîne, love gladdeth yonge and olde;
Love is withouten pine, as lovers han me tolde;   50
Love is a gostly wine that maketh bigge and bolde;
Of love no thing shal tine that it in hert wil holde.

Love is the swetest thing that man in erth hath tone;
Love is Goddes derling, love bindeth blood and bone.
In love be our living—I wot no better wone;   55
For me and my loving love maketh both be one.

But fleshly love shal fare as doth the flowr in May,
And lasting be no mare than it wer but a day;
And soroweth sethen ful sare her proudehede and her
    play,
When they been casten in care til pine that lasteth ay.   60

When erth and air shal bren, then may they quake and
    drede,
And up shal rise al men to answer for her dede.

on earth except that which could cast down your love; for love is strong as
death, love is hard as hell.

Love is a light burden, love gladdens young and old; love is without
pain, as lovers have told me; love is a spiritual wine that makes (men)
strong and brave; through love nobody shall lose who is willing to hold
it in his heart.

Love is the sweetest thing that man on earth has received; love is most
dear to God, love binds blood and bone. Let our life be in love—I know no
better dwelling; for love unites both me and my beloved.

But fleshly love must pass as does the flower in May, and last no more
than but a day, as it were; and afterwards (fleshly lovers) shall regret most
bitterly their pride and their pleasure, when in sorrow they are cast into
torment that lasts for ever.

When earth and air shall burn, then may they quake and fear, and all

If they been seen in sin, as now her lif they lede,
They shal sit hell within, and derkness have to mede.

Rich men her hand shal wring and wicked werkės bye;   65
In flaume of fire knight and king with sorow and shame
   shal lye.
If thou wil love, then may thou sing to Crist in melodye;
The love of Him overcometh al thing, in love we live
   and dye.

78   *All Other Love is Like the Moon*

ALL other love is like the moone
    That wexth and waneth as flowr in plain,
As flowr that faireth and falweth soone,
    As day that clereth and endth in rain.

All other love biginth by blisse,   5
    In wop and wo makth his ending;
No love ther n'is that evre habbė lisse
    But what areste in Hevene-King,

Whos love is fresh and evre greene
    And evre full without wanying;   10

77. men must rise up to answer for their deeds. If they are detected in sin, as
they lead their life now, they shall sit inside hell, and have darkness as
reward.

    Great men shall wring their hands and pay for their wicked acts; in the
flame of fire knight and king shall lie with sorrow and shame. If you are
willing to love, then you may sing melodiously to Christ; love of Him
overcomes all things, in love we live and die.

78. 3 faireth: grows beautiful   falweth: fades   4 clereth: is bright
6 wop: weeping   7 f. there is no love that may always have joy
except that which is fixed upon the King of Heaven   10 wanying:
lessening

His love sweeteth withouté teene,
  His love is endless and a-ring.

All other love I flee for thee;
  Tell me, tell me where thou list.
'In Marìè mild and free   15
  I shall be found, ac more in Crist'.

79 *Hand by Hand We Shall us Take*

HAND by hand we shule us take,
  And joye and blissé shule we make;
For the devel of helle man hath forsake,
And Godés Son is maked our make.

A child is boren amongés man,   5
And in that child was no wam:
That child is God, that child is man,
And in that child oure lif bigan.
    Hand by hand then shule us take, *etc.*

Sinful man, be blithe and glad: 10
For your mariage thy peis is grad
  When Crist was boren.
Com to Crist, thy peis is grad;
For thee was His blood y-shad,
    That were forloren.   15
    Hand by hand then shule us take, *etc.*

78. 11 His love sweetens without giving pain   12 a-ring: infinite
14 list: liest   15 free: gracious   16 ac: but

79. 1 shule: must   3 for man has renounced the devil of hell
4 make: spouse   6 wam: blemish   11 peis: peace   grad:
prepared   14 y-shad: shed   15 who were damned

Sinful man, be blithe and bold,
For heven is both bought and sold,
  Evereche fote.
Com to Crist, thy peis is told,   20
For thee He yaf a hundrefold,
    His lif to bote.
        Hand by hand then shule us take, *etc.*

80   *Choristers Training*

UNCOMLY in cloistre I cowre ful of care;
   I looke as a lurdein and—listne til my lare—
The song of the ce-sol-fa dos me siken sare
And sitte stotiand on a song a moneth and mare.

I ga gouland aboute al so dos a gooke.   5
Many is the sorwful song I sing upon my booke;
I am holde so harde, unnethes dare I looke.
Al the mirthe of this mold for God I forsooke.

I goule on my grayel and rore as a rooke;
Litil wiste I therof when I therto tooke!   10
Some notes arn shorte and some a long nooke,
Some crooken away-ward as a flesh-hooke.

79. 19 Evereche: every   20 told: proclaimed   21 yaf: gave
22 to bote: as atonement

80. Unfitted for the cloister I skulk full of misery; I look like a dolt, and—
listen to my tale—the singing of high C makes me sigh bitterly and sit
stuttering over a song a month and more.

I go wailing about like a cuckoo. There's many a wretched song that I
sing in my book: I am kept so hard at it I scarcely dare look up. All the
joys of this world I gave up for God.

I wail over my gradual and caw like a rook; little I knew about it
when I began! Some notes are short and some a long angle-shape, some
bend away like a meat-hook.

When I can my lesson, to my maister wil I gone
That heres me my rendre he wenes I have wel done.
'What hast thou done, Daun Water, sin Saterday at
    none?   15
Thou holdest nought a note, by God, in right tone!

'Way me! leve Water, thou werkes al til shame,
Thou stumblest and stikes fast as thou were lame!
Thou tones nought the note ilke by his name;
Thou bitest asunder be-quarre, for be-mol I thee blame.

'Way thee! leve Water, thou werkes al to wonder!   21
As an old caudron biginnest to clonder!
Thou tuchest nought the notes, thou bites hem on sunder.
Hold up, for shame! thou letes al under.'

Then is Water so wo that wel ner wil he blede,   25
And wendes him til William and bit him wel to spede.
'God it wot', says William, 'therof hadde I nede!
Now wot I how *judicare* was set in the Crede!

When I know my lesson, I go to my master, who hears me (repeat) my lesson which he expects me to have done well. 'What have you been doing, Master Walter, since Saturday at noon? You don't hold a note, by God!, at the right pitch!

'Oh! (*lit.* woe is me) my dear Walter, your performance is a disgrace, you stumble and stick fast as if you were a cripple! You don't sing each note distinctly; You bite apart (*i.e.* distort the pitch of) B natural, I criticize you for B flat.

'Woe to you, my dear Walter, you do your work abominably! Like an old cauldron you begin to rumble! You don't hit the notes, you distort their pitch. Hold up, for shame! you go all flat.'

Then Walter is so wretched that he very nearly bleeds (*i.e.* ? is heartbroken), and he goes along to William and wishes him luck. 'God knows', says William, 'I needed it! Now I know what punishment is! (*cf.* no. 215, l. 20).

'Me is wo so is the bee that belles in the walmes:
I donke upon David til my tonge talmes.   30
I ne rendrede nought sithen men beren palmes.
Is it al so mikel sorwe in song so is in salmes?'

'Ya, by God! thou reddes! and so it is wel werre.
I sol-fe, and sing after, and is me nevere the nerre;
I horle at the notes and heve hem al of herre!   35
Alle that me heres wenes that I erre.

'Of be-mol and of be-quarre, of both I was wel bare
When I went out of this world and—liste til my lare—
Of ef-fa-uts and e-la-mi ne coud I never are;
I faile faste in the fa, it files al my fare.   40

'Yet ther been other notes, sol and ut and la,
And that froward file that men clepes fa:
Often he dos me liken ille and werkes me ful wa;
Might I him never hitten in tone for to ta.

'I'm as wretched as the bee buzzing in the water: I pound away at the
psalms till my tongue tires. I've not been able to repeat my lesson since
Palm Sunday. Is there as much misery in song (*i.e.* vocal music in general)
as there is in the psalms?'

'Yes, by God! you've said it! and indeed it's much worse. I practise the
scale, and sing afterwards, and I'm never any the nearer: I rush at the notes
and heave them right off their hinges! Everyone who hears me thinks I'm
blundering.

'Of B flat and B natural, of both I was quite ignorant when I gave up
secular life, and—listen to my tale—of F and E I never knew anything
before; I go wrong in the "fa", it wrecks everything I do.

'And there are other notes too, "sol" and "ut" and "la", and that
troublesome wretch that they call "fa": often he makes me miserable and
causes me great distress; I could never hit him so as to get him in tune.

'Yet ther is a streinant with two longe tailes; 45
Therfore has oure maister ofte horled my kailes.
Ful litel thou kennes what sorwe me ailes:
It is but childes game that thou with David dailes!

'When ilke note til other lepes and makes hem asaut,
That we calles a moison in ge-sol-re-uts en haut. 50
Il hail were thou boren if thou make defaut;
Then says oure maister "que vos ren ne vaut".'

81 *Alexander and the Gymnosophists*

'FOR I have founde you folk faithful of speche
Me to lere of your lif withoute les tale,
Yernes now of my yift that you leve were,
And, what it be that ye bidde, your boones I graunte.'
Thenne saide they: 'Wordlich weiy, we wishe of thy
yifte 5
Ay-lastinge lif to lachen upon erthe;
That us derye no deth desire we nouthe,
For other worldliche won at wille we have.'
'Nay, certes,' saide the noble, 'that may not be graunted

---

80. 'And also there is a breve with two long tails; because of it our master
has often knocked down my skittles (*i.e.* bowled me out, blown me up).
Very little you know about the misery I suffer: what you're doing with
the psalms is mere child's play!

'When every note leaps at the other and they clash together, that we
call a melody in high G. You would be unlucky to be born if you make a
mistake: then our master says that you're no good.'

81. 1 For: since   2–4 in telling me of your way of life without false-
hood, ask now as my gift for what you please, and, whatever you ask, I
shall grant your requests   5–9 Wordlich . . .: Honoured sir, we wish
as your gift to obtain everlasting life upon earth; that no death should
harm us (is what) we now desire, since of other earthly good we have all
we want

Of me that mighteless am myself so to kepe.   10
I am siker of myself to suffre min ende;
I ne have no lordshipe of lif to lengthe my dayes.'
'Seg,' saide they again, 'sin thou so knowest
That thee is demed the deth to dure nought longe,
Why farest thou so fightinge folk to destroye,   15
And for to winne the world wendest so roume?
How might thou kepe thee of scathe with skile and
      with trouthe
Ayeins right to bereve regnes of kinges?'
Thenne again saide the gome with a good chere:
'Through the grace of God I gete that I have.   20
They han demed me or deth, through dintes of mighte,
Of erthe to be emperour in everich a side.
Sin I have grace of that graunt grimmest to worthe,
I wroughte wrechely now, and wrathede Drighten,
If I for dul of any deth my destiné fledde   25
That is marked to me and to no mo kinges.
Men seeth wel that the see seseth and stinteth
But when the wind on the water the wawes arereth;
So wolde I reste me rathe and ride ferthe,
Nevere to gete more good no no gome derye,   30

10 by me who am powerless so to preserve myself   11 siker of
myself: certain for my part   12 lordshipe of: power over   lengthe:
lengthen   13–19 'Sir,' they replied, 'since you know that you are
destined to suffer death soon, why do you go fighting in this way to destroy
people, and journey so widely to conquer the world? How can you
escape blame in reason and truth for unjustly depriving realms of their
kings?' Then the man replied with good humour   20 that: what
21–51 They (the gods) have ordained that before death, through mighty
battles, I should be emperor of the whole earth. Since I am privileged by
that decree to be the most formidable man, I should now have acted despi-
cably, and have angered the Lord, if I for fear of any death fled from my
destiny which is ordained for me and for no kings besides. Men see well
that the sea is still and lies quiet except when the wind on the water raises
up the waves; so would I readily rest and ride away, never to win any

Bute as the heie hevene-goddes with hertely thoughtes
So awechen my wit and my wil chaungen
That I may stinte no stounde stille in o place,
That I ne am temted ful tid to turne me thennes.
And sin we witen her wil to worchen on erthe,   35
We mowe be soothliche y-said her servauntes hende.
If God sente every gome that goth upon molde
Worldliche wisdom and wittes y-liche,
Better mighte no burn be than an other;
Apere mighte the pore to parte with the riche.   40
Thenne ferde the worlde as a feeld that ful were of
    bestes,
When every lud liche wel livede upon erthe.
For that enchesoun God ches other chef kinges,
That sholde maistres be made over mene peple;
And me is marked to be most of alle othere: 45
For-thy I chase to cheve as chaunce is me demed.'

more possessions nor injure any man, were it not that the gods of the high
heaven with resolute purpose so rouse my mind and change my will that
I cannot for any length of time stay still in one place, without being impelled
immediately to go elsewhere. And since we know we must do their will
on earth, we can truly be said to be their trusty servants. If God sent to
every man that lives on earth equal worldly wisdom and intelligence, no
man could be better than another; the poor might seem to share with the
rich. Then the world would fare like a field full of beasts, if every man on
earth lived equally well. For that reason God has chosen other great kings,
who were to be made masters over common people; and I am destined to
be the greatest of all: therefore I strive to succeed as my lot is determined.

82   *The Five Joys*

HAIL be thou, Mary, maiden bright!
   Thou techė me the wayės right.
I am a sorful drery wight,
   As thou may see:
Quer I sal in the hardė pine of hellė be?   5

My sinful saulė sighės sare;
Lived I have in sin and care;
Leve I wil and do na mare.
   My levedy free,
Saul and body, lif and dede, beteche I thee.   10

Ther thou lay in thy bright bowr,
Levedy, quite as lily-flowr,
An angel com fra hevene-towr,
   Sant Gabriėl,
And said: 'Levedy ful of blis, ay worth thee wel!'   15

Stil thou stood, ne stint thou nought;
Thou said til him the bodword brought:
'Al His wil it sal be wrought
   In His ancele.'
Levedy, befor thy swetė Sonė mak us lele.   20

The tother joy I wat it was,
As sunnė shinės thoru the glas

3 sorful: sorrowful   5 must I be in the cruel pain of hell
6 sare: bitterly   8 leve: desist   mare: more   9 my gracious
lady   10 dede: death   beteche: commit to   11 Ther: where
12 quite: white   13 com: came   15 ay . . .: may you always
prosper   16 stint: paused   17 you said to him who brought the
message   18 sal: shall   19 ancele: handmaid   20 lele: faithful
21 The tother: the second   wat: know

Swa art thou, levedy, wemlas
  And ay sal be.
Levedy, for that swetė joy, thou rew on me.   25

The thriddė joy, I understand,
Three kingės com of thrinnė land
To fal thy swetė Son til hand,
  And gaf Him gift,
Mirrė, recles, and gold red, as it was right.   30

The King was rich, the gold was red,
The recles fel til His godhed,
Mir to man that sal be ded
  For ourė sake.
Levedy, to thy swetė Son at ane us make.   35

The ferth it is al thoru His grace
Quen He fra dede to lifė ras,
Quen He swa hardė swungen was
  On roodė-tree.
Levedy, of our sinnės al thou make us free.   40

The fift, thou was til heven brought—
The Juws thee sought and fand thee nought,
As thy swetė Son it wrought,
  Almighty King.
Levedy Mary, be our help at our ending.   45

23 Swa: so   wemlas: spotless   25 rew on: pity   27 of . . . :
from three lands   28 to pay homage to your sweet Son   30
recles: incense   gold red: red gold   31 rich: mighty   32 fel til:
was fitting for   33 myrrh (was fitting) for the man who must die
35 at ane: reconciled   36 ferth: fourth   37 Quen: when   ras:
rose   38 swungen: scourged   42 fand: found

THE FIVE JOYS

Levedy, for thy joyės five,
Thou kith thy might and help us swithe,
Levedy Mary, moder o live!
   With flowr and fruit,
Rose and lily thou sprede ay wide and help thy suit.   50

Levedy Mary, wel thou wast
The feendės fraistės me ful fast;
Wel I hope I sal thaim cast
   Thoru might of thee:
Quen I neven thy swetė name I ger thaim flee.   55

Thir joys ar said as I can say,
My site, my sorow I cast away.
Now help me, levedy—wel thou may—
   And be my spere;
Fra the hardė pain of hellė thou me were.   60

All that singės thee this song
And all that liggės in painės strong,
Thou lede thaim right ther thay ga wrong,
   And have mercỳ
On all that trows that God was born of thee, levedỳ.   65

---

47 kith: show   swithe: greatly   48 moder . . .: living mother
50 suit: followers   51 wast: know   52 fraistes: tempt   53
hope: trust   cast: overthrow   55 neven: name   ger: make
56 Thir: these   57 site: grief   60 were: defend   62 ligges: lie
63 ther: where   65 trows: believe

JOHN BARBOUR

c. 1320–95

83   *Bruce Meets Three Men with a Wether*

AND the gud King held forth the way,
Betwix him and his man, quhill thay
Passit out throu the forest war.
Sin in the more thay enterit thar,
That was bath hye and lang and brad;   5
And or thay half it passit had,
Thay saw on side three men cumand,
Lik to licht men and waverand;
Swerdis thay had and axis als,
And ane of tham apon his hals   10
A mekill boundin wether bar.
Thay met the King and halsit him thar,
And the King tham thair halsing yald,
And askit tham quhether thay wald.
Thay said Robert the Bruce thay soucht,   15
For meet with him if that thay moucht;
Thair dwelling with him wald thay ma.
The King said: 'If that ye will swa,
Haldis forth your way with me,

1 held . . .: continued on his way   2 he and his man together,
until they   3 war: were   4 Sin: then   more: moor   thar:
there   5 brad: broad   6 or: before   7 on side: to one side
cumand: coming   8 who looked like disreputable vagrants   9
als: also   10 f. and one of them upon his neck carried a large wether
trussed up   12 halsit: greeted   13 thair . . .: returned their
greeting   14 quhether . . .: where they were going   16 For:
to   moucht: might   17 they wanted to stay with him   18 will
swa: want to do so   19 Haldis forth: continue

And I sall ger you soon him see.'   20
Thay persavit by his speking
That he was the selven Robert King,
And chaungit contenance and late,
And held noucht in the first state;
For thay war fayis to the King,   25
And thoucht to cum into sculking,
And dwell with him quhill that thay saw
Thair point, and bring him then of daw.
Thay grantit till his spek for-thy.
But the King, that was witty,   30
Persavit well by thair having
That thay lufit him na thing,
And said: 'Fellòwis, ye mon all three,
Furthir aquent till that we be,
All by yourselvin forouth ga,   35
And on the samin wise we twa
Sall folow you behind well ner.'
Quod thay: 'Sir, it is na mistèr
To trow intill us any ill.'
'Nane do I', said he, 'but I will   40
That ye ga forouth thus, quhill we
Better with othir knawin be.'
'We grant', thay said, 'sin ye will swa';
And forth apon thair gate gan ga.

---

20 sall ger: shall cause   22 the . . .: King Robert himself   23
late: manner   24 and did not continue their first way of approach
25 fayis: foes   26 into sculking: *i.e.* hiding their purpose   27
quhill: until   28 f. their opportunity, and then kill him. They agreed
to his proposal therefore   30 witty: shrewd   31 having: manner
32 lufit . . .: loved him not at all   33 mon: must   34 aquent:
acquainted   35 forouth ga: go ahead   36 and in the same way
we two   38 f. Said they: 'Sir, there is no need to suspect any harm
in us'   40 Nane do I: I do not   42 othir: each other   43 f.
sin . . .: since you wish it; and they set out on their way

Thus yeed thay till the nicht was ner,   45
And then the formast cumin wer
Till a waist husbandes hous, and thar
Thay slew the wethir that thay bar,
And slew fire for to rost thair mete,
And askit the King if he wald ete,   50
And rest him till the mete war dicht.
The King, that hungry was, ik hicht,
Assentit till thair spek in hy;
But he said he wald anerly
At a fire, and thay all three   55
On na wise with tham tillgiddre be;
In the ende of the hous thay suld ma
An other fire: and thay did swa.
Thay drew tham in the hous end,
And half the wethir till him send;   60
And thay rostit in hy thair mete,
And fell richt freshly for till ete;
For the King well lang fastit had,
And had richt mekill travaill mad:
Tharfor he ete full egrely.   65

And quhen he had etin hastily,
He had to sleep sa mekill will
That he mot set na let thar-till;
For quhen the vanis fillit ar,

---

45 yeed: went   46 f. the . . . hous: those ahead came to a deserted
farmhouse   49 slew: struck   51 dicht: prepared   52 ik
hicht: I promise you   53 spek in hy: proposal promptly   54
wald anerly: wanted (to be) alone   55 a: one   56 were not to
be together with them at all   57 suld ma: were to make   59
they withdrew to the end of the house   60 send: sent   61 hy:
haste   62 and began to eat hungrily   64 and had made a very
long journey   67 f. he had such a great desire to sleep that he could
not resist it   69 vanis: veins

Men worthis hevy evermar,   70
And to slepe drawis hevynes.
The King, that all for-travaillit wes,
Saw that him worthit sleep needways.
Till his foster brother he says:
'May I traist in thee me to wak,   75
Till ik a litill sleeping tak?'
'Ya, sir', he said, 'till I may dree.'
The King then winkit a litill wee,
And sleepit not full encrely,
But gliffnit up oft sudanly;   80
For he had dreed of tha three men
That at the tother fire war then;
That thay his faïs war he wist:
Tharfor he sleepit as fowl on twist.

    The King sleepit but a litill than,   85
Quhen sic a sleep fell on his man
That he micht not hald up his ey
But fell in sleep and routit hey.
Now is the King in gret perìle:
For sleep he swa a litill quhile,   90
He sall be ded foroutin dreed;
For the three traitoures tuk gud heed
That he on sleep was, and his man.
    In full gret hy thay ras up than

---

70 f. people always become drowsy, and drowsiness induces sleep
72 for-travaillit: over-wearied   73 saw that he must inevitably sleep
74 Till: to   75 traist in: trust to   wak: guard   76 Till: while
77 till . . .: while I'm alive   78 winkit . . .: closed his eyes a short
time   79 encrely: deeply   80 gliffnit: glanced   81 tha: those
82 the tother: the other   83 he knew they were his foes   84 as
. . .: like a bird on the bough   85 than: then   86 sic: such
87 hald up: keep open   88 in . . .: asleep and snored loudly   90
sleep he swa: should he sleep like that   91 foroutin dreed: without
doubt   92 tuk . . .: observed well   94 hy: haste   ras: rose

And drew thair swerdis hastily   95
And went toward the King in hy
Quhen that thay saw he sleepit swa,
And sleepand thoucht thay wald him sla.
The King up blenkit hastily
And saw his man sleepand him by   100
And saw cumand the tother three.
Deliverly on fute gat he,
And drew his swerd out and tham met,
And as he yeed his fute he set
Apon his man well hevily.   105
He waknit and ras disily;
For the sleep maisterit him swa
That, or he gat up, an of tha
That com for to sla the King
Gaf him a strak in his rising,   110
Swa that he micht help him no mar.
The King sa straitly stad was thar
That he was never yet sa stad;
Ne war the arming that he had,
He had been ded foroutin wer.   115
But not-for-thy on sic manèr
He helpit him in that bargàin
That tha three traitoures he has slain,
Throu Goddès grace and his manhede.
His foster brother thar was dede.   120

98 sla: kill   99 up blenkit: looked up   102 he quickly got to his feet   106 disily: dizzily   107 maisterit: mastered   108 that, before he got up, one of those   110 gave him a blow as he was getting to his feet   111 so that he could fight no more   112 The King was so hard pressed there   114–17 had it not been for the armour he had, he would have been dead without doubt. But nevertheless in such a manner did he defend himself in that fight   118 tha: those   119 manhede: valour

84 *Christ's Love*

L OVE me broughte
And love me wroughte,
Man, to be thy fere.
Love me fedde
And love me ledde   5
And love me letted here.

Love me slow
And love me drow
And love me laide on bere.
Love is my pes;   10
For love I ches
Man to byen dere.

Ne dred thee nought;
I have thee sought
Bothen day and night.   15
To haven thee
Wel is me:
I have thee wonnen in fight.

85 *Lovely Tear of Lovely Eye*

L OVELY ter of lovely eye,
Why dost thou me so wo?
Sorful ter of sorful eye,
Thou brekst myn herte a-two.

84. 3 fere: companion   6 letted: stopped   7 slow: slew   8
drow: drew   10 pes: peace   11 ches: chose   17 Wel is me:
i.e. makes me happy

85. 2 why do you cause me such distress   3 Sorful: sorrowful

Thou sikest sore,   5
Thy sorwe is more
   Than mannès mouth may telle;
Thou singest of sorwe
Mankin to borwe
   Out of the pit of helle.   10

I proud and kene,
Thou meke and clene
   Withouten wo or wile;
Thou art ded for me,
And I live through thee—   15
   So blissed be that while! . . .

Thyn herte is rent,
Thy body is bent
   Upon the roodè-tree;
The weder is went,   20
The devel is shent,
   Crist, through the might of thee.

86 *King I Sit*

'KING I sitte, and looke aboute;
  To-morwen I may been withoute.'

'Wo is me, a king ich was;
This world, ich lovede but that, alas!
Nought longè gon I was ful riche;   5
Now is riche and poure y-liche.'

85. 5 sikest: sigh   9 to redeem mankind   **11 kene: bold**
13 wo: evil   20 the storm is past   21 shent: destroyed
86. 2 withoute: cast out   3 ich: I   5 gon: ago   **6 y-liche:**
alike

'Ich shal be king, that men shulle see,
When thou, wrechè, ded shalt be.'

87 *The Virgin's Song*

JESU, swetè sonè dere,
  On porful bed list thou here,
    And that me greveth sore;
For thy cradel is as a bere,
Oxe and assè beeth thy fere: 5
  Weepe ich may therfòre.

Jesu, swetè, be not wroth,
Though ich n'abbè clout ne cloth
  Thee on for to folde,
Thee on to foldè ne to wrappe,   10
For ich n'abbè clout ne lappe;
But lay thou thy feet to my pappe,
  And wite thee from the colde.

88 *The Life of this World*

THE lif of this world
  Is ruled with wind,
Weepinge, drede,
  And steryinge:
With wind we blowen,   5
  With wind we lassen;

86. 7 shulle: shall

87. 2 porful: wretchedly poor   list: liest   4 bere: byre   5 fere:
companions   6 ich: I   8 n'abbe: have not   9 on: in
11 lappe: fold of a garment   13 wite: keep

88. 2 wind: breathing   4 steryinge: commotion   5 blowen:
flourish   6 lassen: fade

With weepinge we comen,
   With weeping we passen;
With steryinge we beginnen,
   With steryinge we enden;   10
With drede we dwellen,
   With drede we wenden.

89   *Love*

I AM a fool, I can no good:
  Who that me loveth, I holde him wood.
I brenne hot, I smite sore:
Who that me loveth shal thee no more.
Dredful deth out of me sprong,   5
   For I am welle of wo;
I slow a wise king, fair and strong,
   And yet I shal slee mo.

90   *The Poacher*

IN the monethe of Maye when mirthes been fele
 And the seson of somere when softe been the wedres,
As I went to the wode my weirdes to dreghe,
Into the shawes myself a shotte me to gete
At an hert or an hinde, happen as it mighte;   5

88. 11 dwellen: live   12 wenden: depart

89. 1 can . . .: have no wisdom   2 wood: mad   3 brenne: burn
4 thee: thrive   5 sprong: sprang   6 welle: source   7 slow:
slew   8 slee mo: slay more

90. In the month of May when delights are many and the season summer
when the weather is mild, as I went to the forest to try my luck, alone into
the woods to get myself a shot at a stag or a hind, as chance might fall; and

And as Drighten the day drove from the heven,
As I abode on a bank by a brime side,
There the grise was grene, growen with flowres—
The primrose, the pervinke, and piliole the riche—
The dewe upon daiseys donkede full faire,   10
Burgons and blossoms and braunches full swete,
And the mery mistes full mildely gan falle;
The cukkowe, the cowshote, kene were they bothen,
And the throstils full throly threpen in the bankes;
And eche fowl in that frith fainere than other   15
That the derke was done and the day lightenede.
Hertes and hindes on hilles they gouen,
The fox and the fulmart they flede to the erthe;
The hare hurkles by hawes and harde thider drives
And ferkes faste to hir fourme and fetils hir to sit.   20
    As I stood in that stede on stalking I thoughte:
Bothe my body and my bowe I buskede with leves,
And turnede towardes a tree and tariede there a while;
And as I lokede to a launde a littil me beside
I segh an hert with an hed, an high for the nones;   25
All unburneshed was the beme, full borely the midle,
With eche feetur as thy fote, forfrayed in the greves,

as the Lord drove up the day from the heaven, and I halted on a bank by
the edge of a stream, where the grass was green, covered with flowers—the
primrose, the periwinkle, the noble penny-royal—the dew lay damp on
the daisies glistening brightly, buds and blossoms and boughs were lovely,
and the fair-weather mists came down softly; the cuckoo, the wood-
pigeon, they both (sang) clear, and the thrushes lustily vied in song on the
slopes; and in that wood each bird rejoiced more than the other that the
dark was done and the day dawned. Stags and hinds ?gaze at the hills,
the fox and the pole-cat fled to the earth; the hare crouches by hedges and
dashes quickly to them and runs fast to her form and settles down to sit.
    As I stood in that place I planned my stalking: I covered both my body
and my bow with leaves, and turned towards a tree and tarried there a
while; and as I was looking towards a clearing close beside me I saw a stag
with an exceptionally tall head; the main horn was all in velvet, very

With auntlers on eithere side egheliche longe.
The ryalls full richely raughten from the middes,
With surryals full semely upon sides twaine;   30
And he assommet and sett of six and of five,
And therto borely and brode and of body grete,
And a coloppe for a king, cache him who mighte.
But there sewed him a sowr that served him full yerne,
That woke and warned him when the wind failede,   35
That none so slegh in his slepe with sleghte sholde him dere,
And went the wayes him before when any wothe tide.

  My lyame then full lightly let I down falle,
And to the bole of a birche my berselett I cowchede.
I waited wisly the winde by wagging of the leves,   40
Stalkede full stilly no stikkes to breke,
And crepite to a crabtree and coverede me ther-under.
Then I bende up my bowe and bownede me to shote,
Tighte up my tilere and taisede at the hert.
But the sowr that him sewed set up the nese,   45
And waitede wittily aboute and windede full yerne.

massive at the middle, with each ?tine as long as your foot, well rubbed in
the thickets, with brow-antlers on either side amazingly long. The 'royals'
(*i.e.* second branches) spread magnificently from the middle, with fine
'surroyals' upon both sides; and he was fully developed and furnished with
six antlers on one horn and five on the other, and besides (he was) massive
and broad and huge in body, and a (fit) morsel for a king, if anyone could
catch him. But there went with him a sore (*i.e.* fourth-year stag) which
served him very zealously, which kept watch and warned him when the
wind dropped, so that nobody should be so crafty as to injure him in his
sleep by cunning, and which went ahead of him when any danger
threatened.

  My leash I quickly let drop then, and made my dog lie down by the
bole of a birch. I observed the wind carefully from the movement of the
leaves, stalked very quietly so as to break no sticks, and crept to a crab-tree
and took cover under it. Then I bent my (cross-)bow and prepared to shoot,
lifted my bow-stock and took aim at the stag. But the sore that accom-
panied him raised his nose, and looked about warily and sniffed the wind

Then I moste stande as I stood and stirre no foot ferrere,
For had I minted or movede or made any sines
All my laik hade been lost that I hade longe waitede;
But gnattes gretely me grevede and gnewen min eyne: 50
And he stotaide and stalked and starede full brode;
But at the laste he louted down and laughte till his mete,
And I hallede to the hokes and the hert smote.

91   *Pearl*

P ERLE, plesaunte to prynces paye
      To clanly clos in golde so clere,
Oute of oryent, I hardyly saye,
   Ne proved I never her precios pere:
So rounde, so reken in uche araye,   5
   So smal, so smothe her sydès were,
Quere-so-ever I juggèd gemmès gaye,
   I sette hyr sengely in synglère.
      Allas! I leste hyr in on erbère:
         Thurgh gresse to grounde hit fro me yot.   10
      I dewyne, fordolked of luf-daungère
         Of that pryvy perle wythouten spot.

90. carefully. Then I had to stand where I stood and stir no foot further, for
had I taken aim or moved or made any signs all my sport would have
been lost that I had long watched for; gnats, however, troubled me
greatly and stung my eyes: and he hesitated and moved cautiously and
stared with eyes wide open; but in the end he bent down and took to his
grazing, and I ? pulled back the catches and shot the stag.

91. Pearl, that a prince would delight to set chastely in purest gold, I say
truly that I never found her equal in worth from out of the Orient: so
round, so shapely in every way, so slender and smooth were her sides,
wherever I judged bright gems, I placed her apart in peerless beauty. Alas!
I lost her in a garden: she went from me through the grass to the earth. I
pine away, wounded by love's power, for that Pearl of mine without flaw.

Sythen in that spote hit fro me sprange,
   Ofte haf I wayted, wyschande that wele
That wont was whyle devoyde my wrange   15
   And heven my happe and al my hele:
That dos bot thrych my hertė thrange,
   My breste in bale bot bolne and bele.
Yet thoght me never so swete a sange
   As styllė stounde let to me stele.   20
    For sothe ther fleten to me fele,
     To thenke hir color so clad in clot.
   O moul! thou marres a myry juèle,
    My privy perle wythouten spot.

That spot of spyses mot nedės sprede,   25
   Ther such rychès to rot is runne.
Blomės blayke and blwe and rede
   Ther schynes ful schyr agayn the sunne.
Flor and fryte may not be fede
   Ther hit doun drof in moldės dunne;   30
For uch gresse mot grow of graynės dede—
   No whete were ellės to wonės wonne.
    Of goud uche goude is ay bygonne:
    So semly a sede moght fayly not

Since it slipped from me in that spot, I have often watched there, longing
for the treasure that once used to dispel my sorrows, and raise my happiness
and all my well-being: this does but oppress my heart sorely and makes
my breast swell and burn in grief. Yet it seemed to me no song was so
sweet as that which the quiet hour let steal to me. In truth many thoughts
came to me, thinking on her fairness so wrapped in clay. O earth! thou
spoilest a lovely jewel, my own Pearl without flaw.

    That spot where such treasure has mouldered away must needs be
overgrown with spices. Blossoms white and blue and red shine brightly
there in the sun. Flower and fruit cannot fail where it sank down into the
dark earth; for every plant must grow from dead seeds—else no wheat
would be carried home to the barns. Good is always sprung from good:

That spryngande spyces up ne sponne   35
   Of that precios perle wythouten spot.

To that spot that I in speche expoun
   I entred in that erber grene,
In Auguste in a hygh seysòun,
   Quen corne is corven wyth crokès kene.   40
On huyle ther perle hit trendeled doun
   Schadowed this wortes ful schyre and schene:
Gilofre, gyngure, and gromylyoun,
   And pyonys powdered ay bytwene.
Yif hit was semly on to sene,   45
   A fayr reflayr yet fro hit flot.
Ther wonys that worthyly, I wot and wene,
   My precious perle wythouten spot.

Bifore that spot my honde I spenned
   For care ful colde that to me caght;   50
A devely dele in my hertè denned,
   Thagh resoun sette myselven saght.
I playned my perle that ther was spenned
   With fyrcè skylles that fastè faght;
Thagh kynde of Kryst me comfort kenned,   55

with so fair a seed, springing spices could not fail to shoot from that precious Pearl without flaw.

   I entered into that green garden, to the spot I describe, in August on a high festival, when corn is cut with sharp sickles. The mound where my Pearl rolled down was shaded with these spice-plants, brilliant, and beautiful: gillyflower, ginger, and gromwell, with peonies dotted everywhere among them. If it was pleasant to look upon, pleasant too was the fragrance that rose from it. There dwells that priceless one, I know for sure, my precious Pearl without flaw.

   Before that spot I clenched my hands because of the cold sorrow that seized me. A desolate grief lay hid in my heart, though reason calmed me. I lamented my Pearl imprisoned there with turbulent thoughts that rebelled stubbornly. Though Christ's nature taught me comfort, my

My wreched wylle in wo ay wraght.
I felle upon that floury flaght;
    Suche odour to my hernès schot
I slode upon a slepyng-slaght
    On that precios perle wythouten spot.   60

Fro spot my spyryt ther sprang in space;
    My body on balke ther bod in sweven.
My goste is gon in Godès grace
    In àventure ther mervayles meven.
I ne wyste in this worlde quere that hit wace,   65
    Bot I knew me keste ther klyfès cleven.
Towarde a foreste I bere the face,
    Where rychè rokkes wer to dyscreven.
    The lyght of hem myght no mon leven,
        The glemande glory that of hem glent;   70
    For wern never webbes that wiyès weven
        Of half so dere adubbèment.

Dubbed wern alle tho downès sydes
    Wyth crystal klyffes so cler of kynde.
Holtewodes bryght aboute hem bydes   75
    Of bolles as blwe as ble of Ynde;

wretched will ever suffered in misery. I fell down on that flowery turf;
such scents rose to my brain that I dropped into a deep sleep above that
precious Pearl without flaw.

From that spot my spirit sprang up soon; my body remained there
asleep on the mound. My spirit was gone in God's grace on a venturous
journey to a place of wonders. I had no notion where it was, but I knew I
was set down where cliffs ?rose sheer. I set my face towards a forest where
rich rocks could be seen. No man could believe their radiance, the gleaming
glory that glinted from them; for tapestries that men weave were never of
half such rich splendour.

Adorned were all those hillsides with cliffs of crystal so clear by nature.
Sun-lit woods stand about them with trunks as blue as indigo. The leaves

As bornyst sylver the lef onslydes,
   That thike con trylle on uch a tynde:
Quen glem of glodes agayns hem glydes,
   Wyth schymeryng schene ful schrylle thay schynde.   80
The gravayl that on grounde con grynde
   Wern precious perles of oryent—
The sunnébemes bot blo and blynde
   In respecte of that adubbément.

The adubbement of tho downés dere   85
   Garten my goste al greffe foryete.
So frech flavòres of frytès were
   As fode hit con me fayre refete.
Fowles ther flowen in fryth in fere,
   Of flaumbande hwes, bothe smale and grete;   90
Bot sytole-stryng and gyternère
   Her reken myrthe moght not retrete;
   For quen those bryddes her wyngès bete,
      Thay songen wyth a swete asent:
   So gracios gle couthe no mon gete   95
      As here and se her adubbément.

So al was dubbet on dere asyse
   That fryth ther fortune forth me feres:

that quiver thick on every twig unfurl like burnished silver: when the light
from clear sky falls upon them they shine dazzlingly with a beautiful
shimmering. The gravel that crushed on the ground was of precious orient
pearls—the sunbeams were dark and dim in comparison with that splendour.
   The splendour of those glorious downs made my spirit forget all its grief.
The savours of fruits were so refreshing that they restored me as food does.
Birds of flaming colour, small and great, flew in flocks in the woods there;
but citole-string and cithern-player could not match their gay song; for
when these birds beat their wings they sang with sweet harmony: no man
could have such delightful entertainment as to hear and see their splendour.
   Thus was all that wood where fortune led me arrayed in rich manner:
no man that has tongue is equal to describing its rare beauty. I walked

The derthe therof for to devyse
　　N'is no wy worthé that tongé beres.　　　　　100
I welke ay forth in wely wyse
　　(No bonk so byg that did me deres);
The fyrre in the fryth, the feier con ryse
　　The playn, the plonttes, the spyse, the peres,
And rawes and randes and rych revères—　　　105
　　　As fyldor fyn her bonkés brent.
　　I wan to a water by schore that scheres—
　　　Lorde, dere was hit adubbément!

The dubbemente of tho derworth depe
　　Wern bonkés bene of beryl bryght.　　　　110
Swangeande swete the water con swepe,
　　Wyth a rownande rourde raykande aryght.
In the founce ther stonden stonés stepe,
　　As glente thurgh glas that glowed and glyght,
As stremande sternes, quen strothe-men slepe,　　115
　　Staren in welkyn in wynter nyght;
　　For uche a pobbel in pole ther pyght
　　　Was emerad, saffer, other gemmé gente,
　　That alle the loghé lemed of lyght,
　　　So dere was hit adubbément.　　　　　120

ever onward happily (there was no bank so steep as to hinder me); the
farther into the wood, the fairer appeared the level ground, the plants, the
spices, the pear-trees, and hedge-rows and stream-borders and noble
rivers—their banks gleamed like fine gold thread. I reached a stream that
curved along its shore—Lord, how rich was its splendour!

　The splendour of those rich depths was fair banks of bright beryl.
Swirling sweetly the water swept by, meandering on with a murmuring
noise. At the bottom gleam shining stones that glowed and glinted like
a sunbeam through glass, as shining stars, when men are asleep, glitter in
the sky on a winter's night; for every pebble lying there in the pool was
emerald, sapphire, or noble gem, so that the whole pool shone with light,
so rich was its splendour.

The dubbement dere of doun and dales,
    Of wod and water and wlonkė playnes,
Bylde in me blys, abated my bales,
    Fordidden my stresse, dystryed my paynes.
Doun after a strem that dryghly hales   125
    I bowed in blys, bredful my braynes.
The fyrre I folwed those floty vales,
    The more strengthe of joye myn hertė straynes.
    As fortune fares ther as ho fraynes,
        Whether solace ho sende other ellės sore,   130
    The wy to wham her wylle ho waynes
        Hyttes to have ay more and more.

More of wele was in that wyse
    Then I cowthe telle thagh I tom hade;
For urthely herte myght not suffyse   135
    To the tenthė dole of tho gladnes glade.
For-thy I thoght that Paradyse
    Was ther over gayn tho bonkės brade.
I hoped the water were a devyse
    Bytwenė myrthes by merės made.   140
    Biyonde the broke, by slente other slade,
        I hoped that motė merkėd wore.

    The rich splendour of down and dales, of wood and water and fertile plains, raised happiness in me, abated my sorrows, dispelled my grief, destroyed my pain. Down along a rushing stream I went in delight, thoughts crowding my brain. The farther I followed those watery valleys, the stronger the sense of joy that swelled my heart. Fortune does (?) as she chooses, whether she sends solace or pain; so the man to whom she gives her favour strives to gain ever more and more.

    More weal was there in that scene than I could tell, though I had leisure; for an earthly heart could not appreciate a tenth part of those joyful joys. And so I thought that Paradise was over beyond those broad banks. I supposed the water was a division between delightful places made ?by streams. Beyond the brook, by slope or valley, I supposed God's city

Bot the water was depe, I dorst not wade,
    And ever me longed ay more and more.

More and more, and yet wel mare,   145
    Me lyste to se the broke biyonde;
For if hit was fayr ther I con fare,
    Wel loveloker was the fyrrė londe.
Abowte me con I stote and stare;
    To fynde a forthe faste con I fonde;   150
Bot wothės mo iwysse ther ware
    The fyrre I stalkėd by the stronde.
And ever me thoght I schulde not wonde
    For wo ther weles so wynnė wore.
Thenne newė note me com on honde   155
    That meved my mynde ay more and more.

More mervayle con my dom adaunt:
    I segh biyonde that myry mere
A crystal clyffe ful rėlusaunt;
    Mony ryal ray con fro hit rere.   160
At the fote therof ther sete a faunt,
    A mayden of menske, ful debonere;

stood. But the water was deep, I dared not cross, and ever I longed, always
more and more.

  More and more and still much more I longed to see beyond the brook;
for if it was fair where I walked, much lovelier was the farther side. I stood
and gazed about me; I tried hard to find a ford; but truly the dangers (of
crossing) grew more the farther I walked along the bank. And still I
thought I should not draw back for fear of harm where delights were so
entrancing. Then a new sight appeared to me that stirred my mind ever
more and more.

  A greater wonder overpassed my reason: I saw beyond that beautiful
water a crystal cliff sparkling bright; many a brilliant light sprang from it.
At its foot sat a child, a gracious and gentle maiden; shining white was her

Blysnande whyt was hyr bléaunt.
  I knew hyr wel—I hade sen hyr ere.
  As glysnande golde that man con schere,   165
    So schon that schene anunder shore.
  On lengthe I lokèd to hyr there;
    The lenger, I knew hyr more and more.

The more I frayste hyr fayrè face
  (Her fygure fyn quen I had fonte)   170
Suche gladande glory con to me glace
  As lyttel byfore therto was wonte.
To calle hyr lyste con me enchace,
  Bot baysment gef myn hert a brunt:
I segh hyr in so strange a place.   175
  Such a burre myght make myn hertè blunt.
  Thenne veres ho up her fayrè frount,
    Hyr vysayge whyt as playn yvòre:
  That stonge myn hert ful stray atount,
    And ever the lenger, the more and more.   180

mantle. I knew her well—I had seen her before. Like glistening gold when it is cut, that maiden sat radiant at the foot of the bank. Long I gazed on her there, and the longer (I gazed), I knew her more and more.

The more I studied her fair face (when I had scanned her graceful form), such gladdening glory stole upon me as had rarely enough come to me before. Desire urged me to call her, but astonishment struck a blow at my heart: I saw her in surroundings so strange. Such a shock of surprise was enough to dumbfound me. Then she turned upwards her lovely face, her visage white as smooth ivory: it stunned my senses with amazement, and ever the longer, more and more.

92 *Jonah is Cast into the Sea*

ANON out of the north-est the noys bigynes,
    When bothe brethes con blowe upon blo watteres.
Rogh rakkes ther ros wyth rudnyng anunder;
The see soughed ful sore, gret selly to here.
The wyndes on the wonne water so wrastel togeder   5
That the wawes ful wode waltered so highe
And efte busched to the abyme, that breed fysches
Durst nowhere for rogh arest at the bothem.
When the breth and the brok and the bote metten,
Hit was a joyles gyn that Jonas was inne: 10
For hit reled on roun upon the roghe ythes;
The bur ber to hit baft that braste alle her gere.
Then hurled on a hepe the helme and the sterne;
Furst to-murte mony rop and the mast after;
The sayl sweyed on the see. Thenne suppe bihoved   15
The coge of the colde water, and thenne the cry ryses.
Yet corven thay the cordes and kest al ther-oute.
Mony ladde ther forth lep to lave and to kest;
Scopen out the scathel water that fayn scape wolde:
For be monnes lode never so luther, the lyf is ay swete.   20

  At once the din begins from the North-East, when both winds [Eurus and Aquilo] blew upon the leaden waters. Ragged clouds rose up there, with red beneath them; the sea roared mightily, a great marvel to hear. The winds so wrestle together on the dark water that the raging waves rolled so high and plunged again (so low) into the depths that the terrified fishes dared nowhere lie at the bottom because of the turmoil. When wind and water and ship met, it was a joyless craft that Jonah was in: for she reeled around upon the wild waves; the gale drove behind her so that all their gear broke. Then helm and rudder were flung in a heap; first many a rope broke, and afterwards the mast; the sail flopped on the sea. Then the ship had to sup the cold water, and then a great cry rises. Still they cut the ropes and cast all overboard. Many a man sprang forward to bale and to clear (the wreckage); intent on escaping, they scooped out the destroying water: for however hard a man's living may be, life is ever sweet.

Ther was busy over-borde bale to kest,
Her bagges and her fether-beddes and her bryght wedes,
Her kysttes and her coferes, her caraldes alle,
And al to lyghten that lome, yif lethe wolde schape.
Bot ever was i-lyche loud the lot of the wyndes,　　　25
And ever wrother the water and wodder the stremes.
Then tho wery for-wroght wyst no bote,
Bot uchon glewed on his god that gayned hym beste:
Summe to Vernagu ther vouched avowes solemne,
Summe to Diana devout and derf Nepturne,　　　30
To Mahoun and to Mergot, the Mone and the Sunne,
And uche lede as he loved and layde had his hert.
　　Thenne bispeke the spakest, dispayred wel nere:
'I leve here be sum losynger, sum lawles wrech
That has greved his god, and gos here amonge uus.　　　35
Lo! al synkes in his synne and for his sake marres.
I louue that we lay lotes on ledes uchone,
And whoso lympes the losse, lay hym ther-oute;
And quen the gulty is gon, what may gome trawe
Bot he that rules the rak may rwe on those other?'　　　40
This was sette in asent, and sembled thay were,

There was toiling to throw overboard bales of cargo, their bags and
their feather-beds and their gay clothes, their chests and their coffers and
all their casks, all to lighten the ship to see if an easing would follow. But
the roar of the winds was as loud as ever, and ever angrier the sea and
wilder the waves. Then those men, tired out with toil, knew of no
remedy, but each called on the god that pleased him best: some there made
solemn vows to Vernagu, some to sacred Diana and stern Neptune, to
Mahomet and Magog, to the Moon and the Sun, each man to the one he
loved, where he had given his heart.

Then the wisest spoke, near to despair: 'I believe there is here some
miscreant, some lawless wretch who has angered his god, and is here
among us. See! all sinks with his sin and perishes because of him. I recom-
mend that we set lots on every man, and whoever is the loser, throw him
overboard; and when the guilty one is gone, what should a man believe
but that he who rules the storm will have pity on the rest?' This was

Heryed out of uche hyrne to hent that falles;
A lodesmon lyghtly lep under hachches
For to layte mo ledes and hem to lote bryng.

   Bot hym fayled no freke, that he fynde myght,   45
Saf Jonas the Jewe, that jowked in derne:
He was flowen for ferde of the flode-lotes
Into the bothem of the bot, and on a brede lyggede,
Onhelde by the hurrock, for the heven-wrache,   49
Slypped upon a sloumbe-slepe, and slomberande he routes.
The freke hym frunt wyth his fot and bede hym ferk up:
'Ther Ragnel in his rakentes hym rere of his dremes!'
Bi the here haspede he hentes hym thenne,
And broght hym up by the brest and upon borde sette,
Arayned hym ful runyschly what raysoun he hade   55
In such slaghtes of sorwe to slepe so faste.

   Sone haf thay her sortes sette and serelych deled,
And ay the lote upon laste lymped on Jonas.
Thenne ascryed thay hym skete and asked ful loude:
'What the devel has thou don, doted wrech?   60
What seches thou on see, synful schrewe,

agreed, and they were assembled, dragged from every corner to take what should befall them; a pilot quickly jumped down under the hatches to search for more men and bring them to the lot-casting.

But no man was missing, that he could find, save Jonah the Jew, who lay asleep in a hiding-place: he had fled for fear of the roaring waters into the bottom of the boat, and lay on a plank, huddled up in the stern-part, because of heaven's vengeance, fallen into a deep sleep and snoring as he slumbered. The pilot kicked him with his foot and bade him rouse up: 'May Ragnel (the Devil) in his fetters wake him from his dreams!' Seizing him by the hair, he drags him thence, and brought him up (?)gripping him round the chest and set him on the deck, asked him angrily what excuse he had for sleeping so sound in such onsets of calamity.

They at once arranged their lots and distributed them severally, and always in the end the lot fell on Jonah. Then at once they cried out against him and loudly demanded: 'What the devil have you done, witless wretch? Why should you seek on the sea, sinful villain, to destroy us all by your

Wyth thy lastes so luther to lose uus uchone?
Has thou, gome, no governour ne god on to calle,
That thou thus slydes on slepe when thou slayn worthes?
Of what londe art thou lent? What laytes thou here?   65
Whyder in worlde that thou wylt, and what is thyn arnde?
Lo! thy dom is the dyght for thy dedes ille.
Do gyf glory to thy godde er thou glyde hens.'
    'I am an Ebru', quoth he, 'of Israyl borne.
That wiye I worchyp, i-wysse, that wroght alle thynges—   70
Alle the worlde wyth the welkyn, the wynde and the
          sternes,
And alle that wones ther wythinne, at a worde one.
Alle this meschef for me is made at thys tyme,
For I haf greved my God and gulty am founden.
For-thy beres me to the borde and bathes me ther-oute: 75
Er gete ye no happe, I hope forsothe.'
    He ossed hym, by unnynges that thay undernomen,
That he was flawen fro the face of frelych Dryghtyn.
Thenne such a ferde on hem fel and flayed hem wythinne
That thay ruyt hym to rowe, and letten the rynk one.   80
Hatheles hiyed in haste wyth ores ful longe,

wicked crimes? Have you, man, no guardian power or god to call on,
that you fall asleep like this when you are about to be drowned? From
what land are you come? What seek you here? Where in the world do
you want to go, and what is your errand? See! your doom is settled because
of your ill-deeds. Give glory to your god before you pass hence.'
    'I am a Hebrew,' said he, 'of Israel born. I worship that One, surely,
who created all things—all the world with the sky, the wind and the
stars, and, in a word, all that lives therein. All this trouble is made at this
time on my account, because I have angered my God and am found guilty.
So carry me to the side and plunge me overboard: before that you may
have no good fortune, I truly believe.'
    He showed them by signs which they understood that he had fled from
the face of the glorious Lord. Then such a fear fell upon them and terrified
their hearts that they (?) hastened to row, and let the man alone. Men made

Syn her sayl was hem aslypped, on sydes to rowe;
Hef and haled upon hyght to helpen hymselven.
Bot al was nedles note: that nolde not bityde.
In bluber of the blo flod bursten her ores;   85
Thenne hade thay noght in her honde that hem help
     myght.
Thenne nas no coumfort to kever ne counsel non other
Bot Jonas into his juis jugge bylyve.

Fyrst thay prayen to the Prynce that prophetes serven
That he gef hem the grace to greven hym never   90
That thay in baleles blod ther blenden her handes,
Thagh that hathel wer his that thay here quelled.
Tyd by top and bi to thay token hym synne,
Into that lodlych loghe thay luche hym sone.
He was no tytter out-tulde that tempest ne sessed;   95
The se saghtled ther-with as sone as ho moght.

Thenne thagh her takel were torne that totered on ythes,
Styffe stremes and streght hem strayned a whyle,
That drof hem dryghlych a-doun the depe to serve,
Tyl a swetter ful swythe hem sweyed to bonk.   100

haste with long oars to row at the ship's sides, since their sail had been
lost; they heaved and pulled mightily to help themselves. But all was
useless effort: it would not succeed. In the seething of the dark sea their
oars broke; then they had nothing at their disposal which could help them.
Then there was no relief to be had and no other counsel except to adjudge
Jonah to his doom forthwith.

First they pray the Prince whom prophets serve to give them grace
never to anger him because they dipped their hands in innocent blood,
though the man they slew there should be his servant. Quickly by head
and by toe they took him then, they pitched him forthwith into that
terrible sea. No sooner was he flung overboard than the tempest ceased;
the sea quietened at that as soon as it might.

Then, though their gear was torn and swaying on the waves, strong and
unvarying currents drove them for a time, which forced them relentlessly
to keep the deep sea, till a more favourable current swung them swiftly
towards the shore.

Ther was loving on lofte, when thay the londe wonnen,
To oure mercyable God, on Moyses wyse,
Wyth sacrafyse up-set and solempne vowes;
And graunted hym on to be God, and graythly non other.

93 *Gawain and the Lady of the Castle*

THUS laykes this lorde by lynde-wodes eves,
   And Gawayn the god mon in gay bed lyges,
Lurkes quyl the daylyght lemed on the wowes,
Under covertour ful clere, cortyned aboute.
And as in slomeryng he slode, sleyly he herde   5
A littel dyn at his dor, and dernly upon;
And he heves up his hed out of the clothes,
A corner of the cortyn he caght up a lyttel,
And waytes warly thiderwarde quat hit be myght.
Hit was the ladi, loflyest to beholde,   10
That drow the dor after hir ful dernly and stylle,
And bowed towarde the bed. And the burne schamed,
And layde hym doun lystyly, and let as he slepte.
And ho stepped stilly and stel to his bedde,

92. There praise was raised up, when they had gained the land, to our merciful God, in Moses's fashion, with sacrifice set up and solemn vows; and they proclaimed him alone to be God, and surely no other.

93. So this lord hunts at the fringe of the forest, and the good knight Gawain lies in his rich bed, till the daylight shone on the chamber-walls, lies quiet under the bright coverlet, curtained all about. And as he was falling into a doze, he heard a faint noise made stealthily at his door, and heard it open quietly; and he raises his head from the bed-clothes, lifts a corner of the curtain a little, and looks warily in that direction to see what it could be. It was the lady, loveliest to behold, who closed the door after her stealthily and silently, and moved towards the bed. And the knight felt embarrassed, and lay down again feigning, and pretended he was asleep. And she came forward quietly and stole towards his bed, lifted up

Kest up the cortyn and creped withinne,   15
And set hir ful softly on the bed-syde,
And lenged there selly longe to loke quen he wakened.
The lede lay lurked a ful longe quyle,
Compast in his concience to quat that cace myght
Meve other amount: to mervayle hym thoght.   20
Bot yet he sayde in hymself: 'More semly hit were
To aspye wyth my spelle in space quat ho wolde.'
Then he wakenede, and wroth, and to hir warde torned,
And unlouked his yye-lyddes, and let as hym wondered,
And sayned hym, as bi his sawe the saver to worthe,   25
  with hande.
 Wyth chynne and cheke ful swete,
 Bothe quit and red in blande,
 Ful lufly con ho lete
 Wyth lyppes smal laghande.   30

'God moroun, Sir Gawayn', sayde that gay lady,
'Ye ar a sleper unsliye that mon may slyde hider.
Now ar ye tan astyt! Bot true uus may schape
I schal bynde yow in your bedde, that be ye trayst.'
Al laghande the lady lanced tho bourdes.   35

the curtain and crept within it, and sat down gently on the side of his bed,
and remained there a very long time to watch when he wakened. The
knight lay still for a long while, and pondered in his mind what this
happening might lead to or mean: it seemed to him very strange. But yet
he said to himself: 'It would be more seemly to find out at once what she
wishes by asking her.' Then he roused, stretched himself, turned towards
her, and opened his eye-lids, and pretended that he was amazed, and
crossed himself with his hand, as if to be the safer for that prayer. With
sweet chin and cheek, both white and red mingled, she looked very lovely
with her delicate smiling lips.

'Good morning, Sir Gawain', said that gay lady, 'you are a careless
sleeper that anybody can slip in here. Now you are taken prisoner in a
trice! Unless there can be a truce between us I shall bind you in your bed,
of that you may be sure.' All smiling the lady spoke these jesting words.

'Goud moroun, gay', quoth Gawayn the blythe,
'Me schal worthe at your wille, and that me wel lykes;
For I yelde me yederly, and yeye after grace;
And that is the best, be my dome, for me byhoves nede.'
And thus he bourded ayayn with mony a blythe laghter. 40
'Bot wolde ye, lady lovely, then leve me grante,
And deprece your prysoun, and pray hym to ryse,
I wolde bowe of this bed, and busk me better,
I schulde kever the more comfort to karp yow wyth.'
'Nay for sothe, beau sir', sayd that swete,   45
'Ye schal not rise of your bedde; I rych yow better:
I schal happe yow here that other half als,
And sythen karp wyth my knyght that I kaght have;
For I wene wel, iwysse, Sir Wowen ye are,
That alle the worlde worchipes quere-so ye ride.   50
Your honour, your hendelayk is hendely praysed
With lordes, wyth ladyes, with alle that lyf bere.
And now ye ar here, iwysse, and we bot oure one;
My lorde and his ledes ar on lenthe faren;
Other burnes in her bedde, and my burdes als;   55
The dor drawen and dit with a derf haspe.
And sythen I have in this hous hym that al lykes,

'Good morning, gay lady', said light-hearted Gawain, 'I must be at your
will, and that pleases me well; for I surrender at once, and ask for grace;
and that, I think, is the best course; for needs I must.' So he jested in return
with many a glad laugh. 'But if, lovely lady, you would then grant me
leave, and release your prisoner, and bid him rise, I would get up from this
bed, and array myself better, and should have the greater pleasure in
talking with you.' 'No indeed, good sir', said the sweet lady, 'you shall
not rise from your bed; I prescribe a better way for you: here I shall bind you
fast on the other side too, and then talk with my captive knight; for indeed
I believe well that you are Sir Gawain, whom all the world honours
wherever you ride. Your honour, your courtesy, are highly praised by
lords, by ladies, by every living man. And now you are here, to be sure,
and we are by ourselves; my lord and his party are gone far away; the
other men are in their beds, and my women too; the door is closed and

I schal ware my whyle wel, quyl hit lastes,
    with tale.'
  'Ye ar welcum to my cors,   60
  Yowre awen won to wale;
  Me behoves of fyne force
  Your servaunt be, and schale.

'In god fayth', quoth Gawayn, 'gayn hit me thynkkes,
Thagh I be not now he that ye of speken.   65
To reche to such reverence as ye reherce here
I am wiye unworthy—I wot wel myselven.
Bi God, I were glad, and yow god thoght,
At sawe other at servyce that I sette myght
To the plesaunce of your prys: hit were a pure joye.'   70
'In god fayth, Sir Gawayn', quoth the gay lady,
'The prys and the prowes that pleses al other,
If I hit lakked other set at lyght, hit were littel daynté.
Bot hit ar ladyes innowe that lever wer nowthe
Haf the, hende, in hor holde (as I the habbe here)—   75
To daly with derely your daynté wordes,
Kever hem comfort and colen her cares—

fastened with a stout hasp. And since I have in this house the knight who
is admired by all, I must make good use of my time, while it lasts, in
conversation.' 'You are welcome to me, to do as you choose; I must needs
be your servant, and I shall be.

'In good faith', continued Gawain, 'it seems agreeable to me, though
indeed I am not the paragon you describe. To attain to such honour as
you tell of here, I am a man unworthy—I know it well myself. By God,
I should be glad, if it seemed good to you, to do, in word or deed, some-
thing that would please your worthiness: it would be a pure joy.'

'In good faith, Sir Gawain', said the gay lady, 'if I dispraised or thought
lightly of the honour and prowess that pleases everybody else, it would
do me little credit. But there are ladies enough who would rather at this
instant have you, noble knight, in their power (as I have you here)—to
enjoy fully your courteous words, to win solace for themselves and lighten

Then much of the garysoun other golde that thay haven.
Bot I louue that ilk Lorde that the lyfte haldes
I haf hit holly in my honde that al desyres,   80
    thurghe grace.'
  Scho made hym so gret chere,
  That was so fayr of face.
  The knyght with speches skere
  Answared to uche a cace.   85

'Madame', quoth the myry mon, 'Mary yow yelde!
For I haf founden, in god fayth, yowre fraunchis nobele,
And other ful much of other folk fongen hor dedes;
Bot the daynté that thay delen for my disert nysen:
Hit is the worchyp of yourself, that noght bot wel connes.'
'Bi Mary', quoth the menskful, 'me thynk hit an other.   91
For were I worth al the wone of wymmen alyve,
And al the wele of the worlde were in my honde,
And I schulde chepen and chose to cheve me a lorde,
For the costes that I haf knowen upon the, knyght, here,   95
Of bewté and debonerté and blythe semblaunt,
And that I haf er herkkened and halde hit here true—
Ther schulde no freke upon folde bifore yow be chosen.'

their cares—than much of the treasure or gold that they have. But I praise
that Lord who rules the heavens that I have wholly in my hands what all
desire, by grace.' So welcome she made him, she who was so fair of face.
The knight with blameless words answered each thing she said.

'Madam', replied the man gallantly, 'Mary reward you! For, in good
faith, I have found your generosity noble, and received a great many
other (?) courtesies from other people; but the honour they accord me (?)
is not because of my desert: it reflects the honour of yourself, who can
only do right.' 'By Mary', said the noble lady, 'it seems to me otherwise.
For if I were worth all the multitude of living women, and if all the
wealth of the world were in my hands, and if I could bargain and choose to
get myself a lord, because of the qualities that I have recognized in you
here, knight, of beauty, courtesy, and joyous bearing, and because of what
I have heard before and hold here confirmed—no man in the world

'Iwysse, worthy', quoth the wiye, 'ye haf waled wel better;
Bot I am proude of the prys that ye put on me, 100
And, soberly your servaunt, my soverayn I holde yow,
And yowre knyght I becom, and Kryst yow foryelde!'
Thus thay meled of muchquat til myd-morn paste;
And ay the lady let lyk as ho hym loved mych.
The freke ferde with defence and feted ful fayre. 105
'Thagh I were burde bryghtest', the burde in mynde hade,
'The lasse luf in his lode' (for lur that he soght
  boute hone,
The dunte that schulde hym deve;
And nedes hit most be done). 110
The lady thenn spek of leve,
He granted hir ful sone.

Thenne ho gef hym god day, and wyth a glent laghed,
And as ho stod, ho stonyed hym wyth ful stor wordes:
'Now He that spedes uche spech this disport yelde yow! 115
Bot that ye be Gawan, hit gos in mynde.'
'Querfore?', quoth the freke, and freschly he askes,
Ferde lest he hade fayled in fourme of his castes;

would be chosen before you.' 'In truth, good lady', said the knight,
'you have made a much better choice; but I am proud of the worth you
assign to me; and, devotedly your servant, I hold you as my sovereign,
and I become your knight, and Christ reward you!' Thus they talked of
many things till mid-morn passed; and all the while the lady acted as if
she loved him greatly. The knight responded guardedly and behaved
faultlessly. 'Though I were the fairest of women', thought the lady, 'the
less love-making would there be in his company' (that was because of the
destruction he was going to without delay, the return blow that was to
strike him down; and inevitably it had to be done). The lady then spoke of
taking leave, and he granted it at once.
 Then she bade him good day, and flashed him a smile, and as she stood,
she astonished him with words of reproach: 'Now, may He who blesses
every conversation repay you for this pleasure! But doubt stirs in my
mind that you can be Gawain.' 'Why?' asked the knight, and he spoke

Bot the burde hym blessed, and bi this skyl sayde:
'So god as Gawayn gaynly is halden,   120
And cortaysye is closed so clene in hymselven,
Couth not lyghtly haf lenged so long wyth a lady,
Bot he had craved a cosse, bi his courtaysye,
Bi sum towch of summe tryfle at sum tales ende.'
Then quoth Wowen: 'Iwysse, worthe as yow lykes: 125
I schal kysse at your comaundement, as a knyght falles,
And no fire, lest he displese yow—so plede hit no more.'
Ho comes nerre with that and caches hym in armes,
Loutes luflych adoun and the leude kysses.
Thay comly bykennen to Kryst ayther other.   130
Ho dos hir forth at the dore withouten dyn more;
And he ryches hym to ryse and rapes hym sone,
Clepes to his chamberlayn, choses his wede,
Bowes forth, quen he was boun, blythely to masse.
And thenne he meved to his mete that menskly hym
     keped;   135
And made myry al day, til the mone rysed,
    with game.
    Was never freke fayrer fonge
    Bitwene two so dyngne dame,

quickly, afraid lest he had been at fault in the manner of his words. But the lady blessed him and said as follows: 'So good a knight as Gawain is rightly held to be, and one in whom courtesy is so purely embodied, could not well have been so long with a lady, without craving a kiss of his courtesy, by some hint, on some slight opportunity, at some pause in the talk.' Then said Gawain: 'Certainly, let it be as you please: I must kiss at your command, as befits a knight, and not otherwise, lest he displease you—pray bring this charge no more.' At that she comes nearer and clasps him in her arms, bends down lovingly and kisses the knight. They graciously commend each other to Christ. She lets herself out of the door without more noise; and he prepares to get up, and hastens at once, calls to his chamberlain, chooses his clothes, and, when dressed, goes forth gladly to mass. And then he went to his food, which entertained him well; and made merry joyfully all day till the moon rose. Never was a man better received in

The alder and the yonge;   140
Much solace set thay same. . . .

*[In the evening the lady's husband, the lord of the castle, returns home
after a successful deer-hunt]*

Thenne comaunded the lorde in that sale to samen alle the
    meny,
Bothe the ladyes on loghe to lyght with her burdes
Bifore alle the folk on the flette. Frekes he beddes
Verayly his venysoun to fech hym byforne,   145
And al godly in gomen Gawayn he called,
Teches hym to the tayles of ful tayt bestes,
Schewes hym the schyre grece schorne upon rybbes.
'How payes yow this play? Haf I prys wonnen?
Have I thryvandely thonk thurgh my craft served?'   150
'Ye iwysse', quoth that other wiye, 'here is wayth fayrest
That I segh this seven yere in sesoun of wynter.'
'And al I gif yow, Gawayn', quoth the gome thenne,
'For by acorde of covenaunt ye crave hit as your awen.'
'This is soth', quoth the segge, 'I say yow that ilke: 155
That I haf worthyly wonnen this wones wythinne
Iwysse with as god wylle hit worthes to youres.'

the company of two such noble ladies, the older and the young; they made
very merry together. . . .
  Then the lord commanded all the household to assemble in the hall, and
both ladies to come down with their maidens in the presence of all the
company there. He bids his men bring in before him his carcases truly
counted, and courteously and merrily he called Gawain, draws his attention
to the tails of prime carcases, shows him the white fat cut through on their
ribs. 'How do you like this sport? Have I earned praise? Have I fully
deserved thanks by my skill?' 'Yes indeed', said the other knight, 'here is
the finest bag that I have seen this seven-year in the winter season.' 'And
I give you it all, Gawain,' then said his host, 'for by the terms of our agree-
ment you claim it as your own.' 'That is true', replied the knight; 'I say the
same to you: what I have honourably won in this house certainly becomes

He hasppes his fayre hals his armes wythinne,
And kysses hym as comlyly as he couthe avyse.
'Tas yow there my chevicaunce, I cheved no more;   160
I vowche hit saf fynly, thagh feler hit were.'
'Hit is god', quoth the godmon, 'grant-mercy therfore.
Hit may be such hit is the better, and ye me breve wolde
Where ye wan this ilk wele bi wytte of yorselven.'
'That was not forward', quoth he, 'frayst me no more;   165
For ye haf tan that yow tydes, trawe ye non other
          ye mowe.'
     Thay laghed and made hem blythe
     Wyth lotes that were to lowe;
     To soper thay yede as-swythe,   170
     Wyth dayntés newe innowe.

94   *Ipomadon Plays the Fool at Court*

H E made his master to cutte his hore,
     Hye behinde and lowe before,
   Wonder ille-faringly;
A blak, sooty sheeld he gat—
Seven yere before (I wot well that)   5
   It had hange up to dry;

93. yours with as good will'. He clasps his host's fair neck in his arms and kisses him as prettily as he could contrive. 'Take there my winning—I won no more: I would grant it without reserve though it were a greater thing.' 'It is good', said the master of the house, 'my best thanks for it. It may turn out to be the better winning, if you would tell me where you gained this prize by your own skill.' 'That was not our compact', he replied, 'ask me no more; since you have taken what is due to you, be assured that you are entitled to take no more.' They laughed and made merry with words worthy of praise; they went at once to their supper of many rare dainties.

94. 1 master: tutor (*see textual note*)   hore: hair   3 very grotes-
quely   4 gat: got

An old rusty swerd he hadde,
His sperė was a plough gadde,
  A full unbright briny;
Upon that o legge a broken boote,   10
A rent hose on the other foote,
  Two tatres hanging by.

His helme was not worth a bene,
His hors might unnethe go for lene—
  It was an olde croked mere;   15
An uncomely sadel behinde siker;
His bridel was a wrethė wiker—
  Of othere rekkes he ne're.
'Master, ye muste to the cité fare
And privily take your innė thare,   20
  That no man wit what ye ere.'
Thalamewe did his comaundement;
Ipomadon to the court is went,
  Ill-farand was his gere.

The king was newly set to mete,   25
The quene and other ladies grete
  And knightės many one;
Ipomadon among them all
Come riding in to the hall
  His croked mere upon;   30
So short his steropes lethers wore,
His knees stood half a foot and more
  Aboven his horses mane;

8 gadde: goad (for oxen)   9 briny: corslet   10 that o: the one   14 his horse could scarcely walk for leanness   15 croked mere: decrepit mare   16 siker: assuredly   17 wrethe wiker: twisted withy   18 he does not care to have anything else   20 inne: lodging   21 ere: are   24 his appearance was grotesque   25 king: *i.e.* Mellengere   29 Come: came   31 wore: were

Crokand with his back he rade.
Of his atire wonder they hade, 35
  Knightès big of bane.

His hors was wonder hard of lere;
With spores and wand he stroke the mere,
  He betès on her bones;
And ever the faster that he dang, 40
The more softly wold she gang,
  She wold not stere on the stones.
Their knives out of their handes gan fall,
With so good will loughe they all
  That were within that wones; 45
To laughing made he no sembland;
There was none a cuppe might hold in hand,
  So loughe they all at ones.

About him he began to stare
In every hirne here and thare, 50
  Half wood as he were;
Knightes at his atire lough,
And some of them was ferd ynough,
  Ladies chaunged their chere.
Though it were long, yet at the last 55
A word of folie out he cast:
  'God looke thee, Mellengere!

34 **he** rode with his back doubled up   35 atire: get-up   36
bane: bone   **37** lere: flank   38 with spurs and stick he struck
the mare   40 dang: hit   42 the slower she would go   42
stere: move   43 gan fall: fell   44 so heartily they all laughed
45 wones: place   46 he showed no sign of laughing   48 at ones:
together   50 hirne: corner   thare: there   51 as if he were half
mad   53 ferd: frightened   54 chaunged . . .: i.e. turned pale
56 folie: nonsense   57 looke: watch over

I am the best knight under sheeld,
There no man cometh in the feeld—
　　That bought thou ones full dere!'　　　　　　60

'When was that?' quod the king.
'Wot thou not?' 'Nay, no thing!'
　　'Sir, no more wot I!'
Then all men up a laughter caste,
That nere their hertes asunder braste　　　　　65
　　Both on bench and by.
Ipomadon said after that
To the quene there she sat:
　　'God looke you, faire lady!
Madame, that have ye seen　　　　　　　　　70
That ye wold full blithe have been
　　To kiss us curtesly!'

The quene wax rede for shame;
The king said: 'Is it thus, madame?'
　　'Sir, I saw him never are!'　　　　　　　75
'Foole,' quod Cananeüs thenne,
'I pray thee, where was that and whenne?'
　　'A, sir, are ye thare?
I can not tell, verily, what day,
But on the land, I hope, ye lay,　　　　　　80
　　And lost your hors, every hare!'
'When was that? I wot no why!'
'No, in faith, no more wot I!'
　　Then lough both less and more.

59 There: as long as　　　60 you paid very dear for it once　　61
quod: said　　62 no thing: not at all　　65 nere: **nearly**　　braste:
burst　　66 both on and beside the benches (*i.e.* everywhere in the hall)
68 there: where　　70 that . . .: you have known (the time)　　73
wax: grew　　75 are: before　　78 are . . .: ? do you remember
80 land: ground　　hope: am sure　　81 every hare: *i.e.* completely
82 why: occasion　　84 both . . .: *i.e.* everybody

'Sir king, if it be thy wille,   85
I pray thee, make these folk be stille
   That jangles thus like a jay.
So worthy as I am one
Under heven, I trow, is none
   Where freke men flees away.   90
I hate peace and love the werre:
Thou may see by my glittrand gere
   And by my rich aray!
So good as I may no man be;
And if thou wilt withholdė me   95
   Herke what I shall say!

'If I dwell, withouten faile,
Thou must graunte me the firste battaile
   That is asked of thee;
And if me likės I will fight,   100
And if me likes not, by this light,
   Turne my bak and flee!'
The king to laughė might not fine:
'I shall thee graunt the first derine,
   And thou wilt bide and be.'   105
Ipomadon said: 'Sir, it is but lawe.'
Then all men lough and said their sawe:
   'A noble foole is he!'

---

86 stille: quiet   88–90 So worthy a man as I am does not exist
under heaven, I believe, wherever brave men flee   91 werre: war
92 glittrand gere: glittering armour   95 withholde me: retain me in
your service   97 dwell: stay   98 battaile: battle   100 me
likes: it pleases me   101 by . . .: *i.e.* certainly   103 fine: cease
104 derine: combat   105 if you are willing to stay   106 it . . .:
it is only right   107 said . . .: declared

He fared as he were wrothe ynough
That they him to scorné lough,   110
   And he said in that hall:
'I pray God gif you all mischaunce,
When ye maketh any destaunce
   Or foole shuld me call,
But the king, withouten doute;   115
In faith I take no mo withoute,
   Not one among you all,
But if it be my lady the quene,
For the grete love that between us hath bene.'
   Then lough bothe grete and small.   120

'Sir,' quod Cananeüs than,
'I redé you withhold this man;
   I shall say you for-why:
So noble a foole as this is
Among men doth good, y-wis,   125
   When hertes been ofte hevy.
At their wordes is mikel merthe,
Many time they slake the wrethe:
   Withhold him for-thy.'
Ipomadon sore angerd was,   130
But never the less he let it pass,
   That none perseved there-by.

'Cananeüs, at my scoole
In faith ye held me for no foole,
   When ye lay on the lande!'   135

109 fared as: behaved as if   113 destaunce: trouble   115
But: except   116 take . . .: exempt no one else   118 But if:
unless   121 than: then   122 rede: advise   123 for-why:
why   125 y-wis: indeed   128 slake . . .: appease wrath
129 for-thy: therefore   132 there-by: by his manner   133 at . . .:
? *i.e.* when I dealt with you

'When was that, I you pray?'
'I can not verily tell the day,
    Whether it were pul or pande.
That time the quene loved me wele
And I again her never a dele   140
    In fay, if she me fande!'
They lough all, bothe less and more;
They said: 'To wit, when that it wore
    Is right a good demande.'

Sir Segamus said: 'When was that?'   145
'A, sir, when ye had a squat,
    I am avisèd now;
What day it was, I am not graith.'
Segamus said: 'Sir, no, in faith,
    No more am I, I trow!'   150
'Sir king, where is Cabanus?
Certes, I were not taried thus
    Had he been here with you:
And he wiste what I wore,
I trow it wold mirth him more   155
    Than othere oxe or cow.

'For onès I made him adred,
That fro my handès faste he fled,
    But I wot never what day.'
There all men lough on hee   160
And saiden: 'In faith, no more wot we,
    Savely dare we say!'

138 pul . . .: *unexplained*   140 f. and I (loved) her in return not
in the least, indeed, had she tested me   143 f. To . . .: to be sure,
when that was is a fair question   146 squat: fall   147 I recollect
it now   148 graith: able to say   152 indeed, I would not have
been kept waiting so   154 had he known who I was   155
mirth: delight   156 othere: either   157 ones: once   160 on
hee: aloud   162 we dare safely say

'Good sir, when?' quod Manastus.
'Sin me nedès tell you bus,
　　On the lande when ye lay　　　　　　　165
And I myself down you bare.'
Then loughe bothe less and mare;
　　They said: 'That is no nay!'

Cabanus, the soothe to say,
Was on hunting all that day　　　　　　　170
　　And wiste nothing of this.
'Have done, sir king, I pray thee,
If thou wilt withholdè me—
　　Elles I dwell not, y-wis.
Wiste thou what maistries I couthe make,　　175
My service wold thou not forsake,
　　As have I joye and blis!
Lordes, knightes, prayth for me now:
What de'ell! is ther no helpe at you?
　　Why sayes none of you yis?'　　　　　180

Loude he crièd on the quene:
'In faith, madame, that day hath bene
　　Ye wold for me have prayed;
And so I trow ye wold do yit,
But all afar fro thee am I flit—　　　　　185
　　That maketh you all afraid.'
At him they all had joye ynough,
The quene at his wordès lough,
　　And to the king she said:

164 since I must needs tell you　　　167 mare: greater　　　168
That . . .: there's no denying that　　　　170 on hunting: hunting
174 otherwise I am not staying, indeed　　　175 if you knew what feats
I could perform　　　176 forsake: refuse　　　178 prayth: plead
179 de'ell: the devil　　at: from　　　180 yis: yes　　　184 yit: yet
185 but I have been wholly apart from you　　　186 all: much

'Sin I have lovèd him, I moste   190
Prayè for him nedès coste,
  If ye wold hold you paid.'

All men prayes for him so fast,
The king him graunted at the last;
  Then at the first he light: 195
'My hors myself kepe I will',
He said, 'Come hider to me, Gill!'
  Then lough they all aright.
He shoved the waiker with his arme;
Every man said: 'It were grete harme,   200
  And we had forgone this sight!'
Amides the flore he made his sete;
With trenchours and with broken mete
  They sayd that noble knight.

95   *Jesu Christ, my Leman Swete*

JESU Crist, myn leman swete,
    That for me diedes on roodè-tree,
  With al myn herte I thee biseke
For thy woundès two and three,
That al so faste into myn herte   5
  Thy lovè rooted motè be
As was the spere into thy side,
  When thou suffredes ded for me.

94. 190 Sin: since   moste: must   191 nedès coste: necessarily
192 if it were your pleasure   195 then for the first time he dis-
mounted   196 kepe: look after   199 waiker: withy bridle
200 harme: shame   201 And: if   204 sayd: ?pelted

95. 3 biseke: beseech   5 al so: just as   into: in   6 motè: may
8 ded: death

96   *Mercy*

MERCY is hendest where sinne is mest,
   Mercy is lattere there sinne is lest;
Mercy abideth and loketh al day
When man fro sinne wille turnen away;
Mercy saveth that lawe wolde spille: 5
Mercy asketh but Godès wille.

97   *Divine Love*

CRIST made to man a fair presènt,
   His bloody body with love y-brent;
That blisful body His lif hath lent
For love of man whom sinne hath blent.
O love, love, what hast thou ment?   5
Me thinketh that love to wrathe is went.
Thy loveliche handes love hath to-rent,
And thy lithe armes wel streite y-tent;
Thy brest is bare, thy body is bent,
For wrong hath wonne and right is shent.   10

Thy mildè bones love hath to-drawe,
Thy nailes, thy feet been al to-gnawe.
The Lord of love love hath now slawe—
When love is strong, love hath no lawe.

96. 1 hendest: readiest   mest: greatest   2 lattere: slower   there: where   3 loketh . . .: watches always (for the time)   5 that: him whom   spille: destroy   6 mercy requires God's will alone

97. 2 y-brent: afire   3 lent: given   4 blent: blinded   6 went: turned   7 loveliche: lovely   to-rent: torn to pieces   8 lithe: gentle   streite y-tent: cruelly stretched   10 shent: destroyed   11 to-drawe: drawn apart   12 to-gnawe: mutilated   13 Love has now slain the Lord of love

His herte is rent, His body is bent,   15
   Upon the roodè-tree;
Wrong is went, the devel is shent,
   Crist, thorugh the might of thee.

For thee that herte is laid to wedde.
Swich was the love that herte us kedde,   20
That hertè brast, that hertè bledde,
That hertè-blood oure soulès fedde.

That herte He yef for treuthe of love;
Therfore in Him one is trewe love.
For love of thee that herte is yove;   25
Keep thou that herte, and thou art above.

Love, love, wher shalt thou wone?
Thy woning-stede is thee binome.
For Cristès herte, that was thyn home;
He is ded, now hast thou none.   30

Love, love, why dost thou so?
Love, thou brekest myn herte a-two.

Love hath shewed his gretè might,
For love hath made of day the night.
Love hath slawe the King of right,   35
And love hath ended the strongè fight.

So muchel love was nevere non;
That witeth ful wel Marìe and Jhon,

17 went: overthrown   19 laid . . .: pledged   20 Swich: such
kedde: showed   21 brast: burst   23 yef: gave   24 one:
alone   25 yove: given   26 above: victorious   27 wone:
dwell   28 your dwelling-place is taken from you

And also witeth they everichon
That love with Him hath made at on.   40

Love maketh, Crist, thyn hertè myn;
So maketh love myn hertè thyn.
Thenne shal my love be trewe and fyn,
And love in love shal makè fyn.

98   *Separated Lovers*

MY lefe is faren in londe;
  Allas! why is she so?
And I am so sore in bonde
I may not come her to.
She hath my hert in hold   5
  Where-ever she ride or go,
With trew love a thousandfold.

WILLIAM LANGLAND

fl. c. 1375

99   *The Field Full of Folk*

IN a somer seson whenne softe was the sunne
  I shop me into a shroud as I a shep were,
In habite as an hermite unholy of werkes,
Wente wide in this world wondres to here.
But on a May morwening upon Malverne hilles   5
Me befel a ferly, of fairye me thoughte;

97. 39 everichon: each one   40 whom love has made at one with
Him   43 fyn: perfect   44 make fyn: make his peace

98. 1 My dear one has gone away   3 in bonde: confined   5 in
hold: captive   6 go: walk

99. 1 softe: warm   2 I dressed myself in a garment as if I were a
shepherd   3 In . . .as: clothed like   6 a marvellous thing befell
me, by magic as it seemed to me

I was wery ofwandred and wente me to reste
Under a brod bank by a bournes side;
And as I lay and lenede and lookede on the watres,
I slomerede into a sleeping, it swyede so merye.   10
Thenne gan I mete a merveillous swevene:
That I was in a wildernesse, wiste I nevere where;
Ac as I beheld into the Est on high to the sunne
I saw a towr on a toft tryely y-maked;
A deep dale benethe, a dungeoun thereinne   15
With deepe dikes and derke and dredful of sight.

A fair feeld ful of folk fand I there-betwene,
Of alle maner of men, the mene and the riche,
Worching and wandringe as the world asketh.
Some putte hem to plow, playede ful selde,   20
In setting and sowing swunke ful harde,
Wonne that these wastours with glotonye destroyeth.
And some putte hem to pride, aparailede hem thereafter,
In countenaunce of clothing comen disgised.
In prayers and penaunce putten hem manye,   25
Al for love of oure Lord livede wel straite,
In hope for to have hevene-riche blisse,
As ancres and hermites that holden hem in celles,

---

7 wery ofwandred: weary from wandering   8 by . . .: by the side of
a stream   9 lenede: rested   10 I dozed to sleep, it sounded so
pleasant   11 Then I dreamed a wonderful dream   12 wiste:
knew   13 Ac: but   14 toft: hill   tryely: excellently   16
dredful . . .: of terrifying aspect   17 fand: found   18 the
mene . . .: the lowly and the great   19 Worching: working   asketh:
requires   20 putte . . . plow: devoted themselves to ploughing   selde:
seldom   21 setting: planting   swunke: toiled   22 Wonne
that: gained what   destroyeth: consume   23 f. And some de-
voted themselves to pride, dressed themselves up accordingly, went about
in fantastic guises to show off their clothes   26 wel straite: very
austerely   27 trusting to have the bliss of the kingdom of heaven
28 As ancres: such as anchorites   holden hem: keep themselves

Coveite not in cuntré to cairen aboute
For no likerous liflode here likam to plese.   30
And some chosen to chaffare, they chevede the betere,
As it seemeth to oure sight that suche men thriven.
And some merthes to make, as minstrales cunne,
And gete gold with here glee giltles, I trowe.
Ac japeres and jangleres, Judas children,   35
Fonden hem fantasies and fooles hem make,
And have wit at wille to worche if hem list.
That Poule precheth of hem I dar not prove it here:
Qui loquitur turpiloquium is Luciferes hine.
Bidderes and beggeres faste aboute yede   40
Til here bely and here bagge were bratful y-crammed;
Flite thenne for here foode, foughten at the ale;
In glotonye, God wot, go they to bedde,
And risen up with ribaudrye as Robertes knaves;
Sleep and sleuthe seweth hem evere.   45
Pilgrimes and palmeres plighten hem togedere
For to seke Saint Jame and saintes at Rome;
Wenten forth in here way with many wise tales,
And hadde leve to lye al here lif after.
Hermites on an heep, with hookede staves,   50

29 Coveite: desire   cairen: go   30 for the sake of any delightful way of life to gratify their bodies   31 And some took to trading, they prospered the better   32 As: for   33 And some took to entertaining, as minstrels know how to   34 with . . .giltles: for their music without sin   35–40 But tricksters and idle talkers, Judas's children, invent false tales and play the fool, and have the brains at their command to work if they please. What Paul preaches about them I dare not expound here: he who speaks obscenity is Lucifer's servant. Mendicants and beggars went about busily   41 bratful: chock-full   42 Flite for: wrangled over   44 ribaudrye: iniquity   Robertes knaves: lawless vagabonds   45 sleuthe: sloth   seweth: follow   46 plighten hem: pledge themselves   47 Saint Jame: *i.e.* of Compostela   48 in here: on their   49 lye: tell lies   50 on an heep: in a crowd

Wenten to Walsingham, and here wenches after;
Grete lobies and longe, that loth were to swinke,
Clothede hem in copes to be knowen from othere,
Shopen hem hermites here ese to have.
I fand there freres, alle the foure ordres,   55
Preching the peple for profit of the wombe;
Glosede the gospel as hem good likede,
For coveitise of copes construede it as they wolde.
Many of these maistres may clothe hem at liking,
For here mony and here marchaundise meten togedere.   60
Sithen charité hath been chapman and chief to shrive
        lordes,
Manye ferlies han fallen in a fewe yeres.
But Holy Church and hy holden bet togedere,
The moste mischief on molde is mounting up faste.
There prechede a pardoner, as he a preest were,   65
Broughte forth a bulle with bishopes seeles,
And saide that himself mighte assoile hem alle
Of falsnesse of fasting and of avowes broken.
Lewede men levede it wel and likede his speche,
Comen up kneelinge to kissen his bulle.   70
He buncheth hem with his brevet and blereth here eye,
And raughte with his raggeman ringes and broches.

51 after: following them   52 Grete . . . longe: great lanky louts
swinke: work   53 knowen . . .: distinguished   54 Shopen hem:
made themselves   55 freres: friars   56 wombe: belly   57
interpreted the gospel as it suited them   58 For . . . of: in their desire
for   59 maistres: gentry   at liking: as they like   60 for their money
and their trade go together   61 Since love has turned pedlar and been
most active in shriving lords   62 ferlies han fallen: strange things have
occurred   63 f. Unless Holy Church and they work together better,
the greatest disaster on earth is . . .   65 as: as if   67 assoile:
absolve   68 of evading their fasts and of broken vows   69 Lewede:
ignorant   levede: believed   71 buncheth: thumps   brevet:
Papal Indulgence   72 raughte: procured   raggeman: document

Thus they given here gold glotones to helpe
And leneth it loseles that lecherie haunten.
But were the bishop y-blissed and worth bothe his eres,   75
His seel shulde not be sent to deceive the peple.
It is not al by the bishop that the boy precheth,
Ac the parish preest and the pardoner parte the silver
That the pore peple of the parish shulde have if they ne
    were.
Persones and parish preestes plainede hem to here bishop
That here parish was pore sithe the pestilence time,   81
To have a licence and leve at Londoun to dwelle,
To singe for simonye—for silver is swete.
There hovede an hundred in houves of silk,
Serjauntes it seemede that servede at the barre;   85
Pleten for penies and poundes the lawe,
And nought for love of oure Lord unlose here lippes
    ones.
Thou mightest betere mete mist on Malverne hilles
Thanne gete a mom of here mouth til mony be shewed.
I saw bishopes bolde and bacheleres of divin   90
Become clerkes of acountes the king for to serve;
Archedekenes and denes, that dignités haven
To preche the peple and pore men to feede,

---

74 and give it to profligates who practise lechery   75 y-blissed:
worthy to be blessed   worth . . .: *i.e.* making proper use of his
two ears   77 It is not entirely by the connivance of the bishop
that the rascal preaches   78 parte: share   silver: money
79 they . . .: it were not for them   80 Persones: parsons   plainede
hem: complained   81 sithe . . .: since the time of the Black Death
82 To: (pleaded) to   83 To . . . simonye: *i.e.* to be hired to sing
masses for the dead   84 hovede: lingered   houves: caps
85 Serjauntes: barristers   86 Pleten: (they) plead   87 unlose:
open   88 mete: measure   89 mom: mumble   90 divin:
divinity   92 dignités: official duties

Been y-lope to Londoun by leve of here bishop,
And been clerkes of the Kinges Bench the cuntré to
    shende.   95
Barouns and burgeis and bondage also
I saw in that semblé, as ye shulen here after,
Baxteres and bocheres and brewsteres manye,
Wollene websteres and weveres of linen,
Taillours and tanneres and tokkeres bothe,   100
Masones, minours, and manye othere craftes,
As dikeres and delveres that doth here deede ille
And driveth forth the longe day with *Dieu save Dame Emme*!
Cookes and here knaves crieth 'hote pies, hote!
Goode gees and gris! Go we dine, go we!'   105
Taverners to hem tolde the same:
'Whit wyn of Osay and wyn of Gascoyne,
Of the Ryn and of the Rochel, the rost to defye!'
Al this I saw sleeping and seven sithes more.

100   *Belling the Cat*

T HEN ran ther a route of ratones, as it were,
   And smale mys with hem, mo than a thousand,
Comen til a conseil for here comune profit;

99. 94 Been y-lope: have run off   95 the cuntré . . .: to the detriment
of the country   96 bondage: bondsmen   97 semblé: assembly
shulen here: shall hear   98 many bakers and butchers and brewers
99 Wollene websteres: weavers of wool   100 tokkeres bothe: fullers
too   102 such as ditchers and diggers who do their work badly
103 driveth forth: pass away   104 knaves: boys   105 gris:
sucking pigs   106 to hem: ? besides them   107 Osay: Alsace
Gascony   108 of the Rhine and La Rochelle, to digest the roast meat
109 sithes: times

100. 1 route of ratones: crowd of rats   2 hem: them   mo: more
3 Comen til: came to   here: their

For a cat of a court cam when him likede
And overlep hem lightliche and laghte hem alle at wille,   5
And playde with some perilously, and putte hem ther him
    likede;
'And if we gruche of his game, he wil greve us sore,
To his clees clawe us and in his cloches us holde,
That us lotheth the lyf er he lette us passe.
Mighte we with any wit his wille withsitte,   10
We mighte be lordes alofte, and live as us liste.'

   A ratoun of renown, moste resonable of tonge,
Saide: 'I have seyen grete sires in citees and in townes
Bere beighes of brighte gold al aboute here nekkes,
And colers of crafty werk, bothe knightes and squieres.   15
Were ther a belle on here beigh, by Jesu, as me thinketh,
Men mighte y-wite where they wente and here way
    roume.
Right so', quod the ratoun, 'reson me sheweth
A belle to biggen of bras or of bright silver,
And knitten it on a coler for oure comune profit,   20
And hangen it aboute the cattes halse; thenne here we
    mowe
Wher he rit othere reste or rometh to playe;
And if him list for to laike, then loke we mowe,

---

4 For: because   him likede: he pleased   5 and pounced on them
swiftly and caught them at will   6 ther: where   7 gruche of:
complain about   greve: injure   8 f. . . .: grab us in his claws
and hold us in his clutches, so that life is hateful to us before he lets us go
10 If we could by any scheme thwart his will   11 alofte: on high
us liste: we pleased   12 moste . . .: with a very persuasive tongue
13 seyen: seen   sires: lords   14 beighes: rings   15 crafty
werk: skilled workmanship   17 here way roume: clear out of their
way   18 Right so: similarly   quod: said   sheweth: tells
19 biggen: buy   20 knitten: tie   21 halse: neck   mowe: can
22 Wher . . . reste: whether he is on the warpath (*lit.* rides) or resting
23 laike: play   loke: watch

And apere in his presence the while him playe liketh;
And if him wratheth, been we ware, and his way roume.' 25
  Alle this route of ratones to this reson they assentede;
Ac tho the belle was y-broughte and on the beigh hanged,
Ther ne was non of al the route, for al the reame of
    Fraunce,
That durste have y-bounde the belle aboute the cattes
    nekke,
Ne have hanged it aboute his halse, al Engeland to winne; 30
And leten here labour y-lost and al here longe study.
  A mous that muche good couthe, as me tho thoughte,
Strok forth sturnely and stood before hem alle,
And to the route of ratones rehersede these wordes:
'Though we hadde y-kild the cat, yet shulde ther come
    another 35
To crache us and alle oure kinde, though we crope under
    benches.
For-thy I conseile for our comune profit, let the cat
    y-worthe,
And be nevere so bold the belle him shewe;
For I herde my sire sayn, sevene yeer y-passed,
"Ther the cat is but a kitoun, the court is full elinge"; 40
Wittenesse at Holy Writ, who so can rede,
Ve terre ubi puer est rex!
I saye it for me', quod the mous, 'I see so muche after,
Shal never the cat ne kitoun by my conseil be greved,

Ne carpen of here colers that costede me nevere;   45
And though it costed my catel, biknowen I ne wolde,
But suffre and say nought, and that is the beste,
Til that mischief amende hem, that many man chasteth.
For many mannes malt we mys wolde destroye,
And the route of ratones of reste men awake,   50
Ne were the cat of the court and yonge kitones toward;
For hadde ye ratones youre reed, ye couthe not reule
    youselven.

101   *Long Will in London*

THUS I awakede, wot God, when I wonede in
    Cornehille,
Kitte and I in a cote, y-clothed as a lollare,
And litel y-let by, leveth me for soothe,
Amonges lollares of Londone and lewede hermites;
For I made of tho men as Resoun me taughte.   5
For as I cam by Consience, with Resoun I mette,
In an hot hervest, whenne I hadde myn hele,
And limes to labory with, and lovede wel-fare,
And no dede to do but to drinke and to slepe.

---

100. 45 f. nor mention be made of their collars, for which I would never
have subscribed; and even if it had cost me my money, I would not
proclaim it   48 till misfortune, which chastens many men, teaches
them better   50 *second* of: from   51 if the cat and young kittens
of the court were not about   52 reed: policy, way   couthe: would
not know how to

101. 1 wonede: lived   2 cote: hovel   lollare: idle vagabond
3 and little esteemed, believe me truly   4 lewede: ignorant   5
for I regarded those men as Reason taught me   6 by: past   7
hele: health   8 limes: limbs   wel-fare: easy living

In hele and in inwitt, one me apposede,   10
Rominge in remembraunce thus Resoun me aratede:
'Can thou serven', he saide, 'or singen in a churche,
Or coke for my cokeres, or to the cart piche,
Mowen or mywen, or make bond to sheves,
Repe, or been a ripe-reve, and arise erly,   15
Or have an horn and be hayward, and ligge theroute
     nightes,
And kepe my corn in my croft fro pikares and theves,
Or shap shoon or cloth, or sheep and kine kepe,
Heggen or harwen, or swin or gees drive,
Or any other kines craft that to the comune nedeth,   20
Hem that bedreden be bileve to finde?'
'Certes', I saide, 'and so me God helpe,
I am to waike to werke with sikel or with sythe,
And to long, leve me, lowe to stoupe,
To worche as a werkeman any while to duren.'   25
'Thenne hast thou landes to live by', quod Resoun, 'or
     linage riche,
That finde thee thy foode? For an idel man thou
     semest,
A spendour that spene mot, or a spille-time,
Or beggest thy bileve aboute at mennes haches,

10 f. being sound in body and mind, one questioned me, as I roamed
in recollection Reason berated me thus   12 serven: serve at mass
13 or make haycocks for my harvesters, or pitch (hay) on to the cart
14 mow or stack, or make binding for sheaves   15 ripe-reve: harvest
overseer   16 hayward . . .: hedge-keeper, and lie out of doors at
night   17 pikares: pilferers   18 shap . . . cloth: make shoes or
clothing   19–21 hedge or harrow, or tend pigs or geese, or any other
kind of skill necessary for the community, to provide food for those that
are bedridden   23 waike: weak   24 long, leve me: tall, believe
me   25 to last any time working as a labourer   26 linage:
family   27 finde thee: provide you with   28 f. a spender who
must spend, or a time-waster, or go about begging your food at men's
doors

Or faitest upon Fridayes or feste-dayes in churches,   30
The whiche is lollarne lif, that litel is praised
There Rightfulnesse rewardeth right as men deserveth:
Reddet unicuique iuxta opera sua.
Or thou art broke, so may be, in body or in membre,
Or y-maimed thorgh som mishap whereby thou mighte
    be excused.'   35
'When I yong was', quod ich, 'many yeer hennes,
My fader and my frendes founde me to scole,
Til I wiste witterly what Holy Writ menede,
And what is beste for the body, as the Book telleth,
And sikerest for the soule, by so I wil continue;   40
And fond I ne're, in faith, sith my frendes deyede,
Lif that me likede, but in these longe clothes.
And if I by labour sholde liven and liflode deserven,
That labour that I lerned beste therwith liven I sholde:
In eadem vocacione qua vocati estis, sitis.   45
And so I live in London and upeland bothe;
The lomes that I labore with and liflode deserve
Is *Pater Noster* and my Primer, *Placebo* and *Dirige*,
And my Sauter som time, and my Sevene Psalmes.
These I segge for here soules of suche as me helpeth;   50
And tho that finden me my foode vouchen saf, I trowe,

30 faitest: beg under false pretences   31 lollarne: idlers'   32
There: where   right: exactly   33 Ps. 62. 12 (A.V.)   34
broke: crippled   36 quod: said   hennes: ago   37 frendes . . .:
relatives maintained me at school   38 witterly: clearly   menede:
meant   40 and safest for the soul, provided that I am willing to
continue   41 fond I nere: I never found   sith: since   42 me
likede: pleased me   but: except   43 liflode deserves: earn my
living   45 cf. I Cor. 7. 20   46 upeland: in the country
47 lomes: tools   48 Primer: prayer-book for laymen   *Placebo . . .*
parts of the office for the Dead   49 Sauter: Psalter   Sevene
Psalmes: the Penitential Psalms   50 segge: say   here . . . suche:
the souls of such   51 f. and those who provide me with my food

To be welcome when I come otherwhile in a monthe,
Now with him, now with her. On this wise I begge,
Withoute bagge or botel but my wombe one.
And also, moreover, me thinketh, Sire Resoun,   55
Me sholde constraine no clerc to no knaves werkes;
For by the lawe of *Levitici*, that oure Lord ordainede,
Clerkes y-crowned, of kinde understandinge,
Sholde nother swinke ne swete, ne swerien at enquestes,
Ne fighte in no vaunewarde, ne his foe greve: 60
Non reddas malum pro malo.
For it been heires of hevene alle that been y-crowned,
And in quoer and in kirkes Cristes ministres:
Dominus pars hereditatis mee &c; et alibi: *Clemencia non
    constringit.*
It becometh for clerkes Crist for to serve,   65
And knaves uncrownede to carte and to worche.
For sholde no clerke be crowned but if he come were
Of frankeleines and free men, and of folke y-wedded.
Bondemen and bastardes and beggares children,
These belongeth to labory, and lordes kin to serve   70
God and good men, as here degree asketh;
Some to singe masses, or sitten and writen,
Reden and receiven that Resoun oughte to spene.
Ac   sithe bondemen barnes han be made bishopes,

graciously allow (me) to be welcome when I come from time to time
during a month   54 but . . .: except my belly only   56 no
educated man should be forced to do menial work   58 Clerkes
y-crowned: tonsured clerics   kinde: natural   59 swinke: toil
swerien . . .: give evidence on oath at inquests   60 vaunewarde:
vanguard   greve: injure   61 1 Thess. 5. 15   62 for all who
are tonsured are heirs to heaven   63 quoer: choir   64 Ps. 16. 5
(A.V.)   65 becometh for: befits   66 knaves uncrownede:
untonsured menials   67 but if: unless   70 belongeth: ought
71 (to serve) God and good men, as their rank requires   72 Some
to: *i.e.* priests (ought) to   73 to read and accept what Reason should
dispense   74 Ac . . . han: but since bondsmen's children have

And barnes bastardes han be archedekenes,   75
And soutares and here sones for silver han be knightes,
And lordes sones here laborers, and laide here rentes to
          wedde,
For the righte of this reume riden ayein oure enemies,
In confort of the comune and the kinges worshipe,
And monkes and moniales, that mendenants sholde finde,   80
Y-made here kin knightes, and knightes fees y-purchased,
Popes and patrones pore gentel blood refused
And taken Simondes sones seintuarie to kepe:
Lif-holynesse and love hath be longe hennes,
And wil til it be wered out or otherwise y-chaunged.   85
     For-thy rebuke me righte noughte, Resoun, I you
          praye,
For in my consience I knowe what Crist wolde I
          wroughte.
Prayeres of a perfit man and penaunce discrete
Is the levest labour that oure Lord pleseth.
Non de solo', I saide, 'for soothe *vivit homo*,   90
Nec in pane et in pabulo, the *Pater Noster* wittenesseth:
Fiat voluntas Dei, that fint us alle thinges.'
Quod Consience: 'By Crist, I can not see this lieth;
Ac it seemeth no sad perfitnesse in citees to begge,

75 barnes bastardes: bastard children   76 soutares: cobblers
77–80 and lords' sons (have been) their labourers, and have mortgaged their
estates, have ridden against our enemies in the just cause of this realm, in
support of the common good and the king's honour, and monks and nuns,
who ought to maintain beggars   81 knightes fees: estates held by
knightes in return for armed service   83 and entrusted Simon's sons
(*i.e.* simoniacs) with ministering in sanctuaries   84 hennes: absent
85 it . . . out: this is over   86 For-thy: therefore   87 wolde:
would wish that   88 perfit: righteous   penaunce discrete: fitting
penance   89 levest: most pleasing   90 ff. cf. Matt. 4. 4, 6. 10
92 fint us: provides for us   93 lieth: is tenable   94 f. but
begging in cities does not seem to be true righteous conduct, unless one is
an obedientiary in priory or monastery

But he be obediencer to prior or to ministre.' 95
'That is sooth', I saide, 'and so I beknowe
That I have y-tint time and time mis-spened;
Ac yet I hope, as he that ofte hath y-chaffared,
And ay loste and loste, and at the laste him happed
He boughte suche a bargain he was the bet evere, 100
And sette al his los at a leef at the laste ende,
Suche a winning him warth thorgh werdes of grace:
Simile est regnum celorum thesauro abscondito in agro;
Mulier que invenit dragmam.
So hope I to have of Him that is almighty 105
A gobet of His grace, and biginne a time
That alle times of my time to profit shal turne.'
 'I rede thee', quod Resoun tho, 'rape thee to biginne
The lif that is lowable and leele to thy soule';
'Ye, and continue', quod Consience; and to the kirke I
  wente. 110

102 *Glutton in the Tavern*

NOW biginneth Glotoun for to go to shrifte,
 And caires him to kirke-ward his conpte to shewe.
Fasting on a Friday forth gan he wende

101. 96 beknowe: acknowledge 97 y-tint: wasted mis-spened:
misspent 98 hope: trust y-chaffared: made deals 99 him
happed: it chanced (that) 100 bet: better 101 f. and in the end
reckoned all his losses of no consequence (*lit.* worth a leaf), such a profit
accrued to him through the power of grace 103 f. Matt. 13. 44, Luke
15. 9   106 gobet: piece biginne . . .: enter upon a time
108 'I advise you', said Reason then, 'to hasten to begin 109 lowable:
praiseworthy leele: true

102. 2 and betakes himself towards the church to render his account
3 gan . . .: he went

By Betene hous the brewestere, that bad him good
    morwen,
And whiderward he wolde the brew-wif him askede.   5
'To holy churche,' quod he, 'for to here masse,
And sennes sitte and be shrive, and sinege no more.'

    'I have good ale, gossip. Glotoun, wilt thou assaye?'
'Hast thou', quod he, 'any hote spices?'
'I have peper and pionie and a pound of garleke,   10
A ferthing-worth fenkel-sedes, for fasting-dayes I boughte
    it.'

    Thenne goth Glotoun in, and grete othes after.
Sesse the souteress sat on the benche,
Watte the warnere and his wif drunke,
Timme the tinkere and twaine of his knaves,   15
Hicke the hackenayman and Hewe the nedlere,
Clarice of Cockes Lane, and the clerc of the churche,
Sire Peres of Prydie and Purnele of Flaundres,
An hayward, an heremite, the hangeman of Tybourne,
Dawe the dikere with a doseine harlotes   20
Of portours and of pike-purses and of pilede tooth-
    draweres,
A ribibour and a ratoner, a rakere and his knave,

4 By . . . brewestere: past the house of Beten, the ale-wife   5
And . . wolde: and where he was going   6 quod; said   7
and afterwards sit and make confession, and sin no more   8 gossip:
friend   assaye: try (it)   10 pionie: peony-seeds   11 fenkel-:
fennel   12 grete . . .: coarse oaths follow   13 souteress:
cobbler-woman   14 warnere: game-keeper   drunke: were drinking
15 knaves: servants   16 hackenayman: keeper of horses for hire
nedlere: needle-maker   17 Cock Lane (where women of ill fame
were lodged)   clerc: *i.e.* clerk in minor orders   18 Sir Piers (*i.e.* a
priest) of ?Priddy (Som.) and Petronella (*i.e.* a wanton woman) of Flanders
19 hayward: hedge-keeper   20 dikere: ditcher   harlotes: scoundrels
21 pilede: bald-headed   22 a rebeck-player, a rat-catcher, a scavenger
and his boy

A ropere and a redingkinge, and Rose the dishere,
Godefray the garlek-monger and Griffith the Walshe,
And of upholderes an heep, erly by the morwe   25
Geven Glotoun with glad chere good ale to hanselle.
   Clement the coblere cast off his cloke,
And to the newe faire nempnede forth to selle;
Hicke the hackenayman hit his hood after,
And bade Bitte the bochere been on his side.   30
There were chapmen y-chose this chaffare to praise,
That who so hadde the hood sholde not have the
   cloke,
And that the bettere thing, by arbitreres, bote sholde the
   worse.
Tho risen up rape and rouned togideres,
And praisede this penyworthes apart by hem selve,   35
And there were othes an heep for on sholde have the
   worse.
They couthe not, by here consience, acorden for
   treuthe,
Til Robin the Ropere arise they bisoughte
And nempned him for an oumper, that no debat were.
Hicke the hostiler hadde the cloke,   40

---

23 ropere: rope-maker   redingkinge: *unexplained*   dishere: dish-seller
24 Walshe: Welshman   25 and a great number of dealers in second-
hand goods, early in the morning   29 Geven to hanselle: gave as a
token of good will   28 and proffered it for sale at the New Fair (?
i.e. by barter)   29 hit . . .: then tapped his hood   30 bochere:
butcher   31 Bargainers were chosen there to value these articles
32 *see textual note*   33–39 and that (whoever got) the better thing,
assessed by arbitrators, should compensate (him who got) the worse.
They (the bargainers) hastily got up and whispered together, and valued
these bargains apart by themselves, and there were plenty of oaths because
one was getting the worse bargain. They could not honestly agree, indeed,
till they asked Robin the rope-maker to stand up and nominated him as an
umpire, so that there should be no wrangling.   40 hostiler: ostler

In covenaunt that Clement sholde the cuppe fille,
And have Hickes hood the hostiler, and holde him
    y-served;
And who so repentede him rathest sholde arise after
And grete Sire Glotoun with a galoun of ale.
    There was laughing and lowring and 'Let go the
        cuppe!'   45
Bargaines and bevereges bigan tho to awake;
And seten so til evensong, and sungen umbywhile,
Til Glotoun hadde y-globbed a galoun and a gille.

103   *Our Needy Neighbours*

A C that most needen aren oure neighebores, and we
    nime good heede,
As prisones in pittes, and pore folk in cotes
Charged with children and chief lordes rente;
That they with spinning may spare, spenen it on hous-hire,
Bothe in milke and in mele to make with papelotes   5
To aglotye with here girles that greden after foode.
And hemselve also suffre muche hunger,

102. 41–3 on condition that Clement should fill his cup (at Hick's expense),
and have Hick the ostler's hood, and consider himself satisfied; and the first
person to repudiate the bargain should stand up afterwards   44 grete:
reward   45 There was laughing and scowling and 'Pass round the
cup!'   46 tho to awake: to flow then   47 seten so: so they
went on   umbywhile: at times   48 y-globbed: gulped down

103. 1 f. But those who are most in need are our neighbours, if we pay
due attention, such as prisoners in dungeons   2 cotes: hovels   3
Charged: burdened   chief lordes: landlord's   4 whatever they can
save, by spinning, they spend on house-rent   5 f. in: on   to . . .:
with which to make porridge, to satisfy their children who cry for food
7 hemselve: themselves

And wo in winter-times, and waking on nightes
To rise to the reule to rokke the cradel,
Bothe to carde and to kembe, to cloute and to washe,   10
And to ribbe and to rele, rushes to pilye,
That reuthe is to rede or in rime shewe
The wo of these women that wonieth in cotes;
And of manye other men that muche wo suffren,
Bothe afingred and afurste, to turne the faire outward,   15
And been abashed for to begge and willen not be aknowe
What them needede at here neighebores at noon and at
     eve.
This I wot witterly, as the world techeth,
What other behoveth that hath many children,
And hath no catel but his craft to clothe hem and to
     feede,   20
And fele to fonge ther-to, and fewe pens taketh.
There is pain and peny-ale as for a pitaunce y-take,
And colde flesh and fish as venison were bake;
Fridays and fasting-days a ferthing-worth of musceles
Were a feste with suche folk, or so fele cockes.   25

8 waking: being awake   9 reule: space between bed and wall
10 kembe: comb (wool)   cloute: patch   11 f. and to scrape flax
and reel thread, to peel rushes (for rushlights), so that it is pitiful to relate
or to describe in verse   13 wonieth: live   15 afflicted by both
hunger and thirst, so as to keep up appearances   16 abashed:
ashamed   be aknowe: admit   17 hem needede at: they needed
from   18 f. This I certainly know, as experience teaches, what
another needs who has many children   20 catel: assets   craft:
trade   21 and has many claims upon his income, and earns very
little   22 there bread and small beer seems a treat   23 as . . .:
like roast venison   24 f. on Fridays and fast-days a farthing's worth
of mussels, or as many cockles, would be a feast for such people

The Trinity

FOR to a torche or to a taper the Trinité is likened,
As wax and a wike were twined togederes,
And thenne flauming fyr forth of hem bothe;
And as wax and wike and warm fyr togederes
Fostren forth a flaume and a fair leye,   5
That serveth these swinkeres to see by a-nightes,
So doth the Sire and the Sone and Saint Spirit togederes
Fostren forth amonges folke fyn love and beleve,
That alle kinne cristene clenseth of sinne.
And as thou seest some time sodeinliche of a torche   10
The blase be y-blowen out, yet brenneth the wike,
Withouten leye and lighte lith fyr in the mache,
So is the Holy Gost God and grace withouten mercy
To alle unkinde creatures that coveiten to destruye
Leel licame and lyf that oure Lord shupte.   15
And as glowing gledes gladeth not these werkmen
That worchen and waken in winteres nightes
As doth a kix or a candle that caught hath fyr and blaseth,
No more doth Sire ne the Sone ne Saint Spirit togederes
Graunten any grace ne forgivenesse of sinnes   20
Til that the Holy Gost ginne to glowe and blase:
So that the Holy Gost gloweth but as a glede

2 As: as if   togederes: together   3 and then fire flaming forth
from them both   5 engender a flame and a fine blaze   6 swin-
keres: workers a-nightes: at night   7 Saint: Holy   8 fyn: pure
9 which cleanses all kinds of Christians of sin   10 sodeinliche:
suddenly   11 brenneth: burns   12 lith: lies mache: wick
14 f. to all wicked creatures that desire to destroy the faithful body and
life which our Lord created   16 gledes: live coals   17 worchen:
work waken: keep awake   18 kix: dry stalk   21 ginne: begins

Til that love and beleve leliche to him blowe;
And thenne flaumeth he as fyr on Fader and on *Filius*,
And melteth mighte into mercy, as we may see a winter   25
Isekeles in evesinges thorgh hete of the sunne
Melteth in a mint-while to mist and to water;
So grace of the Holy Gost the grete mighte of the Trinité
Melteth al to mercy to merciable and to non othere.
And as wax withouten more upon a warm glede   30
Wil brennen and blasen, be they togederes,
And solacen that mowen not see sitting in derknesse,
So wil the Fader foryive folke of milde hertes
That reufulliche repenten and restitucion make
In as muche as they mowen amenden and payen;   35
And if it sufficeth not for asseth that in such a will deyeth,
Mercy, for his mekenesse, wil maky good the remenaunt.
And as the wike and warm fyr wil make a faire flaume
For to murthe men with that in merke sitten,
So wil Crist of His curtesye, and men crien Him mercy,   40
Bothe foryive and foryete, and yet bidde for us
To the Fader of hevene foryivenesse to have.
Ac hewe fyr at a flint foure hundred winter,
Bute thou have tasch to take it with, tender and broches,
Al thy labor is loste and al thy longe travaile: 45

23 till love and faith blow steadfastly upon him   25 a: in
26 Isekeles in evesinges: icicles in the eaves   27 mint-while: space of
a minute   28 f. so the grace of the Holy Ghost completely melts the
great might of the Trinity to mercy for the merciful and for no others
30 more: anything else   31 be they: if they are   32 that mowen
not: those who cannot   33 milde: humble   35 mowen: can
36 and if anyone has not enough to make full reparation and dies intending
it   37 for: because of   39 murthe (with): gladden   merke:
darkness   40 and: if   41 f. bidde To: intercede with   43 Ac
hewe at: but strike from   44 unless you have touchwood to kindle
it, tinder and sticks

For may no fyr flaume make, faile it his kinde.
So is the Holy Gost God and grace withouten mercy
To alle unkinde creatures, as Crist Himselve witnesseth:
Amen dico vobis, nescio vos.

GEOFFREY CHAUCER

c. 1340–1400

105 *Jove's Eagle Carries Chaucer into Space*

THIS egle, of which I have you told,
That shone with fethres as of gold,
Which that so highè gan to sore,
I gan beholdè more and more,
To see the beauté and the wonder.   5
But never was ther dint of thonder,
Ne that thing that men callè fouder,
That smote sometime a towr to powder
And in his swiftè coming brende,
That so swithè gan descende   10
As this fowl, when it beheld
That I a-roum was in the feld.
And with his grimmè pawès stronge,
Within his sharpè nailès longe,
Me, fleyinge, in a swap he hente,   15
And with his sours again up wente,
Me carying in his clawès starke
As lightly as I were a larke,
How high I can not tellè you,

---

104. 46 faile . . .: if it lacks the conditions proper to it   49 Matt. 25. 12
105. 2 whose feathers shone like gold   4 I was watching more and
more intently   6 dint: clap   7 fouder: thunderbolt   9 and
burnt (it) in its swift passage   10 swithe: quickly   12 a-roum:
in the open   14 nailes: talons   15 in . . .: he seized at one strike
16 sours: upward flight   18 as easily as if I were a lark

For I came up, I n'isté how.   20
For so astonyed and aswevéd
Was every vertu in my hevéd,
What with his sours and with my drede,
That al my feeling gan to dede,
For-why it was to grete affray.   25
  Thus I longe in his clawés lay,
Til at the last he to me spake
In mannés vois, and saide: 'Awake!
Aṅd be not agast, for shame!'
And callèd me tho by my name,   30
And, for I shulde the bet abraide,
Me mette, 'Awake!' to me he saide,
Right in the samé vois and stevene
That useth one I coudé nevene;
And with that vois, sooth for to sayn,   35
My mindé came to me agayn;
For it was goodly said to me,
So n'as it never wont to be.
  And here-withal I gan to stere,
And he me in his feet to bere,   40
Til that he felt that I had hete
And felt eke that myn herté bete.
And tho gan he me to disporte
Aṅd with wordés to comfòrte,
And saidé twyès: 'Sainté Mary!   45
Thou art noyous for to cary,

20 n'iste: did not know   21 f. for so stunned and stupefied was
every faculty in my head   24 f. that all my senses became deadened,
because the terror was too great   30 tho: then   31 and, to
rouse me more effectively   32 Me mette: I dreamt   33 Right:
exactly   stevene: accent   34 that someone I could name uses
35 sooth . . .: to tell the truth   37 goodly: kindly   38 as it
never used to be   39 stere: stir   41 hete: vital heat   43 dis-
porte: entertain   45 twyes: twice   46 noyous: troublesome

And nothing nedeth it, pardee!
For also wis God helpė me
As thou none harm shalt have of this;
And this cas that betid thee is   50
Is for thy lore and for thy prow.
Let see, darst thou yet lookė now?
Be ful assurėd, boldėly,
I am thy frend.' And therwith I
Gan for to wondren in my minde: 55
'O God', thought I, 'that madest kinde,
Shal I none other wayės dye?
Wher Jovės wil me stellifye?
Or what thing may this signifye?
I neither am Ennok, ne Elye,   60
Ne Romulus, ne Ganymede,
That was y-bore up, as men rede,
To hevene with Daun Jupiter,
And made the goddės botiller.'
Lo, this was tho my fantasÿe!   65
But he that bare me gan espye
That so I thought, and saidė this:
'Thou demest of thyself amis,
For Jovės is not theraboute—
I dare wel putte thee out of doute—   70
To make of thee as yet a sterre.
But er I bere thee muché ferre,
I wil thee tellė what I am,

---

47 and, indeed, it's quite unnecessary   48 f. also . . . As: as surely
as God may help me   50 cas: happening   betid is: has befallen
51 lore: instruction   prow: benefit   52 Let see: let's see   53
boldely: confidently   56 kinde: nature   58 does Jove mean to
make me into a star   60 Enoch   Elijah   63 with Daun: by
Master   64 botiller: butler   68 you are mistaken about yourself
69 theraboute: intending   71 sterre: star   72 ferre: farther

And whider thou shalt, and why I cam
Tò do this, so that thou take   75
Good herte, and not for ferè quake.'
'Gladly', quod I. 'Now wel', quod he;
'First, I, that in my feet have thee,
Of which thou hast a fere and wonder,
Am dwelling with the god of thonder,   80
Which that men callen Jupiter,
That doth me flee ful oftè fer
To do al his comaundèment.
And for this cause he hath me sent
To thee. Now herkè, by thy trouthe!   85
Certain, he hath of thee routhe,
That thou so longè trewèly
Hast servèd so ententifly
His blindè nevew Cupido,
Aǹd fairè Venùs alsò,   90
Withoutè guerdon ever yit,
And never-the-less hast set thy wit,
Although that in thy hed ful lit is,
To makè bookès, songès, ditees,
In rime, or ellès in cadènce,   95
As thou best canst, in reverence
Of Love, and of his servantes eke,
That have his service sought, and seke:
And painest thee to praise his art,
Although thou haddest never part.   100
Wherfore, also God me blesse,

---

74 whider thou shalt: where you are going   77 quod: said   82
who very often makes me fly far   86 routhe: pity   88 ententifly:
devotedly   91 yit: yet   93 lit: little   94 ditees: poems
95 ellès: else   cadence: ? rhythmic pattern   99 painest thee:
you take pains   101 also . . .: so may God bless me

Jovės halt it gret humblesse,
And vertu eke, that thou wilt make
A-night ful oft thyn hed to ake,
In thy studye so thou writest,   105
And ever-mo of Love enditest,
In honour of him and in praisinges,
And in his folkės furtheringes,
And in her matere al devisest,
And nought him nor his folk despisest,   110
Although thou maist go in the daunce
Of hem that him list not avaunce.
  Wherfore, as I saide, y-wis,
Jupiter considereth this,
And also, beau sir, other thinges: 115
That is, that thou hast no tidinges
Of Lovės folk, if they be glade,
Ne of nought ellės that God made;
And nought only fro fer contree
That ther no tiding comth to thee,   120
But of thy verray neighėbores,
That dwellen almost at thy dores,
Thou herest neither that ne this;
For when thy labour don al is,
And hast made alle thy rekeninges,   125
In stede of reste and newė thinges
Thou gost home to thy house anon,
And, also domb as any ston,

102 Jove considers it great humility   103 wilt: are willing to
106 ever-mo: evermore   108 f. and in helping his followers, and
recount every detail in their affairs   111 f. although you may go in
the band of those he is not pleased to help   113 y-wis: indeed
115 beau: good   119 nought: (it is) not   fer: far   125
rekeninges: accounts (*i.e.* Chaucer's daily work)   126 newe thinges:
change   127 anon: at once   128 also: as

Thou sittest at another book,
Til fully daswėd is thy look;   130
And livest thus as an herėmite,
Although thyn abstinence is lite.
    And therfore Jovės, thurgh his grace,
Wil that I bere thee to a place
Which that hight the House of Fame,   135
To do thee some disport and game,
In some recompensacioun
Of labour and devocioun
That thou hast had, lo causėless,
To Cupido the rechėless.   140

106   *The Eagle Converses with Chaucer*

'HOW farest thou?' quod he to me.
    'Wel', quod I. 'Now see', quod he,
'By thy trouthė, yond a-down,
Wher that thou knowest any town,
Or house, or any other thing.   5
And when thou hast of ought knowing,
Lookė that thou warnė me,
And I anon shal tellė thee
How fer that thou art now therfro.'
    And I a-down to looken tho,   10
Aṅd beheld feldes and plaines,

105. 130 daswed: dazed   132 lite: little   135 hight: is called
136 to give you some entertainment and pleasure   138 Of: for
140 recheless: heedless

106. 1 quod: said   3 yond a-down: down there   4 Wher that:
whether   6 hast . . .: recognize anything   7 see that you tell
me   8 anon: at once   9 fer: far   therfro: from there
10 and I looked down then

And now hilles, and now mountàines,
Now valèyès, now forèstes,
And now, unnethès, gretè bestes;
Now rivèrès, now citees,   15
Now townès, and now gretè trees,
Now shippès sailling in the see.
  But thus soone in a whilè he
Was flowèn fro the ground so hye
That al the world, as to myn eye,   20
No morè seemèd than a prikke;
Or ellès was the air so thikke
That I ne mightè not discerne.
With that he spak to me as yerne,
And saidè: 'Seest thou any town   25
Or ought thou knowest yonder down?'
I saidè 'Nay', 'No wonder n'is,'
Quod he, 'for half so high as this
N'as Alixandrè Macedo;
Ne the king, Daun Scipio,   30
That saw in dreem, at point devis,
Hell and erthe and Paradis;
Ne eke the wrechè Dedalus,
Ne his child, nice Ycarus,
That fleigh so highè that the hete   35
His wingès malt, and he fel wete
In-mid the see, and ther he dreint,
For whom was makèd much compleint.
  'Now turn upwàrd', quod he, 'thy face,
Aǹd behold this largè space,   40

14 unnethes: hardly   20 as to: to   22 elles: else   24 as
yerne: eagerly   29 N'as: was not   30 Daun: Master   31
at . . .: perfectly   34 nice: foolish   35 fleigh: flew   36 malt:
melted   37 in-mid: amid   dreint: drowned   38 compleint:
lamentation

This air; but lookè thou ne be
A-drad of hem that thou shalt see;
For in this regioun certèin,
Dwelleth many a citezèin
Of which that speketh Daun Platò: 45
These been the airish bestès, lo!'
And so saw I all that meynee
Bothè gon and also flee.
'Now', quod he tho, 'cast up thyn eye.
See yonder, lo, the Galaxie   50
Which men clepth the Milky Way,
For it is white (and some, parfay,
Callen it Watlingè Strete)
That onès was y-brent with hete,
When the sunnès son, the rede,   55
That hightè Pheton, woldè lede
Algate his fader carte, and gye.
The carte-hors gunnè wel espye
That he coude no governaunce,
And gunnè for to lepe and launce,   60
And beren him now up, now doun,
Til that he sey the Scorpioun,
Which that in heven a signe is yit.
And he, for ferdè, loste his wit
Of that, and let the reinès gon   65
Òf his hors; and they anon

---

41 looke: see that   42 A-drad of hem: frightened by them
43 certein: indeed   46 airish: of the air   47 meynee: company
48 gon: walk   flee: fly   49 tho: then   51 men clepth: is called
52 For: because   parfay: indeed   54 ones: once   y-brent: scorched
55 rede: fiery   56 f. who was called Phaeton, wished to drive his
father's chariot and control it whatever the risk   58 f. the chariot-
horses soon perceived that he did not know how to control them   60
gunne: began   launce: rear   62 sey: saw   63 yit: still   64 f.
for . . . that: in terror, lost his head because of that   66 anon: at once

Gunne up to mounte and down descende,
Til bothe the air and erthe brende;
Til Jupiter, lo, atte laste,
Him slow, and fro the carte caste.   70
Lo, is it not a grete mischaunce
To lete a fool han governaunce
Of thing that he can not demayne?'
And with this word, sooth for to sayne,
He gan upper alway for to sore,   75
And gladded me ay more and more,
So faithfully to me spak he.

    Tho gan I looken under me
And beheld the airish bestes,
Cloudes, mistes, and tempestes,   80
Snowes, hailes, raines, windes,
And th' engendring in her kindes,
All the way through which I cam.
'O God', quod I, 'that made Adàm,
Muche is thy might and thy noblesse!'   85
And tho thought I upon Boèsse,
That writ: 'A thought may flee so hye
With fetheres of Philosophye,
To passen everich element;
And when he hath so fer y-went,   90
Then may be seen behinde his bak
Cloude'; and al that I of spak.

    Tho gan I wexen in a were,

68 brende: caught fire   70 slow: struck down   72 han: have
73 of something he does not know how to manage   74 sooth . . .:
to tell the truth   75 upper alway: higher and higher   76
gladded: reassured   77 faithfully: convincingly   82 and the
begetting of each of them   85 noblesse: greatness   86 Boesse:
Boethius   87 writ: writes   flee: fly   89 so as to pass through
every sphere   90 fer: far   92 al . . .: I spoke of all that   93
Then I began to grow perplexed

And saide: 'I wot wel I am here;
But wher in body or in gost   95
I n'ot, y-wis; but God, thou wost!
For moré clere entendément
N'as me never yet y-sent.'
And then thought I on Marcian,
And eke on Anteclaudian,   100
That sooth was her descripsioun
Of alle the hevens regioun,
As fer as that I sey the preve:
Therfore I can hem now beleve.

    With that this egle gan to crye: 105
'Let be', quod he, 'thy fantasye!
Wilt thou lere of sterrès aught?'
'Nay, certainly', quod I, 'right naught.'
'And why?' 'For I am now to old.'
'Ellès wold I thee have told',   110
Quod he, 'the sterrès namès, lo,
And al the hevens signes therto,
And which they been.' 'No fors', quod I.
'Yis, pardee!' quod he. 'Wost thou why?
For when thou redest poetrye,   115
How goddès gunnè stellifye
Brid, fish, beest, or him or here,
As the Raven, or either Bere,
Or Arionès harpè fine,

95 wher: whether   gost: spirit   96 I do not know certainly;
but God, thou knowest   97 entendement: understanding   99
Martianus Capella   100 *Anticlaudianus* by Alanus de Insulis   101
her: their   103 insofar as I had seen the evidence   107 lere: learn
sterres: stars   109 For: because   to: too   110 Elles: otherwise
113 and of what kind they are.' 'No use', said I   114 Yis, pardee: yes,
indeed (*lit.* by God)   116 gunne . . .: turned into stars   117
Brid: bird   or . . .: man or woman   118 As: such as   119
Ariones harpe: Lyra

Castor, Pollux, or Delphìne,   120
Or Athalantès doughtres sevene,
How allè these arn set in hevene;
For though thou have hem ofte on hande,
Yet n'ost thou not wher that they stande.'
'No fors', quod I, 'it is no nede.   125
I leve as wel, so God me spede,
Hem that write of this matère,
As though I knew her places here;
And eke they shinen here so brighte,
It shuldè shenden al my sighte   130
To looke on hem.' 'That may wel be',
Quod he. And so forth bare he me
A while, and then he gan to crye,
That never herd I thing so hye:
'Now up the hed! for al is wel;   135
Saint Julian, lo, bon hostèl!
See here the House of Famè lo!
Mayst thou not herèn that I do?'
'What?' quod I. 'The gretè soun',
Quod he, 'that rumbleth up and doun   140
In Famès House, full of tidinges,
Bothe of fair speche and chidinges,
And of fals and sooth compouned.
Herkè wel; it is not rouned.
Herest thou not the gretè swough?'   145
'Yis, pardee!' quod I, 'wel ynough.'

---

120 Delphine: Dolphin   121 Athalantes: Atlas's   123 f. for though you often have to deal with them, yet you do not know where they are   126 I trust as surely, so help me God   130 shenden: ruin 134 That: so that hye: loud   136 bon hostel: (grant us) good lodging   138 that: what   139 soun: sound   143 compouned: compounded   144 rouned: whispered   145 swough: rushing sound

'And what soun is it like?' quod he.
'Peter! like beting of the see',
Quod I, 'again the roches holowe,
When tempest doth the shippès swalowe; 150
And let a man stand, out of doute,
A milè thens, and here it route.
Or ellès like the last humblinge
After a clappe of a thundringe,
When Jovès hath the air y-bete— 155
But it doth me for ferè swete!'
'Nay, dred thee not therof', quod he:
'It is no thing will biten thee;
Thou shalt non harm have, trewèly.'

107 *Old Books*

A THOUSAND timès have I herd men telle
That ther is joy in heven and paine in helle,
And I acordè wel that it is so;
But nathèless yet wot I wel alsò
That ther n'is none dwelling in this contree 5
That either hath in hell or heven be,
Ne may of it none other wayès witen
But as he hath herd said or found it writen:
For by assay ther may no man it preve.

106. 149 again: against roches: rocks 151 if a man were to stand,
indeed 152 route: roar 153 humblinge: rumbling 156 but
it makes me sweat with fear 157 dred thee: be afraid 158 will:
(which) will

107. 3 acorde: agree 7 f. Ne . . . as: nor can know about it in any
other way but by what 9 assay: trial preve: prove

But God forbedè but men shuldè leve   10
Wel morè thing than men harr seen with eye!
Men shal not wenen every thing a lye
But if himself it seeth or ellès dooth:
For, God wot, thing is never the lessè sooth,
Though every wight ne may it not y-see: 15
'Bernard the monk ne saugh not all', pardee!
    Then motè we to bookès that we finde,
Thurgh which that oldè thingès been in minde,
And to the doctrine of these oldè wise
Yivè credènce, in every skilful wise,   20
That tellen of these olde apprevèd stories
Of holyness, of reignès, of victòries,
Of love, of hate, of other sundry thinges
Of which I may not maken rèhersinges.
And if that oldè bookès were awey,   25
Y-lorèn were of rèmembraunce the key.
Wel ought us then honòurèn and beleve
These bookès, ther we han none other preve.
    And as for me, though that I can but lite,
On bookès for to rede I me delite,   30
And to hem yive I faith and ful credènce,
And in myn hert have hem in reverence
So hertèly, that ther is gamè non
That fro my bookès maketh me to gon,

---

10 But God forbid that men should not believe   11 thing:
things   han: have   12 Men shal not wenen: one must not suppose
13 unless one sees it oneself or else experiences it   16 'St. Bernard did
not see everything', to be sure   17 mote: must   19 wise: wise
men   20 give credence in every reasonable way   21 approved:
authenticated   22 reignes: realms   24 which I cannot enumerate
26 Y-loren: lost   27 ought us: we ought (to)   28 ther: where
preve: evidence   29 can . . .: know but little   31 hem: them
32 f. have . . . hertely: hold them in such deep respect   33 game:
diversion

But it be seldom on the holyday;   35
Save, certainly, when that the month of May
Is come, and that I here the fowlès singe,
And that the flowrès ginnen for to springe,
Farewel my book and my devocioun!

108   *Criseyde sees Troilus return from Battle*

B UT as she sat allone and thoughtè thus,
  Ascry aros at scarmuch al withoute,
And men cride in the strete: 'See, Troïlus
Hath right now put to flight the Grekès route!'
  With that gan al hir meyné for to shoute: 5
    'A, go we see! cast up the yatès wide!
    For through this strete he mot to paleis ride:

'For other way is fro the yatè non
  Of Dardanus, there open is the chaine.'
With that com he and al his folk anon   10
  An esy pas riding, in routès twaine,
  Right as his happy day was, sooth to sayne,
    For which, men sayn, may nought destourbèd be
    That shal betiden of necessitee.

107. 35 But it be seldom: except occasionally

108. 2 shouting broke out at a skirmish just outside   4 route: army
5 gan: began   meyné: household   6 cast . . .: open the gates up
wide   7 mot: must   8 f. For . . . there: for there is no other
way from the gate of Dardanus, where   10 com: came   anon: at
once   11 routes: companies   12–14 as befitted his fortunate
day, to tell the truth, on which account, they say, nothing can be altered
that must, of necessity, happen

This Troïlus sat on his bayė steede,   15
    Al armėd, save his hed, ful richėly;
And wounded was his hors and gan to bleede,
    On which he rod a pas ful softėly.
        But swich a knightly sightė, trewėly,
            As was on him, was nought, withouten faile,   20
            To looke on Mars, that god is of bataile:

So like a man of armės and a knight
    He was to seen, fulfilled of heigh prowesse;
For bothe he hadde a body and a might
    To don that thing, as wel as hardinesse;   25
        And eek to seen him in his gere him dresse,
            So fresh, so yong, so weldy seemėd he,
            It was an heven upon him for to see!

His helm to-hewėn was in twenty places,
    That by a tissew heng his bak behinde;   30
His sheeld to-dashėd was with swerdes and maces,
    In which men mightė many an arwė finde
        That thirlėd haddė horn and nerf and rinde.
            And ay the peple cride: 'Here comth our joye,
            And, next his brother, holder up of Troye!'   35

For which he wex a litel red for shame,
    When he the peple upon him herdė cryen,

---

17 gan . . . : was bleeding   18 a pas: at a walking pace   19 ff.
But truly Mars, the god of battle, would indeed not be such a knightly
sight as he was to look upon   22 f. He looked such a fine man of
arms and a knight, perfect in noble valour   25 that thing: *i.e.*
knightly deeds   hardinesse: courage   26 him dresse: arm himself
27 weldy: vigorous   29 to-hewen: hewn to pieces   30 **heng:**
hung   31 to-dashed: shattered   33 which had pierced horn (of
the shield) and sinew and skin   35 next: after   36 wex: **grew**

That to beholde it was a noble game,
How sobrelich he castè down his eyen.
Criseÿda gan al his chere aspyen,   40
    And let it so softe in hir hertè sinke
    That to hirself she sayde: 'Who yaf me drinke?'

109   *Troilus Laments Criseyde's Absence*

THERWITH, when he was ware and gan beholde
    How shet was every window of the place,
As frost, him thoughte, his hertè gan to colde;
For which with chaungèd dedlich palè face,
Withouten word, he forthby gan to pace;   5
    And, as God wolde, he gan so fastè ride
    That no wight of his contenaunce espide.

Then saide he thus: 'O palais desolat,
    O hous, of houses whilom best y-hight,
O palais empty and disconsolat,   10
    O thou lantèrne of which queint is the light,
    O palais, whilom day, that now art night,
    Wel oughtest thou to falle, and I to dye,
    Sin she is went that wont was us to gye!

'O palais, whilom crowne of houses alle,   15
    Enluminèd with sunne of allè blisse!

108. 38 game: sight   40 chere: demeanour   42 Who . . .: *i.e.*
who has given me a love potion?

109. 1 gan beholde: beheld   2 shet: shut   3 him thoughte: it
seemed to him   gan . . .: grew cold   4 dedlich: deathly   5
forthby: by   7 that nobody noticed his expression   9 of . . .:
formerly called best of houses   11 queint: extinguished   14 Sin:
since gye: rule

O ring, fro which the ruby is out falle,
  O cause of wo, that cause hast been of lisse!
Yet, sin I may no bet, fain wolde I kisse ·
    Thy coldè dorès, dorste I for this route;   **20**
    And farewel shrine of which the saint is oute!'

110   *Go, Little Book*

GO, litel book, go, litel myn tragèdy,
    Ther God thy makere yet, er that he die,
So sendè might to make in some comèdy!
  But litel book, no making thou n'envìe,
  But subgit be to allè poësie;   **5**
    And kiss the steppès where as thou seest pace
    Virgìle, Ovìde, Omèr, Lucàn, and Stace.

111   *O Yonge Freshe Folkes*

O YONGÈ freshè folkès, he or she,
    In which that love up groweth with youre age,
Repaireth home fro worldly vanité,
  And of youre herte up casteth the visàge

109. 18 lisse: joy   19 sin . . . bet: since I can do no better   **20**
dorste . . .: if I dared in spite of this crowd

110. 2 f. May God yet send your author, before he dies, the power to write
a poem on some happy theme!   4 no . . .: do not try to rival any poem
5 subgit be: pay homage to   6 where . . .: where you see pass
7 Omer: Homer   Stace: Statius

111. 1 freshe: lively   2 which that: whom   3 Repaireth: return
4 and lift up the countenance of your heart

To th'ilkė God that after His imàge   5
    You made, and thinketh al n'is but a faire
This world, that passeth soone as flowrės faire.

And loveth Him, the which that right for love
    Upon a crois, oure soulės for to beye,
First starf, and rose, and sit in hevene above;   10
    For He n'il falsen no wight, dare I seye,
    That wil his herte al holly on Him leye.
        And sin He best to love is, and most meeke,
        What needeth feinede lovės for to seeke?

Lo here, of payens cursėd oldė rites!   15
    Lo here, what alle her goddės may availle!
Lo here, these wreched worldės appetites!
    Lo here, the fin and guerdoun for travàille
Of Jove, Appollo, of Mars, of swich rascaille!
        Lo here, the forme of oldė clerkės speche   20
        In poetrie, if ye her bookės seche!

O moral Gower, this book I directe
    To thee, and to thee, philosophical Strode,
To vouchen sauf, ther nede is, to correcte,
    Of youre benignités and zelės gode.   25
        And to that soothfast Crist, that starf on rode,
        With al myn herte, of mercy evere I praye,
        And to the Lord right thus I speke and saye:

6 f. thinketh . . . world: consider all this world is but a fair (*i.e.* short-
lived)   8 loveth: love   9 crois: cross   beye: redeem   10
starf: died   sit: sits   11 n'il . . . wight: will not fail anyone
12 wil: is willing to   holly: wholly   13 sin: since   meeke:
gracious   14 what need is there to seek feigned loves   15 payens:
pagans   16 her: their   18 fin: result   19 rascaille: rabble
20 forme: style   clerkes: writers   21 seche: search   24 f. so
that you may graciously correct it where necessary, out of your kindness
and devotion   26 rode: the cross   27 of: for

Thou one, and two, and three, eterne on live,
　　That regnest ay in three, and two, and one,　　30
Uncircumscript, and al mayst circumscrive,
　　Us from visible and invisible fone
　　Defende, and to thy mercy, everichone,
　　　So make us, Jesus, for thy mercy digne,
　　　For love of maide and moder thyn benigne!　　35

112 *The Prioress*

THER was also a Nonne, a Prioresse,
　　That of hir smiling was ful simple and coy;
Hire gretteste oth was but by saint Loy;
And she was cleped Madame Eglentine.
Ful wel she sang the service divine,　　　　　　5
Entuned in hir nose ful semely;
And Frensh she spak ful faire and fetisly
After the scole of Stratford-atte-Bowe—
For Frensh of Paris was to hir unknowe.
At mete wel y-taught was she with-alle:　　　　10
She let no morsel from hir lippes falle,
Ne wette hir fingres in hir sauce depe;
Wel coude she carie a morsel and wel kepe
That no drope ne fille upon hir brest.

111. 29 eterne . . .: ever-living　　　31 uncircumscribed, and canst
circumscribe all　　　32 fone: foes　　　33 f. and . . .: and, Jesus, in thy
mercy, make every one of us worthy of thy mercy

112. 2 of: in　coy: demure, well-bred　　　3 gretteste: coarsest　Loy:
Eligius　　　4 cleped: called　　　6 Entuned: intoned　　　7 fetisly:
elegantly　　　8 Stratford . . .: *i.e.* the nunnery of St. Leonard's, Brom-
ley, near Stratford le Bow　　　12 depe: deeply　　　13 coude: knew
how to　kepe: take care　　　14 fille: fell

In curteisie was set ful muchel hir lest: 15
Hir over-lippė wipėd she so clene
That in hir cuppe ther was no ferthing sene
Of grecė, when she dronken hadde hir draughte.
Ful semėly after hir mete she raughte.
And sikerly she was of greet desport,   20
And ful plesàunt, and amiable of port,
And peinėd hir to countrefetė chere
Of court, and been estatlich of manère,
And to been holden digne of reverence.
But, for to speken of hir conscience,   25
She was so charitable and so pitòus
She woldė wepe if that she saugh a mous
Caught in a trappe, if it were deed or bledde.
Of smalė houndės hadde she that she fedde
With rosted flesh, or milk and wastel-breed;   30
But sore wepte she if one of hem were deed,
Or if men smote it with a yerdė smerte;
And al was conscience and tendrė herte.
Ful semėly hir wimpel pinchėd was;
Hir nosė tretis, hir eyèn greye as glas,   35
Hir mouth ful smal, and therto softe and reed;
But sikerly she hadde a fair forhèed!
It was almost a spannė brod, I trowe;
For, hardily, she was not undergrowe.
Ful fetis was hir cloke, as I was war.   40

---

15 lest: mind   17 ferthing: smallest spot   18 grece: grease
19 most becomingly she reached for her food   20 sikerly: certainly
desport: gaiety   22 and she took pains to imitate the manners
23 estatlich: dignified   24 digne: worthy   25 conscience:
sensibility   26 she was so kind and so tender-hearted   27 saugh:
saw   29 Of: *i.e.* some   houndes: dogs   30 wastel-breed: fine
white bread   32 yerde: stick   smerte: sharply   34 pinched:
pleated   35 tretis: shapely   39 hardily: certainly   40 fetis:
elegant   was war: observed

Of smal coràl aboute hir arm she bar
A peire of bedès, gauded al with grene,
And theron heng a brooch of gold ful shene,
On which ther was first writ a crownèd A,
And after *Amor vincit omnia*.   45

113   *The Clerk of Oxford*

A CLERK ther was of Oxenford alsò
   That unto logik haddè longe y-go;
As leenè was his hors as is a rake,
And he n'as not right fat, I undertake,
But lookèd holwe and therto sobrely.   5
Ful thredbare was his overeste courtèpy,
For he hadde geten him yet no benefice
Ne was so worldly for to have offìce;
For him was levere have at his beddes heed
Twènty bookès clad in blak or reed   10
Of Aristotle and his philosophie
Than robès riche, or fithele or gay sautrie.
But al be that he was a philosòphre
Yèt hadde he but litel gold in cofre!
But al that he mighte of his frendès hente   15
On bookès and on lerninge he it spente,
And bisily gan for the soulès praye

112. 42 a rosary, with green beads as gauds (*i.e.* the large beads)   43
heng: hung   shene: beautiful   44 crowned: with crown above
45 *cf.* Virgil, Eclog. X. 69

113. 1 Clerk: scholar   5 sobrely: serious   6 overeste courtepy:
outermost jacket   7 geten him: got for himself   8 for . . .: as to
have secular employment   9 him was levere: he would rather
10 clad: bound   12 fithele: fiddle   sautrie: psaltery   13 al be
that: although   philosophre: philosopher (*also* alchemist)   15 hente:
get   17 bisily: fervently

Of hem that yaf him wherwith to scolaye;
Of studie took he most cure and most heede.
Nought o word spak he morė than was neede,   20
And that was said in forme and reverence
And short and quik and ful of hy sentènce;
Sowninge in moral vertu was his speche,
And gladly wolde he lerne and gladly teche.

114   *The Wife of Bath*

A GOOD Wif was ther of bisidė Bathe,
    But she was somdel deef, and that was scathe.
Of cloth-making she haddė swich an' haunt
She passėd hem of Yprès and of Gaunt.
In al the parishe wif ne was ther non   5
That to the offringe bifore hir sholdė gon;
And if ther dide, certàin so wroth was she
That she was out of allė charitee.
Hir coverchiefs ful finė were of ground;
I dorstė swere they weyèden ten pound   10
That on a Sonday weren upon hir heed!
Hir hosen werèn of fin scarlet reed,
Ful straite y-teyd, and shoes ful moiste and newe.

---

113. 18 hem: them   yaf: gave   scolaye: study   19 his studies
were his greatest interest and concern   20 o: one   21 in . . .:
with propriety and deference   22 quik: acute   hy sentence: deep
significance   23 Sowninge in: inclining to

114. 1 of biside: from near   2 somdel deef: rather deaf   scathe:
a pity   3 swich . . .: such skill   4 passed hem: surpassed them
Gaunt: Ghent   9 coverchiefs: head-dresses   ground: texture
12 scarlet: material   13 straite y-teyd: tightly laced   moiste: ?
supple

Bold was hir face, and fair, and reed of hewe.
She was a worthy womman al hir live;   15
Housbondes at chirchė-dore she haddė five,
Withouten other compaignye in youthe—
But therof nedeth not to speke as nowthe.
And thriës hadde she been at Jèrusalem;
She haddė passėd many a straungė strem;   20
At Rome she haddė been, and at Boloigne,
In Galice at Saint Jame, and at Coloigne:
She coudė muchel of wandringe by the waye.
Gat-toothėd was she, soothly for to saye.
Upon an amblere esily she sat,   25
Y-wimpled wel, and on hir heed an hat
As brod as is a bokeler or a targe;
A foot-mantel aboute hir hipės large,
And on hir feet a paire of sporès sharpe.
In felaweship wel coude she laughe and carpe.   30
Of Remedies of Love she knew perchaunce,
For she coude of that art the oldė daunce.

115   *The Wife's Fifth Husband*

'WHAT sholde I saye? but, at the monthės ende,
    This joly clerk Jankin, that was so hende,
Hath wedded me with grete solempnitee;
And to him yaf I al the land and fee

114. 17 Withouten: apart from   18 but there is no need to speak of
that now   20 many . . .: many distant waters   21 Boulogne
23 coude: knew   24 Gat-toothed: gap-toothed   28 foot-mantel:
wrap from waist to feet   30 felaweship: company   carpe: chatter
31 *cf.* Ovid's *Remedia Amoris*   perchaunce: doubtless   32 the olde
daunce: all the tricks

115. 2 hende: pleasant   4 yaf: gave   fee: possessions

That evere was me yeven ther-before.   5
But afterward repented me ful sore!
He n'oldė suffrė nothing of my list;
By God! he smote me onės on the list—
For that I rente out of his book a leef—
That of the stroke myn erė wax al deef.   10
Stibourn I was as is a leonesse,
And of my tonge a verray jangleresse,
And walke I wolde as I had doon beforn
From hous to hous, although he had it sworn;
For which he oftentimės woldė preche   15
And me of oldė Romain gestės teche:
How he Simplicius Gallus lefte his wif
And hir forsook for terme of al his lif,
Nought but for open-heveded he hir say
Looking out at his dore upon a day.   20
    Another Romain tolde he me by name
That, for his wif was at a someres game
Withoute his witing, he forsook hir eke.
And then wolde he upon his Bible seke
That ilkė proverbe of Ecclesiaste   25
Where he comandeth and forbedeth faste
Man shal not suffre his wif go roule aboute.
Then wolde he saye right thus, withouten doute:
"Whoso that buildeth his hous al of salwes
And priketh his blindė hors over the falwes   30

5 me yeven: given to me   6 repented me: I regretted it   7
he would not allow any of my pleasures   8 ones: once   list: ear
9 For that: because   10 of: from   wax: became   11 Stibourn:
stubborn   12 and with my tongue a real prattler   14 although . . .:
even though he had sworn (I should not)   16 gestes: stories   19
only because he saw her bare-headed   22 for: because   23
witing: knowing   25 Ecclesiasticus 25: 25   26 faste: strictly
27 roule: roll   29 salwes: willows   30 priketh: rides   falwes:
ploughed fields

And suffreth his wif to go seeken halwes
Is worthy to been hanged on the galwes."
But al for nought—I settė nought an hawe
Of his provèrbės n'of his oldė sawe,
Ne I woldė not of him corrected be: 35
I hate him that my vices telleth me,
And so do mo, God wot, of us than I.
This made him with me wood al outrely:
I n'oldė nought forbere him in no cas.

    Now wil I say you sooth, by Saint Thomàs,   40
Why that I rente out of his book a leef,
For which he smote me so that I was deef.

    He had a book that gladly, night and day,
For his disport he woldė rede alway;
He cleped it Valerie and Theofraste,   45
At which book he lough alway ful faste.
And eke ther was somtime a clerk at Rome,
A cardinal, that hightė Saint Jerome,
That made a book again Jovinian;
In which book eke ther was Tertulan,   50
Crisippus, *Trotula*, and Helowis
That was abbèssė not fer fro Parìs;
And eke the Parables of Salomon,
Ovìdės "Art", and bookės many on,
And allė these were bounden in o volùme.   55

31 halwes: saints' shrines   33 sette . . .: did not care a haw
34 Of: for   35 of: by   37 mo: more   38 wood . . .:
utterly furious   39 forbere: defer to   45 cleped: called
Valerie: Walter Map's *Epistola Valerii ad Rufinum de non Ducenda Uxore*
Theofraste: Theophrastus, *Liber de Nuptiis*   46 lough: laughed
faste: much   48 highte: was called   49 again: against   50
Tertullian   51 Chrysippus (mentioned by Jerome)   *Trotula*: *i.e.*
medical work compiled by Trottus, a doctor of Salerno   Heloise   52
fer: far   54 Ovid's *Art of Love*, and many (other) books   55 o:
one

And every night and day was his custùme,
When he had leiser and vacacioun
From other worldly occupacioun,
To reden on this book of wikked wives.
He knew of hem mo legendès and lives   60
Than been of goodè wivès in the Bible.
For trusteth wel, it is an impossìble
That any clerk wil spekè good of wives,
But if it be of holy saintès lives,
Ne of none other womman never the mo.   65
Who painted the leòn, tel me who?
By God! if wommen haddè writen stories,
As clerkès han withinne her oratories,
They wolde han writen of men more wikkednesse
Than al the mark of Adam may redresse.   70
The children of Mercùrie and Venùs
Been in her werking ful contrarius:
Mercùrie loveth wisdom and sciènce,
And Venus loveth riot and dispence;
And for her diverse disposicioun   75
Ech falleth in otheres exaltacioun;
And thus, God wot, Mercùrie is desolat
In Pisces, wher Venùs is èxaltat;
And Venus falleth ther Mercùrie is raised.
Therfore no womman of no clerk is praised.   80
The clerk, when he is old and may nought do

57 vacacioun: freedom   59 reden on: read   wives: women
60 hem: them   mo: more   62 For believe (me), it is an impossibility
64 But if: unless   65 never the mo: *i.e.* at all   66 painted:
depicted (*i.e.* in Æsop's fable of the Man and the Lion)   68 han: have
her: their   70 the mark of Adam: *i.e.* males   72 her: their
73 science: learning   74 dispence: extravagance   75 for her:
because of their   76 each is 'dejected' (*i.e.* exerts least influence) in
the 'exaltation' (*i.e.* time of greatest influence) of the other   77 deso-
lat: 'dejected'   80 of: by

Of Venus werkes worth his olde sho,
Then sit he down and writ in his dotàge
That wommen can not kepe her mariàge!
   But now to purpos, why I tolde thee   85
That I was beten for a book, pardee!
Upon a night Jankin, that was our sire,
Redde on his book, as he sat by the fire,
Of Eva first, that for hir wikkednesse
Was al mankinde brought to wrechednesse;   90
For which that Jesu Crist Himself was slain,
That boughte us with His herte-blood again.
Lo, here expres of wimmen may ye finde
That womman was the los of al mankinde.
   Tho redde he me how Sampson loste his heres: 95
Sleeping, his lemman kitte it with hir sheres,
Thùrgh which tresoun loste he bothe his eyen.
   Tho redde he me (if that I shal not lyen)
Of Hercules and of his Dianyre,
That caused him to sette himself afire.   100
   Nothing forgat he the sorwe and the wo
That Socrates had with his wivès two:
How Xantippa caste pisse upon his heed.
This sely man sat stille as he were deed;
He wiped his heed, namore dorste he sayn   105
But "er that thonder stinte comth a rain".
   Of Phasipha, that was the queene of Crete,
For shrewednesse, him thoughte the tale swete;

82 *i.e.* any good as a lover   83 sit: sits   writ: writes   84 her:
their   85 to purpos: (to come) to the point   86 pardee: by God
87 sire: husband   89 that for hir: on account of whose   92 boughte
again: redeemed   93 expres . . .: you can find it explicitly stated
of women   94 los: ruin   95 Tho: then   heres: hair   96
lemman: sweetheart   kitte: cut   99 Deianira   104 sely:
innocent   106 stinte: stops   107 Pasiphae   108
shrewednesse: wickedness   him thoughte: seemed to him

Fy! spek namore—it is a grisly thing—
Of hir horrible lust and hir liking.   110
    Of Clitermystra, for hir lecherye
That falsly made hir housband for to dye—
He redde it with ful good devocioun.
    He tolde me eke for what occasioun
Amphiorax at Thebès loste his lif: 115
Myn housband had a legende of his wif
Eriphilem, that for an ouche of gold
Hath privily unto the Grekès told
Wher that hir housband hidde him in a place,
For which he had at Thebès sory grace.   120
    Of Livia tolde he me, and of Lucye:
They bothè made her housbandes for to dye—
That one for love, that other was for hate.
Livia hir housband, on an even late,
Empoisoned hath, for that she was his fo;   125
Lucia likerous loved hir housband so
That, for he sholde alway upon hir thinke,
She yaf him swich a maner lovè-drinke
That he was deed er it were by the morwe.
And thus algatès housbandès han sorwe.   130
    Then tolde he me how one Latumius
Complained unto his felawe Arrius
That in his gardin growèd swich a tree
On which he saide how that his wivès three
Hangèd hemself for hertès despitus.   135

111 Clytemnestra   113 ful . . .: great relish   115 Amphiaraus
117 Eriphyle   ouche: necklace   120 sory grace: a wretched fate
121 Livia, wife of Drusus   Lucilia, wife of Lucretius   123 That: the
125 for that: because   126 likerous: wanton   127 for: so that
128 yaf: gave   swich a maner: of such a kind   129 er . . .: before
the next morning   130 algates: in every way   han: have   135
for . . .: because of their spiteful hearts

"O leevė brother", quod this Arrius,
"Yif me a plante of th'ilkė blissėd tree,
And in my gardin planted it shal be."
  Of latter date of wivės hath he red
That some han slain her housbandes in her bed,   140
And lete hir lechour dighte hir al the night,
When that the corps lay in the floor upright.
And some han drivė nailės in her brain
Whil that they slepte, and thus they han hem slain.
Some han hem yevė poisoun in her drinke.   145
He spak more harm than hertė may bethinke;
And therwithal he knew of mo provèrbes
Than in this world ther growėn gras or herbes:
"Bet is", quod he, "thyn habitacioun
Be with a leoun or a foul dragòun   150
Than with a womman using for to chide."
"Bet is", quod he, "hye in the roof abide
Than with an angry wif down in the hous;
They been so wikked and contrarious,
They haten that her housbandes loveth ay."   155
He saide "a womman cast hir shame away
When she cast of hir smok"; and forthermo,
"A fair womman, but she be chast alsò,
Is like a gold ring in a sowės nose."
Who woldė wene or who woldė suppose   160
The wo that in myn hertė was, and pine?
  And when I saugh he woldė nevere fine

---

136 leeve: dear   quod: said   137 plante: cutting   blissed:
blessed   141 dighte: lie with   142 in . . .: flat on the floor
146 bethinke: conceive   147 mo: more   148 herbes: plants
149 Bet is: it is better   150 leoun: lion   151 using . . .: always chiding
155 that: what   156 cast: casts   157 of: off   forthermo:
furthermore   158 but: unless   160 wene: imagine   161
pine: suffering   162 saugh: saw   fine: cease

To reden on this cursed book al night,
Al sodeinly three levès have I plight
Out of his book, right as he redde, and eke   165
I with my fist so took him on the cheke
That in our fyr he fil bakward a-down.
And he up stirte as doth a wood leòun,
And with his fist he smote me on the heed,
That in the floor I lay as I were deed.   170
And when he saugh how stillè that I lay,
He was agast and wolde han fled his way,
Til attè laste out of my swough I braide.
"O! hast thou slain me, falsè theef?" I saide,
"And for my land thus hast thou mordred me?   175
Er I be deed, yet wil I kissè thee."
    And neer he cam, and knelèd faire a-down,
And saidè: "Deerè sister Alisoun,
As help me God, I shal thee nevere smite.
That I have done, it is thyself to wite;   180
Foryeve it me, and that I thee beseke!"
And yet eftsoones I hitte him on the cheke,
And saidè "Theef! thus muchel am I wreke;
Now wil I die, I may no lenger speke."
But attè laste, with muchel care and wo,   185
We fille acorded by us selven two:
He yaf me al the bridel in myn hand,
To han the governaunce of hous and land,
And of his tonge and of his hand alsò;

---

164 plight: plucked   166 took: hit   167 fil: fell   168 stirte:
jun·ped   wood: raging   173 swough: swoon   braide: came to
177 neer: nearer   180 for what I have done you are yourself to
blame   181 Foryeve: forgive   beseke: beseech   182 eftsoones:
immediately after   183 wreke: avenged   184 lenger: longer
185 care: sorrow   186 we were reconciled, between the two of us
188 governaunce: control

And made him brenne his book anon right tho.   190
And when that I had geten unto me,
By maistrye, al the soverainetee,
And that he saide "myn owne trewe wif,
Do as thee lust the terme of al thy lif,
Keep thyn honòur and keep eke myn estate"—   195
After that day we hadden nevere debate.
God help me so, I was to him as kinde
As any wif from Denmark unto Inde,
And also trewe, and so was he to me.
I pray to God, that sit in magestee,   200
So blesse his soule for His mercy deere.
   Now wil I say my tale, if ye wil heere.'

Beholde the wordes betwene the Somnour and the Frere

   The Frere lough when he had herd al this:
'Now dame', quod he, 'so have I joye or blis,
This is a long preamble of a tale!'   205
And when the Somnour herde the Frere gale,
'Lo,' quod the Somnour, 'Goddes armes two!
A frere wil entremette him everemo.
Lo, goode men, a flye and eke a frere
Wil falle in every dish and eke matère.   210
What spekest thou of preambulacioun?
What! amble or trotte or pees or go sit down!
Thou lettest our disport in this manère.'

'Ye, wilt thou so, sir Somnour?' quod the Frere,
'Now, by my faith, I shal, er that I go,   215
Telle of a Somnour swich a tale or two
That al the folk shal laughen in this place.'
  'Now ellès, Frerè, I beshrewe thy face',
Quod this Somnour, 'and I beshrewè me,
But if I tellè talès two or three   220
Of frerès, er I come to Sidingborne,
That I shal make thyn hertè for to morne—
For wel I wot thy pacience is gon'.
  Our Hostè cridè 'Pees! and that anon!'
And saidè, 'Let the womman telle hir tale.   225
Ye fare as folk that drunken been of ale.
Do, dame, telle forth your tale, and that is best.'
  'Al redy, sire,' quod she, 'right as you lest,
If I have licence of this worthy Frere.'
  'Yis, dame,' quod he, 'tel forth, and I wil heere.'   230

116   *The Reeve*

THE Revè was a slendrè colerik man;
    His berd was shave as ny as ever he can,
His heer was by his eres ful round y-shorn,
His top was dokkèd lyk a preest biforn;
Ful longè were his leggès and ful leene,   5
Y-lyk a staf, ther was no calf y-seene.
Wel coude he kepe a gerner and a binne—

115. 214 Ye: indeed   218 elles: otherwise   beshrewe: curse
220 But if: unless   221 Sittingbourne   224 Pees: be silent
anon: at once   226 fare: behave   228 lest: please

116. 1 Reve: estate manager and account keeper   2 ny: close
3 heer: hair   4 the hair on his crown was cut short in front like a
priest   7 He well knew how to manage a granary and a bin (for grain)

Ther was non auditour coude of him winne;
Wel wiste he by the droughte and by the rain
The yeeldinge of his seed and of his grain.   10
His lordès sheep, his neet, his dayèrye,
His swin, his hors, his stor, and his pultrỳe
Was hoolly in this Revès governing;
And by his covenant yaf the rekening
Sin that his lord was twenty yeer of age.   15
There coude no man bringe him in àrrerage.
Ther n'as baillif ne hierde nor other hine
That he ne knew his sleighte and his covine:
They were adrad of him as of the deeth!
His woning was ful faire upon an heeth;   20
With grenè treès shadwed was his place.
He coudè bettre than his lord purchàse;
Ful riche he was astorèd prively:
His lord wel coude he plesen subtilly,
To yeve and lene him of his owenè good   25
And have a thank and yet a cote and hood.
In youthe he haddè lerned a good mistèr:
He was a wel good wrighte, a carpenter.
This Revè sat upon a ful good stot
That was al pomely-grey and hightè Scot.   30
A long surcote of pers upon he hade,
And by his side he bar a rusty blade.

---

8 coude . . .: who knew how to get the better of him   9 wiste:
knew   11 neet: cattle   12 stor: stock   13 hoolly: wholly
14 yaf: he gave   15 Sin that: since   16 nobody could make him
short in his accounts   17 hierde: herdsman   hine: servant   18
whose trickery and deceit he did not know   19 adrad: afraid
deeth: Plague   20 woning: dwelling   22 purchase: get rich
23 he was very richly provided secretly   24 subtilly: craftily
25 give or lend him what was rightfully his (the lord's)   26 yet: as
well   27 mister: trade   29 stot: horse   30 pomely: dappled
highte: was called   31 he wore a long outer coat of Persian blue

Of Northfolk was this Reve of which I telle,
Biside a town men clepen Baldéswelle.
Tukkéd he was as is a frere aboute,   35
And evere he rode the hindreste of oure route.

117   *The Mill at Trumpington*

A T Trumpingtoun, not fer fro Cantébrigge,
       Ther goth a brook, and over that a brigge,
Upon the whiché brook ther stant a melle,
And—this is verray sooth that I you telle—
A millere was ther dwelling many a day.   5
As any pecok he was proud and gay;
Pipen he coude, and fishe, and nettés beete,
And turné cuppés, and wel wrastle and sheete;
And by his belt he bar a long panade,
And of a swerd ful trenchant was the blade.   10
A joly poppere bar he in his pouche—
Ther was no man for peril dorste him touche—
A Sheffeld thwitel bar he in his hose.
Round was his face and camuse was his nose;
As piléd as an apé was his skulle.   15
He was a market-betere atté fulle:
Ther dorsté no wight hand upon him legge
That he ne swor he sholde anon abegge.

116. 34 near a village they call Bawdeswell   35 he was girdled like a
friar   36 hindreste: rearmost   route: company

117. 1 fer . . .: far from Cambridge   3 stant: stands   melle: mill
4 verray sooth: the real truth   7 beete: mend   8 and turn
(wooden) cups, and wrestle well and shoot (with the bow)   9 bar:
carried   panade: cutlass   10 a: *i.e.* his   11 poppere: dagger
13 thwitel: knife   14 camuse: snub   15 piled: ?bristly
16–18 he was a constant trouble-maker at markets: nobody dared lay a
hand upon him without him swearing instant reprisal

A theef he was forsoothe of corn and mele,
And that a sly, and usaunt for to stele.   20
His name was hote 'deynous Simekin'.
A wif he hadde, y-comen of noble kin:
The person of the town hir fader was.
With hir he yaf ful many a panne of bras
For that Simkin sholde in his blood allye.   25
She was y-fostred in a nonnerye;
For Simkin wolde no wif, as he saide,
But she were wel y-norissed and a maide,
To saven his estaat of yomanrye.
And she was proud and pert as is a pye.   30
A ful fair sighte was it upon hem two:
On halydayes biforn hir wolde he go
With his tipet bounde aboute his heed,
And she cam after in a gyte of reed,
And Simekin hadde hosen of the same—   35
Ther dorste no wight clepen hir but 'dame'.
Was non so hardy that wente by the waye
That with hir dorste rage or ones playe,
But if he wolde be slayn of Simekin
With panade or with knif or boidekin;   40
For jalous folk been perilous everemo—
Algate they wolde her wives wenden so!

20 usaunt . . .: in the habit of stealing   21 hote: called
deynous: scornful   23 person: parson   town: village   24 f.
the parson gave many brass pans with her so that Simkin should marry her
28 But: unless   y-norissed: brought up   29 to keep up his position as
a yeoman   30 pye: magpie   31 upon hem two: to see these two
33 his tipet: pendant from his hood   34 gyte: mantle   36 nobody
dared call her anything but 'madam'.   37–9 nobody passing by the
way was so bold as to dare make love to her or make a single pass at her,
unless he wanted to be killed by Simkin   40 boidekin: dagger
41 everemo: always   42 at least they would like their wives to
think so

And eek, for she was somdel smoterlich,
She was as digne as water in a dich,
And ful of hoker and of bisèmare.   45
Hir thoughtè that a lady sholde hir spare,
What for hir kinrede and hir nortelrye
That she hadde lernèd in the nonnerye.

A doughter haddè they bitwixe hem two
Of twenty yeer, withouten any mo   50
Savinge a child that was of half yeer age;
In cradel it lay and was a proprè page.
This wenchè thikke and wel y-growèn was,
With camuse nose and eyèn greye as glas,
Buttokès brode, and brestès rounde and hye;   55
But right fair was hir heer—I wil not lye.

This person of the town, for she was feir,
In purpos was to maken hir his heir
Bothe of his catel and his mesuàge,
And straunge he made it of hir mariàge.   60
His purpos was for to bestowe hir hye
Into som worthy blood of auncetrye—
For holy chirches good mot been despended
On holy chirches blood that is descended—
Therfore he wolde his holy blood honòure,   65
Though that he holy chirchè sholde devoure.

43 f. and also, because of her somewhat disreputable origin, she put
on airs and was as offensive as foul ditch-water   45 hoker: scorn
bisemare: disdain   46 it seemed to her that a lady should ?keep her-
self apart   47 kinrede: birth   nortelrye: education   49 hem two:
the two of them   50 withouten any mo: and no more (children)
52 propre page: fine boy   53 thikke: sturdy   56 heer: hair
57 person: parson   for: because   58 In purpos was: intended
59 catel: goods   60 and he made difficulties about her marriage
62 auncetrye: high lineage   63 f. for holy church's riches must be
spent on the blood descended from holy church   66 devoure: con-
sume (the riches of)

Greet sokene hath this millere, out of doute,
With whete and malt of al the land aboute,
And namėliche ther was a greet collègge
Men clepen the Soler Halle at Cantėbregge;   70
Ther was her whete and eek her malt y-grounde.
And on a day it happėd in a stounde
Sik lay the maunciple on a maladye;
Men wenden wisly that he sholdė dye.
For which this millere stal bothe mele and corn   75
An hundred timė morė than biforn;
For ther-biforn he stal but curteisly,
But now he was a theef outrageously;
For which the wardeyn chidde and madė fare,
But therof sette the millere not a tare,   80
And craketh bost and swor it was not so.

Thenne were ther yongė povrė clerkės two
That dwelten in this halle of which I saye;
Testif they were and lusty for to playe,
And, only for her mirthe and reverye,   85
Upon the wardeyn bisily they crye
To yeve hem levė but a litel stounde
To gon to mille and seen her corn y-grounde;
And hardily they dorstė laye her nekke

67 Greet sokene: far-reaching right of milling   out of doute: without
doubt   68 malt: barley   69 nameliche: particularly   70
which they call the Soler Hall (now part of Trinity College)   71 her:
their   72 and one day it happened that at the time   73 on: of
74 people thought he was sure to die   75 stal: stole   77 curteisly:
discreetly   78 outrageously: beyond all bounds   79 f. at which
the warden (of Soler Hall) complained and made a fuss, but the miller
cared nothing (not a tare) for that   81 craketh bost: bluffs   82
clerkes: students   84–6 they were impetuous and eager to enjoy
themselves, and, purely for their fun and amusement, they appeal pressingly
to the warden   87 stounde: time   89 hardily: confidently
laye: pledge

The millere sholde not stele hem half a pekke   90
Of corn by sleightė, ne by force hem reve;
And at the laste the wardeyn yaf hem leve.
John highte that oon and Alayn highte that other;
Of o town were they born, that hightė Strother,
Fer in the north—I can not tellė where.   95
　This Alayn maketh redy al his gere,
And on an hors the sak he caste anon.
Forth goth Alàyn the clerk and also John
With good swerd and with bokeler by her side.
John knew the way—hem nededė no gide—   100
And at the mille the sak adown he layth.
Alàyn spak first: 'Al hail, Simond, i fayth!
How fares thy fairė doughter and thy wif?'
　'Alàyn, welcòme', quod Simkin, 'by my lif!
And John alsò. How now, what do ye heer?'   105
　'Simond,' quod John, 'by God, nede has na peer:
Him boės serve himselve that has na swayn,
Or elles he is a fool, as clerkės sayn.
Oure manciple, I hope he wil be deed,
Swa werkės ay the wangės in his heed;   110
And for-thy is I come, and eek Alàyn,
To grinde oure corn and carye it ham agayn.
I pray you spede us heythen that ye may.'
　'It shal be don', quod Simkin, 'by my fay!
What wil ye don whil that it is in hande?'   115

'By God, right by the hoper wil I stande',
Quod John, 'and see howgates the corn gas in.
Yet saugh I nevere, by my fader kin!
How that the hoper waggès til and fra.'
    Alàyn answèrdè: 'John, and wilt thou swa?   120
Thenne wil I be binethè, by my crown!
And see how that the melé fallès down
Into the trough; that sal be my disport.
For John, i faith, I may been of youre sort:
I is as ille a millere as ar ye.'   125
    This millere smilèd of her nicetee
And thoughte: 'Al this n'is doon but for a wile:
They wenè that no man may hem begile.
But, by my thrift, yet shal I blere her eye
For al the sleighte in her philosophye!   130
The morè queintè crekès that they make,
The morè wil I stelè when I take:
In stede of flour yet wil I yeve hem bren.
"The gretteste clerkès been nought wisest men",
As whilom to the wolf thus spak the mare.   135
Of al her art ne counte I nought a tare.'
    Out at the dore he goth ful prively,
When that he saugh his timè, softèly.
He looketh up and down til he hath founde
The clerkès hors, ther as it stood y-bounde   140
Bihinde the mille under a levèsel,
And to the hors he goth him faire and wel.

117 howgates: how   gas: goes   118 saugh: saw   fader: father's
119 til and fra: to and fro   120 swa: so   123 sal: shall   125
ille: bad   126 of...: at their simplicity   127 wile: ruse   129
by my thrift: *i.e.* indeed   blere her eye: hoodwink them   130
sleighte: wisdom   131 queinte crekes: clever tricks   133 bren:
bran   134 clerkes: scholars   136 All their cleverness isn't worth
a tare, I reckon   140 ther as: where   141 levesel: shady tree
142 goth him: goes

He stripeth off the bridel right anon,
And when the hors was laus, he ginneth gon
Toward the fen ther wildē marēs renne,   145
And forth with 'wehee' thurgh thikke and thurgh
    thenne.
    This millere goth again, no word he sayde,
But doth his note, and with the clerkes playde
Til that her corn was faire and wel y-grounde.
And when the mele is sakkēd and y-bounde   150
This John goth out and fint his hors away,
And gan to crye 'harrow!' and 'waylaway!
Oure hors is lost! Alàyn, for Goddēs banes,
Step on thy feet! Com off, man, al at anes!
Allas! oure wardeyn has his palfrey lorn.'   155
This Alayn al forgat bothe mele and corn;
Al was out of his minde his housbondrye.
'What! whilk way is he gaan?' he gan to crye.
    The wif cam lepinge inward with a ren.
She sayde: 'Allas! youre hors goth to the fen   160
With wildē mares, as faste as he may go.
Unthank come on his hand that bond him so,
And he that bettrē sholde han knit the reine!'
    'Allas!', quod John, 'Alàyn, for Cristēs peine,
Lay down thy swerd, and I wil myn alswa.   165
I is ful wight, God waat, as is a raa;
By Goddēs herte, he sal not scape us bathe!

---

143 right anon: straightaway   144 laus: loose   ginneth gon:
sets off   145 ther: where   renne: run   146 thenne: thin
147 again: back   148 note: job   playde: joked   151 fint: finds
152 waylaway: alas   153 banes: bones   154 Com . . .: Come on,
man, at once!   155 lorn: lost   158 whilk: which   gaan: gone
gan . . .: cried   159 inward . . .: in at a run   162 Unthank: a
curse   bond: tied   163 han knit: have tied   165 alswa: also
166 I'm very fast, God knows, like a roe   167 bathe: both

Why n'ad thou pit the capul in the lathe?
Il hail! By God, Alàyn, thou is a fonne!'
 These sely clerkės han ful faste y-ronne   170
Toward the fen, bothe Alayn and eek John.
 And when the millere saugh that they were gon
He half a bushel of her flour hath take,
And bad his wif go knede it in a cake.
He sayde: 'I trowe the clerkės were aferd.   175
Yet can a millere make a clerkės berd,
For al his art! Now let hem gon her waye!
Lo wher they gon! Ye, let the children playe!
They gete him not so lightly, by my crown!'
 These sely clerkės rennen up and down   180
With 'keep! keep! stand! stand! jossa! warderere!
Ga, whistle thou, and I sal keep him here.'
But shortly, til that it was verray night,
They coudė not, though they do al her might,
Her capul cacche—he ran alway so faste—   185
Til in a dich they caughte him attė laste.
 Wery and weet as beest is in the rayn
Comth sely John, and with him comth Alàyn.
'Allas', quod John, 'the day that I was born!
Now are we drive til hething and til scorn.   190
Oure corn is stoln: me wil us foolės calle,
Bathė the wardeyn and oure felawes alle,
And namėly the millere, waylaway!'
 Thus plaineth John as he goth by the way

168 Why didn't you put the horse in the barn?   169 Il hail: What
a disaster!   fonne: fool   170 sely: poor   175 aferd: on their
guard   176 make . . .: outwit a student   178 Ye: well   179
gete . . . lightly: won't catch him so easily   181 keep: look out
jossa: down here   warderere: watch behind you   182 Ga: go
keep: watch for   183 verray night: quite dark   187 weet: wet
190 now we've been made a laughing-stock and butt   191 me: they
(*lit.* one)   193 namely: particularly   194 plaineth: laments

Toward the mille, and Bayard in his hand.　　　195
The millere sittinge by the fyr he fand,
For it was night, and forther mighte they nought;
But, for the love of God, they him bisought
Of herberwe and of ese, as for her peny.
　　The millere sayde again: 'If ther be eny,　　　200
Swich as it is, yet shal ye have youre part.
Myn hous is strait, but ye han lernèd art:
Ye konne by argumentès make a place
A milè brod of twenty foot of space.
Let see now if this placè may suffise,　　　205
Or make it roum with speche, as is your gise.'
　　'Now Symond', saydè John, 'by Saint Cutbèrd!
Ay is thou mirie, and this is faire answèrd.
I have herd said "man sal taa of twa thinges:
Slik as he findes or taa slik as he bringes".　　　210
But specially I pray thee, hostè deere,
Get us som mete and drinke and make us cheere,
And we wil payè trewely attè fulle.
"With empty hand men may nane hawkès tulle":
Lo, here oure silver, redy for to spende.'　　　215
　　This millere into town his doughter sende
For ale and breed, and rosted hem a goos,
And bond her hors, it sholdè not gon loos;
And in his owenè chaumbre hem made a bed
With sheetès and with chalons faire y-spred.　　　220

195 Bayard: *i.e.* the horse　　　196 fand: found　　　197 forther . . .:
they could go no further　　　199 for lodging and hospitality for which
they would pay　　　200 again: in reply　　　201 Swich: such　　　202
strait: small　　　203 konne: know how to　　　206 roum: roomy
206 gise: way　　　207 St. Cuthbert　　　208 Ay . . . mirie: you always
have a joke　　　209 f. man . . .: a man must take one of two things:
what he finds or take what he brings (*cf.* no. 311. i)　　　212 make . . .:
entertain us　　　213 atte fulle: in full　　　214 tulle: lure　　　215
silver: money　　　216 sende: sent　　　220 chalons: coverlets

Nought from his owenĕ bed ten foot or twelve
His doughter haddĕ a bed, al by hir selve,
Right in the samĕ chambrĕ by and by—
It mightĕ be no bet, and causĕ why?
Ther was no roumer herberwe in the place.   225
They soupen and they speke, hem to solàce,
And drinken evere strong ale attĕ beste.
Aboutĕ midnight wentĕ they to reste.

118   *Three Revellers Search for Death*

THESE riotòurĕs three, of which I telle,
Longe erst er primĕ rong of any belle,
Were set hem in a tavernĕ to drinke,
And as they sat they herde a bellĕ clinke
Beforn a cors, was caried to his grave.   5
That one of hem gan callen to his knave:
'Go bet', quod he, 'and axĕ redily
What cors is this that passeth heer forby,
And looke that thou reportĕ his namĕ weel.'

    'Sire', quod this boy, 'it nedeth never-a-deel: 10
It was me told er ye cam heer two houres.
He was, pardee, an old felàwe of youres;
And sodeinly he was y-slain to-night,

---

117. 223 by and by: alongside   224 bet: better   225 roumer:
more roomy   227 evere: continually   atte beste: of the best

118. 1 riotoures: revellers   2 long before any bell rang for prime
3 Were set hem: had settled themselves   5 in front of a corpse
which was being carried to its grave   6 f. one of them called to his
servant: 'go at once', said he, 'and quickly ask   8 forby: by   9
reporte: tell (us)   10 it . . .: there is no need at all   12 pardee:
indeed   felawe: companion

Fordronke, as he sat on his bench upright.
Ther cam a privee theef men clepeth Deeth,   15
That in this contree al the peple sleeth,
And with his spere he smote his herte a-two,
And wente his way withouten wordès mo.
He hath a thousand slain this pestilence;
And, maister, er ye come in his presènce,   20
Me thinketh that it werè necessàrie
For to be ware of swich an adversàrie.
Beeth redy for to meete him everemore;
Thus taughtè me my dame—I say namore.'
'By Saintè Marie!' saide this tavernère,   25
'The child saith sooth, for he hath slain this yere,
Henne over a mile, withinne a greet villàge,
Both man and womman, child, and hine, and page;
I trow his habitacioun be there.
To been avisèd greet wisdom it were,   30
Er that he dide a man a dishonòur.'

   'Ye, Goddès armès!' quod this riotòur,
'Is it swich peril with him for to meete?
I shal him seeke by way and eek by streete,
I make avow to Goddès dignè bones!   35
Herkneth, felàwès, we three been al ones;
Let ech of us holde up his hand til other,
And ech of us bicomen otheres brother,
And we wil sleen this falsè traitour Deeth.
He shal be slain, he that so many sleeth,   40
By Goddès dignitee, er it be night!'

14 Fordronke: dead drunk · 15 privee: stealthy   men clepeth: one calls   16 sleeth: slays   17 a-two: in two   18 mo: more   25 tavernere: inn-keeper   26 child: servant   27 Henne over a mile: over a mile from here   28 hine: labourer   page: servant-boy   30 it would be very wise to be forewarned   34 by way . . .: in the highways and by-ways   35 digne: glorious   36 al ones: of one mind   37 til other: to the others   39 sleen: slay

Togidres han these three her trouthes plight
To live and dyen ech of hem for other,
As though he were his owene y-boren brother.
And up they stirte, al dronken, in this rage,   45
And forth they gon towardes that villàge
Of which the taverner hadde spoke beforn;
And many a grisly oth thenne han they sworn,
And Cristes blessed body they to-rente:
Deeth shal be deed, if that they may him hente!   50
    When they han gon not fully half a mile,
Right as they wolde han troden over a stile,
An old man and a povre with hem mette.
This olde man ful mekely hem grette,
And saide thus: 'Now, lordes, God you see!'   55
The proudeste of these riotoures three
Answerde again: 'What, carl, with sory grace!
Why art thou al forwrapped save thy face?
Why livest thou so longe in so greet age?'
    This olde man gan looke in his visàge,   60
And saide thus: 'For I ne can not finde
A man, though that I walked into Inde,
Neither in citee nor in no villàge,
That wolde chaunge his youthe for myn age;
And therfore mot I han myn age stille,   65
As longe time as it is Goddes wille.
Ne Deeth, allas, ne wil not han my lyf!
Thus walke I lyk a resteless caitìf,

42 Togidres: together   han: have   her: their   44 y-boren:
born   45 stirte: jumped   rage: mad mood   49 to-rente:
dismembered (in their oaths)   50 hente: catch   52 Right ...
troden: just as they were about to step   53 povre: poor   54
grette: greeted   55 God ...: God watch over you   57 again:
back   with ...: curse you!   58 forwrapped: wrapped up   61
For: because   62 Inde: India   65 mot: must   68 caitif:
captive

And on the ground, which is my modres gate,
I knokkė with my staf, bothe erly and late,   70
And sayė "Leevė moder, let me in!
Lo how I vanishe, flesh, and blood, and skin!
Allas! when shul my bonės been at reste?
Moder, with you wolde I chaunge my cheste
That in my chambre longė time hath be,   75
Ye, for an hairė-clout to wrappė me!"
But yet to me she wil not do that grace,
For which ful pale and welkėd is my face.

   But, sires, to you it is no curteisye
To speken to an old man vileinye,   80
But he trespàsse in word or elles in dede.
In Holy Writ ye may yourself wel rede:
"Agains an old man, hor upon his heed,
Ye sholde arise"; wherfore I yeve you reed,
Ne doth unto an old man non harm now,   85
Namore than that ye wolde men did to yow
In agė, if that ye so longe abide.
And God be with you, where ye go or ride!
I mot go thider as I have to go.'

   'Nay, oldė cherl, by God, thou shalt not so!'   90
Saidė this other hasardour anon;
'Thou partest not so lightly, by Saint John!
Thou spak right now of th'ilkė traitour Deeth
That in this contree alle oure frendės sleeth.

---

69 modres: mother's   71 Leeve: dear   72 vanishe: waste
away   74 chaunge . . .: exchange my chest of clothes   76 yes,
for a hair-cloth to wrap round me   77 grace: favour   78
welked: shrunken   79 to: in   80 vileinye: rudeness (*i.e.* rudely)
81 unless he offends in word or else in deed   83 Agains: in the pre-
sence of   hor: grey   84 yeve you reed: give you advice   85 Ne
doth: do not do   88 where . . .: wherever you walk or ride   89
I . . . as: I must go where   91 hasardour: player at dice   anon: at
once   92 lightly: quickly

Have heer my trouthe, as thou art his espye,   95
Telle where he is, or thou shalt it abye,
By God and by the holy sacrement!
For soothly thou art one of his assent
To sleen us yongė folk, thou falsė theef!'
   'Now, sires', quod he, 'if that you be so leef   100
To findė Deeth, turne up this croked way;
For in that grove I lefte him, by my fay,
Under a tree, and there he wil abide;
Nought for youre bost he wil him nothing hide.
See ye that ok? Right there ye shal him finde.   105
God savė you, that boughte again mankinde,
And you amende!' Thus saide this oldė man.
And everich of these riotòurės ran
Til he cam to that tree, and ther they founde
Of florins fine of gold y-coinėd rounde   110
Wel ny an eightė bushels, as hem thoughte.
No lenger thennė after Deeth they soughte,
But ech of hem so glad was of that sighte,
For that the florins been so faire and brighte,
That down they sette hem by this precious hord.   115
The worste of hem, he spak the firstė word:
'Bretheren', quod he, 'take kepe what that I saye;
My wit is greet, though that I bourde and playe.
This tresor hath Fortùne unto us yiven,
In mirthe and joliftee oure lyf to liven,   120

95 espye: spy   96 abye: pay for   98 one . . .: in collusion
with him   100 if . . .: if it is so pleasing to you   102 fay: faith
104 he will not wish to hide himself at all because of your threats
106 boughte again: redeemed   108 everich: each   110 florins:
nobles (worth 6s. 8d.)   y-coined rounde: rounded in the minting
111 very nearly eight bushels, as it seemed to them   112 lenger:
longer   114 For that: because   115 sette hem: sat   117
take kepe: pay attention to   118 wit: intelligence   bourde: joke
playe: fool   120 joliftee: merriment

And lightly as it comth, so wil we spende.
Ey! Goddès precious dignitee! who wende
To-day that we sholde han so fair a grace?
But mighte this gold be caried fro this place
Home to myn hous, or ellès unto youres—   125
For wel ye wot that al this gold is oures—
Thenne werè we in heigh felicitee.
But trewèly, by daye it may not bee:
Men woldè sayn that we were thevès stronge,
And for oure owenè tresor don us honge.   130
This tresor moste y-caried be by nighte
As wisely and as slyly as it mighte.
Wherfore I rede that cut among us alle
Be drawe, and let see wher the cut wil falle;
And he that hath the cut, with hertè blithe,   135
Shal rennè to the town, and that ful swithe,
And bringe us breed and wyn ful prively.
And two of us shul kepen subtilly
This tresor wel; and if he wil not tarie,
When it is night, we wil this tresor carie,   140
By one assent, where as us thinketh best.'
    That one of hem the cut broughte in his fest,
And bad hem drawe, and looke where it wil falle;
And it fil on the yongeste of hem alle,
And forth toward the town he wente anon.   145
And also soone as that he was a-gon,
That one of hem spak thus unto that other:

121 and we will spend it as easily as it comes   122 wende:
thought   123 grace: fortune   124 mighte this gold: if this
gold could   129 stronge: flagrant   130 don . . .: get us hanged
131 moste: must   132 as discreetly and secretly as possible   133
rede: propose   cut: lots   134 let see: let (us) see   136 renne:
run   swithe: fast   138 shul . . .: shall secretly guard   141 by
common agreement, wherever seems to us best   142 fest: fist   144
fil: fell   145 anon: at once   146 also: as

'Thou knowest wel thou art my sworèn brother;
Thy profit wil I tellè thee anon.
Thou wost wel that oure felawe is a-gon;   150
And heere is gold, and that ful greet plentee,
That shal departed been among us three.
But natheles, if I can shape it so
That it departed were among us two,
Hadde I not don a frendès turn to thee?'   155
    That other answèrde: 'I n'ot how that may be.
He wot wel that the gold is with us twaye.
What shal we don? What shal we to him saye?'
'Shal it be conseil?', saide the firstè shrewe,
'And I shal tellen in a wordès fewe   160
What we shal don, and bringe it wel aboute.'
'I grauntè', quod that other, 'out of doute,
That, by my trouthe, I wil thee not biwraye.'
'Now', quod the firste, 'thou wost wel we be
        twaye,
And two of us shul strenger be than on.   165
Looke, when that he is set, that right anon
Aris as though thou woldest with him playe,
And I shal rive him thurgh the sidès twaye
Whil that thou strogelest with him as in game;
And with thy daggere looke thou do the same.   170
And thenne shal al this gold departed be,
My deerè frend, bitwixen me and thee.
Thenne may we bothe oure lustès all fulfille,
And playe at dees right at oure owenè wille.'

150 wost: know   152 departed: divided   153 shape:
manage   156 n'ot: do not know   157 twaye: two   159
conseil: a secret   shrewe: scoundrel   162 grauntè: agree
out...: certainly   163 biwraye: betray   165 strenger: stronger
on: one   166 when he has sat down, see that you immediately
168 rive: stab   173 lustes: desires   174 dees: dice

And thus acorded been these shrewès twaye   175
To sleen the thridde, as ye han herd me saye.
   This yongeste, which that wentè to the town,
Ful ofte in herte he rolleth up and down
The beautee of these florins newe and brighte.
'O Lord', quod he, 'if so were that I mighte   180
Have al this tresor to myself allone,
Ther is no man that liveth under the trone
Of God that sholdè live so merye as I!'
And attè last the feend, oure enemy,
Putte in his thought that he sholde poison beye,   185
With which he mightè sleen his felawes tweye;
For-why the feend fond him in swich livinge
That he hadde levè him to sorwè bringe:
For this was outrely his fulle entente,
To sleen hem bothe, and nevere to repente.   190
And forth he goth— no lenger wolde he tarie—
Into the town, unto a pothecarie,
And prayèd him that he him woldè selle
Som poison, that he mighte his rattès quelle;
And eek ther was a polcat in his hawe,   195
That, as he saide, his capouns hadde y-slawe,
And fain he woldè wreke him, if he mighte,
On vermin that destroyèd him by nighte.
   The pothecarie answèrde: 'And thou shalt have
A thing that, also God my soulè save,   200
In al this world ther is no creätùre
That ete or dronke hath of this confiture

---

176 thridde: third   182 trone: throne   185 beye: buy
187 f. because the devil found his way of life to be such that he had (God's)
leave to bring him to a bad end   189 outrely: absolutely   191
lenger: longer   192 pothecarie: apothecary   194 quelle: kill
195: hawe: yard   196 y-slawe: killed   197 wreke him: avenge
himself   200 also: so may   202 confiture: concoction

Nought but the montance of a corn of whete,
That he ne shal his lyf anon forlete;
Ye, sterve he shal, and that in lessė while   205
Than thou wilt gon a-paas not but a mile,
The poisoun is so strong and violent.'

This cursėd man hath in his hand y-hent
This poisoun in a box, and sith he ran
Into the nextė strete unto a man,   210
And borwed of him largė botels three;
And in the two his poison pourėd he.
The thridde he keptė clenė for his drinke;
For al the night he shoop him for to swinke
In caryinge of the gold out of that place.   215
And when this riotour, with sory grace,
Hadde filled with wyn his gretė botels three,
To his felàwes again repaireth he.

What nedeth it to sermone of it more?
For right as they hadde cast his deeth bifore,   220
Right so they han him slain, and that anon.
And when that this was don, thus spak that on:
'Now let us sitte and drinke and make us merye,
And afterward we wil his body berye.'
And with that word it happėd him, per cas,   225
To take the botel ther the poison was,
And drank, and yaf his felawe drinke alsò,
For which anon they storven bothė two.

<hr />

203 a quantity no bigger than a grain of wheat   204 who does
not lose his life forthwith   205 Ye . . . shal: Yes, die he must
206 than it will take you to walk no more than a mile   208 y-hent:
taken   209 sith: then   214 shoop . . .: intended to work hard
216 with sory grace: curse him   219 sermone: speak   220 cast:
plotted   222 that on: the one   225 it . . .: he happened, by
chance   226 ther: in which   227 yaf . . .: gave (it) to his
companion to drink also   228 storven: died

119 *The Former Age*

A BLISFUL lyf, a paisible and a swete
 Ledden the peples in the former age;
They helde hem payed of fruitès that they ete,
Which that the feeldès yave hem by usàge;
They ne were not forpampred with outràge;   5
 Unknowèn was the quern and eek the melle;
They eten mast, hawès, and swich pounàge,
And dronken water of the coldè welle.

Yet n'as the ground not wounded with the plough,
 But corn up-sprang, unsowe of mannès hand, 10
The which they gniden, and ete not half ynough.
 No man yet knew the furwès of his land;
 No man the fyr out of the flint yet fand;
 Uncorven and ungrobbèd lay the vine;
 No man yet in the morter spices grand   15
 To clarré ne to sause of galantine.

No madder, welde, or wode no litestère
 Ne knew; the flees was of his former hewe;
No flesh ne wiste offence of egge or spere;
 No coin ne knew man which was fals or trewe; 20

---

1 paisible: peaceable   3 helde . . . of: were content with
4 yave . . .: customarily gave them 5 they were not over-pampered
by excess 6 melle: mill 7 they ate mast, haws, and such pannage
11 gniden: rubbed (in their hands) 12 furwes: furrows 13
fand: had discovered 14 the vine was unpruned and uncultivated
15 grand: ground 16 for clary (spiced drink) or for galantine-sauce
17–20 No dyer knew about madder, weld, or woad; wool was its original
colour; no flesh knew any injury from blade or spear; nobody had learnt to
distinguish a false coin from a true

No ship yet carf the wawès grene and blewe;
　No marchaunt yet ne fette outlandish ware;
No trompès for the werrès folk ne knewe,
　No towrès hye and wallès rounde or square.

What sholde it han availèd to werraye?　　　　　　　25
　Ther lay no profit, ther was no richesse;
But cursèd was the time, I dare wel saye,
　That men first dide her swety bisinesse
To grobbe up metal, lurking in darknesse,
　And in the riverès first gemmès soughte.　　　　30
Allas! then sprang up al the cursednesse
　Of covetise, that first our sorwè broughte!

These tyraunts putte hem gladly not in pres
　No wildnesse ne no bushes for to winne
Ther poverte is, as saith Diogenes,　　　　　　　35
　Ther as vitàile is eek so scars and thinne
That nought but mast or apples is therinne.
　But ther as baggès been and fat vitàile,
Ther wil they gon, and sparè for no sinne
　With al her host the cité for t'assaile.　　　　40

Yet were no palais-chaumbres ne non halles;
　In cavès and in wodès softe and swete
Slepten this blissèd folk withoutè walles
　On gras or levès in parfìt quiète.

21 carf: carved　　wawes: waves　　　　22 marchaunt: merchant
fette: fetched　　23 trompes: trumpets　　werres: wars　　25 werraye:
make war　　28 dide . . .: *i.e.* sweated and toiled　　32 covetise:
avarice　　　　33–6 These tyrants had no desire to exert themselves to
conquer a wilderness and some bushes where there is no wealth, as Diogenes
says, and where food also is so scarce and meagre　　　38 but where
there are money-bags and abundant food　　　39 f. spare . . .: have no
compunction in attacking the city with all their forces　　　43 withoute
walles: outside　　44 parfit: perfect

No down of fetheres ne no blechèd shete   45
   Was kid to hem, but in surté they slepte.
Her hertès were al one, withoutè galles;
   Everich of hem his faith to other kepte.

Unforgèd was the hauberk and the plate;
   The lambish peple, void of allè vice,   50
Hadden no fantasyè to debate,
   But ech of hem wolde other wel cherìce;
   No pridè, non envỳe, non avarice,
     No lord, no tailage by no tyrannye;
   Humblesse and pees, good faith, the empèrice,   55
    .   .   .   .   .

Yet was not Jupiter the likerous
   That first was fader of delìcacye,
Come in this world; ne Nembrot, dèsirous
   To regnen, had not made his towrès hye.
Allas, allas! now may men wepe and crye!   60
   For in our dayès n'is but covetise,
   Doublenesse, and tresoun, and envỳe,
     Poisòun, manslàughtre, and mordre in sondry wise.

---

46 kid: known   surté: security   47 one: united   galles:
rancour   48 Everich: each   49 plate: plate-armour   50 lamb-
ish: *i.e.* innocent   51 had no inclination to quarrel   52 wolde . . .:
wanted to cherish his neighbour   54 tailage: tax   55
Humblesse: humility   emperice: empress   56 likerous: lecherous
delicacye: luxury   58 Nimrod   61 n'is . . .: there is nothing
but avarice   63 mordre . . .: murder in various forms

120   *Now Welcome, Summer*

NOW welcome, somer, with thy sunnĕ softe,
   That hast thes wintres wedres overshake
And driven away the longĕ nightĕs blake!

Saint Valentin, that art ful hy o-lofte,
Thus singen smalĕ fowlĕs for thy sake: 5
   'Now welcome, somer, with thy sunnĕ softe,
   That hast thes wintres wedres overshake!'

Wel han they causĕ for to gladden ofte,
Sith ech of hem recovered hath his make;
Ful blissful mowe they singĕ when they wake: 10
   'Now welcome, somer, with thy sunnĕ softe,
   That hast thes wintres wedres overshake
   And driven away the longĕ nightĕs blake!'

121   *To Adam, his Scribe*

ADAM scrivein, if ever it thee bifalle
   Boèce or *Troilus* for to writen newe,
Under thy long lokkes thou most have the scalle
   But after my making thou write more trewe!
   So ofte a-daye I mot thy werk renewe,   5
      It to correcte and eek to rubbe and scrape;
      And al is through thy negligence and rape.

120. 1 softe: warm   2 wedres: storms   overshake: shaken off
4 o-lofte: above   8 f. they have good reason to rejoice often, since
each of them has got his mate   10 mowe: may

121. 1 scrivein: scribe   2 *Boece*: Chaucer's translation of Boethius
3–5 you deserve to get the scab under your long hair unless you copy more
faithfully what I compose! so often I have to re-do your work   7 rape:
haste

Truth

FLEE fro the prees and dwell with soothfastnesse;
 Suffice unto thy thing, though it be smal;
For hord hath hate, and climbing tikelnesse,
 Prees hath envỳe, and welè blent overal;
 Savour no more than thee behovè shal.   5
  Wirche wel thyself, that other folk canst rede;
  And trouthè shal delivere, it is no drede.

Tempest thee not al crokèd to redresse,
 In trust of hir that turneth as a bal—
For grete rest stant in litel bisinesse;   10
 And eek be ware to sporne ayenst an al;
 Strive not as doth the crokkè with the wal.
  Dauntè thyself, that dauntest otheres dede;
  And trouthè shal delivere, it is no drede.

That thee is sent, receive in buxumnesse;   15
 The wrestling for this worlde asketh a fal:
Here n'is none home, here n'is but wildernesse:
 Forth, pilgrim, forth! Forth, beest, out of thy stal!
 Know thy countree, look up, thank God of al.
  Hold the high way and let thy gost thee lede;   20
  And trouthè shal delivere, it is no drede.

1–7 Flee from the throng and dwell with truth; be satisfied with what you have, though it be little: for hoarding brings hate, and climbing insecurity, the throng has envy, and prosperity blinds entirely; desire no more than you need. Act well yourself, you who know how to advise other people; and truth shall set (you) free, there is no doubt. 8–13 Do not distress yourself to set right all that is awry, trusting to her who spins like a ball—great rest lies in little agitation; also beware of kicking against an awl; do not strive like the earthen pot against the wall. Govern yourself, you who govern another's doings. 15 Receive what is sent to you in submissiveness 16 asketh: asks for 19 Know thy contree: know (heaven as) your country of: for 20 gost: spirit

123   *Hide, Absalom, thy Gilt Tresses*

HIDE, Absolon, thy giltė tresses clere;
    Ester, lay thou thy meekness al a-down;
Hide, Jonathas, al thy frendly manère;
    Penelope and Marcia Catoun,
    Make of your wifhood no comparisoun;   5
      Hide ye your beautés, Isoude and Eleine:
      My lady comth, that al this may disteine.

Thy fairė body let it not appere,
    Lavine; and thou, Lucresse of Romė toun,
And Polixene, that boughten love so dere,   10
    And Cleopatre, with al thy passioun,
    Hide ye your trouthe of love and your renoun;
      And thou, Tisbé, that hast for love swich peine:
      My lady comth, that al this may disteine.

Hero, Dido, Laodamia, alle y-fere,   15
    And Phillis, hanging for thy Demophoun,
And Canacee, espiėd by thy chere,
    Ysiphilee, betraisėd with Jasòun,
    Make of your trouthė neither bost ne soun;
      Nor Ypermestre or Adriane, ye tweine: 20
      My lady comth, that al this may disteine.

---

1 gilte . . .: shining golden tresses   2 Esther, resign your claim
to graciousness   4 Marcia, wife of Cato of Utica   6 Isoude:
Isolde   Eleine: Helen   7 disteine: outshine, make dim
9 Lavinia   12 trouthe: fidelity   13 swich: such   15 y-
fere: together   17 and Canace (daughter of Aeolus), found out by
your appearance   18 Hypsipyle, betrayed by Jason   19 make
neither boast nor vaunt of your fidelity   20 Hypermnestra   Ariadne

124   *Complaint of Chaucer to his Purse*

TO you, my purse, and to none other wight
  Complain I, for ye be my lady dere;
I am so sory, now that ye been light,
  That certès, but ye make me hevy chere,
  Me were as leef be laid upon my bere.   5
    For which unto your mercy thus I crye:
    Beeth hevy again, or ellès mot I dye!

Now voucheth sauf this day, or it be night,
  That I of you the blisful soun may here,
Or see your colour like the sunnè bright,   10
  Thàt of yelownesse hadde never pere.
  Ye be my life, ye be myn hertès stere,
    Quene of comfòrt and of good companye:
    Beeth hevy again, or ellès mot I dye!

Now purse, that been to me my livès light   15
  And saviour, as down in this world here,
Out of this townè helpe me thurgh your might,
  Sin that ye wil not been my tresorère;
  For I am shave as nye as any frere.
    But yet I pray unto your curtesye: 20
    Beeth hevy again, or ellès mot I dye!

---

4 f. that indeed, unless you show me heaviness (of heart), I would as
soon be laid upon my bier   7 be heavy again, or else I must die
8 Now graciously grant this day, before it is night   9 soun: sound
11 pere: peer   12 stere: pilot   18 Sin: since   tresorere: treasurer
19 for I am as close-shaved as any friar

COMPLAINT TO HIS PURSE

L'envoy de Chaucer

O conquerour of Brutės Albion,
Which that by line and free eleccion
  Been verray king, this song to you I sende;
  And ye, that mowėn alle oure harmes amende,   25
Have minde upon my supplicacion!

?GEOFFREY CHAUCER

Merciless Beauty

I

YOUR eyėn two wil slee me sodenly;
  I may the beauté of them not sustene,
So woundeth it thourghout my hertė kene.

And but your word wil helen hastily
My hertės woundė, while that it is grene,   5
  Your eyėn two wil slee me sodenly;
  I may the beauté of them not sustene.

Upon my trouthe I say you faithfully
That ye been of my life and deth the quene;
For with my deth the trouthė shal be sene.   10
  Your eyėn two wil slee me sodenly;
  I may the beauté of them not sustene,
  So woundeth it thourghout my hertė kene.

II

So hath your beauté fro your hertė chaced
Pité, that me n'availeth not to plaine;   15
For Daunger halt your mercy in his chaine.

124. 22 conquerour: *i.e.* Henry IV   Brutes: Brutus's (legendary
founder of Britain)   23 line: lineage   24 verray: true
25 mowen: have power to   26 Have minde upon: bear in mind
125. 1 slee: slay   3 so cruelly does it wound me right through the
heart   4 but: unless   8 faithfully: truthfully   15 plaine: complain
16 Daunger: Aloofness   halt: holds

Giltless my deth thus han ye me purchàced;
I say you sooth, me nedeth not to faine;
   So hath your beauté fro your hertè chaced
   Pité, that me n'availeth not to plaine.   20

Alas! that Nature hath in you compàssed
So grete beauté, that no man may attaine
To mercy, though he stervè for the paine.
   So hath your beauté fro your hertè chaced
   Pité, that me n'availeth not to plaine;   25
   For Daunger halt your mercy in his chaine.

III

Sin I fro Love escapèd am so fat,
I never thenk to been his prisoun lene;
Sin I am free, I counte him not a bene.

He may answère and sayè this and that;   30
I do no fors, I speke right as I mene.
   Sin I fro Love escapèd am so fat,
   I never thenk to been his prisoun lene.

Love hath my name y-strike out of his slat,
And he is strike out of my bookès clene   35
For evermo—ther is non other mene.
   Sin I fro Love escapèd am so fat,
   I never thenk to been his prisoun lene;
   Sin I am free, I counte him not a bene.

17 Thus you have contrived my death, guiltless though I am   18
me . . .: I do not need to pretend   23 sterve: die   27 Sin: since
28 thenk: intend   prisoun: prisoner   29 counte . . .: reckon him
not worth a bean   31 do no fors: I do not care   34 y-strike . . .:
struck off his slate   36 for evermore—there is no alternative

d. 1408

126　　　　　*Ceix and Alceone*

THIS finde I write in Poësìe:
　　Ceïx the king of Trocinie
Hadde Alceònė to his wif,
Which as hir ownė hertės lif
Him loveth; and he hadde alsò　　　　　5
A brother, which was clepėd tho
Dedalion, and he per cas
Fro kinde of man forshapė was
Into a goshauk of liknesse;
Wherof the king gret hevynesse　　　　　10
Hath take, and thoughte in his coràge
To gon upon a pelrinage
Into a strangė regioun,
Wher he hath his devocioun
To don his sacrifice and praye,　　　　　15
If that he mighte in any waye
Toward the goddės findė grace
His brother helė to purchàce,
So that he mightė be reformed
Of that he haddė be transformed.　　　　　20

1 write: written　　　2 Trocinie: Trachis (in Thessaly)　　　3
Halcyone　　　6 cleped tho: called then　　　7 per cas: by chance
8–11 was turned from human form into the likeness of a goshawk; at
which the king was greatly grieved, and resolved in his heart　　　12
pelrinage: pilgrimage　　　14 devocioun: earnest desire　　　17 Toward:
in the eyes of　　　18 to obtain his brother's restoration　　　19 f.
reformed . . .: changed back to his original form from that into which he
had been transformed

To this purpòs and to this ende
This king is redy for to wende,
As he which woldè go by shipe;
And for to don him felawshipe
His wif unto the see him broughte,   25
With al hir herte and him besoughte
That he the time hir woldè sain
When that he thoughtè come ayain:
'Withinne', he saith, 'two monthè day.'
And thus in al the haste he may   30
He took his leve, and forth he saileth,
Weepende and she hirself bewaileth,
And turneth home ther she cam fro.
   But when the monthès were ago
The whiche he sette of his cominge,   35
And that she herdè no tidinge,
Ther was no carè for to seche:
Wherof the goddès to beseche
Tho she began in many wise,
And to Junò hir sacrifise   40
Above alle othrè most she dede;
And for hir lord she hath so bede
To wite and knowe how that he ferde,
That Juno the goddèsse hir herde;
Anon and ùpon this matère   45
She bad Irìs hir messagère
To Sleepès hous that she shal wende,

---

22 wende: go   23 f. being determined to go by ship; and to
keep him company   26 and begged him with all her heart   28
thoughte . . .: expected to come back   29 two . . .: two months'
time   32 and weeping she laments her lot   33 ther: where
34 ago: past   35 which he had fixed for his return   37 there
was no lack of anxiety   41 dede: made   42 bede: begged
43 ferde: fared   45 Anon and: and immediately

And bidde him that he make an ende,
Be swevene and shewèn al the cas
Unto this lady, how it was.   50
    This Iris, fro the highè stage
Which undertake hath the messàge,
Hir rainy copè dede upon,
The which was wonderly begon
With colours of divèrsè hewe,   55
An hundred mo than men it knewe;
The hevene lich unto a bowe
She bende, and so she cam down lowe,
The god of Sleep wher that she fand;
And that was in a strangè land   60
Which marcheth upon Chimerie:
For ther, as saith the Poësie,
The god of Sleep hath made his hous,
Which of entaille is marveilous.
    Under an hill ther is a cave,   65
Which of the sunnè may nought have,
So that no man may know aright
The point between the day and night:
Ther is no fyr, ther is no sparke,
Ther is no dorè which may charke,   70
Wherof an eyè sholde unshette,
So that inward ther is no lette.
And for to speke of that withoute,

48 make an ende: end the matter   49 and in a dream reveal all
the circumstances   51 highe . . .: high places (of the gods)   53
dede upon: put on   54 wonderly begon: wonderfully adorned
56 mo: more   it knewe: knew of   57 lich: like   59 fand:
found   61 which borders on Cimmeria (land of darkness)   64 of
entaille: in its fashioning   66 which can get no sun   68 point:
? distinction   70 charke: creak   71 which might cause an eye to
open   72 inward: inside   lette: hindrance (to sleep)   73 that . . .:
the outside

319

Ther stant no grete tree nigh aboute
Wher-on ther mightė crowe or pie   75
Alightė, for to clepe or crie;
Ther is no cok to crowė day,
Ne beestė non which noisė may;
The hill but al aboutė round
Ther is growende upon the ground   80
Popy, which berth the seed of sleep,
With othrė herbės suche an heep.
A stillė water for the nones
Rennende upon the smalė stones,
Which hightė of Lethės the rivère,   85
Under that hill in such manère
Ther is, which yifth grete appetit
To sleep. And thus full of delit
Sleep hath his hous; and of his couche
Withinne his chambre if I shal touche,   90
Of hebenus that sleepy tree
The bordės al aboutė be;
And for he sholdė sleepė softe,
Upon a fethre-bed alofte
He lith with many a pilwe of down.   95
The chambre is strowėd up and down
With swevenes many thousendfold.
     Thus cam Irìs into this hold,
And to the bed, which is al blak,
She goth, and ther with Sleep she spak,   100

---

74 stant: stands   76 clepe: call   78 noise: make a noise   79
but all round about the hill   81 berth: bears   82 with a host of
other such plants   83 a very quiet stream   84 Rennende: running
85 which is called the river Lethe   87 yifth . . .: gives a great desire
(for)   90 shal touche (of): am to touch on   91 hebenus: ebony
93 for: so that   95 lith: lies   pilwe: pillow   97 swevenes:
dreams   98 hold: abode

And in the wise as she was bede
The message of Junò she dede.
Ful ofte hir wordès she reherceth
Ere she his sleepy erès perceth;
With muchel wo but atè laste   105
His slombrende eyèn he upcaste
And saide hir that it shal be do.

  Wherof among a thousend tho
Withinne his hous that sleepy were,
In speciäl he ches out there   110
Three, which sholden do this dede:
The firste of hem, so as I rede,
Was Morpheüs, the whos natùre
Is for to takè the figùre
Of what persònè that him liketh,   115
Wherof that he ful ofte entriketh
The lif which sleepè shal be nighte;
And Ithecus that other highte,
Which hath the vois of every soun,
The chere and the condicioun   120
Of every lif, what so it is;
The thriddè suiende after this
Is Panthasas, which may transforme
Of every thing the rightè forme,
And change it in an other kinde.   125

---

101 and as she was bidden   **102** dede: did   **103** reherceth: repeats   **105** but at last with great reluctance   **108** Wherof: wherefore   tho: then   **110** in special: specially   ches: chose   **112** the first of them, as I learn from reading   **113** the whos: whose   **114** figure: shape   **115** of whatever person he pleases   **116** Wherof that: whereby   entriketh: deceives   **117** lif: person   **118** and the second was called Ithecus (*i.e.* Icelos)   **119** f. who can reproduce every sound, look and quality   **122** the third following after this   **123** Phantasos   may: has power to   **125** in: into

Upon hem three, so as I finde,
Of swevenes stant al th'àpparence,
Which other while is evidence,
And other while but a jape.

But natheless it is so shape 130
That Morpheüs by night al one
Appiereth until Alceòne
In liknesse of hir housèbande
Al naked ded upon the strande;
And how he dreinte in special 135
These othrè two it shewèn al:
The tempeste of the blakè cloude,
The woodè see, the windès loude,
Al this she mette, and sigh him dien;
Wherof that she began to crien, 140
Sleepende a-beddè ther she lay,
And with that noise of hir affray
Hir women sterten up aboute,
Whiche of here lady were in doute,
And axen hir how that she ferde; 145
And she, right as she sigh and herde,
Hir swevene hath told hem everydel;
And they it halsen allè wel
And sain it is a tokne of good.

But til she wiste how that it stood 150
She hath no confort in hir herte,

126–9 On these three, I gather, depends all that appears in dreams,
which is sometimes a reliable indication, sometimes a mere delusion
130 shape: contrived   132 until: to   135 and exactly how he
drowned   138 woode: raging   139 mette: dreamed   sigh: saw
140 Wherof that: wherefore   141 ther: where   142 affray: terror
143 sterten: jump   144 who were afraid for their mistress   145
axen: ask   146 right: just   sigh: saw   147 everydel: in every
detail   148 and they all interpret it favourably

Upon the morwe and up she sterte,
And to the see, wher that she mette
The body lay, withouté lette
She drough, and when that she cam nigh,   155
Stark ded, hise armés spred, she sigh
Hir lord fletende upon the wawe.
Wherof hir wittés been withdrawe,
And she, which took of deth no kepe,
Anon forth lepte into the depe   160
And wolde have caught him in hir arm.
  This infortune of double harm
The goddés fro the hevene above
Behelde, and for the trouthe of love
Which in this worthy lady stood,   165
They have upon the salté flood
Hir dreinté lord and hir alsò
Fro deth to livé turnéd so
That they been shapen into briddes
Swimmende upon the wawe amiddes.   170
And when she sigh hir lord livende
In liknesse of a brid swimmende,
And she was of the samé sort,
So as she mighté do disport,
Upon the joyé which she hadde   175
Hir wingés bothe abrod she spradde,
And him, so as she may suffise,

152 and in the morning up she jumped   153 mette: dreamed
154 lette: delay   155 drough: went   157 fletende: floating
wawe: wave   158 At which she was bereft of her senses   159
took . . .: was regardless of death   160 Anon: straightway   162
infortune: ill fortune   164 trouthe: fidelity   167 dreinte:
drowned   169 shapen . . .: turned into birds   170 upon . . .:
in the midst of the waves   174 so that she could show her
pleasure   175 Upon: because of   176 abrod: out wide
spradde: spread   177 so . . .: as far as she is capable

Beclipte and kiste in such a wise
As she was whilom wont to do:
Hir wingès for hir armès two   180
She took, and for hir lippès softe
Hir hardè bille, and so ful ofte
She fondeth in hir briddès forme,
If that she mighte hirself conforme,
To do the plesance of a wif,   185
As she dede in that other lif:
For though she had hir power lore
Hir will stood as it was tofore,
And serveth him so as she may.

Wherof into this ilkè day   190
Togedre upon the see they wone,
Wher many a doughter and a sone
They bringen forth of briddès kinde;
And for men sholden take in minde
This Alceòun the trewè queene,   195
Hir briddès yet, as it is seene,
Of Alceòun the namè bere.

127   *Medea's Magic*

THUS it befell upon a night,
When ther was nought but sterrèlight,
She was vanìsht right as hir liste,

---

126. 178 Beclipte: embraced   183 fondeth: endeavours   184
conforme: adapt   187 lore: lost   188 tofore: before   189
And: and (she)   190 wherefore to this very day   191 wone: dwell
194 and so that men should remember   197 Alceoun: *i.e.* halcyon

127. 2 sterre-: star   3 right . . .: just as she wished

That no wight but hirself it wiste,
And that was atė midnight tide: 5
The world was stille on every side.
With open hed and foot al bare,
Hir her to-spred, she gan to fare—
Upon hir clothės gert she was—
Al spechėles and on the gras   10
She glode forth as an addrė doth;
Non otherwisė she ne goth
Til she cam to the freshė flood,
And there a whilė she withstood.
Thriės she turnėd hir aboute,   15
And thriės eek she gan down loute,
And in the flood she wette hir her,
And thriės on the water ther
She gaspeth with a dreching ande,
And tho she took hir speche on hande.   20
First she began to clepe and calle
Upwàrd unto the sterrès alle,
To wind, to air, to see, to land
She praide, and eek held up hir hand,
To Echatės and gan to crye,   25
Which is goddesse of sorcerye.
She saidė: 'Helpeth at this nede,
And as ye maden me to spede
When Jason cam the flees to seche,
So help me now, I you beseche.'   30

---

4 That: so that   wight: creature   7 open: uncovered   8 her hair
flowing, she set out   9 Upon: in   gert: dressed   10–12 and
without a word she glided out onto the grass like an adder; she continues
in the same fashion   13 freshe flood: *i.e.* the river   14 with-
stood: stopped   15 Thriės: thrice   hir: herself   16 gan loute:
bowed   19 dreching ande: harrowing gasp   20 and then she
started to speak   21 clepe: cry   25 and cried to Hecate
27 Helpeth: help

With that she looketh and was war
Down fro the sky ther cam a char,
The which dragòuns aboutè drowe.
And tho she gan hir hed down bowe,
And up she stigh, and faire and wel   35
She drof forth bothè char and whel
Above in th'air among the skies.
The land of Crete and tho partìes
She soughte, and fastè gan hir hie;
And there upon the hillès highe,   40
Of Othrin and Olimpe alsò
And eek of othre hillès mo,
She fand and gadreth herbès swote;
She pulleth up som by the rote,
And manye with a knif she sherth,   45
And alle into hir char she berth.
Thus when she hath the hillès sought,
The floodès ther foryat she nought,
Eridian and Amphrisos,
Peneìe and eek Spercheïdos;   50
To hem she wente and ther she nom
Bothe of the water and the fom,
The sand and eek the smalè stones,
Whiche as she ches out for the nones,
And of the Redè See a part   55
That was behovelich to hir art
She took; and after that aboute

31 war: aware that   32 char: chariot   33 drowe: drew
34 tho: then   35 stigh: mounted   36 whel: wheel   38 tho
parties: those parts   41 from Othrys   42 mo: besides   43
fand: found   swote: sweet   45 sherth: cuts   46 berth: carries
48 floodes: rivers   foryat: forgot   49 Eridian: Eridanus
Amphrysus   50 Peneus   Spercheos   51 hem: them
nom: took   54 which she selected for her purpose   56 behovelich
to: necessary for

She soughtė sondry sedės oute
In fieldės and in many greves,
And eek a part she took of leves; 60
But thing which might hir most availe
She fand in Crete and in Thessàile.
 In dayės and in nightės nine,
With gret travàile and with gret pine,
She was purveyd of every piece, 65
And turneth homward into Grece.
Before the gatės of Esòn
Hir char she let away to gon,
And took out first that was therinne.
For tho she thoughtė to beginne 70
Such thing as semeth impossìble,
And made hirselven invisìble,
As she that was with air enclosed
And mighte of no man be desclosed.
She took up turvės of the land 75
Withoutė help of mannės hand,
Al helėd with the grenė gras,
Of which an alter made ther was
Unto Echàtės, the goddesse
Of art magìque, and the maistresse; 80
And eft another to Juvente,
As she which dide hir hole entente.
Tho took she fieldwode and vervaine—
Of herbes be nought betre twaine—
Of which anon withoutė let 85

59 greves: groves   64 pine: pains   65 she had provided
herself with every item   67 Aeson   69 that: what   73 f.
being enveloped in vapour and unable to be exposed to view by anyone
77 heled: covered   81 eft: then   Juventa, goddess of Youth
82 like one who was taking every care   83 fieldwode: *see textual note*
84 f. there are no two better herbes—with which at once without delay

These alters been aboutè set.
Two sondry pittès fastè by
She made, and with that hastèly
A wether which was blak she slough,
And out therof the blood she drough   90
And dide into the pittès two;
Warm milk she putte alsò therto
With hony meind; and in such wise
She gan to make hir sacrifice;
And cride and praidè forth withal   95
To Pluto the god ìnfernal,
And to the queenè Proserpine.
And so she soughte out al the line
Of hem that longen to that craft—
Behindè was no namè laft—   100
And praide hem alle, as she wel couthe,
To grante Esòn his firstè youthe.

This olde Esòn brought forth was tho;
Away she bad alle othrè go,
Upon perìl that mightè falle;   105
And with that word they wenten alle
And leften there hem two alone.
And tho she gan to gaspe and gone,
And madè signès many on,
And saide hir wordès therupon;   110
So that with spelling of hir charmes
She took Esòn in both hir armes
And made him for to sleepè faste,

87 sondry: separate   89 slough: killed   90 drough: drew
91 dide: put (it)   93 meind: mixed   98 line: series   99
longen to: are associated with   100 no name was left out   101
couthe: knew how to   105 for fear of what might happen to them
108 gone: gape   109 many on: many   111 spelling of: uttering

And him upon hir herbès caste.
The blakè wether tho she took,   115
And hew the flesh as doth a cook;
On either alter part she laide,
And with the charmès that she saide
A fyr down fro the sky alighte
And made it for to brennè lighte.   120
But when Medea saugh it brenne,
Anon she gan to sterte and renne
The firy alters al aboute.
Ther was no bestè which goth oute
More wildè than she semeth ther: 125
Aboute hir shuldres hing hir her,
As though she were oute of hir minde
And turnèd in another kinde.
Tho lay ther certain wodè cleft,
Of which the pieces now and eft   130
She made hem in the pittès wete,
And put hem in the firy hete,
And took the brand with al the blase,
And thriès she began to rase
Aboute Esòn, ther as he slepte;   135
And eft with water, which she kepte,
She made a cercle aboute him thries,
And eft with fyr of sulphrè twies;
Ful many an other thing she dede,
Which is nought writen in this stede.   140

114 him upon: upon him   116 hew: cut up   119 alighte:
descended   120 brenne lighte: burn brightly   121 saugh: saw
122 f. she immediately leapt forward and ran all round the flaming altars
124 goth oute: roves   126 hing . . .: hung her hair   128 and
had been turned into a different creature   129 certain . . .: some
split wood   130 now . . .: again and again   131 made wete:
wetted   134 rase: run quickly   135 ther as: where   139 dede:
did   140 stede: place

But tho she ran so up and down,
She madè many a wonder soun,
Somtimè lich unto the cock,
Somtime unto the laverock,
Sometimè cakleth as a hen,   145
Somtimè spekth as don the men;
And right so as hir jargoun strangeth,
In sondry wise hir formè changeth:
She semeth faye and no wommàn.
For with the craftès that she can   150
She was, as who saith, a goddesse,
And what hir listè, more or lesse,
She dide (in bookès as we finde)
That passeth over mannès kinde.
But who that wil of wondres here,   155
What thing she wroughte in this matère
To make an ende of that she gan—
Such merveil herdè neverè man.

Apointed in the newè mone,
When it was timè for to done,   160
She sette a caldron on the fire,
In which was al the hole atire,
Wheron the medicinè stood,
Of juse, or water, and of blood,
And let it buile in such a plit   165
Til that she saugh the spumè whit;

141 tho: while   142 soun: sound   143 lich: like   147
and just as her speech grows strange   149 faye: supernatural
150 can: knows   151 as who saith: as they say   154 which is
beyond the natural power of man   155-8 But if anyone wants to
hear wonders, (to hear) what things she did in this process so as to conclude
what she had begun—nobody ever heard such a marvel   159 the
new moon being the time appointed   160 done: act   162 atire:
preparation   163 of which the medicine consisted   165 buile:
boil   plit: way

And tho she caste in rinde and roote,
And seed and flowr that was for boote,
With many an herbe and many a stone,
Wherof she hath ther many one;   170
And eek Cimpheius the serpènt
To hir hath alle his scalès lent;
Chelidre hir yaf his addres skin,
And she to builen caste hem in;
A part eek of the hornèd owle,   175
The which men here on nightès howle;
And of a raven, which was told
Òf nine hundred winter old,
She took the hed with al the bille;
And as the medicine it wille,   180
She took therafter the bowèle
Of the seewolf, and for the hele
Of Eson, with a thousand mo
Of thingès that she haddè tho,
In that caldroun togedre as blive   185
She putte; and took thenne of olìve
A dryè branche hem with to stere,
The which anon gan flowre and bere
And waxe al fresh and grene ayein.
When she this vertu haddè sein,   190
She let the lestè drope of alle
Upon the barè flor down falle;
Anon ther sprang up flowr and gras,

168 for boote: efficacious   171-3 *see textual note*   173 yaf:
gave   177 told: reckoned (to be)   180 it wille: requires   182
seewolf: fabulous amphibious beast   hele: treatment   183 mo: more
185 as blive: immediately   186 putte; put (it)   187 hem . . .: to
stir them with   188 bere: bloom   190 vertu: miraculous power
sein: seen   191 the . . .: the least possible drop   193 gras:
herbage

Where as the dropė fallė was,
And wox anon al medwė-grene,   195
So that it mightė wel be sene.
Medea thennė knew and wiste
Hir medicine is for to triste,
And goth to Eson ther he lay,
And took a swerd was of assay,   200
With which a wounde upon his side
She madė, that therout may slide
The blood withinnė, which was old
And sek and trouble and feble and cold.
And tho she took unto his use   205
Of herbės al the bestė juse,
And pourėd it into his wounde;
That made his veinės fulle and sounde.
And tho she made his woundė close,
And took his hand, and up he rose;   210
And tho she yaf him drinke a draughte,
Of which his youth ayein he caughte,
His hed, his herte, and his visàge
Lich unto twenty winter age;
His horė herės were away,   215
And lich unto the freshė May,
When passėd been the coldė showres,
Right so recovereth he his flowres.

---

194 Where as: where   195 wox: grew   medwe-: meadow-
198 for . . .: to be trusted   199 ther: where   200 was . . .:
(which) was of proven quality   204 and unhealthy and disordered
and thin and cold   205 unto his use: for use upon him   211
drinke: to drink   212 from which he recovered his youth   214
Lich: like   215 hore: grey   218 flowres: youthful vigour

128 *Adrian and Bardus*

TO speke of an unkindė man,
  I finde how whilom Adrian,
Of Romė which a gret lord was,
Upon a day as he per cas
To wode in his huntingė wente,   5
It hapneth at a soudein wente,
After his chace as he poursuieth,
Thurgh hap, the which no man eschuieth,
He fell unware into a pet,
Wher that it mightė nought be let.   10
The pet was deep and he fell lowe,
That of his men non mightė knowe
Wher he becam, for non was nigh
Which of his fall the mischief sigh.

And thus al onė ther he lay   15
Clepende and criende al the day
For socour and deliverance,
Til ayein eve it fell per chance,
A while er it began to nighte,
A povere man, which Bardus highte,   20
Cam forth walkendė with his asse,
And haddė gadrėd him a tasse

---

1 unkinde: ungrateful   4 per cas: by chance   6 at . . .: suddenly   7 as he was pursuing his game   8 hap: chance 9 unware: unawares   pet: pit   10 let: prevented   13 Wher he becam: what became of him   14 mischief: mishap   sigh: saw 15 al one: all by himself   16 clepende: calling   18 ayein: towards 19 nighte: grow dark   20 povere: poor   highte: was called 22 and had gathered himself a pile

Of grenė stickės and of drye
To sellė, who that wolde hem bye,
As he which haddė no liflode   25
But whenne he mightė such a lode
To townė with his assė carie.
And as it fell him for to tarie
That ilkė timė nigh the pet,
And hath the trussė fastė knet,   30
He herde a vois, which cridė dimme,
And he his erė to the brimme
Hath laid, and herde it was a man,
Which saide: 'Ha! help here Adrian,
And I wil yiven half my good.'   35
   The povere man this understood,
As he that woldė gladly winne,
And to this lord which was withinne
He spak and saide: 'If I thee save,
What sikernessė shal I have   40
Of covenant, that afterward
Thou wilt me yivė such reward
As thou behightest now tofore?'
   That other hath his othės swore
By hevene and by the goddės alle,   45
If that it mightė so befalle
That he out of the pet him broughte,
Of all the goodės whiche he oughte
He shal have evene halvendel.

---

24 f. who . . . : (if) anyone wanted to buy them, being one who had
no livelihood   26 But: except   28 it fell him: he happened
30 trusse: bundle   knet: tied   31 dimme: faintly   35 yiven:
give   good: possessions   37 being one who was glad to earn
something   40 sikernesse: security   43 as you promised
just now   48 oughte: possessed   49 he is to have exactly
half

This Bardus saide he woldė wel;   50
And with this word his asse anon
He let untrusse, and therupon
Down goth the corde into the pet,
To which he hath at th'ende knet
A staf, wherby, he saide, he wolde   55
That Adrian him sholdė holde.
But it was tho per chancė falle,
Into that pet was also falle
An apė, which at th'ilkė throwe,
When that the cordė cam down lowe,   60
Al sodeinly therto he skipte
And it in bothe his armės clipte.
And Bardus with his asse anon
Him hath updrawe, and he is gon.
But when he sigh it was an ape,   65
He wende al haddė been a jape
Of faiërie, and sore him dradde;
And Adrian eftsonė gradde
For help, and cride and praidė faste,
And he eftsone his cordė caste;   70
But when it cam unto the grounde,
A gret serpènt it hath bewounde,
The which Bardùs anon up drough.
And thenne him thoughtė wel ynough
It was fantòsme, but yet he herde   75

50 wolde wel: was very willing   51 anon: at once   52
let untrusse: unloaded   54 knet: tied   56 him . . .: should hold
on   57 but by chance it happened then   59 th'ilke throwe: that
very moment   62 clipte: clasped   65 sigh: saw   66 he
supposed it had all been a trick   67 faierie: magic   him dradde:
was afraid   68 eftsone gradde: again cried out   69 faste: urgently
71 grounde: bottom   72 bewounde: wound itself round   73
drough: drew   74 and then he felt sure   75 fantosme: an
illusion   yet: still

The vois, and he therto answèrde:
'What wight art thou, in Godès name?'
    'I am', quod Adriàn, 'the same,
Whos good thou shalt have evene half.'
Quod Bardus: 'Thenne, a Godès half,   80
The thriddè time assaye I shal';
And caste his cordè forth withal
Into the pet, and when it cam
To him, this lord of Rome it nam,
And therupon him hath adressed,   85
And with his hand ful oftè blessed,
And thenne he bad to Bardus hale.
And he, which understood his tale,
Between him and his asse, al softe,
Hath drawe and set him up alofte   90
Withouten harm, al esily.
    He saith nought onès, 'Grant merci',
But straughte him forth to the cité,
And let this povere Bardus be.
And natheless this simple man   95
His covenant, so as he can,
Hath axèd; and that other saide,
If so be that he him umbraide
Of ought that hath be speke or do,
It shal been vengèd on him so   100
That him were betrè to be ded.

---

78 quod: said   80 a . . .: in God's name   81 thridde: third
84 nam: seized   85 and has attached himself to it   86 blessed:
crossed himself   87 hale: haul   88 tale: words   89 with
the help of his ass, very gently   91 esily: smoothly   92 f. he does
not once say 'thank you very much', but hurried off to the city   96
covenant: agreed reward   so as: as best   97 axed: asked for
98 umbraide (of): reproached (with)   99 speke: spoken   100
venged: revenged

And he can tho non other red,
But on his asse ayain he caste
His trusse, and hieth homward faste;
And when that he cam home to bedde,   105
He tolde his wif how that he spedde.
But finaly, to speke ought more
Unto this lord he dradde him sore,
So that a word ne durste he sain.
And thus upon the morwe ayain,   110
In thĕ manère as I recorde,
Forth with his asse and with his corde
To gadrĕ wode, as he dide ere,
He goth; and when that he cam nere
Unto the placĕ where he wolde,   115
He hath his ape anon beholde,
Which haddĕ gadred al aboute
Of stickĕs here and there a route,
And laide hem redy to his hand,
Wherof he made his trusse and band.   120
Fro day to day and in this wise
This apĕ profreth his servìse,
So that he hadde of wode ynough.
Upon a time and as he drough
Toward the wode, he sigh beside   125
The gretĕ gastly serpent glide,
Til that she cam in his presènce,
And in hir kinde a reverence
She hath him do, and forth withal
A stone mor bright than a cristàl   130

102 and he then knows no other course   103 ayain: again
106 spedde: fared   108 dradde him: was afraid   115 wolde:
used to go   118 route: number   120 band: tied it up
121 And day by day in this manner   124 and once as he was going
125 sigh...: saw nearby   128 kinde: own way   129 hath do: made

337

Out of hir mouth tofore his waye
She let down falle, and wente awaye
For that he shal nought been adrad.
Tho was this povere Bardus glad,
Thankendė God and to the ston   135
He goth and takth it up anon,
And hath gret wonder in his wit
How that the beste him hath aquit,
Wher that the mannės son hath failed,
For whom he haddė most travàiled.   140
  But al he putte in Godės hand,
And turneth home, and what he fand
Unto his wif he hath it shewed;
And they, that werėn bothė lewed,
Acorden that he sholde it selle.   145
And he no lengere woldė dwelle,
But forth anon upon the tale
The stone he profreth to the sale;
And right as he himself it sette,
The jueler anon forth fette   150
The gold and made his payėment;
Therof was no delayėment.
  Thus when this stone was bought and sold,
Homward with joyė manifold
This Bardus goth; and when he cam   155
Home to his hous and that he nam
His gold out of his purs, withinne
He fand his stone alsò therinne;

131 tofore . . .: in front of him   133 so that he should not be
frightened   134 Tho: then   135 Thankende God and: and
thanking God   138 aquit: requited   142 fand: found   144
lewed: ignorant   145 Acorden: agree   146 lengere: longer
dwelle: delay   147 but immediately after their talk   148 to the
sale: for sale   149 sette: priced   150 fette: fetched   156 nam:
took

ADRIAN AND BARDUS

Wherof for joye his hertè plaide,
Unto his wif and thus he saide: 160
'Lo, here my gold, lo here my ston!'
His wif hath wonder therupon,
And axeth him how that may be.
'Now, by my trouthe, I n'ot', quod he,
'But I dare swere upon a book   165
That to my merchant I it took,
And he it haddè when I wente:
So knowe I nought to what entente
It is now here, but it be grace.
For-thy tomorwe in other place   170
I wille it fondè for to selle,
And if it wil nought with him dwelle,
But crepe into my purs ayain,
Then dare I saufly swere and sain
It is the vertu of the stone.'   175
    The morwè cam, and he is gone
To seche aboute in other stede
His stone to selle, and he so dede,
And lefte it with his chapman there.
But when that he cam ellèswhere   180
In presence of his wif at hom,
Out of his purs and that he nom
His gold, he fand his stone withal.
And thus it fell him overal,
Where he it solde in sondry place,   185
Such was the fortune and the grace.

159 plaide: jumped   160 and to his wife he said   164 n'ot:
do not know   166 took: gave   168 to what entente: why
169 but: unless   170 For-thy: therefore   171 fonde: try
174 saufly: safely   175 vertu: peculiar property   177 seche: seek
stede: place   178 dede: did   179 chapman: merchant   182
and took out of his purse   184 fell: befell   overal: everywhere
185 Where: wherever

But so wel may nothing been hid
That it n'is atė lastė kid:
This famė goth aboutė Rome
So ferforth that the wordės come   190
To th'Emperour Justinian;
And he let sendė for the man
And axede him how that it was.
And Bardus tolde him al the cas,
How that the worm and eek the beste, 195
Although they maden no beheste,
His travail hadden wel aquit;
But he which hadde a mannės wit,
And made his covenant by mouthe,
And swor therto al that he couthe,   200
To parte and yiven half his good,
Hath now foryete how that it stood,
As he which wil no trouthė holde.

 This Emperour al that he tolde
Hath herd, and th'ilke unkindėnesse 205
He saide he wolde himself redresse.
And thus in court of juggėment
This Adrian was thenne assent.
And the querèle in audience
Declarėd was in the presènce   210
Of th'Emperour and many mo;
Wherof was muchel spechė tho
And gret wondring among the press.

188 kid: made known 189 fame: story 190 ferforth: widely
come: came 192 let sende: sent 194 al . . .: the whole story
195 worm: snake 196 beheste: promise 197 aquit: repaid
200 and swore besides by every oath he could think of 202 foryete:
forgotten 203 refusing to keep his word 205 unkindenesse:
ingratitude 208 assent: sent for 209 querele: complaint
in audience: at a formal hearing 211 mo: more 212 tho: then
213 press: people

But atè lastè natheless
For the partỳè which hath plained   215
The lawe hath demèd and ordained,
By hem that were avisèd wel,
That he shal have the halvendel
Thurghout of Adrianès good.

And thus of th'ilke unkindè blood   220
Stant the memòire into this day,
Wherof that every wise man may
Ensamplen him and take in minde
What shame it is to been unkinde;
Ayain the which resòn debateth,   225
And every creäture it hateth.

JOHN TREVISA

d. 1402

129   *Prologue to a Translation*

A CROIS was made al of reed
   In the biginning of my book
That is clepèd 'God me speed'
   In the first lessoun that I took.

Thenne I lernède A and Be   5
   And other lettres by her names;
But alwày 'God speedè me'
   That is me needful in alle games.

128. 215 plained: complained   217 by (the decision of) men of
sound judgement   218 halvendel: half part   219 of Adrian's
entire property   220 unkinde blood: ungrateful man   221
Stant: endures   into: to   222 f. from which every wise man can take
warning and remember   225 which reason opposes

129. 1 crois: cross   reed: red   3 cleped: called   6 her: their

If I playde in feeld other meedes,
   Outher stille outher with nois   10
I prayėde help in allė deedes
   Of Him that diėde on the crois.

Now diverse playės in His name
   I shal lete passe forth and fare,
And aventure to playe o long game;   15
   Also and I shal spare

Bothė woodės, meedes, and feeldes,
   Place that I have playėd inne;
And in His name, that al thing weeldes,
   This gamė now I shal biginne.   20

And prayė help, counseil, and reede
   To me that He willė sende;
And this gamė rule and leede
   And bring it to a good ende.

130   *On the Death of Edward III*

A! DERE God, what may this be,
   That alle thing weres and wasteth away?
Frendship is but a vanité:
   Unnethe it durės al a day.

129. 9 other: or   10 either silently or aloud   14–16 I must let pass
and go by, and venture to play one long game (*i.e.* the translation); and
also I must forgo   19 weeldes: rules   21 reede: advice   23
rule: direct   leede: conduct

130. 1 what: how   2 weres: decays   4 it scarcely lasts a whole
day

They be so sliper at assay,   5
  So leef to han and loth to lete,
And so fikel in her fay,
  That selden y-seye is soone foryete.

I say it not withouten a cause,
  And therfore takės right good hede;   10
For if ye construwe wel this clause,
  I put you holly out of drede
That for pure shame your hertes wil blede,
  And ye this matere wisly trete:
He that was our mostė spede   15
  Is selden y-seye and soone foryete.

Sum time an English ship we had,
  Nobel it was and heigh of towr;
Thorgh al Cristendam it was drad,
  And stif wolde stande in ech a stowr,   20
And best durst bide a sharp showr,
  And other stormės smale and grete.
Now is that ship, that bar the flowr,
  Selden seye and soone foryete.

Into that ship ther longed a rother   25
  That steered the ship and governed it;
In al this world n'is such another,
  As me thinketh in my wit.

5 f. They (*i.e.* friends) are so slippery when put to the test, so anxious
to have and loath to forgo   7 her fay: their fidelity   8 y-seye:
seen   foryete: forgotten   10 takes: take   11 clause: text
12 I fully assure you   14 if you consider this matter carefully
15 mostė spede: greatest cause of success   18 heigh . . .: with high
fighting top   19 drad: dreaded   20 and would stand firm in
every battle   21 bide . . . .: stand a fierce squall   23 bar . . .:
surpassed all   25 To that ship there belonged a rudder

Whil ship and rother togeder was knit
  They dredde nouther tempest drye nor wete;   30
Now be they bothe in sunder flit,
  That selden seye is soone foryete.

Sharpė wawes that ship has sailed,
  And sayed alle sees at àventure.
For wind ne wederes never it failed   35
  Whil the rother mighte endure.
    Though the see were rough or elles demure,
      Goode havenes that ship wolde gete.
    Now is that ship, I am wel sure,
      Selde y-seye and soone foryete.   40

This goodė ship I may remene
  To the chivalrye of this lande;
Sum time they counted nought a bene
  By al Fraunce, ich understande.
    They took and slough hem with her hande,   45
      The power of Fraunce, both smal and grete,
    And brought the king hider to bide her bande:
      And now right soone it is foryete.

That ship hadde a ful siker mast,
  And a sail strong and large,   50
That made the goode ship never agast
  To undertake a thing of charge;

30 nouther: neither   31 in . . . : parted   33 Sharpe wawes: fierce waves   34 and explored all seas whatever the danger   35 wederes: storms   37 elles demure: else calm   41 remene: compare   42 chivalrye: men-at-arms   43 f. once they reckoned all France not worth a bean, I understand   45 took . . . hem: set about killing them   46 power: forces   47 and brought the king (John of France) here to be their prisoner   49 siker: secure 52 of charge: important

And to that ship ther longed a barge
    Of al Fraunce yaf nought a clete;
To us it was a siker targe,   55
    And now right clene it is foryete.

The rother was nouther ok ne elm—
    It was Edward the Thridde, the noble knight.
The Prince his sone bar up his helm,
    That never scoumfited was in fight.   60
    The King him rode and rouwed aright;
        The Prince dredde nouther stok nor strete.
    Now of hem we lete ful light:
        That selde is seye is soone foryete.

The swifte barge was Duk Henri,   65
    That noble knight and wel assayed;
And in his leggaunce worthily
    He abode many a bitter brayd.
    If that his enemys ought outrayed,
        To chastise hem wolde he not lete.   70
    Now is that lord ful lowe y-layd:
        That selde is seye is soone foryete.

These goode Comùnès, by the roode!
    I likne hem to the shipès mast,
That with her catel and her goode   75
    Maintened the werre both first and last.

54 which cared nothing for all France   55 targe: shield   59
bar up: held   his helm: its tiller   60 scoumfited: beaten
61 him rode: sailed   62 nouther . . .: *i.e.* nothing   63 Now we
care little about them   64 That: what   65 Henry, first Duke of
Lancaster   66 assayed: tried   67 leggaunce: service to his liege-
lord   68 abode: stood   brayd: onslaught   69 ought . . .:
offended in any way   70 lete: neglect   74 likne: liken   75
catel: property   goode: money   76 supported the war throughout

The wind that blew the ship with blast
    It was goode prayers, I say it atrete.
Now is devoutness out y-cast,
    And many goode dedes been clene foryete.   80

Thus been these lordes y-laid ful lowe:
    The stok is of the samė rote;
An impe biginnės for to growe
    And yet I hope shal been our bote,
    To holde his fomen under fote,   85
    And as a lord be set in sete.
Crist levė that he so mote,
    That selden y-seye be not foryete!

Were that impė fully growe,
    That he had sarry sap and pith,   90
I hope he shulde be kud and knowe
    For conquerour of many a kith.
He is ful liflich in lime and lith
    In armes to travaile and to swete.
Crist levė we so fare him with   95
    That selden seye be never foryete!

And therfore holliche I you rede,
    Til that this impe be fully growe,
That ech a man up with the hede
    And maintene him, bothe heighe and lowe.   100

---

78 atrete: plainly   83 impe: sapling (*i.e.* Richard II)   84 and
I trust shall yet be our salvation   86 set . . .: enthroned   87 leve:
grant   mote: may   90 sarry: ?vigorous   91 kud: famed
92 kith: country   93 He is very vigorous in limb and joint   95
fare . . .: treat him   97 And therefore I advise you whole-heartedly
99 that each man hold up his head   100 maintene: support

The Frenshe men cunne bothe boste and blowe
And with her scornés us to-threte,
And we beeth bothe unkinde and slowe,
That selden seye is soone foryete.

And therfore, goode sires, taketh reward   105
Of your doughty king that diede in age,
And to his soné, Prince Edward,
That wellé was of alle coràge.
Suche two lordes of heigh paràge
I n'ot in erthe when we shal gete;   110
And now her los biginneth to swage,
That selde y-seye is soone foryete.

131   *A Warning to Beware*

Y ET is God a curteis lord,
   And mekéliche can shewe His might;
Fain He wolde bringe til acord
   Mankinde, to live in treuthe aright.
Allas! why set we that lord so light   5
   And al to foule with Him we fare?
In world is none so wise no wight
   That they ne have warning to be ware. . . .

130. 101 cunne: know how to   blowe: bluster   102 f. and castigate
us with their taunts, if we are both disloyal and apathetic   104 That: so
that   105 f. taketh reward Of: remember   108 welle: fount
109 parage: lineage   110 n'ot: know not   111 los: renown
swage: decline

131. 1 Yet: even now   curteis: gracious   2 mekeliche: mercifully
3 till: into   5 f. set . . .: do we have so little regard for that lord and
treat Him all too shamefully   7 no wight: nor brave

When the comùnes began to rise,
    Was none so gret lord, as I gesse,   10
That they in herte bigan to grise,
    And laide her jolité in presse.
    Wher was thenne her worthinesse,
        When they made lordès droupe and dare?
Of alle wise men I take witnesse,   15
    This was a warning to be ware. . . .

And also when this erthè quoke,
    Was none so proud he n'as agast,
And al his jolité forsoke,
    And thought on God whil that it last;   20
And as soone as it was over-past
    Men wox as evil as they dide are.
Eche man in his herte may cast
    This was a warning to be ware.

Forsoothe, this was a lord to drede,   25
    So sudeinly made man agast;
Of gold and selver they took non hede,
    But out of her houses ful soone they past.
    Chaumbres, chimeneys al to-brast,
        Chirches and castels foule gan fare;   30
    Pinacles, steples to grounde it cast;
        And al was warning to be ware.

The moving of this erthe, y-wis,
    That shulde by kinde be ferm and stable,

---

11 **That** : but that   grise: be terrified   12 and put away their gaiety
14 **when they** (the peasants) made lords cringe and cower   17 quoke:
quaked   18 he n'as: (that) he was not   22 wox: grew   are:
before   23 cast: reflect   26 So: (who) so   29 to-brast:
were shattered   30 foule . . .: fared badly   33 y-wis: indeed
34 kinde: nature

A pure, verrày tokning it is   35
   That mennės hertės been chaungàble,
   And that to falsėd they been most able:
    For with good faith wil we not fare.
   Leef it wel withouten fable,
    This was a warning to be ware.   40

The rising of the comùnes in lande,
   The pestilence, and the erthėquake—
These three thinges, I understande,
   Betokenes the grete vengàunce and wrake
   That shuldė falle for sinnės sake,   45
    As these clerkės cunne declare.
   Now may we chese to leve or take,
    For warning have we to be ware. . . .

Be ware, for I can say no more,
   Be ware for vengaunce of trespàs;   50
Be ware, and thenk upon this lore;
   Be ware of this sudein cas.
   And yet be ware while we have spas,
    And thanke that Child that Mary bare,
   Of His gret goodnesse and His gras,   55
    Sende us such warning to be ware.

35 verray: true   37 falsed: falsehood   able: prone   38 fare:
act   39 Believe it well, truly   44 wrake: retribution   45
shulde: were bound to   46 clerkes . . .: learned men declared
47 chese: choose   51 lore: lesson   52 cas: misfortune   53 spas:
time   56 Sende: (who) sent

132 *Deo Gracias*

IN a chirche ther I con knel,
   This ender day is one morwening,
Me liked the servise wonder wel;
   For-thy the lengere can I ling.
I seigh a clerk a book forth bring   5
   That prikkèd was in many a plas;
Faste he soughte what he sholde sing,
   And al was *Deo Gracias*.

Alle the querìstres in that queer
   On that word fast gan they cry: 10
The noise was good, and I drow neer
   And called a preest ful privèly,
   And saide: 'Sire, for your curtesy,
     Tel me, if ye habbeth spas,
   What it meneth, and for-why   15
     Ye singè *Deo Gracias*.'

In silk that comely clerk was clad,
   And over a lettorne leenèd he;
And with his word he made me glad,
   And saide: 'Sone, I shal tellè thee.   20
Fader and Sone in Trinité,
   The Holy Gost, ground of our gras,
Also oftè-sithè thankè we
   As we say *Deo Gracias*.

1 ther . . .: where I knelt   2 the other day one morning
4 therefore I stayed the longer   5 seigh: saw   6 prikked:
marked with muscial notes   7 Faste: eagerly   9 queristres:
choristers   queer: choir   10 fast . . .: they sang out loud   11
drow neer: drew nearer   14 habbeth spas: have time   15 for-
why: why   18 lettorne: lectern   22 ground: source   23 Also
ofte-sithe: as often

'To thanke and blesse Him we been bounde   25
    With al the mirthes that man may minne;
For al the world in wo was wounde
    Til that He crepte into our kinne;
    A lovesum birde He lighte withinne,
        The worthiest that ever was;   30
    And shedde His blood for ouré sinne,
        And therfore *Deo Gracias*.'

Then saide the preest: 'Sone, by thy leve,
    I mosté saye forth my servìse;
I praye thee take it nought in greve,   35
    For thou hast herd al my devìse,
    Because why it is clerkés wise,
        And Holy Chirche minde of it mas,
    Unto the Prince so muchel of prise
        For to singe *Deo Gracias*.'   40

Out of that chirche I wente my way,
    And on that word was al my thought,
And twenty timés I can say:
    'God graunte that I foryete it nought.'
    Though I were out of bonchef brought,   45
        What help were to me to saye 'allas'?
    In the name of God, whatever be wrought,
        I shal say '*Deo Gracias*'. . . .

26 mirthes: gladness   minne: think of   27 wounde: wrapped
28 kinne: kind   29 birde: lady   lighte: alighted   34 moste:
must   35 in greve: amiss   36 devise: explanation   37
Because why: the reason why   wise: custom   38 minde . . .:
records it   39 prise: worth   44 foryete: forget   45 bonchef:
good fortune   46 were: would it be

133 *Think on Yesterday*

WHEN men beeth meriest at her mele,
    With mete and drink to maken hem glade,
With worship and with worldlich wele,
    They been so set they cunne not sade:
They have no deinté for to dele   5
    With thinges that been devoutly made;
They weene her honour and her hele
    Shal ever laste and never diffade.
But in her hertes I wolde they hade,
    When they gon richest men on aray,   10
How soone that God hem may degrade,
    And sum time thenk on yesterday. . . .

Salamon saide in his poisỳ:
    He holdeth wel betere with an hounde
That is liking and jolỳ,   15
    And of seknesse hol and sounde,
Than by a lion, though he ly
    Cold and ded upon the grounde.
Wherof serveth his victory
    That was so stif in eche a stounde?   20

1 her: their   2 hem: them(selves)   3 f. with honour and worldly prosperity, they are so content they cannot have too much   5 deinté: inclination   6 with works of devotion   7 hele: health   8 diffade: fade   9 wolde . . .: wish they would consider   10 when they go about in the greatest splendour   14 holdeth with (by): esteems   15 liking: pleasing   16 hol: whole, free   17 though: if   19 f. What use is his victory, he that was so brave on every occasion

The mosté fool, I herde respounde,
   Is wiser whil he livé may
Than he that had a thousend pounde
   And was buried yesterday. . . .

I have wist, sin I couthe meen,   25
   That children hath by candel-light
Her shadewe on the wal y-seen,
   And runne therafter al the night;
Bisy abouté they han been
   To cachen it with al her might,   30
And when they cachen it best wolde ween,
   Soonest it shet out of her sight:
The shadewe cachen they ne might,
   For no lines that they couthe lay.
This shadewe I may likne aright   35
   To this world and yesterday. . . .

Sum men saith that deth is a theef
   And al unwarned wil on him stele;
And I say nay, and make a preef
   That deth is stedefast, trewe, and lele,   40
And warneth eche man of his greef
   That he wil o day with him dele.
The lif that is to you so leef
   He wil you reve, and eke your hele;
These pointes may no man him repele,   45
   He cometh so boldely to pik his pray.

21 moste: greatest respounde: reply   25 I have known, since I could remember   29 they have busily tried   31 and when they felt surest of catching it   32 shet: shot   34 lines: snares   35 likne: liken   38 unwarned: without warning   39 preef: proof   40 lele: faithful   41 greef: suffering   42 which he will one day allot to him   43 leef: dear   44 reve: rob hele: health   45 no man can withdraw from him these special powers   46 pik: take

When men beeth meriest at her mele
I rede ye thenk on yesterday.

134   *This World Fares as a Fantasy*

WHICH is man who wot, and what,
   Whether that he be ought or nought?
Of erthe and air groweth up a gnat,
   And so doth man, when al is sought;
Though man be waxen gret and fat,   5
   Man melteth away so deth a mought.
Mannės might n'is worth a mat,
   But noyeth himself and turneth to nought.
Who wot, save He that al hath wrought,
   Wher man bicometh when he shal dye?   10
Who knoweth by dede ought but by thought?
   For this world fareth as a fantasye.

Dyeth man, and beestės dye,
   And al is on occasioun;
And alle o deth bos bothė drye,   15
   And han one incarnacioun;
Save that men beeth morė slye,
   Al is o comparisoun.

133. 48 rede: advise

134. 1 Who knows of what nature man is, and what he is   4 sought:
examined   5 waxen: grown   6 so . . .: as does a moth
7 mat: *i.e.* worthless mat of straw   8 (it) only harms and destroys
him   10 Wher man bicometh: what becomes of man   11 Who
knows anything? about death (? in fact) except by speculation   12
fantasye: phantom   14 on . . .: a matter of chance   15 and
both must suffer the same death   16 han: have   17 slye:
intelligent   18 all is alike

Who wot if mannès soulè stye
  And beestès soulès sinketh down?   20
Who knoweth beestes entencioun,
  On her creatour how they crye,
Save only God that knoweth her soun?
  For this world fareth as a fantasye.

Eche secte hopeth to be save   25
  Boldèly by her beleeve;
And echone upon God hy crave—
  Why shulde God with hem Him greeve?
Echone troweth that other rave,
  But alle hy cheseth God for cheeve,   30
And hope in God echone they have,
  And by her wit her worching preeve.
Thus many maters men don meeve,
  Sechen her wittès how and why;
But Godes mercy is us alle beheeve,   35
  For this world fareth as a fantasye.

135   *Come out, Lazarus!*

'COM out, Lazer, what-so befalle!'
    Then might not the feend of helle
Lenger make that soule to dwelle;
So dredful was that ilkè cry

134. 19 stye: rise   21 entencioun: meaning   22 what their cries
to their creator mean   23 knoweth . . .: understands their utterance
25 f. hopeth Boldely: trusts confidently   27 hy: they   28 Him
greeve: trouble Himself   29 Each believes the other is mad   30
cheseth: choose   cheeve: chief   32 and justify their practice with
their intellects   33 don meeve: discuss   34 rack their brains as
to how and why   35 is . . .: is necessary for us all

135. 3 Lenger: longer

To that felòun, oure enemy. 5
The Kingès trumpè blew a blast:
'Com out!', it saide, 'be not agast'.
With that vois the feende gan quake
As doth the leef when windès wake.

'Com out' is now a wonder soun: 10
It hath overcome that foule felòun;
And al his carful companye
For drede therof they gunnè crye.
Yet is 'Com out' a wonder song;
For it hath broken the prison strong, 15
Feteres, chaines, and bondès mo,
That wroughten wreched soulès wo.
'Com out!': that Kingès vois so free
It maketh the devel and deth to flee.
Say me now, thou serpent sly, 20
Is not 'Com out' an asper cry?
'Com out' is word of batàile,
For it gan hellè soone to assaile.
Why stoppest thou not, feend, thyn ere,
That this word entre not there? 25
He that saide that word of might
Shop Him felly to the fight;
For with that word He won the feeld,
Withouten spere, withouten sheeld,
And broughte hem out of prison strong 30
That werèn holden there with wrong.
Tel now, tyrant, where is thy might?
'Com out' hath felld it al with fight.

5 feloun: traitor   8 gan quake: quaked   10 wonder soun:
wonderful sound   12 carful: wretched   13 gunne crye: cried
16 mo: besides   17 which afflicted wretched souls   18 free: noble
21 asper: harsh   22 bataile: battle   23 soone: immediately
27 advanced valiantly to the battle   30 hem: them

Quia Amore Langueo

IN the vaile of restless mind
 I sought in mountein and in mede,
Trusting a trew love for to find.
 Upon an hill then took I hede;
 A voise I herd—and nere I yede—   5
  In gret dolòur complaining tho:
 'See, dere soule, my sidès blede,
  Quia amore langueo.'

Upon this mount I fand a tree;
 Under this tree a man sitting;   10
From hede to foot wounded was he,
 His hertè-blood I saw bleding;
 A semely man to be a king,
  A gracious face to looke unto.
 I asked him how he had paining.   15
  He said: '*Quia amore langueo.*

'I am trew love that fals was never:
 My sister, mannes soule, I lovèd her thus;
Bicause I wold on no wise dissever,
 I left my kingdom glorious;   20
 I purveyed her a place full precious;
  She flitt, I folowed; I loved her so
 That I suffred these painès piteous,
  Quia amore langueo.

'My fair love and my spousè bright,   25
 I saved her fro beeting, and she hath me bett;

5 nere: nearer yede: went   6 tho: then   8 S. of S. 2. 5
9 fand: found 15 how: why   19 dissever: be separated   22
flitt: left   26 bett: beaten

I clothed her in grace and hevenly light,
  This bloody surcote she hath on me sett.
  For longing love I will not lett;
    Swetė strokės be these, lo!   30
  I have lovėd ever as I hett,
    Quia amore langueo.

'I crowned her with blisse, and she me with thorne;
  I led her to chambre, and she me to dye;
I brought her to worship, and she me to scorne;   35
  I did her reverence, and she me vilanye.
  To love that loveth is no maistrỳe;
    Her hate made never my love her fo;
  Ask then no mo questions whye,
    Quia amore langueo.   40

'Looke unto myn handės, man!
  These gloves were given me when I her sought;
They be not white, but rede and wan,
  Embrodred with blood, my spouse them bought;
  They will not off, I leve them nought,   45
    I wowe her with them where ever she go;
  These handes full frendly for her fought,
    Quia amore langueo.

'Marvell not, man, though I sit still;
  My love hath shod me wonder straite;   50
She bukled my feet, as was her will,
  With sharpė nailes—well thou maist waite!

---

29 For: because of   lett: cease   31 hett: promised   35
worship: honour   36 vilanye: indignity   37 that: one who
maistrye: hard task   39 mo : more   43 wan: discoloured
44 Embrodred: decorated   45 leve . . .: am never without them
46 wowe: woo   47 frendly: lovingly   50 wonder . . .: wonder-
fully tight   52 waite: see

In my love was never dessaite,
 For all my membres I have opend her to;
My body I made her hertès baite,   55
 Quia amore langueo.

'In my side I have made her nest;
 Looke in me how wide a wound is here!
This is her chambre, here shall she rest,
 That she and I may sleepe in fere.   60
 Here may she washe, if any filth were,
  Here is socour for all her wo;
 Cum if she will, she shall have chere,
  Quia amore langueo.

'I will abide till she be redy,   65
 I will her sue if she say nay;
If she be rechèless, I will be redy,
 If she be daungerous, I will her pray.
 If she do weepè, then bid I nay;
  Myn armes been spred to clip her me to; 70
 Cry onès; I cum. Now, soule, assay!
  Quia amore langueo.

'I sit on an hille for to see farre,
 I looke to the vaile; my spouse I see:
Now rinne she away-ward, now cometh she narre, 75
 Yet fro myn eye-sight she may not be.
 Some waite their prey to make her flee;
  I rinne tofore to chastise her fo.

---

53 dessaite: concealment 55 her . . .: bait for her heart 60
in fere: together 63 chere: welcome 66 sue: follow 67
recheless: thoughtless redy: prudent 68 daungerous: reluctant
69 bid . . .: I shall beg her not to 70 clip: clasp 71 ones: once
assay: try 75 rinne: runs narre: nearer 77 waite: lie in wait
for 78 tofore: ahead

Recover, my soule, againe to me,
   Quia amore langueo.   80

'My swetė spousė, will we go play?
   Apples been ripe in my gardìne;
I shall clothe thee in new array,
   Thy mete shall be milk, honye, and wine.
Now, dere soule, let us go dine,   85
   Thy sustenance is in my scrippė, lo!
Tary not now, fair spousė mine,
   Quia amore langueo.

'If thou be foule, I shall make thee clene;
   If thou be seke, I shal thee hele;   90
If thou ought mourne, I shall bemene.
   Spouse, why will thou nought with me dele?
Thou foundest never love so lele;
   What wilt thou, soule, that I shall do?
I may of unkindness thee appele,   95
   Quia amore langueo.

'What shall I do now with my spouse?
   Abide I will her gentilnisse.
Wold she looke onės out of her house
   Of fleshly affecciouns and unclennisse,   100
Her bed is made, her bolster is blisse,
   Her chambre is chosen, suche are no mo.
Looke out at the windows of kindnisse,
   Quia amore langueo.

---

79 Recover: return   86 scrippe: bag   90 seke: sick   91
ought: at all   bemene: condole   92 with . . .: love me   93 lele:
faithful   95 I may accuse you of ingratitude   98 gentilnisse:
gracious favour   99 Wold she: if she would   101 bolster: pillow
102 her chamber is choice, there are no more like it

'Long and love thou never so hye,   105
  Yet is my love more than thyn may be;
Thou gladdest, thou weepest, I sit thee bye;
  Yet might thou, spouse, looke onès at me!
    Spouse, shuld I alway feedè thee
      With childès mete? Nay, love, not so!   110
    I preve thy love with adversité,
      Quia amore langueo.

'My spouse is in chambrè, hold youre pease;
  Make no noise, but let her sleepe.
My babe shall suffrè no disease,   115
  I may not here my dere child weepe;
  For with my pappe I shall her keepe.
    No wonder though I tend her to:
    This hole in my side had never been so deepe,
      But *quia amore langueo.*   120

'Wax not wery, myn owne dere wife:
  What meede is aye to live in comfòrt?
For in tribulacion I rin more rife
  Oftentimes than in disport;
  In welth, in wo, ever I support.   125
    Then, dere soule, go never me fro!
    Thy meede is markèd, when thou art mort,
      Quia amore langueo.'

105 hye: deep   111 preve: test   115 disease: discomfort
117 with: close to   118 tend: attend   122 what reward is there
in living always in comfort   123 rin . . .: run (to help) more quickly
124 disport: happiness   125 welth: prosperity   127 markèd:
assigned   mort: dead

137   *Christ's Plea to Mankind*

L O! lemman swete, now may thou see
    That I have lost my lif for thee.
    What might I do thee more?
For-thy I pray thee specially
That thou forsake ill company   5
    That woundès me so sore;

And take mine armès privily
And do them in thy tresory,
    In what stede so thou dwelles;
And, swete lemman, forget thou nought   10
That I thy love so dere have bought,
    And I aske thee nought elles.

138   *Abide, Good Men*

A BIDE, good men, and hald your pays,
    And here what God Himselven says,
    Hingand on the rood:
'Man and woman that by me gase,
Look up to me and stint thy pace;   5
    For thee I shed my blood.

'Behald my body or thou gang,
And think upon my painès strang,
    And still as stane thou stand.

137. 1 lemman: sweetheart   4 For-thy: therefore   7 armes: armour   9 stede: place   12 elles: else

138. 1 hald . . .: hold your peace   3 Hingand: hanging   4 gase: goes   5 stint . . .: stay your step   7 or . . .: before you go   8 strang: severe   9 stane: stone

Behald thyself the sooth, and see   10
How I am hinged here on this tree
And nailèd foot and hand.

'Behald my heved, behald my feet,
And thy misdeedès look thou leet;
   Behald my grisely face.   15
And of thy sins ask àlegeance,
And in my mercy have àffiance,
   And thou shall get my grace.'

139   *Turn Again*

IN a noon-tide of a sumers day—
   The sunne shon ful merye that tide—
I took myn hawk al for to play,
   My spaniel renning by my side.

A feisant hen soone gan I see   5
   Myn hound put up ful fair to flight;
I sente my faukun, I let him flee:
   It was to me a deinteous sight.

My faukun flegh faste to his pray,
   I ran tho with a ful glad chere;   10
I spurnèd ful soone on my way,
   My leg was hent al with a brere.

138. 13 heved: head   14 and see that you leave off your misdeeds
15 grisely: terrible   16 alegeance: remission   17 affiance: trust
139. 4 renning: running   5 gan . . .: I saw (which)   7 flee: fly
8 deinteous: fine   9 flegh: flew   10 tho: then   11 spurned:
stumbled   12 hent: caught   brere: briar

This brere forsoothe dide me greef,
  And soone it made me to turne ayé,
For he bare written in every leef   15
  This word in Latin, *revertere*.

I kneeled and pulled the brere me fro,
  And redde this word ful hendély;
Myn herte fil down unto my to
  That was wont sitten ful likingly.   20

I let myn hawk and feisant fare,
  My spaniel fil down to my knee;
Thenne took I me with sighing sare
  This new lessòun, *revertere*.

Revertere is as miche to say   25
  In English tunge as 'turne ayèn'.
Turne ayèn, man, I thee pray,
  And thinke hertily what thou hast ben.

Of thy livinge bethinke thee rife,
  In open and in privité;   30
That thou may come to everlasting life,
  Take to thy minde *revertere*.

---

13 dide . . .: hurt me   14 ayé: again   18 hendely: readily
19 fil: fell   20 which used to be untroubled   22 fil . . .: lay
down by my knees   23 me: to myself   sare: grievous   25
miche: much   26 ayen: again   28 hertily: earnestly   29
rife: often

140 *Against Friars*

PREEST ne monk ne yet canòun
   Ne no man of religioun
Given hem so to devocioun
   As don these holy freres.
For some given hem to chivalry,   5
Some to riot and ribaudery;
But freres given hem to grete studỳ,
   And to grete prayères.
     Who-so kepès their rule al
       Both in word and dede,   10
     I am ful siker that he shal
       Have heven-blis to mede.

Men may see by their contenaunce
That they are men of grete penàunce,
And also that their sustenaunce   15
   Simple is and waike.
I have lived now fourty yeres,
And fatter men about the neres
Yet saw I never than are these freres,
   In contreys ther they raike.   20
     Mete-less so megre are they made,
       And penaunce so puttes hem down,
     That echone is an hors-lade
       When he shal trusse of town.

---

3 hem: themselves   5 chivalry: warfare   6 riot . . .:
dissipation and debauchery   11 siker: certain   12 to mede: as
reward   16 waike: poor   18 neres: kidneys   20 ther:
where   raike: rove   21 Mete-less: without food   megre: lean
23 hors-lade: horse-load   24 trusse: pack up and go out

Allas, that ever it shuld be so,   25
Suche clerkes as they about shuld go
Fro town to town by two and two
    To seeke their sustenaunce!
By God that al this world wan,
He that that ordre first bigan,   30
Me think, certès, it was a man
    Of simple ordinaunce.
        For they have nought to livè by
            They wandren here and there,
        And dele with divers mercery,   35
            Right as they pedlers were.

They dele with purses, pinnes, and knives,
With girdles, gloves, for wenches and wives;
But ever bacward the husband thrives
    Ther they are haunted till: 40
For when the good-man is fro hame,
And the frere comes to our dame,
He spares nawther for sinne ne shame
    That he ne dos his will.
        If they no help of houswives had,   45
            When husbandes are not inne,
        The frerès welfare were ful bad,
            For they shuld brew ful thinne.

Some freres beren pelùre aboute
For grete ladys and wenches stoute,   50

---

26 clerkes: religious   29 wan: won   32 ordinaunce: habits
33 For: because   35 mercery: wares   36 Right as: just as if
39 bacward: the worse   40 wherever they resort   41 good-man:
master   hame: home   43 f. he refrains for fear of neither sin nor
shame from doing his will   48 brew . . .: *i.e.* have a poor reception
49 pelure: fur   50 stoute: proud

To reverce with their clothes withoute—
    Al after that they ere—
For some vaire, and some grise,
For some bugee, and for some bise;
And also many a divers spise   55
    In bagges about they bere.
      Al that for women is plesand
        Ful redy, certes, have they;
      But litel give they the husband
        That for al shal pay.   60

Trantes they can, and many jape:
For some can with a pound of sape
Get him a kirtel and a cape
    And somwhat els therto!
Wherto shuld I othès swere?   65
Ther is no pedler that pak can bere
That half so dere can sell his gere
    Than a frere can do.
      For if he give a wife a knife
        That cost but penys two,   70
      Worthe ten knives, so mot I thrife,
        He wil have er he go. . . .

They say that they distroyè sinne,
And they maintene men most ther-inne:
For had a man slain al his kinne,   75
    Go shrive him at a frere,
And for less than a pair of shoone

51 to trim the outside of their clothes   52 according to their rank
53 vaire: striped fur   grise: grey fur   54 bugee: lambskin
bise: dark brown fur   55 spise: spice   61 They know tricks
and many a deception   62 sape: soap   63 kirtel: tunic   65
Wherto: why   68 Than: as   71 so . . .: so may I prosper
76 let him go (and) confess to a friar   77 shoone: shoes

He wil assoil him, clene and soone,
And say the sin that he has doone
   His soule shal never dere.   80
     It semes sooth that men sayn of thaim
      In many divers londe,
     That that caitife cursèd Caim
      First this ordre fonde.

Now see the sooth wheder it be swa,   85
That frerè Carmes come of a K,
The frere Austìnes come of A,
   Frere Iacobines of I,
Of M comen the frere Menòurs:
Thus grounded Caim these four ordòurs   90
That fillen the world ful of erròurs
   And of ypocrisy.
     All wickednes that men can tell
      Regnès hem among;
     Ther shal no soule have roume in hell,   95
      Of freres ther is such throng. . . .

Ful wisely can they preche and say,
But as they preche no thing do thay.
I was a frere ful many a day;
   Therfor the sooth I wate.   100
But when I saw that their living
Acorded not to their preching,
   Off I cast my frere clothing,
     And wightly went my gate.

---

78 he will absolve him, completely and at once   80 dere: harm
83 Cain   84 fonde: founded   85 wheder: whether   swa: so
86 Carmes: Carmelites   88 Iacobines: Dominicans   89 Menours:
Franciscans   90 grounded: founded   100 wate: know   104
and promptly went my way

Other leve ne took I none   105
   Fro hem when I went,
But took hem to the devel echone—
   The prior and the convènt.

Out of the ordre though I be gone,
Apostata ne am I none: 110
Of twelve monethes me wanted one,
   And odde days nine or ten.
Away to wende I made me boun
Or time come of professioun;
I went my way thurghout the toun   115
   In sight of many men.
     Lord God, that with painès ill
      Mankinde bought so dere,
     Let never man after me have will
      For to make him frere!   120

141   *A Dream*

M E thought I was in wildernesse walking al one,
   There bestes were and briddes and no barne elles,
In a cumbe cressing on a crest-wise,
Al gras-grene, that gladed my herte,
By a cliffe un-y-knowe, of Cristes owen making.   5
I lepte forth lightly along by the hegges,
And moved forth merily to maistrie the hilles;

140. 107 took: consigned   113 boun: ready   114 Or: before
come: came   119 will: desire   120 to become a friar

141. 1 al one: alone   2 There: where   briddes . . .: birds and
nobody else   3 in a valley ?rising upwards like a crest   6 lepte:
ran   lightly: quickly   7 maistrie: surmount

For til I came to the coppe couthe I not stinte
Of the highest hille by halfe of alle other.
    I tourned me twyes and toted aboute,   10
Beholding hegges and holts so grene,
The mansions and medwes mowen al newe,
For such was the saison of the same yere.
I lifte up my eye-lides and looked ferther
And saw many swete sights, so me God helpe: 15
The wodes and the waters and the welle-springes,
And trees y-trailed fro toppe to th'erthe,
Curiously y-covred with curtelle of grene;
The flowrs on feeldes flavring swete,
The corn on the croftes y-cropped ful faire,   20
The renning rivière rushing faste,
Ful of fish and of frie of felefold kinde;
The breres with their beries bent over the wayes,
As honysoucles hanging upon eche half;
Chesteines and cheries that children desiren   25
Were logged under leves ful lusty to seen.
The hawthorn so holsum I beheld eeke,
And how the benes blowed and the brome-flowres;
Peres and plummes and pesecoddes grene,
That ladies lusty looken muche after,   30
Were gadred for gomes ere they gunne ripe;
The grapes growed agrete in gardens aboute,

---

8 coppe: summit   couthe . . . : I could not stop   9 by halfe: by far
10 I turned round twice and gazed about   12 mansions: ? lawns
17 y-trailed: decked   18 curiously: beautifully   curtelle: robe
19 flavring: smelling   20 croftes: fields   y-cropped: reaped
21 renning: running   22 felefold kinde: many different kinds
23 breres: briars   24 As: also   eche half: every side   25 chesteines:
chestnuts   26 logged: sheltered   lusty: delightful   27 holsum:
wholesome   28 blowed: blossomed   30 looken after: search for
31 were gathered for men before they ripened   32 2grete: in pro-
fusion

And other fruits felefold in feeldes and closes;
To nempne alle the names it nedeth not here.
   The conings fro covert covred the bankes,   35
And raughte out a raundon and retourned againes,
Played forth on the plaine, and to the pitte after,
But any hound hente them or the hay-nettes.
The hare hied him faste, and the houndes after;
For kissing of his croupe acaunt-wise he wente;   40
For n'ad he tourned twyes, his tail had be licked,
So ernestly Ector iched him after.
The sheepe fro the sunne shadwed themself,
While the lambes laiked along by the hegges.
The cow with hire calfe and coltes ful faire   45
And high hors in haras hurteled togedre,
And praised the pasture that prime-saute them made.
The deere on the dale drowe to their dennes,
Ferked forth to the ferne and felle down amiddes.
Herts and hindes, a hundred togedre,   50
With reindeer and robuc runne to the wodes
For the kenets on the cleere were un-y-coupled;
And buckes ful burnished that baren good grece,
Four hundred on a herd y-heeded ful faire,

33 closes: enclosures   34 nempne: name   it . . .: is unnecessary here   35 conings: rabbits   covred: ranged over   36 and rushed out headlong and returned again   37 to the pitte: (went) to the burrow   38 unless some dog caught them or the rabbit-nets 40 to prevent them kissing his rump he went zig-zagging   41 n'ad . . . twyes: had he not turned twice   42 Ector: *i.e.* a hound iched: itched, sought   44 laiked: played   46 hors in haras: horses at stud   47 praised: appreciated   prime-saute: spirited 48 on: in   drowe: went   49 Ferked: went   felle . . .: dropped down in the middle of it   51 runne: ran   52 because the hunting dogs in the open were uncoupled   53 burnished: having rubbed the velvet from their antlers   baren . . .: carried much fat 54 y-heeded . . .: with very fine antlers

Layen lowe in a launde along by the pale,   55
A swete sight for souvrains, so me God helpe.
  I moved down fro the mote to the midwards,
And so adown to the dale, dwelled I no longer;
But such a noise of nestlings ne so swete notes
I herde not this halfe yere, ne so hevenly sounes   60
As I dide on that dale adown among the hegges;
For in every bush was a brid that in his best wise
Babled with his bille, that blisse was to here,
So cheerly they chirmed and chaunged their notes,
That what for flavour of the fruits and of the somer
      flowres,   65
The smelling smote as spices, me thought,
That of my travail trewly took I no kepe,
For al was vanished me fro through the freshe sightes.

142   *The Blacksmiths*

SWARTE smeked smithes smatered with smoke
  Drive me to deth with din of here dintes.
Swich nois on nightes ne herd men never:
What knavene cry and clatering of knockes!
The cammede kongons cryen after 'col, col'   5
And blowen here bellowes, that al here brain brestes:
'Huf, puf!' saith that one; 'haf, paf!' that other.

---

141. 55 launde: clearing   pale: fence   56 souvrains: princes   57
mote . . .: hill towards the middle   58 dwelled: stayed   60
sounes: sounds   64 cheerly: joyfully   chirmed: sang   65
flavour: scent   66 The . . . spices: the fragrance struck me like spices
67 so that truly I cared not about my troubles   68 freshe: joyous

142. 1 Black smoke-grimed smiths smutted with smoke   2 here
dintes: their blows   3 Swich: such   4 knavene cry: shouting
of workmen   5 cammede kongons: snub-nosed brutes   6
brestes: bursts   7 that one: the one

They spitten and sprawlen and spellen many spelles;
They gnawen and gnachen, they grones togedere,
And holden hem hote with here hard hamers.   10
Of a bulle-hide been here barm-felles;
Here shankes been shakeled for the fire-flunderes;
Hevy hameres they han, that hard been handled,
Stark strokes they striken on a steled stokke:
Lus, bus! las, das! rowten by rowe.   15
Swich dolful a dreme the devil it to-drive!
The maister longeth a litel, and lasheth a lesse,
Twineth hem twain, and toucheth a treble:
Tik, tak! hic, hac! tiket, taket! tik, tak!
Lus, bus! lus, das! swich lif they leden,   20
Alle clothemeres: Crist hem give sorwe!
May no man for bren-wateres on night han his rest.

143   *The Assumption*

              'COM my swetė, com my flowr,
                 Com my culver, myn owne bowr,
              Com my moder now with me,
              For Heven-quene I makė thee.'

142. 8 sprawlen . . .: strain and utter many ?oaths   9 gnawen and
gnachen: grind and gnash (teeth)   10 holden hem: keep themselves
11 barm-felles: leather aprons   12 their shanks are protected against
the fire-sparks   13 han: have   handled: wielded   14 Stark:
stout   steled stokke: steel anvil   15 rowten . . .: crash in turn
16 Devil take such an appalling noise!   17 f. The master smith
lengthens a little piece and beats out a smaller one, twists the two together,
and strikes a treble note   21 clothemeres: horse-clothers   22
bren-wateres: water-sizzlers

143. 2 culver: dove

'My swetė Sone, with al my love 5
I com with thee to thyn above;
Wher thou art now let me be,
For al my love is laid on thee.'

144 *In Praise of Winchester*

M E liketh ever the lengere the bet
By Wingester, that joly cité:
The town is good and wel y-set;
The folk is comely on to see.

The air is good bothe inne and oute; 5
The cité stont under an hille;
The riveres renneth all aboute;
The town is rulėd upon skille.

145 *How Should I Rule Me?*

L ORD, how sholde I roulė me,
Of al men y-praised to be?

If I holde the lowe asise,
And take aray of litel prise,
Then men wil say: 'He is nought wise; 5
He is a fon; let him be.'

143. 6 thyn: ? thy home

144. 1 f. I take more and more pleasure in Winchester, that fine city
3 y-set: situated   4 on . . .: to look at   6 stont: stands
7 renneth . . .: run all round it   8 upon skille: wisely

145. 3 lowe asise: lowly manner   4 and adopt a humble style of
living   6 fon: fool

And if I take the mene astate,
And with none man make debate,
Then men wil say, erly and late,
    That I am worth no maner fee.   10

And if I takė grete aray,
Hors and houndes and clothės gay,
Then men wil say every day
    That I passė my degree.

Then take thou heede of the oxe;   15
Go nought to lowė for the foxe,
Nether to hey til thou be wox,
    For the kite that wolde thee slee.

Therfor looke that thou be sley:
For no thing hew thou to hey,   20
Lest they falle down into thy ey
    The spones that above thee be.

146   *Love Undeclared*

WOLDE God that it were so
    As I coude wishe betwixt us two!

The man that I loved altherbest
In al this contré, ėst other west,

145. 7 mene . . .: middle way   8 make . . .: quarrel   10
worth . . .: worth no kind of reward, *i.e.* of no worth   14 that I
live above my station   16 for: for fear of   17 nor (climb) till
you have risen too high   18 slee: slay   19 sley: discreet   20
on no account hew too high   22 spones: chips

146. 3 altherbest: best of all   4 other: or

To me he is a strangė gest: 5
   What wonder is't though I be wo?

When me were levest that he shold dwell,
   .   .   .   .
He wold nought say onės farewell
   When time was come that he most go.   10

In places ofte when I him mete,
   I dare nought speke, but forth I go;
With herte and eyės I him grete—
   So trewe of love I know no mo.

As he is myn hertė love,   15
   My derward dere, y-blessed he be!
I swere by God that is above,
   None hath my love but only he.

I am y-comforted in every side,
   The coloures wexeth both fresh and newe,   20
When he is come and wil abide—
   I wot ful wel that he is trewe.

I love him trewely and no mo—
   Woldė God that he it knewe!
And ever I hope it shal be so;   25
   Then shall I chaungė for no newe.

---

5 strange gest: distant stranger   7 when I most wished that he
would stay   9 ones: once   10 most: must   12 forth: on
14 no mo: nobody else   15 herte: heart's   16 derward: precious
19 am: shall be   20 wexeth: will grow   22 wot: shall know
25 hope: trust   26 newe: new love

JOHN WALTON

fl. c. 1410

147   *God, the Port of Peace*

N OW cometh alle ye that been y-brought
      In bondès full of busy bitternesse,
Of erthly lust abiding in your thought!
    Here is the rest of all your bisynesse,
    Here is the port of pees and restfulnesse   5
      To them that stand in stormès and disese,
    Refut overt to wreches in distresse,
      And al comfòrt of mischief and misese.

THOMAS HOCCLEVE

c. 1368–1426

148   *Anxious Thought*

M USING upon the restless bisynesse
      The which this troubly world hath ay on hande,
That other thing than fruit of bitternesse
    Ne yeeldeth not, as I can understande,
    At Chestres Inne, right fastè by the Strande,   5
      As I lay in my bed upon a night,
      Thought me bereft of sleep the force and might.

147. 1 cometh: come   4 of: from   6 disese: tribulation   7
Refut: refuge   overt: open   8 mischief . . .: trouble and suffering
148. 2 with which this troublous world is always occupied   7 thought
robbed me of the power and dominion of sleep

And many a day and night that wikked hine
Hadde before vexèd my poorè goste
So grevously, that of anguish and pine   10
   No richer man was never in no coste;
   This dare I say, may no wight make his boste
      That he with thought was bette than I aquainted,
      For he to the deth wel nigh hath me fainted. . . .

So long a night ne felt I never none   15
   As was that samè, to my juggèment.
Whoso that thoughty is, he is wo-begone;
   The thoughtful wight is vessel of torment:
   Ther is no greef to him equipollent;
      He graveth deepest of siknesses alle—   20
      Ful wo is him that in such cas is falle.

What wight that inly pensif is, I trowe,
   His moste desire is to be solitàrie;
That this is sooth in my persòne I knowe,
   For ever whil that freting adversàrie   25
   Mine hertè madè to him tributàrie
      In souking of the freshest of my blood,
      To sorwe soole me thought it did me good. . . .

When to the thoughtful wight is told a tale,
   He heereth it as though he thennès were;   30
His hevy thoughtès so him plukke and hale
   Hider and thider, and him greve and dere,

8 hine: fellow   9 goste: spirit   10 pine: pain   11 coste:
region   12 wight: man   13 bette: better   14 he: *i.e.* thought
to the deth: to death   fainted: weakened   15 felt: experienced   17
thoughty: anxious   19 there is no suffering which affects him so much
20 graveth: digs   21 cas: a plight   22 inly: inwardly   23 moste:
greatest   25 freting: devouring   26 subjugated my heart
27 souking: sucking   28 To sorwe soole: to sorrow alone   30
thennes: elsewhere   31 hale: pull   32 greve . . .: trouble and hurt

Thàt his eres availe him not a pere:
He understandeth nothing what men saye,
So been his wittès gone fro him awaye.   35

The smert of thought I by experience
Knowe also wel as doth any man living:
His frosty swote and firy-hot fervènce
And troubly dremès, drempt al in waking,
My mazèd hed sleepless han of cunning   40
And wit despoilèd, and so me bejaped
That after deth ful often have I gaped.

149   *Lament for Chaucer and Gower*

O MAISTER deere and fader reverent!
    My maister Chaucer, flowr of eloquence,
Mirour of fructuous entendèment,
    O universal fader in sciènce!
Allas that thou thyn excellent prudènce   5
    In thy bed mortal mightest nought bequethè!
What ailèd deth? allas! why wolde he slee thee?

O deth! thou didest nought harme singulèr,
    In slaughter of him; but al this land it smerteth.

148. 33 not . . .: not at all (*lit.* a pear)   34 nothing: not at all   35
his wits have so deserted him   36 smert: pain   37 also: as
38 swote: sweat   40 f. have deprived my sleepless fuddled head of
sense and intelligence, and so deluded me   42 gaped after: longed for

149. 1 reverent: reverend   3 entendement: understanding   6 In
thy bed mortal: on thy death-bed   7 wolde . . .: did he want to slay
you   8 singuler: single   9 smerteth: hurts

But nathéless, yet hast thou no powèr   10
  His namè slee; his high vertù asterteth
Unslain fro thee, which ay us lifly herteth
  With bookès of his òrnat ènditing,
  That is to al this land enlumining.

Hast thou not eek my maister Gower slain,   15
  Whos vertu I am insufficient
For to descrive? I wot wel in certàin
  For to sleen al this world thou hast y-ment;
  But sin our Lord Crist was obedient
    To thee, in faith I can no ferther seye: 20
    His creäturès mosten thee obeye.

150   *I have set my Heart so High*

I HAVE set my hert so hye,
  Me liketh no love that lowere is;
And alle the paines that I may drye,
  Me think it do me good, y-wis.

For on that Lorde that loved us alle   5
  So hertely have I set my thought,
It is my joye on Him to calle.
  For love me hath in balès brought,
  Me think it do me good, y-wis.

149. 11 to slay his reputation; his great excellence escapes   12 lifly
herteth: vitally inspires   13 ornat . . .: polished style   17
descrive: describe   in certain: indeed   18 you have resolved to slay
this whole world   19 sin: since   21 mosten: must

150. 3 drye: endure   4 it seems to me they do me good, indeed
6 hertely: devotedly   8 For: Because

151

The Agincourt Carol

*D*EO *gracias, Anglia,*
  Redde pro victoria.

Our King went forth to Normandy
With grace and might of chivalry;
Ther God for him wrought mervelusly;   5
Wherfore England may call and cry
  '*Deo gracias*'.

He sette a sege, the sooth for to say,
To Harflu town with ryal aray;
That town he wan and made afray   10
That Fraunce shal rewe til domèsday:
  Deo gracias.

Then went our King with alle his host
Thorough Fraunce, for all the Frenshè bost;
He spared no drede of lest ne most   15
Til he come to Agincourt cost:
  Deo gracias.

Then, forsooth, that knight comely
In Agincourt feeld he faught manly.
Thorough grace of God most mighty   20
He had both the feeld and the victory:
  Deo gracias.

4 chivalry: men at arms   **8** sette a sege: laid siege   **9** ryal: royal   **10** wan: won   afray: an attack   **15** he neither spared nor feared the least nor the greatest   **16** come: came   cost: district   **19** manly: manfully

There dukes and erles, lord and baròne
Were take and slain, and that wel sone;
And sume were ledde into Lundòne   25
With joy and merth and gret renone:
 Deo gracias.

Now gracious God He save our King,
His peple, and alle his wel-willing;
Yef him good life and good ending,   30
That we with merth mowe savely sing
 '*Deo gracias*'.

152   *God Speed the Plough!*

T H E merthe of all this land
 Maketh the good husband
  With ering of his plow.
Y-blessed be Cristès sand
That hath us sent in hand   5
  Merthe and joye y-now.

· The plow goth many a gate
 Both erly and eke late
  In winter in the clay,
About barly and whete,   10
That maketh men to swete:
  God spede the plow al day!

151. 26 renone: pomp 29 wel-willing: well-wishers 30 Yef:
give 31 mowe savely: may confidently

152. 1 f. The good farmer creates the happiness of all this land 3 ering:
ploughing 4 sand: dispensation 5 us in hand: to us 7
gate: way 9 clay: earth 10 About: for the cultivation of

Brown, Morel and Gore
Drawen the plow ful sore
  Al in the morwèning;   15
Rewarde hem ther-fòre
With a shefe or more
  Al in the evèning.

When men begin to sowe,
Ful wel her corn they knowe   20
  In the mounthe of May.
However Janiver blowe,
Whether hye or lowe,
  God spede the plow allway!

When men beginneth to wede   25
The thistle fro the sede
  In sumer when they may,
God lete hem wel to spede;
And long good life to lede
  All that for plowmen pray.   30

153

Drinking Song

'TAPPSTER, fill another ale'.
    'Anon have I do'.
'God send us good sale!
Avale the stake, avale!

152. 13 names of horses or oxen   14 sore: laboriously   16 hem:
them   20 her: their   knowe: judge   22 January   28 lete:
grant   29 f. and (may God grant that) all who pray for plowmen
may long lead a happy life

153. 2 I've done it at once   3 sale: fortune   4 Avale: ? prosper
stake: ale-stake, tavern-sign

Here is good ale y-founde!   5
     Drink to me,
     And I to thee,
And let the cupp go rounde!'

154   *For the Night-Mare*

Take a flint stone that hath an hole thorough of his owen growing,
and hang it over the stabil dore, or ell over horse, and ell write this
charm.

> *In nomine Patris, etc.*

SAINT Jorge, our Lady knight,
He walked day, he walked night,
Till that he founde that foule wight;
And when that he her founde,
He her bete and he her bounde,   5
Till trewly ther her trowth she plight
That she sholde not come by night
Within seven rod of lande space
Theras Saint Jeorge y-named was.
     St. Jeorge. St. Jeorge. St. Jeorge.   10

> *In nomine Patris, etc.*

And write this in a bille and hange it in the hors mane.

155   *Rats Away!*

I COMAUNDE alle the ratones that are here aboute,
That none dwelle in this place, withinne ne withoute,
Thorgh the vertu of Jesu Crist, that Mary bare aboute,

154. of his owen growing: naturally formed   ell: (i) else, (ii) also
1 Lady: Lady's   3 wight: creature   9 Theras: where
hors: horse's

155. 3 vertu: power

That alle creätures owen for to loute,
And thorgh the vertu of Mark, Mathew, Luke, an Jon— 5
Alle foure Evangeles corden into on—
Thorgh the vertu of Saint Geretrude, that maide clene,
   God graunte that grace
   That none raton dwelle in the place
That here names were nemeled in; 10
And thorgh the vertu of Saint Kasi,
That holy man, that prayed to God Almighty
   For scathes that they deden
   His meden
By dayes and by night, 15
God bad hem fleen and gon out of every mannes sight.
Dominus Deus Sabaot! Emanuel, that gret Godes name!
I betweche this place from ratones and from alle other
   shame.
God save this place fro alle other wikked wightes,
Bothe by dayes and by nightes! *et in nomine Patris et* 20
   Filii, etc.

156   *The World so Wide*

THE worlde so wide, th'air so remuàble,
   The sely man so litel of statùre,
The grove and ground of clothing so mutàble,
   The fire so hot and subtil of natùre,

155. 4 owen...: ought to revere   6 Evangeles: Gospels   corden...:
accord together   10 here: their   nemeled: named   11 Kasi:
Nicasius   13 f. because of the damage they did his meadows   16
hem: them   18 betweche: ? charm   shame: harm   19 wightes:
creatures

156. 1 remuable: changeable   2 sely: helpless   3 the grove and
the earth so variable in their clothing

The water never in oon—what creätùre,   5
  That made is of these fourè thus flitting,
  May stedfast be as here in his living?

The more I go the ferther I am behinde,
  The ferther behind the neer my wayès ende;
The more I seche the worsè can I finde,   10
  The lighter leve the lother for to wende;
  The bet I serve the more al out of mende.
    Is this fortùne—n'ot I—or ìnfortune?
    Though I go loose, tied am I with a lune.

JOHN AUDELAY

fl. 1426

157   *What Tidings?*

'WHAT tithinges bringest us, messangère,
      Of Cristès birth this New Yeres Day?'

'A babe is born of high natùre,
  A Prince of Pese that ever shal be;
Of heven and erth He hath the cure;   5
  His lordship is eternité—
    Such wonder tithinges ye may here.'
    'What tithinges bringes the messangère?'
    'That God and man is one in fere,
      Our sin had made but feendès prey.   10

156. 5 in oon: the same   6 foure: *i.e.* the elements   flitting: shifting
7 as . . .: as regards his life here   9 neer: nearer   10 seche: seek
11 f. the easier the leave, the more unpleasant it is to go; the better I deserve,
the more completely it is forgotten   13 n'ot I: I know not   14
lune: leash

157. 5 cure: charge   7 wonder: wonderful   9 f. that God is
united with man, (whom) our sin . . .

'A seemly selcouth it is to see
  The burd that had this barn y-born—
This child conseived in high degré—
  And maiden is as was beforn.
    Such wonder tithinges ye may here: 15
    That maiden and moder is one y-fere
    And lady is of high aray.

'A wonder thing is now befall:
  That Lord that made both see and sun,
Heven and earth and angeles all,   20
  In mankind is now becum.'
    'What tithinges bringes the messangère?'
    'A faunt that is but of one yere
    Ever has been and shal be ay.

'This lovely lady con grete her child: 25
  "Hail, Son! Hail, Broder! Hail, Fader dere!"
"Hail, doghter! Hail, sister! Hail, moder mild!"
  This hailsing was on coint manère.
    Such wonder tithinges ye may here:
    This greting was of so high chere   30
    That mannès pine it turned to play.

'That Lord that all thing made of nought
  Is man becum for mannès love;
For with His blood he shal be bought
  From bale to blis that is above—   35
    Such wonder tithinges ye may here.
    That Lord us grant now our prayère,
    To dwel in heven that we may.'

11 selcouth: marvel   12 burd: maiden barn: child   16 y-fere:
together   17 aray: degree   23 faunt: infant   25 con grete:
greeted   28 this salutation was in courteous style   30 so . . .:
such great affection   31 pine: pain play: joy   35 bale: misery

158   *The Fairest Flower*

THERE is a flowr sprung of a tree,
    The roote therof is called Jessé,
  A flowr of price;
Ther is non such in Paradise.

This flowr is fair and fresh of hew;   5
It fadès never, but ever is new;
The blisful branch this flowr on grew
Was Mary mild, that bare Jesù,
    A flowr of grace;
    Agains al sorow it is solàce.   10

The sede hereof was Godès sand,
That God Himself sew with His hand,
In Bedlem, in that holé land,
Mides her herbèr, ther He her fand;
    This blisful flowr   15
    Sprang never but in Marys bowr.

When Gabriel this maidè met,
With 'Ave Mària' he her gret;
Betwene hem two this flowr was set
And kept was (no man shuldè wit)   20
    Hent on a day
    In Bedlem it can spred and spray.

---

11 sand: gift   12 sew: sowed   14 in the middle of her garden, where He found her   18 gret: greeted   19 this flower was planted by the two of them secretly   20 shulde wit: must know
21 Hent: till   22 in Bethlehem it grew and sprang

When that flowr began to sprede
And his blossum forth to bede,
Rich and pore of everé lede,   25
They marveld how this flowr might sprede,
    Til kingės three
    That blisful flowrė came to see.

Angeles ther came out of here towr
To looke upon this freshelé flowr,   30
How fair He was in His colòur,
And how swote in His savòur,
    And to behold
    How such a flowr might spring in gold.

Of lilyė, of rose of rise,   35
Of primrole and of flour-de-lise,
Of al the flowrs, at my devise,
That flowr of Jesse yet bers the prise
    As most of hele
    To slake our sorows everédele.   40

I pray you, flowrs of this cuntré,
Wherever ye go, wherever ye be,
Hold up the flowr of good Jessé
Fore your freshness and your beuté,
    As fairest of al,   45
    And ever was and ever shal.

24 bede: show   25 lede: nation   29 here: their   30
freshelé: beautiful   32 swote: sweet   35 of rise: on the spray
36 primrole: primrose   37 at . . .: in my opinion   38 bers . . .:
is supreme   39 hele: healing power   40 everédele: completely
43 Hold up: exalt   44 Fore: above

159 *The Love of God*

I HAVE a love is Heven-King;
  I love His love for evermore.

For love is love and ever shall be,
  And love has been or we were bore;
For love He askes non other fee   5
  But love again; He kepes no more.
    I say herefore: I have, *etc.*

Trew love is tresoure, trust is store
  To a love to Godes plesing;
But lewdè love makes men y-lore,   10
  To love here lust and here liking.
    I say herefore: I have, *etc.*

In good love there is no sin;
  Without love is heviness:
Herfore to love I n'il not blin,   15
  To love my God and His goodness.
    I say herefore: I have, *etc.*

1 is: (who) is   4 or: before   bore: born   6 again: in
return   kepes: desires   7 herefore: therefore   8 store: precious
possession   9 plesing: liking   10 lewde: *i.e.* earthly   y-lore:
lost, ruined   11 (makes men) love their desire and their pleasure
14 without love there is sadness   15 for this reason I will not cease
to love

For He me loved or I Him knew,
  Therfore I love Him altherbest
(Elles my love I might it rew);   20
    I love with Him to take my rest.
    I say herefore: I have, *etc.*

Of all loveres that ever was born
  His love it passèd everichone.
N'ad He us loved we were forlorn;   25
    Without His love trew love is none.
    I say herefore: I have, *etc.*

160   *Dread of Death*

LADY, helpe! Jesu, mercé!
  Timor mortis conturbat me.

Dred of deth, sorow of sin
  Trobels my hert ful grevously;
My soul it noyth with my lust then—   5
  Passio Christi conforta me.

For blindnes is a hevy thing,
  And to be def therwith only,
To lese my light and my hering—
  Passio Christi conforta me;   10

159. 18 For: Because   or: before   19 altherbest: best of all   20 Elles: otherwise   21 take. . .: dwell   24–26 His love surpassed every love. Had He not loved us, we should have been lost; there is no true love except His love

160. 5 my soul is distressed by my sinful desires then   8 only: especially   9 lese: lose

And to lese my tast and my smelling,
   And to be seke in my body;
Here have I lost al my liking—
   Passio Christi conforta me.

Thus God He yives and takes away,   15
   And, as He wil, so mot it be.
His name be blessed both night and day—
   Passio Christi conforta me.

Here is a cause of gret mourning:
   Of myself nothing I see   20
Save filth, unclenness, vile stinking—
   Passio Christi conforta me.

Into this world no more I brought;
   No more I get with me trewly
Save good deed, word, wil, and thought—   25
   Passio Christi conforta me.

The fivè woundes of Jesu Crist
   My medicine now mot they be,
The feendès power down to cast—
   Passio Christi conforta me.   30

As I lay seke in my langòure,
   With sorow of hert and teere of ye,
This carol I made with gret dolòure—
   Passio Christi conforta me.

Oft with this prayere I me blest: 35
   '*In manus tuas, Domine;*

12 seke: sick	**13 liking**: pleasure	**15 yives**: gives	16
mot: must	**24 get**: acquire to take	**32 ye**: eye	

Thou take my soule into thy rest—
Passio Christi conforta me.'

Mary, moder, merciful may,
  For the joys thou hadest, ladỳ,   40
To thy Son for me thou pray—
  Passio Christi conforta me.

Lerne this lesson of blind Awdlay:
  When bale is highest, then bot may be.
If thou be noyèd night or day,   45
  Say '*Passio Christi conforta me.*'

JOHN LYDGATE

c. 1370–1450

161   *Like a Midsummer Rose*

LET no man boste of cunning nor vertù,
    Of tresour, richesse, nor of sapience,
Of worldly sùpport, for al cometh of Jesù,
Counsàil, confòrt, discrecioun, prudènce,
Provisioun, forsight, and providence,   5
  Like as the Lord of gracè list dispose:
Some man hath wisdom, some man hath eloquence—
Al stant on chaunge like a midsomer rose.

Holsom in smelling be the swotè flowres,
  Ful dèlitable outward to the sight;   10

160. 37 rest: mansion   39 may: maiden   44 When trouble is at
its height, the remedy may come   45 noyed: troubled

161. 1 cunning: learning   5 Provisioun: looking ahead   6 Like as:
just as   8 stant on: is founded on   9 swote: sweet   10 delit-
able: delightful

The thorn is sharp, curèd with fresh colòures:
  Al is not gold that outward sheweth bright.
A stokfish bone in derknesse yeveth a light,
  Tween fair and foul, as God list dispose
A difference atwixen day and night—   15
  Al stant on chaunge like a midsomer rose. . . .

The golden char of Phebus in the air
  Chaseth mistes blak that they dare not appeere,
At whos uprist mountains be made so fair
  As they were newly gilt with his beemes cleere;   20
The night doth folwe, appalleth al his cheere
  When western wawes his streemès over-close.
Rekne al beuté, al freshness that is heere,
  Al stant on chaunge like a midsomer rose.

Constraint of coldè maketh flowrès dare   25
  With winter frostes that they dare not appeere.
Al clad in russet the soil of green is bare;
  Tellus and Jove be dullèd of their cheere
By revolucioun and turning of the yeere.
  As gery March his stoundès doth disclose—   30
Now rein, now storm, now Phebus bright and cleere—
  Al stant on chaunge like a midsomer rose.

Wher is now David, the most worthy king
  Of Juda and Israel, most famous and notàble?

11 cured . . .: covered with bright coloured flowers   13 stokfish:
dried fish   yeveth . . .: gives a light (because rotten)   14 Tween . . .
foul: i.e. which looks fair and is foul   15 atwixen: between   17
char: chariot   19 whos: i.e. the sun's   uprist: rising   20 As:
as if   21 appalleth: dims   cheere: face   22 wawes: waves
streemes: beams   23 freshness: brightness   25 dare: lie hidden
28 earth and heaven are dulled in their appearance   30 as fitful March
shows its varieties (lit. times)

And wher is Solomon most sovereign of cunning,   35
  Richest of bilding, of tresour incomparàble?
Face of Absolon, most fair, most amiàble?
  Rekne up echone, of trouthè make no glose,
Rekne up Jonathas, of frenship immutàble—
  Al stant on chaunge like a midsomer rose.   40

Wher is Julius, proudest in his empìre,
  With his triùmphès most imperial?
Wher is Pirrus, that was lord and sire
  Of al Inde in his estat royàl?
And wher is Alisaunder that conquered al,   45
  Failed leiser his testament to dispose?
Nabugodonosor or Sardanapal?
  Al stant on chaunge like a midsomer rose.

Wher is Tullius with his sugred tunge?
  Or Crisistomus with his golden mouth?   50
The aureat ditees that be red and sunge
  Of Omerus, in Greece both north and south?
The tragedỳès divers and uncouth
  Of moral Senek, the mysteryes to unclose?
By many example this matere is ful couth—   55
  Al stant on chaunge like a midsomer rose.

Wher been of Frauncè al the Dozèpeers
  Which in Gaule hadde the governaunce?
'Vowes of the Pecok', with al their proudè cheers?

35 cunning: wisdom   38 glose: falsification   46 (who) lacked
the leisure to make his will   47 Nebuchadnezzar   Sardanapalus
49 Cicero   50 St. John Chrysostom   51 ditees: compositions
52 Homer   53 uncouth: marvellous   55 ful couth: well known
57 Dozepeers: twelve peers of Charlemagne   59 Vowes of the Pecok:
i.e. martial vows made to a peacock in the Alexander romance *Les Vœux
du Paon*   their . . .: their (the heroes') proud bearing

The Worthy Nine with al their high bobbaunce?   60
Troian knightės, grettest of alliaunce?
  The flees of gold conquerėd in Colchòse?
Rome and Cartàge, most soverein of puissaunce?
  Al stant on chaunge like a midsomer rose. . . .

The rèmembraunce of every famous knight,   65
  Ground cònsidered, is bilt on rightwisnesse.
Race out ech quarel that is not bilt on right;
  Withoutė trouth what vaileth high noblesse?
Laurer of martirs founded on holynesse—
  White was made red their triumphes to disclose: 70
The whitė lillye was their chast clennesse,
  Their bloody suffraunce was no somer rose.

It was the Rose of the bloody feeld,
  Rose of Jericho that grew in Bedleëm;
The five Roses portrayėd in the sheeld,   75
  Splayed in the baner at Jerusalem.
The sonne was clips and derk in every rem
  When Crist Jesù five wellės list unclose
Toward Paradis, called the redė strem,
  Of whos five woundes print in your hert a rose.   80

---

60 bobbaunce: pride   61 grettest . . .: *i.e.* the most united of companies   62 Colchis   66 Ground considered: when the grounds are examined   67 Race out: erase   quarel: claim   68 vaileth: avails   noblesse: nobility   69 Laurer: laurel   71 clennesse: purity   76 Splayed: displayed   77 clips: eclipsed   rem: realm

Froward Maymond

A FROWARD knave plainly to descrive
   And a sluggard shortly to declare:
A precious knave that casteth him never to thrive,
  His mouth wel wet, his sleves right thredbare,
  A turnebroche, a boy for Hogge of Ware,   5
    With louring face, nodding and slumbring,
    Of newe cristened and called Jakke Hare,
     Which of a bolle can plukke out the lining.

This boy Maymond, ful stuborne of his bones,
  Sluggy on morwen his limes up to dresse,   10
A gentel harlot chose out for the nones,
  Son and cheef heir unto Dame Idelnesse,
  Cosin to Wecok, brother to Reklesnesse,
    Which, late at eve and morwe, at his rising
  Ne hath no joye to do no bisinesse,   15
     Save of a tancard to plukke out the lining.

A boy Chekrelic was his sworen brother
  Of every dish a lipet out to take;

---

1 descrive: describe   2 declare: depict   3 a worthless rascal who makes no effort to do well   5 turnebroche: turn-spit   Roger (Hodge) of Ware, *i.e.* the Cook in *The Canterbury Tales*   7 of newe: newly   8 bolle: drinking-bowl   lining: contents   9 ful . . .: a thorough lazy-bones   10 f. sluggish in getting up in the morning, a choice specimen of a born scoundrel   13 Wecok: *unexplained*   15 to . . .: in any activity   17 Chekrelic: ?picker of scraps   18 lipet: morsel

And Fafyntycol was also another
  Of every bribe the cariage for to make.   20
He can wel waiten on an oven-cake
  And of newe ale been at the clensing;
And of purpos his thirst for to slake
  Can of a picher plukke out the lining.

This knave by leiser wil don al his messàge   25
  And holde a tale with every maner wight;
Ful pale drunken, wel vernished of visàge,
  Whos tonge ay faileth when it draweth to night,
Of o candell he weneth two were light;
  As barked lether his face is shining;   30
Glasy-eyed wil claime of due right
  Out of a bolle to plukke out the lining.

He can a-bed an hors-combe wel shake
  Like as he wold coraye his masters hors;
And with his one hand his masters doublet take   35
  And with the tother privily cut his purs.
Alle swiche knaves shul have Cristes curs
  Erly on morwe at their uprising.
To finde a boy I trow ther be none wors
  Out of a pot to plukke out the lining.   40

He may be sold upon warantise
  As for a truant that no thing wil doon:

19 Fafyntycol: *unexplained*   20 ?to carry out any pilfering
21 can . . .on: knows well how to watch for   23 and for the purpose
of slaking his thirst   25 f. This fellow will do all his errands in a
leisurely way and chat with all kinds of people   27 wel . . .: with
his face all glistening   29 he takes one lit candle for two   30
barked: tanned   34 as if he would curry-comb his master's horse(s)
37 swiche: such   shul: shall   39 I am sure there's no worse boy to
be found   41 upon . . .: under guarantee   42 As for a truant: as
an idle rogue

To selle hors-provendre is his cheef marchaundise,
 And for a chevesaunce can plukke off their shoon,
 And at the dise play the mony soon,   45
  And with his winninges he maketh his offring
 At the ale-stakes, sitting again the moon,
 Out of a cup to plukke out the lining.

L'envoye

Wassail to Maymond and to his jousy pate!
 Unthrift and he be togedre met;   50
Late at eve he wil unspere the gate,
 And grope on morwe if Rigges bak be wet
 And if the bak of Togace be out-het;
  His hevy nolle at midmorwe uplifting
 With unwashen hands, not laced his doublèt, 55
 Out of a bolle to plukke out the lining.

163 *From the Epilogue to 'The Fall of Princes'*

AND semblably, though I go not upright,
 But stoupe and halte for lak of elloquence,
Though Omerus held not the torchè light
 To forthre my penne with colours of cadènce,

---

162. 43 hors-provendre: *i.e.* horse-feed stolen from his master marchaundise: trade 44 chevesaunce: illicit profit 47 at the taverns, sitting in the moonlight 49 Here's to Maymond and his sodden pate 50 Unthrift: neglect and waste 51 unspere . . .: leave the door open 52 f. and feel in the morning to see if Rigg's (the dog's) back is wet and if Togace's (the cat's) back is very hot: *i.e.* to see if it is raining and if the fire is still in

163. 1 semblably: similarly 2 halte: limp 3 Omerus: Homer 4 to help my pen with the ornaments of verse

Nor moral Senec, most sad of his sentènec,   5
  Gaf me no part of his moralitees:
Therfore I saye, thus kneeling on my knees

To allè tho that shal this book beholde,
  I them beseke to have compassioun;
And therwithal I pray hem that they wolde   10
  Favoùre the metre and do correccioun;
  Of gold nor asur I had no foisòun,
    Nor other colours, this processe t'enlumìne,
    Sauf white and blak—and they but dully shine.

I never was acquainted with Virgìle,   15
  Nor with the sugred ditees of Omèr,
Nor Darès Frigius with his golden stile,
  Nor with Ovìde, in poetrye most entier,
  Nor with the soverein ballades of Chaucèr,
    Which, among alle that ever were red or sung,   20
    Excelled al other in our English tung.

I can not been a juge in this matèr:
  As I conceive, folwing my fantasye,
In moral mater ful notable was Gowèr,
  And so was Strode in his philosophye;   25
  In 'Parfit Living', which passeth poesye,
    Richard hermìte, contemplatif of sentènce,
    Drough in English *The Prikke of Conscience*.

5 sad . . .: profound in his thought   8 tho: those   9 beseke: beseech   10 hem: them   11 Favoure: look kindly on   12 foisoun: supply   13 processe: work   14 Sauf: save   16 sugred ditees: honeyed verses   17 Frigius: the Phrygian   18 entier: perfect   23 fantasye: opinion   26 Parfit Living: The Form of Perfect Living   passeth: surpasses   27 Richard Rolle   of sentence: thoughtful   28 Drough: (who) translated

As the gold-tressèd brightè somer sunne
  Passeth other sterrès with his beemès clere,　　　　30
And as Lucinia chaseth skyès dunne
  The frosty nightes when Esperus doth appere,
  Right so my maister haddè never pere—
    I mene Chaucer—in stories that he tolde;
    And he also wrote tragedyès olde,　　　　35

The fall of princes gan pitously complaine,
  As Petrark did, and also John Bochàs,
Laureat Franceis, poetes bothè twaine
  Tolde how princes, for their grete trespàs,
  Were overthrowe, rehersing al the cas,　　　　40
    As Chaucer did in the Monkès Tale.
    But I, that standè low down in the vale,

So grete a book in English to translate,
  Did it by constraint and no presumpcioun;
Born in a village which callèd is Lydgate,　　　　45
  By oldè time a famous castel town;
  In Danès time it was betè down,
    Time when Saint Edmond, martir, maide, and king,
    Was slain at Oxne, by record of writing.

I me excuse, now this book is y-do,　　　　50
  How I was never yet at Citheroun,
Nor on the mountain callèd Pèrnaso,
  Where ninè muses have their mansioun.

---

30 sterres: stars　　clere: bright　　　31 Lucina (the moon)　　chaseth:
dispels　　　36 gan complaine: lamented　　　37 Bochas: Boccaccio
38 Franceis: *i.e.* Petrarch　　　40 rehersing . . .: relating all that happened
45 Lidgate (Suffolk)　　　47 bete: battered　　　49 Oxne . . .: Hoxne,
as recorded in writing　　　51 Cithaeron　　52 Parnassus

But to concludė myn entencioun
    I wil procedė forth with white and blak,   55
And where I faile, let Lydgate bere the lak.

164   *Prayer to St. Helena*

S AINT Elėnė, I thee pray
    To helpe me at my lastė day
To sette the crosse and His passiòne
Betwix my sinfull soule and dome,
Now and in the houre of my dede,   5
And bring my soule to requied.

165   *O Man Unkind*

O MAN unkind, have in mind
    My painės smert!
Behold and see that is for thee
    Percėd my hert.

And yet I wold, or than thou shold   5
    Thy soule forsake,
On cros with pain sharp deth again
    For thy love take.

For which I ask none other task
    But love again.   10
Me then to love all thing above
    Thou ought be fain.

163. 54 entencioun: intended task   56 lak: blame
164. 4 dome: judgement   5 dede: death   6 requied: rest
165. 5 or: rather   9 task: payment   10 again: in return

166   *I Went to Death*

'I WENDE to dede, a king y-wis;
   What helps honòur or worldès blis?
Dede is to man the kindè way—
I wendè to be clad in clay.'

'I wende to dede, clerk ful of skill,
That couthe with wordes men mate and still.
So soone has the dede me made an ende—
Bes war with me! to dede I wende.'

'I wende to dede, knight stif in stowr,
Through fight in feeld I won the flowr.   10
No fights me taught the dede to quell—
I wende to dede, sooth I you tell'.

167   *Lyarde is an Old Horse*

LYARDE is an olde horse and may nought wel drawe;
   He shall be put into the parke holyn for to gnawe.
Barefoot withouten shone there shall he go,
For he is an olde horse and may no more do.
Whiles that Lyarde might drawe, the whiles was he loved;   5
They put him to provande, and therwith he proved.
Now he may nought do his dede as he might beforn,

166. 1 dede: death   y-wis: truly   3 kinde: natural   5 clerk:
scholar   skill: wisdom   6 who knew how to subdue and silence
men with words   8 Bes: be   with: by   9 stif . . .: stout in
battle   10 the flowr: pre-eminence   11 quell: slay

167. 2 holyn: holly   3 shone: shoes   5 loved: praised   6 pro-
vande: fodder   proved: throve   7 beforn: before

403

Thay lig before him pese-straw, and beres away the corn.
They lede him to the smethy to pulle off his shone
And puttes him to greenwoode, ther for to gone.   10
Who-so may nought do his dede, he shall to parke,
Barefoot withouten shone, and go with Lyarde.

168   *With I and E*

WHEN Adam dalf and Evè span, go spire—if thou
        may spede—
Where was than the pride of man, that now marres his
        mede?
Of erthe and lam, as was Adàm makede to noye and nede,
We ar, as he, maked to be, whiles we this life shall lede.
    With I and E, borne ar we, as Salomon us highte,   5
      To travell here, whiles we are fere, as fowle unto the
        flighte.

In werlde we ware casten for care, to we ware worthy to
        wende
To wele or wa, ane of thas twa to welde withouten ende.
For-thy, whiles thou may helpe thee now, amend thee, and
        have mende,

167. 8 lig: lay   pese-straw: straw made of dry pea-plants   11 shall:
must (go)

168. When Adam delved and Eve spun, go (and) ask—if you may succeed
—where then was the pride of man, which now deprives him of his reward
(in heaven)? As Adam was made of earth and clay for trouble and distress,
(so) we, like him, are made, as long as we must lead this life. With I and E,
we are born, as Solomon promised us, to labour here, while we are able, as
a bird (is born) to fly.

  In the world we were intended for sorrow, till we had deserved to pass
to bliss or woe, to possess one of these two without end. Therefore, while
you can help yourself now, reform and bear in mind (that), when you

When thou shall ga, he bes thy fa that here was are thy
frende.   10
   With E and I, I rede for-thy, umthinke thee ay of three:
   What we ar, and what we war, and what that we shall be.

Ware thou as wise, praisèd in prise, as was Salomon,
Wel fairer fode of bane and blode that was Absolon,
Strengely and strang to wreke thy wrang as ever was
Sampson,   15
Thou ne might a day, na mare than thay, the dede with-
stand allon.
   With I and E, the dede to thee shall come, as I thee
kenne,
   But thou ne wate in whatkin state, ne how, ne whare,
ne whenne.

When bemes shall blaw rewly on raw, to rekkening bus us
rise,
When He shall come unto that dome, Jesù, to sit justise. 20
That are was leve then mon be greve, when all gastès shall
rise;
I say that than to sinfull man sary bes that assise.

must go, he shall be your foe who before was your friend here. With E
and I, I advise (you) therefore, consider always three things: what we are,
and what we were, and what we shall be.

   Were you as wise, as highly esteemed, as was Solomon, (were you) a
much fairer creature of bone and blood than was Absalom, (were you) as
brave and strong in avenging your wrong as ever Sampson was, (yet) you
could not for one day, any more than they, withstand death alone. With
I and E, death shall come to you, as I tell you, but you do not know in
what circumstances, nor how, nor where, nor when.

   When trumpets shall blow dreadfully in turn, we must rise to render
account, when He, Jesu, shall come to that Judgement to sit as judge. What
before was dear shall then be grievous, when all souls must rise; I declare
that for sinful man that Judgement then shall be grim. With I and E, he

With I and E, he shall nought flee, if all he his giltès fele;
He ne may him hide, but thare abide, ne fra that dome
    appele.

Of all thine aughte that thee was raughte shall thou nought
    have, I hete,   25
But seven fote thare-in to rote, and a winding-shete.
For-thy thou give whiles thou may live, or all gas that thou
    may gete,
Thy gast fra God, thy goodes olòd, thy flesh foldes under
    fete.
    With I and E, full seker thou be that thine executours
    Of thee ne will rekk, but skikk and skekk full baldely in
    thy bowrs.   30

To dome we drawe, the sothe to shawe in life that us was
    lent;
No Latin ne lawe may help an hawe, but rathely us repent.
The croice, the crown, the spere bes bown, that Jesu rugged
    and rent;
The nailès rude shall thee conclude with thine awen argu-
    ment.

shall not escape, if he hide all his offences; he cannot hide himself, but
(must) stay there, nor (can he) appeal against that judgement.

Of all your property that was granted to you, you shall retain nothing, I
promise, but seven foot in which to rot, and a winding-sheet. Therefore
give while you are alive, before everything that you can acquire goes,
(before) your spirit (goes) from God, your goods (are) dispersed, and your
flesh collapses beneath (men's) feet. With I and E, be very certain that your
executors will not care about you, but will rob and pillage quite brazenly
in your home.

To judgement we shall come, to reveal the truth in the life that was
granted us; no Latin nor law can help at all (*lit.* a haw), unless we quickly
repent. The cross, the crown, the spear shall be ready, which tore and
rent Jesus; the coarse nails shall confute you with your own argument.

With E and O, take kepe thare-to, as Crist Himself us
    kende;   35
We come and go to wele or wo that dredfull dome shall
    ende.

Of will, and wit that vesettes it, in word and that we
    wroughte,
Rekken we mon, and yeeld resòn full rathely of our
    thoughte.
Shall no fallàce cover our case, ne consail gette we noughte;
No gift ne grace, nother thare gase, but brouke as we have
    broughte.   40
    With E and I, I rede for-thy, be ware now with thy
        werkes;
    For termes of yere has thou nane here: thy medes shall
        be thy merkes.

What so it be that we here see—the fairhed of thy face,
Thy blee so bright, thy main, thy might, thy mouth that
    mirthès mase—
All mon as wase to powder passe, to grave when that thou
    gase;   45
A grisely gest then bes thou prest in armès for to brace.

With E and O, pay heed to that, as Christ himself told us; we come and
go to weal or woe which the dread judgement shall determine.

Of (our) will, and of the intellect that watches over it, (as expressed) in
word and in what we have done, we must render account, and give an
explanation, without any delay, of our thought. No deception shall conceal
our position, nor shall we get any advocate; neither gift nor favour,
neither will serve there, but we shall fare as we have deserved. With E
and I, I advise (you) therefore, take care in what you do now; for you
have no days of reckoning here: your rewards (there) must be your goal.

What we see here, whatever it is—the fairness of your face, your com-
plexion so lovely, your strength, your power, your mouth that makes
merry—all must, like a straw torch, turn to dust, when you go to the
grave; then you will quickly become a gruesome guest to embrace in

With I and E, for—leve thou me—bes nane, as I thee
    hete,
Of all thy kith dare sleep thee with a night under thy
    shete.

169   *The Rose that bore Jesu*

T HER is no rose of swich vertù
   As is the rose that bare Jesù:
    Alleluya!

For in this rose conteinèd was
Heven and erth in litel space,   5
    Res miranda.

By that rose we may wel see
That He is God in persones three,
    Pari forma.

The aungeles sungen the sheperdes to: 10
   '*Gloria in excelsis Deo*'.
    Gaudeamus!

Leve we al this worldly mirth,
And folwè we this joyful birth:
    Transeamus.   15

168. arms. With I and E, for—believe you me—there shall be nobody, I
promise you, of all your family that will dare sleep with you for a night
under your sheet.

169. 1 swich: such

1394–1437

170   *The Nightingale's Song*

NOW was there maid fast by the towris wall
   A gardin faire, and in the corneris set
An herber grene, with wandis long and small
   Railit about; and so with treïs set
   Was all the place, and hawthorn hegis knet,   5
That lif was none walking there forby
That might within scarse any wight aspy.

So thik the bowis and the levès grene
   Beshadit all the aleyes that there were;
And middis every herber might be sene   10
   The sharpè grenè swetè jenepere,
   Growing so fair with branchis here and there
That, as it seemit to a lif without,
The bowis spred the herber all about.

And on the smallè grenè twistis sat   15
   The litil swetè nightingale, and song
So loud and clere the ympnis consecrat
   Of Lufis use, now soft, now loud among,
   That all the gardin and the wallis rong

---

1 fast: close   2 set: planted   3 herber: arbour   wandis:
stakes   small: slender   4 Railit: enclosed   5 knet: dense
6 that nobody walking by   10 middis: in the middle of   11
sharpe: pungent   jenepere: juniper   13 a lif . . .: anyone outside
15 twistis: twigs   16 song: sang   17 ympnis: hymns   18 Of:
to   among: at times

Right of thair song and of the copill next   20
Of thair swere armony—and lo the text:

'Worshippe, ye that loveris bene, this May,
    For of your bliss the kalendis ar begunne,
And sing with us "Away, winter, away!
    Cum, somer, cum, the swete sesòun and sunne!"   25
    Awake, for shame! that have your hevenis wunne,
And amorously lift up your hedis all;
Thank Luve that list you to his mercy call.'

Quhen thay this song had sung a litil thrawe,
    Thay stent a quhile, and therwith unafraid,   30
As I beheld and kest myn eyne a-lawe,
    From bough to bough thay hippit and thay plaid,
    And freshly in thair birdis kind arraid
Thair fetheris new, and fret thame in the sunne,
And thankit Lufe that had thair makis wunne.   35

171   *Against the Friars*

THOU that sellest the word of God,
    Be thou barfoot, be thou shod,
    Cum nevere here!
In principio erat verbum
Is the word of God all and sum   5
    That thou sellest, lewèd frere.

---

170. 20 indeed with their song and with the verse which follows   23
kalendis: first days   26 hevenis: supreme happiness   28 list: is
pleased to   29 thrawe: time   30 stent: ceased   31 kest . . .:
cast my eyes down   32 hippit: hopped   33 kind: manner
34 fret: preened   35 that: (they) who   makis: mates

171. 4 John 1:1, the friars' greeting   5 is the total word of God
6 lewed: ignorant

It is cursèd simonye
Either to selle or to bye
   Any gostly thing.
Therfore, frere, go as thou come,   10
And hold thee in thy hous at home
   Til we thee almès bring.

Goddès lawè ye reversen,
And mennès houses ye persen,
   As Paul bereth witness;   15
As midday develes going aboute,
For money lowlé ye loute,
   Flattering both more and less.

172   *The Friars' Retort*

A LLAS! what shul we frerès do,
   Now lewèd men cun Holy Writ?
All aboutè where I go
   They aposen me of it.

Then wondreth me that it is so   5
   How lewèd men cun alle wit.
Certenly we be undo
   But if we mo amenden it.

I trow the devel brought it about
   To write the Gospel in English,   10
For lewèd men been now so stout
   That they yiven us neither flesh ne fish.

171. 9 gostly: spiritual   10 come: came   13 reversen: overthrow
14 persen: penetrate   15 2 Tim. 3:6   17 loute: bow

172. 1 shul: shall   2 lewed: lay   cun: know   4 they confront
me with it   5 wondreth me: it amazes me   6 cun . . .: can
know everything   8 unless we can rectify it   11 stout: defiant

When I come into a shoppe
　　For to say 'In principio',
They bidden me 'Go forth, lewèd poppe!　　　15
　　And worch', and win my silver so.

If I say it longeth not
　　For prestes to worchè where they go,
They leggen for hem Holy Writ,
　　And sayèn that Saint Polle did so.　　　20

Then they looke on myn habìte,
　　And sayn: 'Forsooth, withouten othes,
Wher it be russet, black, or white,
　　It is worth all oure wering-clothes!'

I say: 'I biddè not for me,　　　25
　　But for them that havè none.'
They sayn: 'Thou havest two or three;
　　Yeve hem that nedeth therof one.'

Thus our desseitès been aspide
　　In this manèr and many mo;　　　30
Few men bedden us abide,
　　But hey fast that we were go.

If it go forth in this manère,
　　It wil don us muchè gile;
Men shul find unnethe a frere　　　35
　　In Englande within a while.

15 lewed: worthless　　　16 worch: work　　　17 longeth: is
fitting　　　19 they cite as their evidence Holy Writ　　　22 withouten
othes: undoubtedly　　　23 Wher: whether　　　25 bidde: ask
28 Yeve hem: give them　　　30 mo: more　　　31 bedden: ask
32 but to hurry up and be gone　　　33 forth: on　　　34 gile:
treachery　　　35 unnethe: scarcely

173 *Keep the Sea*

NOW then, for love of Crist and of His joye,
Bring yet England out of troble and noye;
Take hert and wit and set a governaunce,
Set many wittes withouten variaunce
To one accord and unanimité   5
Put to good willè for to kepe the see,
First for worship and profìte alsò,
And to rebuke of eche evil-willed fo:
Thus shall richèsse and worship to us long;
Then to the noble shall we do no wrong,   10
To bere that coin in figure and in dede,
To our coràge and our enmies to drede. . . .
   Kepe then the see about in speciàll,
Which of England is the roundè wall,
As though England were likened to a cité   15
And the wall environ were the see.
Kepe then the see, that is the wall of England,
And then is England kept by Goddès sand,
That, as for any thing that is withoute,
England were at ease withouten doute;   20
And thus shuld every land, one with another,
Entrecomòn as brother with his brother,

2 noye: tribulation   3–6 Take heart and thought and establish
a policy, set many minds without dissension to one unanimously agreed
aim directed to a firm determination to guard the sea   7 worship:
honour   8 rebuke of: repulse   9 to . . .: be ours   10 noble:
i.e. standard unit of money   11 f. in bearing that coin symbolically
and in fact, to inspire us with courage and our enemies with fear
13 in speciall: especially   16 environ: surrounding   18 sand:
dispensation   19 f. so that, as far as any threat from abroad is con-
cerned, England should be untroubled without cause for fear   22
Entrecomon: inter-associate

And live togedre werreless in unité
Without rancòur in verry charité,
In rest and peace, to Cristès grete plesàunce,　　25
Withoutè strife, debate and variaunce;
Which peace men shuld enserch with bisinesse
And knit it sadly, holding in holynesse.

174   *An Absent Lover*

NOW wolde I faine sum merthès make,
  Al only for my ladys sake,
    When I her see;
      But nowe I am so far fro her
    It wil not be.　　5

Though I be far out of her sight,
I am her man both day and night,
    And so wil be.
      Therfore I wolde as I love her
    She lovèd me.　　10

When she is mery, then am I glad;
When she is sory, then am I sad;
    And cause is why:
      For he liveth not that lovèd her
    So wel as I.　　15

---

173. 23 werreless: without war   **24** verry: true   **25** plesaunce:
joy   **26** debate: dispute   **27 f.** enserch . . .: seek diligently
and secure it firmly, holding it sacrosanct

174. 1 sum . . .: rejoice   **9** wolde: wish that   **13** and there is
reason why

She saith that she hath seen it writ
That 'selden seen is soone forgit'.
   It is not so:
      For in good faith, save only her,
     I love no mo.   20

Wherfor I pray, both night and day,
That she may cast all care away
   And live in rest;
      And evermor wherever she be
     To love me best.   25

And I to her to be so trew,
And never to chaungė for no new
   Unto my end;
      And that I may in her servìce
     Ever to amend.   30

175   *Go Heart, Hurt with Adversity*

GO hert, hurt with adversité,
  And let my lady thy woundės see,
And say her this, as I say thee:
'Fare wel my joy and welcom pain
Til I see my lady again!'

---

174. 17 forgit: forgotten   **20** no mo: nobody else   **27** new: *i.e.*
new love   30 ever do better

176   *Amend Me*

I PRAY you all with one thought,
Amendeth me and pair me nought.

Holy Writ saith—nothing is sother—
That no man shuld apair other;
Sith in God I am thy brother,   5
    Amendeth me and pair me nought.

The lore in the gospel ilk man may see,
If thy brother trespas to thee:
Between us two snib thou me,
    Amendeth me and pair me nought.   10

If thou see I do amiss,
And no man wot but thou of this,
Make it nought so il as it is:
    Amend me and pair me nought.

God biddes thou shalt no man defame,   15
No apair no mans name;
But, even as thou wold han the same,
    Amend me and pair me nought.

Apair thou no man with thy word,
Nother in ernest ne in bord;   20
Let thy tong, that is thy sword,
    Amend ever and pair nought.

2 Amendeth: correct   pair: injure   3 sother: truer   4 apair:
injure   5 Sith: since   7 ilk: each   9 rebuke me privately
16 No: nor   17 but, just as you would wish to have the same treat-
ment   20 Nother: neither   bord: jest

Now to amend God give us grace
Of rèpentaunce, and verré space
In heven ther to see His face,   25
    Wher we shall mend and pair nought.

177   *The Seven Sins*

WITH a garland of thornès kene
    My hed was crowned, and that was sene;
The stremes of blood ran by my cheke: SUPERBIA
Thou proudè man, lerne to be meke.

When thou art wroth and wolde take wreche   5
Kepe wel the lore that I thee teche.
Through my right hand the nail it goth: IRA
Forgive therfòre and be not wroth.

With a sperè sharp and grill
My hert was wounded, with my will,   10
For love of man that was me dere: INVIDIA
Envious man, of love thou lere.

Rise up, unlust, out of thy bedde!
Think on my feet that are for-bledde   ACCIDIA
And hardè nailed upon a tree: 15
Think theron, man; this was for thee.

Through my left hand the nail was drive:
Think theron if thou wilt live,
And worship God with almès-dede,   AVARICIA
If thou in hevene wilt have thy mede.   20

176. 24 verré space: true opportunity

177. 5 wreche: revenge   6 Kepe: observe   9 grill: cruel   10
with . . .: by my choice   12 of . . .: learn about loving   13 un-
lust: sloth   14 for-bledde: covered in blood

In alle my paines I sufferd on roode
Man gave me drinkè no thing goode,
Eisell and gallè for to drinke: Gula
Gloton, theron ever thou thinke.

Of a maiden I was born   25
To save the folk that were forlorn;
All my body was beten for sin: Luxuria
Lecher, therfor I rede thee blin.

I was beten for thy sake:
Sin thou leve and shrift thou take;   30
Forsake thy sin and lovè me;   Jesus
Amend thee, and I forgive thee.

178   *The Hare*

BY a forrest as I gan fare,
   Walking al myselven alone,
I herd a mourning of an hare;
   Rewfully she made her mone:

'Dereworth God, how shal I live   5
   And leed my life in land?
Fro dale to downe I am y-drive;
   I n'ot where I may sit or stand.

'I may nother rest nor slepe
   By no valley that is so derne;   10

177. 22 drinke: to drink   23 Eisell: vinegar   26 forlorn: doomed
28 rede . . .: advise you to cease
178. 1 gan fare: went   5 Dereworth: glorious   8 n'ot: do not
know   9 nother: neither   10 in the most secluded valley

Nor no covert may me kepe,
    But ever I ren fro herne to herne.

'Hunteres will not heer their masse,
    In hope of hunting for to wende;
They coupeleth their houndes more and lasse   15
    And bringeth them to the feeldès ende.

'Raches rennen on every side
    In furrows that hopè me to find;
Hunteres taketh their horse and ride,
    And cast the contrey by the wind.   20

'Anon as they cometh me behind,
    I sit ful stil and looke a-lowe;
The firstè man that me doth find,
    Anon he cryeth: "So howe! so howe!"

' "Lo", he saith, "where sitteth an hare.   25
    Arise up, Watte, and go forth blive!"
With sorrow and with michè care
    I scape away with my live.

'At winter in the depè snowe
    Men wil me sechè for to trace—   30
And by my steppes I am y-knowe—
    And followeth me fro place to place.

---

12 ren: run   herne: hiding-place   14 in the expectation of going hunting   15 more . . .: greater and smaller, *i.e.* all   17 Raches: hounds   19 horse: horses   20 and search the country up wind   21 Anon as: as soon as   22 looke a-lowe: keep my eyes down   24 Anon: at once   26 Watte: hare's name   blive: quickly   27 miche: great   30 men will seek to track me

'And if I to the towne come or torne,
　　Be it in wortès or in leeke,
Then wil the wivès al so yorne　　　　　　　　35
　　Fleche me with here doggès eeke.

'And if I sit and crop the coule,
　　And the wife be in the waye,
Anon she will swere: "By Cokkès soule!
　　There is an hare in my haye!"　　　　　　40

'Anon she will clepè forth her knave,
　　And looke right wel wher I sitte;
Behind she will with a stave
　　Ful wel purpos me to hitte.

' "Go forth, Watte, with Cristès curse,　　　　45
　　And if I live, thou shalt be take;
I have an hare-pipe in my purse;
　　It shal be set al for thy sake".

'Then hath these wifes two doggès grete—
　　On me she biddeth hem go:　　　　　　　50
And as a shrew she will me threte,
　　And ever she cryeth: "Go, dogge, go!"

'But all way this most I go;
　　By no banke I may abide;
Lord God, that me is wo!　　　　　　　　55
　　Many a hap hath me betide.

33 towne: farm　torne: turn　　　34 wortes: cabbages　　　35
al...: immediately　　36 Fleche: drive out　here: their　　37 coule:
kale　38 in...: about　　39 Cokkes: God's　40 in...: inside
my fence　41 clepe: call　knave: boy　　47 hare-pipe: trap for
hares　purse: bag　　50 hem: them　　53 this: thus　most: must

'There is no beest in the world, I wene—
   Hert, hind, bukke ne do—
That suffres half so michė tene
   As doth the silly Wat—go where he go.   60

'If a gentilman wil have any game,
   And find me in forme where I sitte,
For dred of losing of his name
   I wot wel he wil not me hitte.

'For an aceres bred he will me leve   65
   Or he will let his houndės ren;
Of all the men that beeth alive
   I am most behold to gentilmen.

'As soone as I can ren to the lay
   Anon the grey-houndes wil me have;   70
My bowels beeth y-throwe away,
   And I am bore home on a stave.

'As soone as I am come home
   I am y-hunge hye upon a pin;
With leeke-wortes I am eete anone,   75
   And whelpės playė with my skin.'

179   *Marvels*

H ERKENS to my tale that I shall here shewe,
   For of suche mervels I have herde fewe;
If any of them be a ly that I tell here-efter,
I wolde I were as bare as the bishop of Chester!

178. 59 tene: misery   60 silly: harmless   62 forme: hare's lair
65 bred: breadth   66 Or: before   ren: run   68 behold: obliged
69 lay: open ground   74 pin: peg   75 leeke-wortes: leeks
179. 1 Herkens: listen   shewe: tell   4 bare: poor

As I went fro Dover to Durram I met by the street 5
A fox and a fulmart had fiftene feet.
The skate stalkede on hill and tight off her skin;
The codling cald at the churche-dore and bad let him in.
The samun sang the hy mass, the hering was the clark,
The porpos at the organs—ther was a golly wark! 10
Ther was a gret offering that ilke̍ day,
For ther was alle that I rekon, upon this array:
Waspes and oysteres and gret cart-sadels,
Muskettes in mortrous, caudrons and ladels,
The pikerel and the perche, the minnows and the roche,
The burbottes and the stikelbakes, the flounder and the
    loche. 16
The hadok hid behind, seen wolde he not be;
With him rode the gurnard, seemly for to see.
Yet was ther more, the sooth if I you telle,
The conger and the wesel rode on a plough-whelle; 20
The keling and the thornbake and the gret whalle,
The crabe and the loppester yet were they ther alle.
Eche one tooke a penny of their purs and offerd at the
    mass;
The oyster offerd ii d. and saide he wolde pay no lass.
When they this offring made, the sooth if I you say, 25
The Pame Sonday befel that yere on Midsummer-day. . . .
    All this I saw that I have here tolde
And many mo mervelles upon Cotte̍swolde;
But I them forgat as I went by the way;

6 fulmart: pole-cat   had: (which) had   7 tight: pulled
10 organs: organ   golly wark:? goodly performance   12 rekon . . .:
enumerate, in this order   13 cart-sadels: saddles supporting cart-
shafts   14 sparrow-hawks in stew, cauldrons and ladels   16
loche: loach   20 whelle: wheel   21 the cod and the ray and the
great whale   22 loppester: lobster   yet: also   24 lass: less
28 mo: more

Therfor at this time no more can I tel nor say.   30
But God, as He made us, and mend us He may,
Save us and send us some drink or we dey!

180   *By a Chapel*

M ERY it is in May morning
   Mery wayès for to gon.

And by a chapel as I com,
Met I with Jesu to chircheward gon,
Peter and Paul, Thomas and Jhon,   5
   And His disiples everichon.

Sainte Thomas the belles gan ring,
And Saint Collas the mass gan sing;
Sainte Jhon took that swete offering—
   And by a chapel as I com.   10

Oure Lord offered what He wolde,
A challis all of rich red golde;
Oure lady the crowne off her molde—
   The son out of her bosom shon.

Saint Jorge that is our Lady knight,   15
He tende the taperes fair and bright—
To myn eye a seemly sight—
   And by a chapel as I com.

179. 32 or we dey: before we die

180. 3 com: came   4 to . . .: going to church   6 everichon:
every one   7 gan ring: rang   8 Collas: Nicholas   13 molde:
head   14 son: sun *and* Son   15 Lady: Lady's   16 tende: lit

CHARLES OF ORLEANS

? 1394–1465

181   *A Lover's Confession*

MY gostly fader, I me confesse,
    First to God and then to you,
That at a window—wot ye how?—
I stale a coss of gret sweetnesse,
Which don was out avisènesse;   5
    But it is don, not undon, now.
My gostly fader, I me confesse,
    First to God and then to you.
But I restore it shall doutlesse
    Again, if so be that I mow;   10
    And that to God I make avow,
And els I axe foryefènesse.
My gostly fader, I me confesse,
    First to God and then to you,
That at a window—wot ye how?—   15
I stale a coss of gret sweetnesse.

1 gostly: spiritual   4 stale a coss: stole a kiss   5 out . . .:
without thinking   10 mow: may   11 make avow: promise
12 and otherwise I ask forgiveness

182 *Lost*

IN the forèst of noyous hevynesse,
 As I went wandring in the month of May,
I mette of love the mighty grete goddèsse,
 Which axèd me whither I was away.
 I hir answèrd: 'As fortune doth convey,   5
  As one exiled from joy—al be me loth—
 That passing well all folk me clepen may
  The man forlost, that wot not where he goth.'

Half in a smile ayèn, of hir humblesse,
 She saide: 'My frend, if so I wist, ma fay,   10
Wherefore that thou art brought in such distresse,
 To shape thyn ese I wolde my self assay;
 For heretofore I sett thyn hert in way
  Of grete plesère; I n'ot who made thee wroth;
 It greveth me thee see in such aray,   15
  The man forlost, that wot not where he goth.'

'Allas!' I saide, 'most sovereine good princesse,
 Ye know my case, what needeth to you say?
It is through Deth, that sheweth to alle rudesse,
 Hath fro me tane that I most lovèd ay,   20

---

1 noyous . . .: grievous sadness   4 who asked me where I was
going   5 convey: guide   6 al . . .: hateful though it is to me
7 so that all people may fittingly call me   8 forlost: completely lost
9 ayen: in reply   of . . .: in her graciousness   10 if . . .: if I knew,
indeed   12 shape: bring about   14 plesere: happiness   n'ot:
know not   wroth: sad   15 aray: state   18 what . . .: what need
is there to tell you   19 rudesse: harshness   20 Hath . . . that:
(who) has taken from me what

In whom that all myn hope and comfort lay:
  So passing frendship was betwene us both
That I was not, to fals Deth did hir day,
  The man forlost, that wot not where he goth.

'Thus am I blind—allas and welaway!—   25
Al fer miswent, with my staf grasping way,
  That no thing axe but me a grave to cloth:
For pité is that I live thus a day,
  The man forlost, that wot not where he goth.'

183   *Adam Driven from Eden*

N OW bethink thee, gentilman,
    How Adam dalf and Evė span.

In the vale of Abraham
Crist himself He made Adàm,
And of his ribbe a fair wommàn,   5
  And thus this seemly word began:

'Cum, Adàm, and thou shalt see
The bliss of Paradis, that is so free;
Therin stant an appil tree;
  Leef and frewt groweth theron.   10

'Adam, if thou this appil ete,
Alle these joyes thou shalt foryete,
And the paines of hellė gete.'
  Thus God Himself warned Adàm.

182. 22 passing: great   23 to . . .: till false Death caused her to die
26 f. gone far astray, groping my way with my stick, who ask nothing but
a grave to cover me

183. 2 dalf: delved   6 word: speech   8 free: excellent   9
stant: stands   12 foryete: lose

When God was fro Adam gon,   15
Soone after cam the feend anon;
A fals tretour he was on;
    He took the tree and crep theron.

'What aileth thee, Adam? Art thou wood?
Thy Lord hath taught thee litil good.   20
He woldè not thou understood
    Of the wittès that He can.

'Take the appil of the tree
And ete therof, I biddè thee,
And alle His joyès thou shalt see;   25
    Fro thee He shal hiden non.'

When Adam hadde that appil ete,
Alle his joyès wern foryete;
Non word morè might he speke;
    He stood as naked as a ston.   30

Then cam an aungel with a swerd
And drof Adàm into desèrt;
Ther was Adam sore afèrd,
    For labour coude he werken non.

17 f. he was a singularly false traitor; he went to the tree and crept on
to it   19 wood: mad   21 f. He did not want you to understand
the wise things that he knows   28 foryete: lost   33 aferd: afraid
34 for he did not know how to do any work

184   *My Purse*

S INGE we alle and say we thus:
    'Gramercy, myn owèn purs!'

When I have in myn purs ynow,
I may have bothe hors and plow,
And alsò frendes ynow,   5
    Through the vertu of myn purs.

When myn purs ginneth to slak,
And ther is nought in my pak,
They wil sayn: 'Go, fare wel, Jak!
    Thou shalt none more drinke with us.'   10

Thus is al myn good y-lorn
And myn purs al to-torn;
I may play me with an horn
    In the stede al of myn purs.

Fare wel hors, and fare wel cow;   15
Fare wel cart, and fare wel plow.
As I played me with a bow
    I said: 'God, what is al this?'

---

11 good y-lorn: money lost   12 to-torn: torn to pieces   13 f.
I may amuse myself with a horn (*i.e.* waste my time, do no good) instead
of (with) my purse

185   *Of a Rose, a Lovely Rose*

O F a rose, a lovely rose,
     Of a rose is al myn song.

Listeneth, lordinges, bothe elde and yinge
How this rose began to springe;
Swich a rose to myn liking   5
    In al this world ne knowe I non.

The aungel cam fro hevene towr
To greete Marỳe with gret honòur,
And saidè she shuld bere the flowr
    That shuldè breke the feendès bond.   10

The flowr sprong in high Bedleèm
That is bothè bright and sheen;
The rose is Mary, hevene-queen:
    Out of her bosom the blosmè sprong.

The ferstè branche is ful of might   15
That sprong on Cristèmessè night;
The sterre shon over Bedlem bright
    That is bothè brod and long.

The secunde branchè sprong to helle
The feendès power down to felle;   20
Therin might non sowlè dwelle—
    Blessed be the time the rosè sprong.

    3 Listen, sirs, both old and young   5 a rose so much to my
liking   11 Bedleem: Bethlehem   12 sheen: beautiful   17
sterre: star

The thriddė branche is good and swote;
It sprong to hevene, crop and rote,
Therin to dwellen and been our bote;   25
   Every day it sheweth in preestės hond.

Pray we to her with gret honòur,
She that bar the blessėd flour:
She be our help and our socòur,
   And shild us fro the feendės bond.   30

186   *Truth*

G OD be with trewthė wher he be!
  I wolde he were in this cuntree.

A man that shuld of trewthė telle,
With gretė lordes he may not dwelle;
In trewė story, as clerkės telle,   5
   Trewthe is put in low degree.

In ladyes chaumbers cometh he not;
Ther dare trewthė setten non fot;
Though he woldė, he may not
   Comen among the high menee.   10

With men of lawe he hath none space;
They loven trewthe in nonė place;
Me thinketh they han a rewly grace
   That trewthe is put at swich degree.

185. 23 swote: sweet   24 crop and rote: top and root   25 bote:
salvation   30 shild: protect

186. 1 wher: wherever   10 menee: society   11 space: opportunity
13 f. it seems to me they have sadly ungracious ways in that truth is rated
so low

In holy cherche he may not sitte;　　　　　　15
Fro man to man they shuln him flitte.
It reweth me sore in myn witte;
　　Of trewthe I havė gret pitee.

Religious, that shulde be good,
If trewthe cum ther, I holde him wood:　　　20
They shulden him rendė cote and hood
　　And make him barė for to flee.

A man that shuld of trewthe aspye,
He must　him seeken esilye
In the bosom of Marỳe,　　　　　　　　25
　　For ther he is, forsoothe, pardee!

187　　　　　　*Service is no Heritage*

B E ware, squier, yeman, and page,
For servise is none heritage.

If thou serve a lord of prise,
Be not too boistous in thyn servìse;
Damme not thyn soule is nonė wise,　　　5
　　For servise is none heritage.

Winteres wether and womanes thought
And lordės lovė chaungeth oft;
This is the sooth, if it be sought,
　　For servise is none heritage.　　　　10

186. 16 shuln . . .: will drive him off　　17 reweth: distresses　20
wood: mad　　21 him rende: tear from him　　22 and make him
flee naked　　23 of . . .: discern truth　　24 esilye: gradually
26 pardee: indeed

187. 1 yeman: servant　　3 prise: worth　　4 boistous: overbearing

Now thou art gret, tomorwe shal I,
As lordès chaungen here balỳ;
In thyn welthe werk sekerly,
    For servise is none heritage.

Then serve we God in allè wise;   15
He shal us quiten our servìse
And yiven us yiftès most of prise—
    Heven to been our heritage.

188   *I Sing of a Maiden*

I SING of a maiden
    That is makèles;
King of alle kingès
    To her son she ches.
He cam also stillè   5
    Ther His moder was,
As dew in Aprìlle
    That falleth on the gras.
He cam also stillè
    To His moderes bowr,   10
As dew in Aprìlle
    That falleth on the flowr.
He cam also stillè
    Ther His moder lay,
As dew in Aprìlle   15
    That falleth on the spray.

187. 12 here baly: their bailiff   13 welthe: prosperity   sekerly:
steadily   16 quiten: repay

188. 2 makeles: matchless, mateless   4 she took as her son   5 also
stille: as silently   6 Ther: where

Moder and maiden
　　Was never none but she;
Wel may swich a lady
　　Godès moder be.　　　　　　　　　　20

189　　　　　　　*I have a Gentle Cock*

I HAVE a gentil cok
　　Croweth me day;
He doth me risen erly
　　My matins for to say.

　　I have a gentil cok,　　　　　　　　5
　　　　Comen he is of gret;
　　His comb is of red corèl,
　　　　His tail is of jet.

　　I have a gentil cok,
　　　　Comen he is of kinde;　　　　10
　　His comb is of red corèl,
　　　　His tail is of inde.

　　His leggès been of asur,
　　　　So gentil and so smale;
　　His sporès arn of silver white　　15
　　　　Into the wortèwale.

188. 19 swich: such

189. 1 gentil: fine　2 (who) crows at day-break for me　3 doth: makes
6 gret: great family　10 kinde: noble stock　12 inde: indigo　14 so
graceful and so slender　15 spores: spurs　16 down to the root

His eynen arn of cristal
Loken al in aumber;
And every night he percheth him
In myn ladyes chaumber.   20

190   *A Last Drink*

O MNES *gentes plaudite!*
   I saw many briddes sitten on a tree;
He tooken her flight and flowen away
With *Ego dixi*, have good day!
Many white federes hath the pye—   5
I may none more singen, my lippes arn so drye.
Many white federes hath the swan—
The more that I drinke, the less good I can.
Lay stikkes on the fire, wel mot it brenne!
Yeve us ones drinken er we gon henne.   10

191   *Adam Lay Y-bounden*

A DAM lay y-bounden,
   Bounden in a bond;
Four thousand winter
   Thought he not to long;
And al was for an appel,   5
   An appel that he took,
As clerkès finden writen
   In herè book.

189. 17 eynen: eyes   18 loken: set

190. 1 *Beginning of psalm* 47   2 briddes: birds   3 He: they
her: their   flowen: flew   4 *Ego dixi: beginning of canticle of Hezekiah*
(Isa. 38: 10)   5 pye: magpie   8 good . . .: sense I have   9
mot . . .: may it burn   10 Give us one (last) drink before we go away

191. 4 to: too   7 clerkes: learned men   8 here: their

434

Ne hadde the appel také been,
 The appel také been, 10
Ne haddé never our Lady
 A been hevene-queen.
Blessèd be the time
 That appel také was!
Therfore we moun singen 15
 '*Deo Gracias!*'

192   *I have a Young Sister*

I HAVE a yong suster
 Fer beyonden see,
Many be the drouryes
 That she senté me.

She senté me the cherye 5
 Withouten any stone,
And so she did the dove
 Withouten any bone.

She senté me the brere
 Withouten any rind; 10
She bad me love my lemman
 Withouté longing.

How shuld any cherye
 Be withouté stone?
And how shuld any dove 15
 Been withouté bone?

191. 9 Had not the apple been taken 11 f. our Lady would never have been queen of heaven 15 moun: may

192. 2 Fer: far 3 drouryes: keep-sakes 9 brere: briar 11 lemman: sweetheart

How shuld any brere
  Been withoutė rind?
How shuld I love myn lemman
  Withoutė longing?   20

When the cherye was a flowr
  Then hadde it non stone.
When the dovė was an ey
  Then hadde it non bone.

When the brerė was onbred   25
  Then hadde it non rind.
When the maiden hath that she loveth
  She is without longing.

193   *The Sun of Grace*

AL the merier is that place
    The sunne of grace him shinėd in.

The sunne of grace him shinėd in
  On a day when it was morwe,
When our Lord God borėn was   5
  Withoutė wem or sorwe.

The sunne of grace him shinėd in
  On a day when it was prime,
When our Lord God borėn was—
  So wel He knew His time.   10

192. 23 ey: egg   25 onbred: not germinated
193. 2 him shined: shone   4 morwe: morning   6 wem: stain
8 prime: early morning

The sunne of grace him shinèd in
 On a day when it was noon,
When our Lord God borèn was,
 And on the roodè doon.

The sunne of grace him shinèd in   15
 On a day when it was undern,
When our Lord God borèn was
 And to the hertè stungen.

194   *Robin and Gandelein*

I HERDE a carping of a clerk,
 Al at yon wodès ende,
Of good Robìn and Gandèlein;
 Was ther none other genge.

Stronge theves wern the childeren none,   5
 But bowmen goode and hende;
He wenten to wode to geten hem fleish,
 If God wold it hem sende.

Al day wenten tho childeren two
 And fleish founden he none,   10
Til it were again even;
 The childeren wold gon home.

Half a hundered of fat falif deer
 He comen ayòn,

193. 14 doon: placed   16 undern: afternoon   18 stungen: pierced
194. 1 carping of: tale by   4 genge: company   5 Stronge: downright   childeren: young men   6 hende: courteous   7 they went to the wood to get themselves meat   9 tho: those   11 again: towards   13 falif: fallow   14 they came upon

And alle he wern fair and fat ynow,   15
    But markèd was ther none.
'By dere God', saide good Robìn,
    'Herof we shul have one.'

Robin bent his joly bowe,
    Therin he set a flo,   20
The fattest deer of alle
    The herte he clef a-two.

He haddè not the deer y-flawe
    Ne half out of the hide,
Ther cam a shrewde arwe out of the west   25
    That felde Robertes pride.
Gandelein looked him est and west
    By every side.

'Who hath myn maister slain?
    Who hath done this dede?   30
Shal I never out of grene-wode go
    Til I see sidès blede.'

Gandelein looked him est and west
    And sought under the sunne;
He saw a litel boy   35
    He clepen Wrennok of Donne;

A good bowe in his hand,
    A brod arwe ther-inne,
And foure and twenty goode arwes
    Trussèd in a thrumme: 40

18 we must have one of these   20 flo: arrow   22 clef: clove
23 y-flawe: flayed   25 shrewde: wicked   34 under . . .: *i.e.*
everywhere   36 He clepen: they call   40 thrumme: bundle

'Be ware thee, ware thee, Gandèlein,
   Her-of thou shalt han summe.

'Be ware thee, ware thee, Gandèlein,
   Her-of thou getst plenté.'
'Ever one for another', saide Gandèlein,   45
   'Misaunter have he shal flee!

'Wherat shal our markè be?'
   Saide Gandèlein.
'Everich at otheres herte',
   Saide Wrennok again.   50

'Who shal yeve the ferstè shote?'
   Saide Gandèlein,
'And I shal yeve thee one beforn',
   Saide Wrennok again.

Wrennok shet a ful good shote—   55
   And he shet not too highe—
Through the sanchothes of his breek;
   It touched neither thighe.

'Now hast thou yoven me one beforn',
   Al thus to Wrennok saide he,   60
'And through the might of our Lady
   A bettere I shal yeve thee.'

Gandelein bent his goode bowe
   And set therin a flo;
He shet through his grene kertel,   65
   His herte he clef on two.

42 han: have   46 Bad luck may he have who flees!   49
Everich: each   51 yeve: give   53 beforn: first   54 again: in
reply   55 shet: shot   57 sanchothes: ? fork   breek: breeches
59 yoven: given

'Now shalt thou never yelpe, Wrennok,
  At alė ne at win,
That thou hast slawe good Robin
  And his knave Gandėlin.   70

'Now shalt thou never yelpe, Wrennok,
  At win ne at ale,
That thou hast slawe good Robin
  And Gandėlin his knave.'

195   *A Henpecked Husband*

HOW, hey! It is none les:
  I dare not sayn when she saith 'Pes!'

Ying men, I warne you everichone,
Eldė wivės take ye none;
For I myself have one at home—   5
  I dare not sayn when she saith 'Pes!'

When I cum fro the plow at noon,
In a riven dish my mete is doon;
I dare not asken our dame a spoon—
  I dare not sayn when she saith 'Pes!'   10

If I aske our damė bred,
She taketh a staf and breketh myn hed,
And doth me rennen under the led—
  I dare not sayn when she saith 'Pes!'

194. 67 yelpe: boast   69 slawe: slain   70 knave: servant
195. 1 les: lie   2 sayn: speak   Pes: peace, *i.e.* be quiet   3 Ying:
young   everichone: every one   4 Elde: old   8 my food is put
on a cracked dish   13 and makes me run under the cauldron

If I aske our damè flesh,   15
She breketh myn hed with a dish:
'Boy, thou art not worth a rish!'—
    I dare not sayn when she saith 'Pes!'

If I aske our damè chese,
'Boy', she saith, al at ese,   20
'Thou art not worth half a pese!'—
    I dare not sayn when she saith 'Pes!'

196   *Penny is a Hardy Knight*

G O bet, peny, go bet, go!
  For thou maght maken both frend and fo.

Peny is an hardy knight;
Peny is mikel of might;
Peny of wrong he maketh right   5
    In every cuntré wher he go.

Though I have a man y-slawe
And forfeted the Kingès lawe,
I shal finden a man of lawe
    Wil taken myn peny and let me go.   10

And if I have to don fer or ner,
And peny be myn messangèr,
Then am I none thing in dwer
    My causè shal be wel y-do.

195. 17 rish: rush   20 al at ese: coolly   21 pese: pea

196. 1 Go bet: get on   2 maght: can   3 hardy: bold   6
wher: wherever   7 y-slawe: killed   8 forfeted: transgressed
11 And if I have business far or near   13 none. . .: in no doubt

And if I have pens both good and fine,   15
Men wil bidden me to the wine;
'That I have shal be thine'—
   Sikerly, they wil sayn so.

And when I have none in my purs,
Peny bet ne peny wors,   20
Of me they holden but litel fors:
   'He was a man, let him go'.

197   *My Baselard*

*P*RENÈGARD, *prenègard!*
  Thus bere I myn basèlard.

Listeneth, lordinges, I you beseke:
Ther is none man worth a leke,
Be he sturdy, be he meke,   5
  But he bere a basèlard.

Myn baselard hath a shede of red
And a clene loket of led;
Me thinketh I may bere up myn hed
  For I bere myn basèlard.   10

My baselard hath a writhen haft;
When I am ful of alè caght

196. 17 That: what   18 Sikerly: certainly   20 bet: better
21 they take but little account of me

197. 1 Prenegard: take care   2 baselard: dagger   3 beseke:
beseech   4 leke: leek   6 But: unless   7 shede: sheath
8 clene loket: neat band   10 For: because   11 writhen: twisted,
decorated   12 when I am tipsy with ale

MY BASELARD

It is gret dred of manslaght,
    For then I bere my baselard.

My baselard hath a silver chape;   15
Therfore I may both gaspe and gape.
Me thinketh I go like none knape
    For I bere a baselard.

My baselard hath a trencher kene,
Fair as rasour, sharp and shene.   20
Ever me thinketh I may be kene
    For I bere a baselard.

As I yede up in the strete
With a cartere I gan mete.
'Felaw', he saide, 'so mot I thee,   25
    Thou shalt forgo thy baselard.'

The cartere his whippe began to take,
And al myn flesh began to quake,
And I was leef for to escape,
    And there I left myn baselard.   30

When I cam forth unto myn damme
Myn hed was broken to the panne;
She saide I was a prety manne
    And wel coude bere myn baselard!

---

13 manslaght: manslaughter   15 chape: scabbard plate   16
gaspe . . .: *i.e.* ? brag   17 knape: menial   19 trencher: blade
20 shene: bright   21 kene: bold   23 yede: went   24 gan
mete: met   25 so . . .: so may I prosper   29 leef: glad
32 panne: brain-pan

198 *Wicked Tongues*

KEEP thy tunge, thy tunge, thy tunge;
Thy wiked tungė werketh me wo.

Ther is none gres that groweth on ground,
Satėnas ne peny-round,
Werse than is a wikked tunge   5
    That speketh bothe evil of frend and fo.

Wikked tunge maketh oftė strif
Betwix a good-man and his wif;
When he shulde lede a merye lif
    Her whitė sidės waxen ful blo.   10

Wikked tunge maketh oftė staunce,
Bothe in Engelond and in Fraunce;
Many a man with spere and launce
    Through wikked tunge to ded is do.

Wikked tungė breketh bone,   15
Though the self havė none;
Of his frend he maketh his fone
    In every place wher that he go.

Good men that sitten in this halle,
I pray you, bothe one and alle,   20
That wikked tungės fro you falle,
    That ye mowen to hevnė go.

---

1 Keep: watch   3 gres: herb   4 Satenas: a poisonous plant
peny-round: pennywort   8 good-man: husband   9 he: they
10 blo: black and blue   11 staunce: dispute   14 ded: death
16 the self: it itself   17 fone: foe   18 wher that: wherever
22 mowen: may

199   *Jolly Jankin*

'KYRIÈ', so 'kyriè',
      Jankin singeth miriè,
With 'aleyson'.

As I went on Yole day
      In oure prosession,   5
Knew I joly Jankin
      By his mery tone—
      Kyrièleyson.

Jankin began the offis
      On the Yolè day,   10
And yet me·thinketh it dos me good,
      So mery gan he say
      '*Kyrièleyson*'.

Jankin red the pistil
      Ful faire and ful wel,   15
And yet me thinketh it dos me good,
      As ever have I sel.
      Kyrièleyson.

Jankin at the *Sanctus*
      Craketh a mery note,   20
And yet me thinketh it dos me good—
      I payèd for his cote.
      Kyrièleyson.

1 *Kyrie: Kyrie eleyson* 'Lord have mercy', used at the beginning of the
Mass   2 mirie: sweetly   3 aleyson: pun on name 'Alison'
12 gan: did   14 pistil: Epistle   17 as I hope always to be happy
20, 24 Craketh: sings in very short notes

445

Jankin craketh notès
   An hunderid on a knot   25
And yet he hakketh hem smallere
   Than wortès to the pot.
   Kyriêleyson.

Jankin at the *Angnus*
   Bereth the pax-brede;   30
He twinkelèd, but said nought,
   And on myn foot he trede.
   Kyriêleyson.

Benedicamus Domino,
   Crist fro shame me shilde!   35
Deo gracias therto—
   Alas, I go with childe!
   Kyriêleyson.

200   *London Lickpenny*

TO London once my stepps I bent,
   Where trouth in no wise should be faint;
To Westminster-ward I forthwith went
To a man of law to make complaint.
I said: 'For Marys love, that holy saint,   5
   Pity the poore that wold proceede!'
But for lack of mony I cood not speede.

And as I thrust the presse among,
   By froward chaunce my hood was gone;

---

199. 25 knot: cluster   26 hem: them   **27** wortes: herbs
29 *Angnus*: *Agnus*   30 pax-brede: pax, osculatory   **31**
twinkeled: winked   35 may Christ shield me from shame

200. 2 faint: falsified   3 To . . . ward: towards Westminster
6 proceede: **go to law**   7 speede: do any good   **9** froward: evil

Yet for all that I stayd not long   10
  Till at the Kinges Bench I was come.
  Before the judge I kneled anon
    And prayd him for Gods sake to take heede;
    But for lack of mony I might not speede. . . .

Unto the Common Place I yode tho   15
  Where sat one with a silken hood;
I did him reverence—for I ought to do so—
  And told my case as well as I cood,
  How my goodes were defrauded me by falshood.
    I gat not a mum of his mouth for my meede,   20
    And for lack of mony I might not speede. . . .

In Westminster Hall I found out one
  Which went in a long gown of ray;
I crouched and kneled before him anon,
  For Maryes love of help I him pray.   25
  'I wot not what thou meanst', gan he say;
    To get me thence he did me beede:
    For lack of mony I cood not speede.

Within this hall neither rich nor yet poor
  Wold do for me ought, although I shold dy;   30
Which seeing, I gat me out of the door,
  Where Fleminges began on me for to cry:
  'Master, what will you copen or by?
    Fine felt hattes, or spectacles to reede?
    Lay down your silver, and here you may
      speede.' . . .   35

15 To the Court of Common Pleas I went then   19 defrauded
me: taken from me by fraud   20 gat: got   mum: word   23 ray:
striped cloth   25 of: for   26 gan . . .: he said   27 beede:
bid   33 copen: purchase

LONDON LICKPENNY

Then unto London I did me hye—
　Of all the land it beareth the prise!
'Hot pescodes!' one began to crye,
　'Strabery ripe!' and 'cherryes in the rise!'
　　One bad me come nere and by some spice;　　40
　　　Peper and saffron they gan me beede;
　　　But for lack of mony I might not speede.

Then to the Chepe I gan me drawn,
　Where mutch people I saw for to stand:
One offred me velvet, silk, and lawn;　　45
　Another he taketh me by the hand,
　'Here is Paris thred, the finest in the land'.
　　I never was used to such thinges in deede,
　　And, wanting mony, I might not speede.

Then went I forth by London Stone,　　50
　Throughout all Canwike Streete:
Drapers mutch cloth me offred anone;
　Then comes me one, cried 'Hot shepes feete!'
　One cried 'Makerell!'; 'Rishes grene!' another
　　　gan greete.
　　One bad me by a hood to cover my head;　　55
　　But for want of mony I might not speed.

Then I hied me into Est Chepe.
　One cries 'Ribbs of befe and many a pie!'
Pewter pottes they clattered on a heape;
　There was harp, pipe, and minstrelsye.　　60
　'Yea, by cock!' 'Nay, by cock!' some began crye.

---

37 beareth . . .: is best　　39 in the rise: on the branch　　41
beede: proffer　　43 gan . . .: betook myself　　50 London Stone
cod in the middle of Cannon St.　　51 Cannon St.　　54 Rishes . . .:
reen rushes!' another yelled　　61 cock: God

448

Some sunge of Jenken and Julian for ther meede.
But for lack of mony I might not speede.

Then into Cornhill anon I yode,
    Where was mutch stolen gere among;   65
I saw where hong mine owne hode
    That I had lost among the throng.
    To by my own hood I thought it wrong—
        I knew it well as I did my Crede:
        But for lack of mony I could not spede.   70

The taverner took me by the sleve:
    'Sir', saith he, 'will you our wine assay?'
I answerd: 'That can not mutch me greve;
    A peny can do no more than it may.'
    I drank a pint and for it did pay;   75
        Yet sore a-hungerd from thence I yede,
        And, wanting mony, I cood not spede.

Then hied I me to Bilingsgate,
    And one cried: 'Hoo! go we hence!'
I prayd a barge-man for Gods sake   80
    That he wold spare me my expence.
    'Thou scapst not here', quod he, 'under two pence;
        I list not yet bestow my almes-deede.'
        Thus, lacking mony, I could not speede.

Then I convayed me into Kent,   85
    For of the law wold I meddle no more;
Because no man to me took entent
    I dight me to do as I did before.

62 for . . .: *i.e.* for money   66 hong: hung   73 greve: hurt
76 yede: went   82 scapst: escape   quod: said   83 I don't want
to give my alms yet   87 to . . .: paid attention to me   88 dight:
prepared

Now Jesus that in Bethlem was bore,
  Save London, and send trew lawyers ther meede! 90
  For whoso wantes mony with them shall not speede.

201   *On the Times (c. 1450)*

NOW is Ingland all in fight;
  Muche peple of consciens light;
Many knightes and litel of might;
Many lawes and litel right;
Many actes of parlament   5
And few kept with tru entent;
Litel charité and fain to plese;
Many a galant penylese;
And many a wonderful disgising
By unprudent and misavising;   10
Grete countenanse and smalle wages;
Many gentilemen and few pages;
Wide gownes and large sleves;
Wel besene and strong theves;
Much bost of their clothes,   15
But wel I wot they lake none othes.

200. 91 wantes: lacks

201. 7 fain: eager   9 disgising: strange fashion in dress   10 mis-
avising: ill-advised people   11 countenanse: show   12 pages:
servants   14 prosperous-looking and flagrant thieves   16 lake . . .:
are not short of oaths

202   *Holly and his Merry Men*

NAY, Ivy, nay, it shal not be y-wis;
Let Holy have the maistry, as the maner is.

Holy stant in the hall faire to behold;
Ivy stant without the dore; she is ful sore a-cold.

Holy and his mery men they daunsen and they sing;   5
Ivy and hir maidenes they weepen and they wring.

Ivy hath a kibe; she caught it with the colde;
So mot they all have ay that with Ivy holde!

Holy hath berys as rede as any rose;
The foster, the hunters keepe hem fro the dos.   10

Ivy hath berys as blake as any slo;
Ther com the oule and ete hem as she go.

Holy hath birdes, a ful faire flok,
The nightingale, the poppingay, the gentil laverok.

Goode Ivy, what birdes hast thou?   15
Non but the howlet that cry 'How, how!'

1 y-wis: indeed   2 maistry: upper hand   3 stant: stands
6 wring: *i.e.* their hands   8 mot: may   10 foster: forester
hem: them   dos: does   12 com: comes   ete: eats   go: goes
14 laverok: lark   16 howlet: (young) owl   cry: cries

203 *Prayer for the Journey*

HERE I am and forth I must,
 And in Jesus Criste is all my trust.
No wicked thing do me no dere,
Nother here nor elleswhere.
The Father with me, the Sone with me,   5
The Holy Gost, and the Trinité,
Be betwixt my gostly enemé and me.
 In the name of the Father and the Son
 And the Holy Gost, Amen.

204 *A Servant-girl's Holiday*

RIBBE ne rele ne spinne ich ne may
 For joy that it is holiday.

Al this day ich han sought;
Spindel ne werve ne fond I nought;
To miché blisse ich am brought   5
 Ayèn this high holiday.

Al unswope is ourè flet,
And ourè fire is unbet;
Oure rushen been unrepè yet
 Ayèn this high holiday.   10

203. 1 must: must (go)   3 let no wicked thing do me any harm
4 Nother: neither   7 gostly: spiritual

204. 1 I cannot scrape flax or reel thread or spin   3 All day I've
been looking for things   4 werve: whorl   fond: found   5
miché: much   6 Ayen: in anticipation of   7 Our floor is all
unswept   8 unbet: not made up   9 unrepe: not cut

Ich mostė fechen worten in;
Predele my kerchef under my chin—
Levė Jakke, lend me a pin
　　To predele me this holiday.

Now it draweth to the none,　　　　　　15
And al my cherrės been undone;
I moste a lite solàs my shone
　　To make hem douse this holiday.

I mostė milken in this pail;
Ought me bred al this shail;　　　　　　20
Yet is the dow under my nail
　　As ich knad this holiday.

Jakke wil bringe me onward in my way,
With me desirė for to play;
Of my dame stant me non ay　　　　　　25
　　On never a good holiday.

Jakke wil pay for my scot
A Sunday at the alė-scot;
Jakke wil sousė wel my throt
　　Evėry good holiday.　　　　　　　　30

Soone he wil take me by the hand,
And he wil legge me on the land
That al my buttockes been of sand
　　Upon this high holiday.

11 moste: must　　worten: vegetables　　12 Predele: ? fasten
13 Leve: dear　　15 Now it's nearly noon　　16 cherres: chores
17 I must soften my shoes a bit　　18 hem: them　　douse: comfortable
20 I ought to spread out (? set to rise) all this ? bowl (of dough)
21 dow: dough　　22 knad: kneaded　　25 f. I'm not afraid of my
mistress on any good holiday　　27 scot: share　　28 A: on　　ale-
scot: *i.e.* feast at which each paid for ale　　32 legge: lay　　land: ground

In he pult and out he drow,   35
And ever ich lay on him y-low:
'By Godes deth, thou dest me wow
   Upon this high holiday!'

Soone my wombe began to swelle
Also gret as a belle;   40
Durst I not my damė telle
   What me betidde this holiday.

205   *I am Forsaken*

CARE away, away, away,
   Murninge away!
I am forsake, another is take;
   No more murne ich may.

I am sory for her sake,   5
   Ich may wel ete and drinke;
When ich slepe ich may not wake,
   So muche on her ich thinke.

I am brought in such a bale
   And brought in such a pine,   10
When ich rise up of my bed
   Me listė wel to dine.

I am brought in suche a pine,
   Y-brought in such a bale,
When ich havė right good wine   15
   Me listė drinke non ale.

204. 35 pult: thrust   36 on . . .: beneath him   37 dest . . .: do
me wrong   40 Also: as   42 betidde: befell
205. 4 ich: I   9 bale: sorrow   10 pine: anguish

206

The Dark Lady

SOME men sayen that I am blac;
　　It is a colour for my prow.
Ther I love ther is no lac;
　　I may not be so white as thou.

Blac is a colour that is good—　　　　　　　5
　　So say I and many mo:
Blac is my hat, blac is my hood,
　　Blac is al that longeth therto.

Blac wil do as good a nede
　　As the white at bord and bedde;　　　　10
And therto also trew in dede,
　　And therto I lay my lif to wedde.

Wind and water may steine the white;
　　Y-wis the blac it may not so;
Ther I see the blac is al my delite;　　　　15
　　I am y-holde by skille therto.

Peper withoute it is wel blac,
　　Y-wis withinne it is not so.
Let go the colour and tak the smac:
　　This I say by me and mo.　　　　　　　20

---

1 blac: dark　　　2 prow: advantage　　　3 in my loving there is
no fault　　6 mo: more　　8 longeth: belongs　　9 do: serve
11 therto also: moreover just as　　12 and on that I stake my life
14 Y-wis: indeed　　15 Ther: where　　16 with reason am I
devoted to it　　17 ff. cf. no. 307. vii　　19 Let go: ignore　smac:
taste　　20 so I say of myself and others

God save alle hem that beeth browne,
   For they beeth trew as any stel;
God kepe hem, bothe in feeld and towne,
   And thenne shal I be kept ful wel.

207   *He is Far*

WERE it undo that is y-do,
   I wold be war.

I lovede a child of this cuntré,
And so I wende he had do me;
Now myself the soothe I see,   5
   That he is far.

He saide to me he wolde be trewe
And chaunge me for none other newe;
Now I sike and am pale of hewe,
   For he is far.   10

He saide his sawes he wold fulfille;
Therfore I let him have al his wille.
Now I sike and mournė stille,
   For he is far.

206. 21 hem: them   browne: dark

207. 2 war: ware   3 child: young man   4 wende: thought
8 newe: new love   9 sike: sigh   11 sawes: promises   13
stille: secretly

ROBERT HENRYSON

fl. c. 1475

208

The Two Mice

E SOPE, mine author, makis mentioun
    Of twa mice, and thay wer sisteris deir,
Of quham the eldest dwelt in ane borrous-toun,
    The uther winnit uponland, weill neir,
    Soliter, quhile under busk, quhile under breir,   5
Quhilis in the corne and uther mennis skaith,
As outlawis dois and levis on thair waith.

This rurall mous into the winter-tide
    Had hunger, cauld, and tholit greit distress.
The uther mous that in the burgh can bide   10
    Wes gild-brother and maid ane free burgèss;
    Toll-free als, but custum mair or less,
And fredome had to ga quhairever sho list
Amang the cheis in ark and meill in kist.

Ane time quhen sho wes full and unfute-sair,   15
    Sho tuke in minde hir sister uponland,
And langit for to heir of hir weilfair,
    To see quhat life sho had under the wand.
    Bairfute, allone, with pikestaf in hir hand,

3 borrous-toun: borough-town   4 the other lived in the coun-
try, very hard   5 Soliter: solitary   quhile: sometimes   busk: bush
breir: briar   6 uther . . .: (doing) damage to others   7 and . . .:
who live by hunting   8 into: in   9 tholit: suffered   10 can
bide: lived   12 als . . .: also, exempt from any tax   14 among the
cheese in the box and meal in the chest   15 Ane: one   unfute-sair:
not foot-sore   18 under . . .: in the open

As pure pilgrime sho passit out of toun 20
To seik hir sister baith over daill and doun.

Furth mony wilsum wayis can sho walk,
Throu mosse and mure, throu bankis, busk and breir,
Sho ran cryand quhill sho come to a balk:
'Cum furth to me, my awin sister deir! 25
Cry "peip" anis!' With that the mous culd heir
And knew hir voice, as kinnisman will do
By verray kind; and forth sho come hir to.

The hartly joy, God! gif ye had seene,
Beis kith quhen that thir sisteris met! 30
And greit kindness was shawin thame betweene:
For quhilis thay leuch, and quhilis for joy thay gret,
Quhile kissit sweit, quhilis in armis plet;
And thus thay fure quhill soberit wes thair mind;
Syne fute for fute unto the chalmer wend. 35

As I herd say, it wes ane sober wane
Of fog and fairn full febilly wes maid—
Ane silly sheill under ane steidfast stane
Of quhilk the entres wes not hy nor braid;
And in the samin thay went but mair abaid, 40

---

20 pure: poor   22 Furth: along   wilsum: bewildering   23
mure :moor   24 cryand: crying   quhill: till   balk: ridge
26 anis: once   28 By verray kind: by very nature   come: came
29 f. God! if you had seen the heartfelt joy shown when these sisters met!
31 kindness: affection   32 leuch: laughed   gret: cried   33 plet:
embraced   34 fure: went on   quhill: till   35 then keeping pace
together they went into the room   36 sober wane: humble dwelling
37 fog: moss   fairn: fern   38 silly sheill: wretched hovel   steid-
fast: firm in its place   39 f. of which the entrance was not high or
broad; and they went into the same without more delay

Withoutin fire or candill birnand bricht—
For commounly sic pikkeris lufis not licht.

Quhen thay wer lugit thus, thir sely mice,
  The youngest sister into hir buttery yide
And brocht furth nuttis and candill insteid of spice— 45
  Gif this wes gude fair, I do it on thame beside.
  The burgess-mous prompit furth in pride,
And said: 'Sister, is this your daily fude?'
'Quhy not?' quod sho, 'Is not this meit richt gude?'

'Na, by my saull! I think it bot ane scorne.' 50
  'Madame', quod sho, 'ye be the mair to blame.
My mother said, sister, quhen we wer borne,
  That I and ye lay baith within ane wame.
  I keip the rate and custume of my dame,
And of my leving into poverty; 55
For landis have we nane in property.'

'My fair sister,' quod sho, 'have me excusit—
  This rude diet and I can not accord:
To tender meit my stomok is ay usit,
  For quhilis I fair als weill as ony lord. 60
  Thir widderit peis and nuttis, or thay be bord,
Wil brek my teith, and mak my wame ful sklender
Quhilk wes before usit to meitis tender.'

---

42 sic pikkeris: such pilferers 43 lugit: lodged   thir sely: these
simple   44 yide: went   46 Gif: if   I . . .: I leave it to them
47 prompit furth: ? burst out   50 ane scorne: contemptible   53
wame: womb   54 f. I keip the style and usage of my mother and
continue to live in poverty   56 in property: of our own   61
widderit: shrivelled   or: before   62 wame: belly

'Weill, weill, sister,' quod the rurall mous,
  'Gif it pleis you, sic thingis as ye see heir,   65
Baith meit and drink, harbery and hous,
  Sal be your awin; will ye remane al yeir
  Ye sall it have with blyth and mery cheir;
And that suld mak the maissis that ar rude,
Amang freindis, richt tender and wonder gude.   70

'Quhat plesure is in the feistis delicate
  The quhilkis ar gevin with ane glowmand brow?
Ane gentill hart is better recreate
  With blyth curàge than seith to him ane cow;
  Ane modicum is mair for till allow,   75
Swa that gude-will be kerver at the dais,
Than thrawin vult and mony spicit mais.'

For all hir mery exhortatioun,
  This burgess-mous had litill will to sing;
Bot hevily sho kest hir browis doun   80
  For all the dainteis that sho culd hir bring.
  Yit at the last sho said, half in hething:
'Sister, this victuall and your royall feist
May weill suffice unto ane rurall beist.

'Lat be this hole and cum into my place.   85
  I sall to you shaw by experience

65 Gif: if   sic: such   66 harbery: lodging   67 Sal: shall
will ye: if you wish to   69 maissis: dishes   70 freindis: relatives
72 glowmand: scowling   73 recreate: refreshed   74 curage:
disposition   than . . .: than by cooking a cow for him   75 for . . .:
to be praised   76 f. as long as goodwill is carver (*i.e.* presides) at the
table, than a sulky face and many spiced dishes   80 hevily: gloomily
81 For: despite   82 hething: raillery

My Gude Friday is better nor your Pace:
   My dish-weshings is worth your haill expence.
   I have housis anew of greit defence;
Of cat nor fall-trap I have na dreid.'   90
'I grant', quod sho; and on togidder thay yeid.

In stubbill array throu gers and corne
   And under buskis prevely couth thay creip;
The eldest wes the gide and went beforne,
   The younger to hir wayis tuke gude keip.   95
   On nicht thay ran, and on the day can sleip;
Quhill in the morning, or the laverok sang,
Thay fand the toun and in blythly couth gang.

Not fer fra thyne unto ane worthy wane
   This burgess brocht thame sone quhar thay suld be.   100
Without 'God speid' thair herbery wes tane
   Into ane spence with vittell greit plentie:
   Baith cheis and butter upon thair skelfis hie,
And fleshe and fishe aneuch, of freshe and salt,
And sekkis full of meill and eik of malt.   105

Efter, quhen thay disposit wer to dine,
   Withoutin grace thay weshe and went to meit

87 nor: than   Pace: Easter   89 anew: enough   90 fall-trap: mousetrap   91 yeid: went   92 In stubbill array: ? in stumbling fashion   gers: grass   93 couth . . .: they crept   95 to . . .: took careful note of her route   96 can sleip: slept   97 Quhill: till or . . .: before the lark sang   98 fand: found   couth gang: went 99 fer: far   thyne: thence   wane: dwelling   101 f. without more ado they took up their quarters in a larder . . .   103 skelfis: shelves 104 aneuch: enough   105 sekkis: sacks   107 weshe: washed

With all coursis that cukis culd devine—
    Muttoun and beif strikin in tailyeis greit;
And lordis fair thus couth thay counterfeit,   110
Except ane thing—thay drank the water cleir
Insteid of wine: bot yit thay maid gude cheir.

With blyth upcast and mery countenance
    The eldest sister sperit at hir gest
Gif that sho by resòne fand difference   115
    Betwix that chalmer and hir sary nest.
    'Ye, dame,' quod sho, 'how lang will this lest?'
'For evermair, I wait, and langer to.'
'Gif it be swa, ye ar at eis', quod sho.

Till eik thair cheir ane subcharge furth sho brocht—   120
    Ane plait of grotis and ane dishe full of meill;
Thraf-caikis als, I trow, sho spairit nocht
    Aboundantly about hir for to deill;
    And mane full fine sho brocht insteid of geill,
And ane quhite candill out of ane coffer stal   125
Insteid of spice to gust thair mouth withal.

This maid thay mery quhill thay micht na mair,
    And 'Haill, Yule! Haill!' cryit upon hy.
Yit efter joy oftimes cumis cair,
    And troubill efter greit prosperity: 130
    Thus as thay sat in all thair jolity

    108 devine: devise   109 strikin . . .: chopped in great slices
110 thus they emulated lords' fare   113 upcast: ? banter   114
sperit at: asked   115 by resone: in fact   116 sary: wretched
117 lest: last   118 I wait: I know   to: too   119 swa: so   at
eis: well off   120 Till eik: to add to   subcharge: extra course
122 Thraf-caikis: oat-cakes   124 mane full fine: excellent white bread
geill: jelly   125 stal: stolen   126 gust: give relish to   127
This: thus   quhill: till   128 upon hy: loudly

The spenser come with keyis in his hand,
Opinit the dure, and thame at denner fand.

Thay taryit not to weshe, as I suppose,
   Bot on to ga quha that micht formest win.   135
The burgess had ane hole, and in sho gois;
   Hir sister had na hole to hide hir in:
   To see that sely mous it was greit sin,
So desolate and will of ane gude reid!
For verray dreid sho fell in swoun neir deid.   140

Bot as God wald, it fell ane happy cace:
   The spenser had na laser for to bide,
Nouther to seik nor serche, to sker nor chace,
   But in he went and left the dure up wide.
   The bald burgess his passing weill hes spide;   145
Out of hir hole sho come and cryit on hie:
'How fair ye, sister? Cry "peip" quhairever ye be!'

This rurall mous lay flatling on the ground,
   And for the deith sho wes full sair dredand,
For till hir hart straik mony wofull stound;   150
   As in ane fever sho trimbillit fute and hand.
   And quhen hir sister in sic ply hir fand,
For verray pity sho began to greit,
Syne confort hir with wordis hunny-sweit.

'Quhy ly ye thus? Rise up, my sister deir!   155
   Cum to your meit: this perell is overpast.'

132 spenser: steward   133 fand: found   135 but made off
as fast as they could   138 sin: shame   139 will . . .: having no
idea what to do   142 laser: leisure   143 sker: scare away
148 flatling: flat   150 for many a woeful pang smote at her heart
152 sic ply: such plight   153 greit: weep   154 Syne: then

The uther answerit hir with hevy cheir:
  'I may not eit, sa sair I am agast;
  I had lever thir fourty dayis fast
With water-caill, and to gnaw beenis or peis,   160
Than all your feist in this dreid and diseis.'

With fair trety yit sho gart hir uprise,
  And to the burde thay went and togidder sat.
And scantly had thay drunkin anis or twise
    Quhen in come Gib Hunter, our joly cat,   165
    And bad 'God speid!' The burgess up with that
And till the hole sho went as fire on flint;
Bawdronis the uther by the bak hes hint.

Fra fute to fute he kest hir to and fra,
  Quhilis up, quhilis doun, als cant as ony kid;   170
Quhilis wald he lat hir rin under the stra,
    Quhilis wald he wink, and play with hir buk-heid.
    Thus to the sely mous greit paine he did,
  Quhill at the last, throu fortune and gude hap,
Betwix ane burde and the wall sho crap.   175

And up in haist behind ane parralling
  Sho clam so hie that Gilbert micht not get hir;

159 lever: rather   160 water-caill: vegetable-broth   161
diseis: uneasiness   162 trety: entreaty   gart: made   163 burde:
table   164 scantly: scarcely   166 up: jumped up   168
Bawdronis: *i.e.* the cat   hint: grabbed   169 kest: tossed   170
cant: frisky   171 stra: straw   172 wink: shut his eyes   buk-
heid: hide-and-seek   173 sely: poor   175 burde: board, *i.e.*
wainscot   crap: crept   176 parralling: partition-wall   177
clam: climbed

Syne by the cluke thare craftely can hing
   Till he wes gane: hir cheir wes all the better.
   Syne doun sho lap quhen thair wes nane to let hir,   180
And to the burgess-mous loud can sho cry:
'Fairweill, sister, thy feist heir I defy!

'Thy mangerie is mingit all with cair:
   Thy guse is gude, thy gansell sour as gall!
The subcharge of thy service is bot sair—   185
   Sa sall thou find heir-efterward, na fall.
   I thank yone courtine and yone perpall wall
Of my defence now fra yone crewell beist.
Almichty God keip me fra sic ane feist!

'Wer I into the kith that I come fra,   190
   For weill nor wo suld I never cum agane.'
With that sho tuke hir leif and furth can ga,
   Quhilis throu the corne and quhilis throu the plane.
   Quhen sho wes furth and free sho wes full fane,
And merily markit unto the mure—   195
I can not tell how weill thairefter sho fure.

Bot I herd say sho passit to hir den
   Als warme as woll, suppose it wes not greit,

178 cluke: claw   can hing: hung   180 lap: leapt   let: stop
182 defy: renounce   183 mangerie: feast   mingit: mingled
184 guse: goose   gansell: sauce   185 the extra course of your meal
is but misery   186 na fall: without fail   187 perpall: partition
188 Of: for   190 into the kith: in the place   193 plane: open
ground   195 markit: made her way   196 fure: fared   198
woll: wool   suppose: although

Full beinly stuffit, baith but and ben,
  Of beinis and nuttis, peis, ry and quheit.   200
  Quhenever sho list sho had aneuch to eit
In quiet and eis withoutin ony dreid;
Bot to hir sisteris feist na mair sho yeid.

209   *This Pretty Woman*

HEREFOR and therefor and therefor I cam,
  And for to praise this praty womàn.
There were three wily, three wily there were:
A fox, a frier, and a womàn.
There were three angry, three angry there were: 5
A wasp, a wesel, and a womàn.
There were three chatering, three chatering there
    were:
A pie, a jaye, and a womàn.
There were three wold be beten, three wold be
    beten there were:
A myll, a stokfish, and a womàn.   10

210   *Lullay, By-by, Lullay*

THIS endris night
  I saw a sight,
    A star as bright as day;

208. 199 beinly: well   but . . .: outer and inner room   200 quheit:
wheat   201 aneuch: enough   202 dreid: anxiety   203 yeid:
went

209. 1 Herefor: for this reason   2 praty: fine   9 wold: needed to
10 myll: *unexplained*

210. 1 the other night

466

And ever among
A maiden song   5
'Lullay, by-by, lullay.'

That lovely lady sat and song
  And to her child can say:
'My son, my broder, my fader dere,
  Why liest thou thus in hay?   10
    My swetė brid,
    Thus it is be-tid,
      Though thou be King verràly;
    But nevertheles
    I wil not ces   15
      To sing "By-by, lullay".'

The child then spak in his talking
  And to his moder said:
'I be kidde for Heven-King
  In crib though I be laid.   20
    For aungeles bright
    Don to me light—
      Thou knowest it is no nay—
    And of that sight
    Thou mayst be light   25
      To sing "By-by, lullay".'

'Now sweet son, sin thou art King,
  Why art thou laid in stall?

---

  4 and all the while   **5** song: sang   **8** can say: said   **11**
  brid: child   **12** thus it has happened   **13** verray: true   **15**
  ces: cease   **19** I am proclaimed as King of Heaven   **22** make
  light for me   **23** you know there is no denying it   **24** of: at
  25 light: glad   **27** sin: since

467

Why n'ere ordainèd thy bedding
  In some gret kingès hall?   30
    Me thinkth it is right
    That king or knight
      Shuld ly in good aray;
    And then among
    It were no wrong   35
      To sing "By-by, lullay".'

'Mary, moder, I am thy child,
  Though I be laid in stall;
Lordes and dukes shal worship me,
  And so shall kingès all.   40
    Ye shall well see
    That kingès three
      Shal come the twelfthè day.
    For this behest
    Give me thy brest,   45
      And sing "By-by, lullay".'

'Now tell me, sweet son, I thee pray—
  Thou art me leve and dere—
How shuld I kepe thee to thy pay
  And make thee glad of chere?   50
    For all thy will
    I wold fulfill,
      Thou wotst full well in fay;
    And for all this
    I will thee kis   55
      And sing 'By-by, lullay".'

29 n'ere: was not   34 and then   44 behest: promise
48 me leve: precious to me   49 kepe: look after   pay: liking
53 fay: truth

'My dere moder, when time it be,
　Thou take me up on loft,
And set me right upon thy knee
　　And handel me full soft;　　　　　　　　60
　　　And in thy arm
　　　Thou hill me warm
　　　　And kepe me night and day;
　　　If I wepe
　　　And may not slepe,　　　　　　　　　65
　　　　Then sing "By-by, lullay".'

'Now, sweet son, sin it is so,
　That all thing is at thy will,
I pray thee graunte me a bon,
　　If it be both right and skill:　　　　　70
　　　That child or man
　　　That wil or can
　　　　Be mery upon my day,
　　　To blis hem bring,
　　　And I shal sing　　　　　　　　　　75
　　　　"Lullay, by-by, lullay".'

211　　　　　　*Ay, Ay, This is the Day*

AY, ay, this is the day
　　That we shal worship ever and ay.

A ferly thing it is to mene
　That a maid a child have borne

210. 58 on loft: aloft　　　62 hill: cover up　　69 bon: request
70 skill: reasonable　　74 hem: them

211. 2 worship: honour　　3 ferly: wondrous　　mene: relate

And sithė was a maiden clene,   5
  As prophetes saiden here-beforne.
Y-wis, it was a wonder thing
That through an aungelės greting
God wold light in a maiden ying,
    With ay,   10
  Ay, ay, I dare well say
Her maidenhed yede no away.

His moder was a maiden mild,
  As Holy Kirk witness and we;
Withouten wem she bar a child,   15
  And so did never non but she.
A ferly thing it shuld befall,
But God hath allė women thrall
In paines to bere her children all,
    With ay,   20
  Ay, ay, I dare well say
She felt none of that aray.

His birth was know that ilkė night
  In all the land thorough and thorough;
Thider they yeden to see that sight,   25
  To Bethleëm, that fairė borough.
Ad angel bad that they shuld go;
He said that 'Betwene beestės two
Godes Sone siker ye find so',
    With ay,   30
  Ay, ay, I dare well say,
In a crib they found Him there He lay.

5 sithe: afterwards   7 Y-wis: certainly   wonder: wonderful
9 ying: young   12 her virginity never went   15 wem: defile-
ment   18 But: though thrall: in bondage   22 aray: condition
24 thorough: through   29 siker: assuredly   32 there: where

Three kingès out of Indè land,
   They cum to seke that ferly fode
With rich presèntès in their hand;   35
   A sterre stifly a-fore hem yode.
A ferly thing it was to see:
That sterre was more than other three;
It held the course to that contree,
     With ay,   40
   Ay, ay, I dare well say,
   They thar not miss of redy way.

When they with that lady met,
   They found her child upon her knee;
Full curtesly they her gret   45
   And prèsent Him with yiftès three.
As King they yave Him gold so rede,
Myrr and cense to His manhede;
Of her offring thus we rede,
     With ay,   50
   Ay, ay, I dare well say,
   They worshipped Him on the twelfthè day.

Mary moder, maiden mild,
   To thee we cry, to thee we call.
Thou be our sucour and our shild;   55
   Us thou save fro mischeves all!
Thou pray thy Sone, that Prince of Pees,
Of all our sinnes He us relees,

---

34 fode: child   36 a star went steadily before them   38
more . . .: *i.e.* more than three times the size of other stars   42 they
had no cause to miss the direct way   45 gret: greeted   46
yiftes: gifts   48 myrrh and incense in homage to him   49 her:
their   55 shild: shield

Out of this world when we shal cees,
    With ay,   60
Ay, ay, so that we may
    Wend with Him at domèsday.

212   *Lullay, my Child*

'LULLAY, my child, and wepe no more,
    Slepe and be now still;
The King of Blis thy fader is,
    As it was His will.'

This endris night   5
I saw a sight,
    A maid a cradel kepe;
And ever she song
And said among:
    'Lullay, my child, and slepe.'   10

'I may not slepe,
But I may wepe,
    I am so wobegone;
Slepe I wold,
But I am cold,   15
    And clothès have I none',

Me thought I herd
The child answèrd;
    And to His moder He said:

211. 59 cees out of: quit

212. 5 endris: other   7 kepe: watch over   8 song: sang   9
among: the while

'My moder dere,   20
What do I here?
  In crib why am I laid?

'I was born
And laid beforn
  Bestes, both ox and ass;   25
My moder mild,
I am thy child,
  But He my Fader was.

'Adams gilt,
This man had spilt;   30
  That sin greved me sore.
Man, for thee
Here shal I be
  Thirty winter and more. . . .

'Here shal I be   35
Hanged on a tree,
  And die, as it is skill;
That I have bought
Lese will I nought:
  It is my Faders will.   40

'A spere so sharp
Shall perse my hert,
  For dedes that I have done.
Fader of Grace,
Whether thou has   45
  Forgeten thy litel sone?' . . .

30 this had destroyed man   37 skill: fitting   38 That:
what   39 Lese: lose   45 have you

213   *For Sore Eyes*

F OR a man that is almost blind:
   Let him go bare-hed all day again the wind
   Till the sunne be sett;
At even wrap him in a cloke,
And put him in a hous full of smoke,   5
   And looke that every hole be well shett.

And when his eyen begine to rope,
Fill hem full of brinston and sope,
   And hill him well and warm.
And if he see not by the next moone   10
As well at midnight as at noone,
   I shall lese my right arm!

214   *Bear a Horn and Blow it not*

I HOLD him wise and wel y-taught
   Can bere an horn and blow it naught.

Blowing was made for grete game;
Of this blowing cometh mikel grame;
Therefor I hold it for no shame   5
   To bere a horn and blow it naught.

Hornes are made both loud and shill;
When time is, blow thou thy fill,

213. 2 again: against   6 shett: stopped   7 rope: stream   8
hem: them   9 hill: cover up   12 lese: lose
214. 2 Can: (who) knows how to   3 game: entertainment   4
grame: harm   7 shill: shrill

And when need is, hold thee still
   And bere a horn and blow it naught.   10

What-so-ever be in thy thought,
Heer and see and say right naught;
Then shall men say thou art well taught
   To bere a horn and blow it naught.

Of al the riches under the sun,   15
Then was there never beter wun
Than is a taught man for to cun
   To bere a horn and blow it naught.

What-so-ever be in thy brest,
Stop thy mouth with thy fist,   20
And look thou think well of 'Had I wist',
   And bere a horn and blow it naught.

And when thou sittest at the ale
And criest like a nightingale,
Beware to whom thou tellest thy tale,   25
   But bere a horn and blow it naught.

215   *Care Away!*

CARE away, away, away,
  Care away for evermore!

All that I may swink or swete
My wife it will both drink and ete;

214. 16 wun: habit   17 than for a man to be trained to know how
21 wist: known

215. 3 All that I can (earn) by toil or sweat

And I say ought, she will me bete: 5
  Careful is my hart therfore.

If I say ought of hir but good,
She looke on me as she were wood,
And will me clout about the hood:
  Careful is my hart therfore.   10

If she will to the good ale ride,
Me must trot all by her side,
And when she drink I must abide:
  Careful is my hart therfore.

If I say it shal be thus,   15
She say: 'Thou lyest, cherl, y-wus!
Weenst thou to overcome me thus?'
  Careful is my hart therfore.

If any man have such a wife to lede,
He shal know how *judicare* cam in the Crede;   20
Of his penàns God do him mede!
  Careful is my hart therfore.

---

5 And: if   ought: anything   6 Careful: sorrowful   8 as...:
as if she were mad   13 abide: be patient   16 y-wus: indeed
17 Weenst thou: do you expect   19 lede: manage   20 *judicare*:
inde venturus est iudicare vivos et mortuos (*i.e.* he shall know what punish-
ment is)   21 may God reward him for his suffering

216 *A Bachelor's Life*

A, a, a, a,
Yet I love whereso I go.

In all this world n'is a meryer life
Than is a yong man withouten a wife;
For he may liven withouten strife   5
    In every place whereso he go.

In every place he is loved over all
Among maidens grete and small,
In dauncing, in piping, and renning at the ball,
    In every place whereso he go.   10

They let light by husbandmen
When they at the ballë ren;
They cast her love to yongë men
    In every place whereso he go.

Then say maidens: 'Farewell, Jack!   15
Thy love is pressed all in thy pack;
Thou berest thy love behind thy back',
    In every place whereso he go.

9 renning: running   ball: ball game (? some kind of hockey)
11 They think little of married men

217   *What is this Why?*

W HY, why, what is this why
       But *virtus verbi Domini*?

When nothing was but God alone,
The Fader, the Holy Gost, with the Sone,
One was three, and three was one.   5
     What is this why?
   To frayn why I hold but foly;
   It is non other certenly
   But *virtus verbi Domini*.

Fiat was a word ful bold,   10
That made al thing as He wold—
Heven and erth and men of mold.
     What is why? *etc.*

The world gan wax and multiply;
The planetes made hem full bisỳ   15
To rewll eche thing by and by.
     What is why? *etc.*

The planetes work nothing in vein,
But, as they be ordeind, so must they reign;
For the word of God wil not agein.   20
     What is why? *etc.*

When Bede had preched the stonės dry,
The might of God made hem to cry

7 frayn: ask   10 *Fiat*: Genesis 1:3   11 wold: wished
12 mold: earth   15 hem: them(selves)   16 to rule each thing
individually   20 will . . .: will not (come) again   22 preched:
preached to

478

'Amen!' (Certes, this is no ly).
    What is why? *etc.*   25

Heretikes wonder of this thing most:
How God is put in the Holy Host,
Here and at Rome and in every cost.
    What is why? *etc.*

218   M and A, R and I

O F M, A, R, I,
        Sing I will a new song.

Of these four letters purpose I,
Of M and A, R and I;
They betoken maid Marỳ;   5
    All our joy of her it sprong.

Withouten wem of her body—
M and A, R and I—
Of her was born a king truly
    The Jewes diden to deth with wrong.   10

Upon the mount of Calvery—
M and A, R and I—
There they beten His bare body
    With scorges that were sharp and long.

Our dere Lady she stood Him by—   15
M and A, R and I—
And weep water ful bitterly
    And teres of blood ever among.

217. 28 cost: country

218. 3 purpose: speak   **7** wem: defilement   10 (whom) the
Jews put . . .   17 weep: wept   18 ever among: all the while

479

219 *Holly and Ivy*

HOLVER and Hivy made a gret party
Who shuld have the maistry
In landės where they go.

Then spake Holver: 'I am fresh and joly;
I wil have the maistry   5
    In landės where we go'.

Then spake Hivy: 'I am loud and proud,
And I wil have the maistry
    In landės where we go'.

Then spak Holver, and set him on his knee: 10
'I pray thee, gentil Hivy,
Say me no vilany
    In landės where we go'.

220 *Ivy, Chief of Trees*

IVY, chefe of trees it is;
    Veni, coronaberis.

The most worthy she is in town—
    He that saith other doth amis—
And worthy to bere the crown: 5
    Veni, coronaberis.

219. 1 party: dispute   2 maistry: upper hand   12 no vilany:
nothing unkind

220. 2 Song of Songs (Vulgate), 4:8   3 in town: *i.e.* in the world
4 other: otherwise

480

Ivy is soft and meek of speech,
  Against all bale she is blis:
Well is he that may her reech;
  Veni, coronaberis.   10

Ivy is green with colour bright;
  Of all trees best she is;
And that I preve well now by right:
  Veni, coronaberis.

Ivy bereth berys black—   15
  God graunt us all His blis!
For there shall we nothing lack;
  Veni coronaberis.

221

An Old Man and his Wife

H EY, how!
  Sely men, God helpe you!

This endres day befel a strife
Totwex an old man and his wife;
She took him by the berd so plite   5
  With hey, how!

She took him by the berd so fast
Till bothe his eyn on water gan brast,
  With hey, how!

---

220. 8 in all sorrow she is a source of joy   9 reech: attain   13
preve: prove

221. 2 Sely: wretched   3 This endres: the other   4 Totwex:
between   5 plite: tangled   8 on . . .: burst into tears

Out at the dore as he can go,　　　　　　10
Met he with his neybres two:
'Neybur, why wepest so?'
　　With hey, how!

'In my hous is swich a smeke—
Go under, and ye shall wete.'　　　　　　15
　　With hey, how!

222　　　　　　　　*Bring us in Good Ale*

BRING us in good ale, and bring us in good ale;
　　For our blessed Lady sake, bring us in good ale.

Bring us in no brown bred, for that is made of brane,
Nor bring us in no white bred, for therin is no game,
　　But bring us in good ale.　　　　　　5

Bring us in no befe, for there is many bones,
But bring us in good ale, for that goth down at ones,
　　And bring us in good ale.

Bring us in no bacon, for that is passing fat,
But bring us in good ale, and give us ynough of that,　10
　　And bring us in good ale.

Bring us in no mutton, for that is often lene,
Nor bring us in no tripes, for they be seldom clene,
　　But bring us in good ale.

221. 10 can go: went　　　　14 swich: such　　　smeke: smoke　　15
under: inside　　wete: know

222. 4 game: pleasure　　　7 ones: once

Bring us in no egges, for there are many shelles,   15
But bring us in good ale, and gives us nothing elles,
   And bring us in good ale.

Bring us in no butter, for therin are many hores,
Nor bring us in no pigges flesh, for that wil make us bores,
   But bring us in good ale. . . .   20

Bring us in no capons flesh, for that is ofté dere,
Nor bring us in no dukkes flesh, for they slober in the
    mere,
   But bring us in good ale.

223   *Doll thy Ale*

D OLL thy ale, doll; doll thy ale, doll!
    Ale make many a man to have a doty poll.

   Ale make many a man to stik at a brier;
   Ale make many a man to ly in the mier;
   And ale make many a man to sleep by the fier.   5
      With doll!

   Alle make many a man to stumbel at a stone;
   Ale make many a man to go drunken home;
   And ale make many a man to brek his tone.
      With doll!   10

222. 18 hores: hairs

223. 1 Doll: ? mull   2 doty poll: fuddled head   3 stik . . .: get
entangled in the brambles (*i.e.* get into trouble)   9 tone: toes

Ale make many a man to draw his knife;
Ale make many a man to make gret strife;
And ale make many a man to bete his wife.
    With doll!

Ale make many a man to wet his chekes;   15
Ale make many a man to ly in the stretes;
And ale make many a man to wet his shetes.
    With doll!

Ale make many a man to stumbel at the blokkes;
Ale make many a man to make his hed have knokkes;   20
And ale make many a man to sit in the stokkes.
    With doll!

Alle make many a man to rin over the falows;
Ale make many a man to swere by God and All Halows;
And ale make many a man to hang upon the galows.   25
    With doll!

224   *Chatterers in Church*

TUTIVILLUS, the devil of hell,
  He writeth her names, sooth to tell,
  Ad missam garulantes.

Bet were be at home for ay
Than here to serve the devil to pay,   5
  Sic vana famulantes.

223. 19 at . . .: over obstacles   23 rin . . .: run across ploughed land
224. 2 her: their   3 (those) chattering at mass   4 Bet: better
5 the . . .: to the devil's liking

These women that sitteth the church about,
They beeth al of the deviles rout,
　　Divina impedientes.

But they be stil, he wil hem quell,　　　　　　　10
With kene crokes draw hem to hell,
　　Ad puteum multum flentes.

For His love that you dere bought
Hold you stil and jangel nought,
　　Sed prece deponentes.　　　　　　　　　　15

The blis of heven then may ye win.
God bring us al to His in
　　'*Amen, amen*' *dicentes!*

225　　　　　　　　*The Months*

JANUAR: By this fire I warme my handes,
　　Februar: And with my spade I delfe my landes.
　　Marche: Here I sette my thinge to springe,
Aprile: And here I heer the fowles singe.
Maii: I am as light as birde in bow,　　　　　　5
Junii: And I weede my corne well ynow.
Julii: With my sithe my mede I mowe,
Auguste: And here I shere my corne full lowe.
September: With my flail I erne my bred,
October: And here I sowe my whete so red.　　　10
November: At Martinesmasse I kille my swine,
December: And at Cristesmasse I drinke red wine.

---

224. 10 unless they are silent, he will destroy them　　**11 kene crokes:**
sharp hooks　　　13 For the love of Him who bought you **dear**　　　15
but (remain) bowing down in prayer　　17 in: lodging

225. 3 At this time I plant my plants to grow　　　5 light: merry

226 *Prayer for Good Dreams*

UPON my right side I me lay,
　Blessid Lady, to thee I pray,
For the terės that ye leete
Upon your swetė Sonės feete,
Send me gracė for to slepe　　　　　　　　　5
And good dremės for to mete,
Sleping, waking, til morowe-day bee.
Our Lord is the frute, our Lady is the tree;
Blessid be the blossom that sprang, Lady, of thee!
In nomine Patris et Filii et Spiritus Sancti　　　10
　　　　　　　　　　　　　　　Amen.

227 *A Woman sat Weeping*

SODENLY afraid, half waking, half sleeping,
　And gretly dismayd: a woman sat weeping,

With favour in her face fer passing my reason,
And of her sore weeping this was the encheason:
Her Son in her lap lay, she said, slain by treason.　　5
If weeping might ripe be, it seemed then in season.
　'Jesu!', so she sobbėd—
　So her Son was bobbėd,
　And of His lif robbėd—
Saying these wordes, as I say thee:　　　　　　10
'Who cannot weepe, come lern at me.'

226. 3 leete: shed　　　　6 mete: dream　　　7 til . . .: till tomorrow
comes

227. 1 afraid: (I was) afraid　　3 with beauty in her face far surpas-
sing my description　　　4 encheason: cause　　　6 ripe: fitting
8 bobbed: buffeted　　11 Who: whoever　at: from

I said I coud not weepe, I was so hard-herted.
She answerd me shortly with wordės that smerted:
'Lo, nature shall move thee; thou must be converted;
Thine own Fader this night is dead'—lo, thus she
       thwerted—   15
   'So my Son is bobbėd,
   And of His lif robbėd.'
   Forsooth then I sobbėd,
  Verifying the wordes she said to me:
 'Who cannot weepe may lern at me'.   20

'Now breke, hert, I thee pray! this cors lith so rewly,
So beten, so wounded, entreted so Jewly.
What wight may me behold and weepe not? None trewly,
To see my dead dere Son ly bleeding, lo, this newly.'
   Ever stil she sobbėd—   25
   So her Son was bobbėd,
   And of His lif robbėd—
  Newing the wordes, as I say thee:
 'Who cannot weepe, com lern at me.'

On me she cast her ey, said 'See, man, thy Brother!'   30
She kissed Him and said 'Swete, am I not thy mother?'
In sowning she fill there—it wolde be none other;
I n'ot which more deadly, the toon or the tother.
   Yet she revived and sobbėd—
   So her Son was bobbėd,   35
   And of His lif robbėd—
 'Who cannot weepe', this was the lay,
 And with that word she vanisht away.

15 thwerted: countered   21 lith . . .: lies so pitifully   22
entreted . . .: treated so Jewishly   24 this: thus   28 Newing: re-
peating   32 f. In a swoon she fell there—she could not help it; I do not
know which looked more deathly, the one or the other

228   *Fragment of a Love Lament*

I HAVE grete marvel of a brid
   That with my love is went away;
She bildes her in another stid:
   Therfore I morn both night and day.
I couth never serve that brid to pay,   5
   Ne frendship with her can I none find,
But fast fro me she flys away—
   Alas that ever she was unkind!

Alas! why is she with me wroth,
   And to that brid I trespast nought?   10
Ye, if she be never so loth,
   She shall nought come out of my thought.
Now of me she gives right nought,
   But bildes her fer under a lind,
In bitter bales she has me brought—   15
   Alas that ever she was unkind! . . .

229   *A Schoolboy's Lot*

WENEST thou, usher, with thyn cointise,
   Eche day beten us on this wise,
As thou were lord of town?
We had lever scole forsake,
And ilche of us another crafte take,   5
Than long to been in thy bandòun.

228. 1 brid: bird, lady   3 she makes her nest in another place
5 I never knew how to serve that bird so as to please her   10 And:
if   11 Ye: indeed   13 f. Now that she cares nothing for me,
but makes her nest far away under a lime-tree   15 bales: sorrows

229. 1 cointise: clever tricks   3 As: as if   4 lever: rather
5 ilche: each   6 bandoun: power

But woldė God that we might ones
Cache thee at the milnė-stones,
   Or at the crabbė-tree!
We shuld leve in thee such a probait,   10
For that thou hast us don and said,
   That alle thy kin shuld rewė thee!

And though Sire Robert, with his cloke,
Wold thee helpe and be thy poke,
   The werrė thou shuldst fare;   15
And for his prayer the rather we wold
Yiven him stripės al uncold,
   Not for him thee spare.

For oftė sorė we abeye
The twinkėlingės of his eye,   20
   The maister, us to bete;
For he and thou are at assent,
Al day yiven agagėment
   To yiven us strokės grete.

230   *Sometime I Loved*

U P, sun and mery wether!
    Sumer draweth nere.

Somtime I loved—so do I yit—
In stedfast wise and not to flit;

229. 7 ones: once   8 milne-: mill   10 probait: testimony
11 For that: because of what   12 rewe: pity   13 Sire Robert:
i.e. the master   14 poke: puck, instigator in wickedness   15
werre: worse   17 Yiven: give   19 abeye: pay for
20 f. the winks of his, the master's, eye to have us beaten   22 f. at . . .:
in collusion, you are always conspiring

230. 4 not . . .: unchangingly

But in dangèr my love was knit,   5
   A pitous thing to here.

For when I offred my servìse,
I to obey in humble wise
As ferforth as I coude devise,
   In conténaunce and chere,   10

Grete paine for nought I dide endure,
Al for that wicked creätùre;
He and no mo, I you ensure,
   Overthrew al my matère.

But now—I thanke God of His sand—   15
I am ascapèd from his band
And free to pas by see and land,
   And sure fro yere to yere.

Now may I etè, drinke, and play,
Walke up and down fro day to day,   20
And herken what these lovers say,
   And laugh at their manère.

When I shal slepe, I have good rest—
Somtime I had not altherbest—
But, ar that I cam to this fest,   25
   I bought it al to dere.

Al that affray is clene a-go;
Not only that, but many mo;

5 *i.e.* but my love was disdained   9 ferforth: far   10 in
conduct and behaviour   13 mo: other   14 upset my life com-
pletely   15 of . . .: for His dispensation   16 band: bond
18 sure: safe   24 altherbest: the best of all   25 ar: before   fest:
happiness   27 affray: distress   a-go: gone   28 mo: more

And sith I am ascapèd so,
I thinke to hold me here.   30

But al the crue that suffren smert,
I wold they sped like youre desert,
That they might sing with mery hert
    This song with us in fere.

231   *Nonsense*

THE cricket and the greshope wenten hem to fight,
    With helme and haburjone all redy dight;
The flee bare the baner as a doughty knight;
The cherubud trumped with all his might.

The hare sete upon the hill and chappind her shone,   5
And swere by the knappes which were ther-upon
That she would not rise ne gon
Till she see twenty houndes and a won.

The milner sete upon the hill,
And all the hennes of the town drew him till.   10
The milner said: 'Shew, henne, shew!
I may not shake my bagge for you.'

230. 29 sith: since   30 hold me: stay   31 crue: band   smert:
anguish   32 I wish they would prosper as you (men) deserve
34 in fere: together
231. 1 greshope: grasshopper   wenten hem: betook themselves   2
dight: arrayed   4 cherubud: beetle   5 sete: sat   chappind . . .:
fastened her shoes   6 knappes: buttons   8 till she saw twenty-
one hounds   9 milner: miller   10 town: village   him till: to
him   12 may: can   for: because of

232 *Letter to 'M'*

I PRAY you, M, to me be trew,
   For I will be trew as long as I lif;
I will not change you for old ne new,
Ne never luf other, whiles that I lif.
And ye be avised, this other yere   5
Ye send me a letter of luf so dere;
I was as glad of your writing
As ever I was of any thing;
For I was sek the day before—
That letter heeled, I was sek no more.   10
M, in space
Comes fortune and grace;
I trist it so for to be
That it shall light on you and me.
M, be stidfast and trew in thought;   15
For luf is the sweeter, the dere that it is bought.
And M, I hope securly
There is none that byes it so dere as we.
And in what place so ever ye be,
As oft as ye will, ye shall me there see.   20
Therefor be ye trew, trew,
Or elles sore I mun it rew.
Be ye stidfast and also trew,
For I will not change for old ne new.
And sithen as we may not togeder speke,   25
By writinge we shall our hertes breke.

---

5 And ye be avised: if you remember   6 send: sent   9 sek:
sick   11 space: time   13 trist: trust   16 dere: dearer
17 hope . . .: trust surely   22 elles: else   mun: may   25 sithen
as: since   26 breke: open

233 *To Keep the Cold Wind Away*

THERE blows a cold wind today, today,
　The wind blows cold today;
Crist suffered His passion for mannes salvacion,
　To kepe the cold wind away.

This wind by reason is called tentacion;　　　　　　5
　It raveth both night and day.
Remember, man, how the Savior was slayn
　To kepe the cold wind away.

Pride and presumcion and fals extorcion,
　That many man doth betray—　　　　　　　　　10
Man, cum to contricion and axe confession
　To kepe the cold wind away.

O Mary mild, for love of the child
　That died on Good Friday,
Be our salvacion from mortal damnacion　　　　　15
　To kepe the cold wind away.

He was nailed, His blood was haled,
　Oure remission for to by;
And for our sinnes all He drank both eisel and gall
　To kepe the cold wind away.　　　　　　　　　20

Slowth, envỳ, covetis, and lecheré
　Blowe the cold wind, as I dare say;
Agene such poison He suffered His passion
　To kepe the cold wind away.

6 raveth: rages　　11 axe: ask　　17 haled: drawn　　19 eisel:
vinegar　　23 Agene: against

O man, remember the Lord so tender   25
   Which died withoute denay;
His handes so smert lay next to His hert
   To kepe the cold wind away.

Now pray we all to the King celestiàll,
   That born He was of may,   30
That we may love so with other mo
   To kepe the cold wind away.

234   *Diversions for an Unhappy Princess*

'TO-MOROWE ye shall on hunting fare,
   And ride, my doughter, in a chare;
It shall be covered with velvet red,
And clothes of fine gold al about your hed,
With damask white and asure-blewe,   5
Wel diapred with lillies newe;
Your pomelles shall be ended with gold,
Your chaines enameled many a fold;
Your mantèl of riche degree,
Purpil palle and ermine free;   10
Jennettes of Spaine, that been so wight,
Trapped to the ground with velvet bright.
Ye shall have harpe, sautrỳ, and song,
And other mirthès you among.

---

233. 26 denay: resistance   27 smert: painful   30 who was born of a maiden   31 other mo: others besides

234. 1 on . . .: go hunting   2 chare: carriage   6 diapred: patterned   7 pomelles: ornamental knobs   8 many a fold: elaborately   9 degree: quality   10 rich crimson cloth and noble ermine   11 Jennettes: small horses   wight: swift   12 Trapped: caparisoned all about you   13 sautry: psaltery   14 and other entertainments

Ye shall have rumney and malmesine,   15
Both ypocrasse and vernage wine,
Mountrose and wine of Greke,
Both algarde and respice eke,
Antioche and bastarde,
Piment also and garnarde,   20
Wine of Greke and muscadell,
Both claré, piment, and rochell;
The red your stomake to defy,
And pottes of osey set you by.
You shall have venison y-bake,   25
The best wilde fowle that may be take;
A lese of grehound with you to strike,
And hert and hinde and other like.
Ye shall be set at such a trist
That hert and hinde shall come to your fist;   30
Your disease to drive you fro
To here the bugles there y-blow,
With their bugles in that place,
And sevenscore raches at his rechase.
Homeward thus shall ye ride,   35
On hauking by the rivers side,

15 rumney: a sweet Greek wine   malmesine: malmsey   16 hip-
pocras (a spiced wine)   vernage: a sweet white Italian wine   17
Mountrose: kind of wine   18 algarde (wine from Algarve, Portugal)
respice: raspis (a red wine)   19 antioch (a medicinal drink)   bastarde:
a sweet Spanish wine   20 Piment: wine with honey and spices
garnarde: wine ?of Granada (?flavoured with pomegranates)   21
muscatel   22 claré: clary (wine with honey and spices)   rochell:
wine from La Rochelle   23 red wine to promote digestion   24
osey: sweet wine of Alsace   27 lese: leash (*i.e.* three)   strike: run
28 other like: the like   29 trist: hunting station   30 to . . .: *i.e.*
within touching distance   31 disease: unhappiness   32 To here:
i.e. you shall hear   33 bugles: ?*for* begles 'beagles'   34 raches:
hunting dogs   at . . .: ? when it (the hart) is turned back   36 On
hauking: a-hawking

With goshauk and with gentil fawcon,
With egle-horne and merlyon.
  'When you come home your men among
Ye shall have revell, daunces and song: 40
Litle children, great and smale,
Shall sing as doth the nightingale.
Then shall ye go to your evensong,
With tenòurs and trebles among;
Threescore of copes of damask bright,   45
Full of perles they shall be pight;
Your aulter-clothes of taffata,
And your sicles all of taffetra.
Your sensòurs shall be of gold,
Endent with asure many a fold.   50
Your quere non organ-song shall want
With countrè-note and discànt;
The other half on orgains playing,
With yonge children full faire singing.
  'Then shall ye go to your suppère,   55
And sitte in tentes in grene arbère,
With clothes of Aras pight to the ground,
With saphires set and diamound.
A cloth of gold about your head,
With popinjayes pight, with pery red;   60
And officers all at your will
All maner delightes to bring you till.

37 gentil: excellent   38 egle-horne: ?kind of hawk   merlyon:
merlin   44 accompanied by tenors and trebles   46 pight: stud-
ded   48 sicles: brocade hangings   taffetra: *unexplained*   49
sensours: censers   50 inlaid with azure intricately   51 Your choir
shall not fail to sing organum (*i.e* part singing)   52 countre-note:
counterpoint   53 orgains: the organ   56 arbere: arbour
57 furnished with Arras tapestries (hanging) to the ground   60 pight:
adorned   pery: precious stones   61 officers: servants   62 you
till: to you

The nightingale sitting on a thorn
Shall singe you notes both even and morn.
An hundreth knightès truly tolde   65
Shall play with bowles in alayes colde;
Your disease to drive awaye
To see the fishes in poolès playe,
And then walke in arbere up and down
To see the flowres of great renown.   70
'To a draw-bridge then shall ye,
The one half of stone, the other of tree;
A barge shall metè you full right
With twenty-four ores full bright,
With trompettes and with clariown,   75
The freshe water to rowe up and down.
Then shall ye go to the salte fome
Your maner to see, or ye come home,
With eighty shippes of largè tour,
With dromedaryes of great honòur,   80
And carackès with sailès two—
The swiftest that on water may go—
With galyes good upon the haven
With eighty ores at the fore-staven.
Your mariners shall singe a-rowe   85
"Hey, how, and rumbylowe".
Then shall ye, doughter, aske the wine,
With spices that be good and fine,
Gentil pottes with ginger grene,

---

65 truly tolde: rightly counted   66 alayes colde: cool alleys
67 disease: unhappiness   68 To see: *i.e.* you shall see   70 of . . . :
glorious   71 shall ye: you shall go   72 tree: wood   73 full
right: in proper style   78 maner: manor   or: before   79
of . . . : with ample fighting-tops   80 with splendid dromonds (large
ships)   81 carackes: galleons   84 fore-staven: bow   85 a-
rowe: together   89 Gentil: excellent

With dates and deinties you betwene;   90
Forty torches breninge bright
At your bridges to bringe you light.
　'Into your chambre they shall you bring
With muchè mirthe and more liking.
Your costerdes covered with white and blewe   95
And diapred with lilies newe;
Your curtaines of camaca all in fold,
Your filiolès all of gold;
Your tester-pery at your head,
Curtaines with popinjayes white and red;   100
Your hillinges with furres of ermìne,
Powdred with golde of hew full fine.
Your blankettes shall be of fustiayne,
Your shetes shall be of cloth of Rayne.
Your head-shete shall be of pery pight   105
With diamondes set and rubyes bright.
When you are laid in bedde so softe,
A cage of gold shall hange alofte,
With longe peper faire burning
And clovès that be swete smelling,   110
Frankensence and olibanum,
That when ye slepe the taste may come.
And if ye no rest may take,
All night minstrelles for you shall wake.'

90 you . . .: about you　　91 breninge: burning　　92 bridges:
?landing stages　　94 mirthe: gaiety　　liking: delight　　95 costerdes:
hangings　　97 camaca: silk　　in fold: pleated　　98 filioles:
ornamental bed-posts　　99 tester-pery: ?jewelled canopy　　101
hillinges: quilts　　103 fustiayne: fustian　　104 cloth . . .: fine
linen of Rennes　　105 head-shete: ?sheet put at the head of the bed
of . . .: studded with jewellery　　109 long pepper (prepared from
the immature fruit-spikes)　　111 olibanum: aromatic resin　　112
taste: scent　　114 wake: stay awake

'Gramercy, father, so mote I thee,   115
For all these thinges liketh not me.'

235   *The Shires*

HERVORDSHIR, shild and spere;
    Wosetershir, wringe pere.
Glowsetershir, shoo and naile;
Bristowshir, ship and saile.
Oxonfordshir, gird mare;   5
Warwikshir, bind beare.
London, globber;
Sothery, great bragger.
Shropshir, my shines been sharpe,
Lay wood to the fire, and yef me my harpe.   10
Lankashir, a fair archer;
Cheshir, thacker.
Northumberland, hasty and hot;
Westmerland, tot for sote.
Yorkeshir, full of knightes;   15
Lincolnshir, men full of mightes.
Cambridgeshir, full of pikes;
Holland, full of dikes.
Suffolk, full of wiles;
Norfolk, full of giles.   20
Essex, good houswives;
Middelsex, full of strives.

234. 115 so . . .: so may I prosper, *i.e.* indeed   116 despite all these
things I am not happy

235. 1 shild: shield   2 press pear   3 shoo: shoe   5 Bristow:
Bristol   5 gird: girth, saddle   *6 refers to the arms of the Earl of
Warwick*   7 glutton   8 Surrey   10 yef: give   12
thatcher   14 fool for fool   18 Holland, Lincs.   22 strives:
quarrels

Kent, as hot as fire;
Sussex, full of mire.
Southampton, drie and wete;   25
Somersetshir, good for whete.
Devinshir, wight and strong;
Dorcetshir will have no wrong.
Willshir, fair and plaine;
Barkshir, fill vaine.   30
Harvodshir, full of wood;
Huntingdonshir, corne full good.
Bedfordshir is not to lack;
Buckinghamshir is his mak.
Northampton, full of love   35
Beneath the girdel and not above.
Nottinghamshir, full of hogges;
Darbyshir, full of dogges.
Leicestershir, full of benes;
Staffordshir, full of shrewd quenes.   40
Cornewall, full of tinne;
Wales, full of gentlemen.

Probata sunt ista omnia

236   *Pilgrims to St. James*

M EN may leve all games
That sailen to Saint James;
For many a man it grames
When they begin to saile.

235. 27 wight: bold   29 plaine: open   30 vaine: **dike**, stream
33 not . . .: beyond reproach   34 his mak: its equal   40
shrewish women

236. 1 **Men** may give up all pleasures   2 St. James of Compostela
3 grames: distresses

For when they have take the see 5
At Sandwiche or at Winchelsee,
At Bristow, or where that it bee,
 Their hertes begin to faile.

Anon the master commaundeth fast
To his shipmen in all the hast 10
To dresse hem soone about the mast
 Their takeling to make.
With 'howe! hissa!' then they cry,
'What howe, mate! thou standest to ny,
Thy felow may not hale thee by'; 15
 Thus they begin to crake.

A boy or twain anon up styen
And overthwart the sail-yerde lyen;
'Y how! tailia!' the remenaunt cryen
 And pull with all their might. 20
'Bestowe the bote, boteswaine, anon,
That our pilgrims may play theron;
For some are like to cough and gron
 Or it be full midnight.

'Hale the boweline! Now vere the shete! 25
Cooke, make redy anon our mete;
Our pilgrims have no lust to ete,
 I pray God yeve hem rest!

7 Bristol where that: wherever 9 Anon: immediately fast:
sharply 11 to post themselves at once round the mast 12 *i.e.*
to handle their ropes 14 to ny: too near 15 hale . . .: haul
next to you 16 crake: shout 17 styen: climb 18 over-
thwart: across 21 Bestowe: get things stowed in 24 Or:
before 25 Hale: pull vere: let out 27 lust: desire 28
yeve: give

Go to the helm! What howe! No nere!
Steward, felow, a pot of bere!' 30
'Ye shall have, sir, with good chere
  Anon all of the best.'

'Y howe! trussa! hale in the brailes!
Thou halest not, by God, thou failes!
O see how well our good ship sailes!' 35
  And thus they say among.
'Hale in the wartake!' 'It shal be don'.
'Steward, cover the borde anon
And set bred and salt there-on,
  And tary not to long.' 40

Then cometh one and saith: 'Be mery!
Ye shall have a storm or a pery.'
'Hold thou thy pees! Thou canst no very;
  Thou medlest wonder sore.'
This mene-while the pilgrims ly 45
And have their bowlés fast them by,
And cry after hot malvèsy,
  'Thou helpe for to restore!'

And some wold have a salted tost,
For they might ete neither sode ne rost; 50
A man might soone pay for their cost
  As for o day or twain.

---

29 Go to the helm: ?put the helm over   nere: nearer the wind
33 brailes: ropes controlling the bunt of the sail   34 thou . . .: you're
slacking   36 among: continually   37 wartake: a rope   38
borde: table   42 pery: squall   43 canst . . .: don't know the truth
44 you talk most gloomily   47 and call for hot malmsey   50
sode: boiled   52 for a day or two

Some laide their bookės on their knee
And rad so long they might not see;
'Allas! mine hede will cleve on three!'   55
    Thus saith another certàin.

Then cometh our owner like a lord,
And speketh many a royal word,
And dresseth him to the high bord
    To see alle thing be well.   60
Anon he calleth a carpentère
And biddeth him bring with him his gere
To make the cabans here and there
    With many a febil cell.

A sak of straw were there right good,   65
For some must lig them in their hood—
I had as lefe be in the wood
    Withoutė mete or drink;
For when that we shall go to bedde,
The pumpe was nigh our beddės hede: 70
A man were as good to be dede
    As smell therof the stink.

fl. c. 1492

237   *Farewell Advent!*

FARE wel Advent! Cristemas is cum;
   Fare wel fro us, both all and sum.

With paciens thou hast us fedde
And made us go hungry to bedde;
For lak of mete we were nigh dedde;   5
   Fare wel fro us, both all and sum.

While thou hast be within oure house.
We ete no puddinges ne no souse,
But stinking fish not worth a louse;
   Fare wel fro us, both all and sum.   10

There was no fresh fish ferre ne nere;
Salt fish and samon was to dere;
And thus we have had hevy chere;
   Fare wel fro us, both all and sum.

Thou hast us fedde with plaices thin,   15
Nothing on them but bone and skin;
Therfore our love thou shalt not win;
   Fare wel fro us, both all and sum.

With muskilles gaping after the moone
Thou hast us fedde at night and noone   20

2 all and sum: one and all   8 souse: pickled meat   11 ferre:
far   13 hevy chere: wretched fare   19 muskilles: mussels
gaping: *i.e.* because stale

FAREWELL ADVENT!

But ones a weke, and that to soone;
    Fare wel fro us, both all and sum.

Our bred was brown, our ale was thin,
Our bred was musty in the bin,
Our ale sour or we did begin;   25
    Fare wel fro us, both all and sum.

Thou art of grete ingratitude
Good mete fro us for to exclude;
Thou art not kind but very rude;
    Fare wel fro us both all and sum.   30

Thou dwellest with us ayenst our will,
And yet thou givest us not our fill;
For lak of mete thou woldest us spill;
    Fare wel fro us, bothe all and sum.

Above all thing thou art a mean   35
To make our chekes both bare and lean.
I wold thou were at Boughton Blean!
    Fare wel fro us, both all and sum.

Come thou no more here nor in Kent,
For, if thou do, thou shalt be shent;   40
It is ynough to fast in Lent;
    Fare wel fro us, both all and sum.

Thou mayst not dwell with none estate;
Therfore with us thou playest chekmate.

---

21 ones: once   25 or: before   27 ingratitude: unkindness
33 spill: destroy   35 mean: means   37 Boughton-under-Blean,
Kent, where there was a hospital for lepers   40 shent: punished
43 estate: class   44 so you discomfit us

Go hens, or we will breke thy pate!   45
  Fare wel fro us, both all and sum.

Thou mayst not dwell with knight nor squire;
For them thou mayst lie in the mire;
They love not thee nor Lent, thy sire;
  Fare wel fro us, both all and sum.   50

Thou mayst not dwell with labouring man,
For on thy fare no skill he can,
For he must ete both now and than;
  Fare wel fro us, both all and sum.

Though thou shalt dwell with monk and frere, 55
Chanòn and nonne ones every yere,
Yet thou shuldest make us better chere;
  Fare wel fro us, both all and sum.

This time of Cristès feest natàll
We will be mery, grete and small,   60
And thou shalt go out of this hall;
  Fare wel fro us, both all and sum.

Advent is gone; Cristemas is cum;
Be we mery now, all and sum!
He is not wise that will be dum   65
  In ortu Regis omnium.

---

48 For them: as far as they are concerned   52 no . . .: he cannot
work   53 than: then   55 frere: friar   56 canon and nun
once every year

? JAMES RYMAN

238

Mary and her Son Alone

M ARY hath born alone
The Son of God in throne.

That maiden mild her child did kepe,
    As moders doth ech one,
But her dere Son full sore did wepe   5
    For sinfull man alone.

She rockèd Him and sung 'Lullay',
    But ever He made grete mone.
'Dere Son', she said, 'tell, I thee pray,
    Why thou dost wepe alone.'   10

'Moder', He said, 'I shall be slain
    That sin did never none,
And suffer deth with wofull pain:
    Therfore I wepe alone.'

'Lullay', she said, 'slepe and be still,   15
    And let be all thy mone,
For all thing is at thine own will,
    In heven and erth, alone.'

'Moder', He said, 'how shuld I slepe?
    How shuld I leve my mone?   20
I have more cause to sob and wepe,
    Sith I shall die alone.'

3 kepe: watch over   11 shall: must   20 leve: cease from
22 Sith: since

'Dere Son', she said, 'the King of Bliss,
  That is so high in throne,
Knoweth that thou didest never amiss.   25
  Why shuldest thou dy alone?'

'Moder', He said, 'only of thee
  I tooke both flesh and bone
To save mankind and make it free
  With my hert-blood alone.'   30

'Dere Son', she said, 'thou art equàll
  To God that is in throne;
For man, therfore, that is so thrall
  Why shuldest thou dy alone?'

'Moder', He said, 'my Faders will   35
  And myn, they be but one;
Therfore by skill I must fulfill
  My Faders will alone.'

'Dere Son', she said, 'sith thou hast take
  Of me both flesh and bone,   40
If it may be, me not forsake
  In care and and wo alone.'

'For man I must the raunsome pay,
  The which to hell is gone,
Moder', He said, 'on Good Friday,   45
  For he may not alone.'

'Dere Son', she said unto Him tho,
  'When thou fro me art gone,

33 **thrall**: enslaved   37 **skill**: reason   41 **me . . .**: do not forsake
me   46 **may not**: cannot (pay)   47 **tho**: then

Then shall I live in care and wo
    Without confòrt, alone.'   50

'Moder', He said, 'take thou no thought,
    For me make thou no mone;
When I have bought that I have wrought,
    Thou shalt not be alone.

'On the third day, I thee behight,   55
    After that I am gone,
I will arise by my grete might
    And confort thee alone.'

239   *The False Fox*

WITH how! fox, how! With hay! fox, hay!
    Come no more unto our house to bere our geese away.

The fals fox came unto our croft,
And so our geese ful fast he sought.

The fals fox came unto our sty   5
And tooke our geese there by and by.

The fals fox came into our yerde,
And there he made the geese aferde.

238. 51 take . . .: do not grieve   53 that: what   55 behight:
promise
239. 4 sought: pursued   5 sty: ?enclosure   6 by and by: one
by one   8 aferde: terrified

The fals fox came unto our gate
And took our geese there where they sate.   10

The fals fox came to our hallè dore
And shrove our geese there in the flore.

The fals fox came into our hall
And assoiled our geese both grete and small.

The fals fox came unto our coupe,   15
And there he made our geese to stoupe.

He took a goose fast by the nek,
And the goose tho began to quek.

The goodwife came out in her smok,
And at the fox she threw her rok.   20

The goodman came out with his flail
And smote the fox upon the tail.

He threw a goose upon his bak,
And forth he went tho with his pak.

The goodman swore, if that he might,   25
He wolde him slee or it were night.

The fals fox went into his denne,
And there he was full mery thenne.

He came ayèn yet the nextè weke
And took away both henne and cheke.   30

12 in: on   14 assoiled: gave absolution to   18 tho: then   19
goodwife: mistress   20 rok: distaff   21 goodman: master
26 slee: kill   or: before   29 ayen: again   30 cheke: chick

The goodman said unto his wife:
'This fals fox liveth a mery life!'

The fals fox came upon a day,
And with our geese he made affray.

He took a goose fast by the nek   35
And made her to say 'wheccumquek'.

'I pray thee, fox', said the goose tho,
'Take of my feders but not of my to.'

240

The Fox and the Goose

'*P*AX *vobis*', quod the fox,
  For I am comen to towne.'

It fell agains the next night
The fox yede to with all his might,
Withouten cole or candel-light,   5
  When that he came unto the towne.

When he came all in the yerde,
Sore the geese were all aferde;
'I shall make some of youre berde
  Or that I go from the towne!'   10

When he came all in the crofte,
There he stalkèd wunderfull softe;

239. 38 feders: feathers

240. 1 quod: said   2 am . . .: have arrived   3 agains . . .: the next evening   4 yede to: went to (work)   6 towne: farm   7 all . . .: right into the yard   8 aferde: frightened   9 I shall outwit some of you   10 Or: before   12 Wunderfull . . .: very quietly

'For here have I be frayed full ofte
When that I have come to towne.'

He hente a goose all by the heye;   15
Faste the goose began to creye.
Oute yede men as they might heye,
  And saide: 'Fals fox, lay it downe!'

'Nay', he saide, 'so mot I thee!
She shall go unto the wode with me; 20
She and I under a tree,
  Among the beryes browne.

I have a wif, and she lieth seke;
Many smale whelpes she have to-eke;
Many bonės they must pike   25
  While they lay adowne.'

241   *At the Tavern*

IS tell you my mind, Annės Tayliur: Dame,
 I deem we lak plesur.
Look here, dame, unlok your dur:
Alack, we have no likur!

Frend, and we ar fer in det   5
For your fine good wine, God wot,
A short gint has a pint pot:
I drank onės, I wold drink yet.

240. 13 frayed: scared 15 hente: seized heye: ?eye 17 as...:
as fast as they could go 19 so...: so may I prosper 23 seke:
sick 24 to-eke: besides 26 lay: lie

241. 1 Is: I Annes: Agnes 3 dur: door 5 and: even if
fer: far 7 gint: ?measure 8 ones: once

242 *Now is Yule Come*

HAY, ay, hay, ay,
Make we meré as we may.

Now is Yole comen with gentil chere;
Of merth and gamen he has no pere;
In every land where he comes nere   5
    Is merth and gamen, I dare wel say.

Now is comen a messingère
Of your lord, Sir Nu Yere,
Bids us all be meré here
    And make as meré as we may.   10

Therefore every man that is here
Sing a carol on his manère;
If he can none, we shall him lere,
    So that we be meré allway.

Whosoever makes hevé chere,   15
Were he never to me dere;
In a dich I wold he were,
    To dry his clothes till it were day!

Mend the fire and make good chere!
Fill the cup, Sir Botélère!   20
Let every man drink to his fere!
    This ends my carol with care away.

3 gentil: kindly   4 gamen: gaiety   12 on . . .: in his own
way   13 can: knows   lere: teach   20 Botelere: butler   21
fere: companion

243 *How the Ploughman Learned his Paternoster*

SOMETIME in Fraunce dwelled a plowman,
  Which was mighty, bold, and strong;
Good skill he coude in husbandry,
And gat his living full merily.
He coude eke sowe and holde a plow,   5
Both dike, hedge, and milke a cow,
Threshe, fane, and geld a swine,
In every season and in time;
To mow and repe both grass and corn
A better labourer was never born;   10
He coude go to plowe with oxe and hors—
With which it were he dide no fors;
Of shepe the wolle off for to shere
His better was founde no where;
Strip hemp he coude to cloute his shone,   15
And set geese a-broode in season of the mone,
Fell wode, and make it as it sholde be;
Of fruite he graffed many a tree;
He coude theche a hous, and daube a wall,
With all thinge that to husbandry dide fall.   20
By these to riches he was brought,
That golde ne silver he lacked nought;
His hall roof was full of bacon flitches;
The chambre charged was with wiches
Full of egges, butter, and chese,   25
Men that were hungry for to ease;
To make good ale, malte had he plentye;

3 he was knowledgeable about farming   4 gat: got   merily: successfully   7 fane: winnow   8 in time: at the proper time   12 he did not mind which   15 cloute . . .: mend his shoes   16 a-broode: to hatch   18 graffed: grafted   24 charged: stacked wiches: boxes

And Martilmas befe to him was not deintye;
Onions and garlike had he ynow,
And good creme, and milk of the cow.   30
Thus by his labour riche was he in dede;
Now to the mater will I procede.

   Grete good he gat and lived yeres fourty,
Yet coude he neither *Pater Noster* nor *Avé*.
In Lenten time the parson dide him shrive;   35
He said: 'Sir, canst thou thy Beleve?'
The plowman said unto the preste:
'Sir, I beleve in Jesu Criste,
Which suffred deth and harowed hell,
As I have herde mine elders tell.'   40
The parson said: 'Man, lete me here
Thee say devoutely thy *Pater Nostèr*,
That thou in it no word do lack'.
Then said the plowman: 'What thing is that
Which ye desire to here so sore?   45
I herde never therof before.'
The preest said: 'To lerne it thou art bound,
Or elles thou livest as an hound:
Without it saved canst thou not be,
Nor never have sight of the Deité;   50
From chirche to be banished aye
All they that can not their *Pater Noster* saye.
Therfore I mervail right gretly
That thy Beleve was never taught thee.
I charge thee, upon pain of deadly sinne,   55
Lerne it, heven if thou wilt winne.'
'I wolde thresh', said the plowman, 'ten yere,

28 Martilmas: Martinmas (11 Nov.)   deintye: rare   33 good: wealth
34 coude: knew   36 canst . . .: do you know your Creed   43
lack: get wrong   48 elles: else   51 to be: shall be

Rather than I it wolde lere.
I pray thee, sir parson, my counseil kepe;
Ten wethers will I give thee of my best shepe,   60
And thou shalt have in the same stounde
Fourty shilinges in grotes rounde
So ye me shewe how I may heven reche.'
  'Well!', said the preest, 'I shall thee teche;
If thou do by my counsèll,   65
To heven shalt thou come right well.'
The husband said: 'If ye will so,
Whatever ye bid me, it shall be do.'
'Well!', said the parson, 'sith thou hast graunt
Truly to kepe this covenaunt,   70
To do as I shall warn thee shortly,
Mark well the wordes that I say to thee:
Thou knowest that of corn is grete scarsnesse,
Wherby many for hungre dye, doubtlesse,
Because they lack their daily brede—   75
Hundredes this yere I have sene dede;
And thou hast grete plentye of whete,
Which men for money now can not gete;
And if thou wilt do after me,
Fourty poore men I shall sende thee,   80
And to eche of them give more or lasse
Or they away fro thee passe.
I shall thee double for thy whete pay
So thou bere truly their names away,
And if thou shewe them all and some,   85
Right in ordre as they do come,

58 before I would learn it   59 counseil: secret   61 stounde: time
63 So: if   67 husband: farmer   69 sith: since   graunt: granted
71 warn: instruct   79 after me: as I advise   82 Or: before
84 So: provided   85 shewe: rehearse   all . . .: one and all

Who is served first and who last of all.'
'In faith!', said the plowman, 'so I shall!
Go when ye will and send them hider;
Fain wold I see that company togider.'   90
   The parson wente to fetch the route,
And gadred poore people all aboute;
To the plowmans hous forth he wente.
The husbandman was well contente
Because the parson was their surety: 95
That made his herte muche more mery.
The preest said: 'See here thy men echone,
Serve them lightly that they were gone.'
The husbandman said to him again:
'The lenger they tary, the more is my pain.'   100
First wente *pater*, feble, lene, and olde—
All his clothes for hungre had he solde:
Two bushelles of whete gat he there;
Unethe for age might he it bere.
Then came *noster* ragged in array: 105
He had his back-burden, and so wente his way.
Two peckes were given to *qui es in celis*;
No wonder if he halted, for kibed were his heles.
Then came *sanctificetur*, and *nomen tuum*:
Of whete amonge them gat an hole tunne—   110
How muche was therin I can not say;
They two laded a carte, and wente their way.
In ordre folowed them other three,
Adveniat, *regnum*, *tuum*, that was dead nye;
They thought to longe that they abode,   115

---

90 togider: together   91 route: crowd   98 serve them
quickly so that they may be gone   99 said again: replied   100
lenger: longer   104 Unethe: scarcely   108 halted: limped
kibed: chilblained   110 amonge: between   tunne: barrel   114
dead nye: nearly dead   115 *i.e.* they could not get away quickly enough

Yet eche of them had an hors-lode.
The plowman cryed: 'Sirs, come away!'
Then wente *fiat, voluntas, tua, sicut, in, celo, et, in,*
terra,
Some blere-eyed, and some lame, with botell and
bagge—
To cover their arses they had not an hole ragge: 120
Aboute ten bushelles they had them amonge,
And in the way homeward full merily songe.
Then came *panem, nostrum, cotidianum, da nobis, hodie;*
Amonge them five they had but one peny
That was given them for Goddes sake;   125
They said therwith that they wold mery make:
Eche had two bushelles of whete that was goode;
They songe going homeward a gest of Robin Hoode.
Et, dimitte, nobis, debita, nostra, came than,
The one sunburned, another black as a pan;   130
They pressed in the hepe, of corne to finde—
No wonder if they fell, for they were all blinde:
Ech of them an hole quartre they had,
And straight to the ale-hous they it lad.
Sicut, et nos, dimittimus, debitoribus, nostris,   135
Came in anon, and dide not miss;
They had ten bushelles, withouten faile,
And laide five to pledge for a kilderkin of ale.
Then came *et, ne, nos, inducas, in, temptationem:*
Amonge them all they had quarters ten;   140
Their brede was baken in a tankard,
And the residue they played at the hazard.
By and by came *sed libera nos a malo;*

119 botell: bundle   128 gest: tale   129 than: then   131
they pushed into the crowd to find some corn   134 lad: took
138 kilderkin: sixteen-gallon cask   141 *i.e.* part was used to buy ale
143 By and by: directly

He was so wery he might not go.
Also *Amen* came renning in anone;   145
He cryed out: 'Spede me, that I were gone!'
He was patched, torn, and all to-rente;
It semed by his langage that he was born in Kente.
   The plowman served them everichone,
And was full glad when thy were gone.   150
But when he saw of corn he had no more,
He wished them at the devil ther-fore.
So long had he meten his corne and whete,
That all his body was in a swete.
Then unto his hous dide he go;   155
His herte was full of pain and wo
To kepe their names and shew them right,
That he rested but litel that night.
Ever he patred on their names faste,
That he had them in ordre at the laste.   160
   Then on the morowe he wente to the parsòn,
And said: 'Sir, for money am I come;
My corn I delivered by the counseil of thee;
Remember thy promis, thou art their suretye.'
The preest said: 'Their names thou must me showe.'   165
The plowman rehersed them on a rowe;
How they were called he kepte in minde;
He said that *Amen* came all behind.
The parson said: 'Man, be glad this day,
Thy *Pater Noster* now canst thou say.'   170
The plowman said: 'Give me my monèye!'
The preest said: 'I owe none to thee to paye;

144 go: walk   145 renning: running   146 Spede me: serve
me quickly   147 to-rente: in shreds   149 everichone: every one
153 meten: measured out   157 shew . . .: state them correctly
159 patred on: repeated   160 That: so that   166 on . . .: in order
172 owe . . .: have no obligation to pay you

Though thou dide thy corn to poore men give,
Thou mayst me blisse while thou dost live;
For by these may ye pay Crist His rente,   175
And serve the Lord omnipotente.'
'Is this the answer', he said, 'that I have shall?
I shall summon thee afore the officiall.'
  So to the courte wente they both in dede;
Not beste of all dide the plowman spede!   180
Unto the officiall the parson tolde all
How it betwene them two dide fall,
And of this *Pater Noster* lerning.
Many to his wordes gave herkening;
They laughed and made sport ynow.   185
The plowman for anger bended his brow,
And said: 'These poor men have away all my corn,
And for my labour the parson doth me scorn.'
The officiall praised gretly the parsòn,
And said right well that he had done;   190
He said: 'Plowman, it is shame to thee
To accuse this gentilman before me.'
He badde him go home, foole as he was,
And ask God mercy for his trespàs.
  The plowman thought ever on his whete,   195
And said: 'Again I shall it never gete.'
Then he wente and to his wife said
How that the parson had him betrayd;
And said: 'While that I live, certàin,
Preest shall I never trust again!'   200
Thus for his corn that he gave there,
His *Pater Noster* dide he lere;
And, after, long he lived withouten strife,

174 blisse: bless   178 officiall: judge in ecclesiastical court
199 certain: certainly   202 lere: learn

Till he went from his mortal life.
The parson deceased after alsò: 205
Their soules I truste to heven dide go;
Unto the which He us bringe
That in heven reigneth eternal Kinge!

244   *A Woman is a Worthy Thing*

> I AM as light as any roe
>   To praise women where that I go.

To unpraise women it were a shame,
For a woman was thy dame;
Our blessed Lady bereth the name   5
  Of all women where that they go.

A woman is a worthy thing:
They do the wash and do the wring;
'Lullay, lullay' she doth thee sing;
  And yet she hath but care and wo.   10

A woman is a worthy wight:
She serveth a man both day and night;
Therto she putteth all her might;
  And yet she hath but care and wo.

245   *My Little Pretty Mopsy*

> 'I PRAY you, cum kiss me,
>   My litle prety mopsé,
> I pray you, cum kiss me.'

244. 1 light: swift   2 where that: wherever   5 bereth . . .:
upholds the reputation   11 wight: creature
245. 2 mopsé: sweetheart

MY LITTLE PRETTY MOPSY

'Alas, good man, must you be kist?
Ye shall not now, ye may me trist;   5
Wherefore go where as ye best list,
    For y-wiss ye shall not kiss me.'

'Y-wiss, sweet hart, if that ye
Had asked a greter thing of me,
So unkind to you I wold not have be;   10
    Wherefore I pray you, cum kiss me.'

'I think very well that ye are kind
Where as ye love and set your mind;
But all your wordes be but as wind,
    Wherefore now ye shall not kiss me.'   15

'I do but talke, ye mow me trust,
But ye take everything at the wurst.'
'Wherefore I say, as I said furst,
    Y-wiss, ye shall not kiss me.'

'I pray you, let me kiss you;   20
If that I shall not kiss you,
Let me kiss your kerches noke;
    I pray you, let me kiss you.'

'All so I say as I furst have said,
And ye will not therewith be dismaid;   25
Yet with that answer ye shall be paid:
    Y-wiss, ye shall not kiss me.'

5 trist: trust   6 where . . .: where you please   7 y-wiss: certainly
16 mow: may   22 your . . .: the corner of your kerchief   24 All
so: just the same   25 if you'll not be vexed at it   26 shall . . .:
must be satisfied

'Now I see well that kisses are dere,
And if I shold labur all the hole yere
I think I shold be never the nere; 30
   Wherefore, I pray you, cum kiss me.'

'Never the nere, ye may be sure;
For ye shall not so soone bring me in ure
To consent unto your nice plesùre,
   Nor, y-wiss, ye shall not kiss me.' 35

'I pray you, com and kiss me,
My litle pretty mopsé;
And if that ye will not kiss me.
   I pray you, let me kiss you.'

'Well, for a kiss I will not stick, 40
So that ye will do nothing but likk;
But, and ye begin on me for to prick,
   Y-wiss, ye shall not kiss me.'

'Now I see well that ye are kind;
Wherefore ye shall ever know my mind, 45
And ever your own ye shall me find,
   At all times redy to kiss you.'

246   *The Forester*

I HAVE been a foster long and many day;
   My lockès been hore.
I shall hang up my horn by the grene wode spray;
   Foster will I be no more.

245. 30 nere: nearer   33 bring . . .: induce me   34 nice: foolish
41 So that: as long as   42 and: if
246. 2 hore: grey

All the whiles that I may my bowe bende   5
  Shall I weddė no wife.
I shall bigge me a bowr at the wodės ende,
  There to lede my life.

247   *Corpus Christi Carol*

LULLY, lulley, lully, lulley;
  The faucon hath born my mak away.

He bare him up, he bare him down,
He bare him into an orchard brown.

In that orchard there was an hall,   5
That was hanged with purpel and pall.

And in that hall there was a bed;
It was hanged with gold so red.

And in that bed there lieth a knight,
His woundės bleeding day and night.   10

By that bedes side there kneeleth a may,
And she weepeth both night and day.

And by that bedes side there standeth a ston,
'Corpus Christi' writen ther-on.

246. 7 bigge: build
247. 2 faucon: falcon   mak: mate   11 may: maid

248   *The Sparrow-Hawk's Complaint*

IN what state that ever I be
   Timor mortis conturbat me.

As I me walked in one morning,
I herd a bird both weep and sing;
This was the tenor of her talking: 5
   Timor mortis conturbat me.

I asked this bird what he ment.
He said: 'I am a musket gent;
For dred of deth I am nigh shent;
   Timor mortis conturbat me.   10

'Jesu Crist, when He shuld die,
To His Fader loud gan He cry:
"Fader", He said, "in Trinity,
   Timor mortis conturbat me."

'When I shall die know I no day;   15
In what place or contrey can I not say;
Therfore this song sing I may,
   Timor mortis conturbat me.'

1 state: rank   3 As I was walking one morning   7, 8 he,
He: she   8 musket gent: noble sparrow-hawk   9 shent: des-
troyed   11 shuld: had to   12 gan: did   15 I do not know
the day when I must die

249 *Stag-Hunt*

AS I walked by a forest side,
I met with a foster; he bad me abide.

At a place where he me set,
He bad me, what time an hart I met,
That I shuld let slip and say 'Go bet!'   5
   With 'Hay! go bet! Hay! go bet! Hay! go bet!
     How!'
   We shall have game and sport ynow.

I had not stond there but a while,
Ye, not the montenance of a mile,
But a gret hart came renning, without any gile.   10
   With 'There he goth! There he goth! There he
     goth! How!'
   We shall have game and sport ynow.

I had no sooner my houndes let go,
But the hart was overthrow.
Then every man began to blow,   15
   With 'Trororo! Trororo! Trororo! Trow!'
   We shall have game and sport ynow.

2 foster: forester   4 what time: when   5 let slip: release
(my dogs)   bet: quick   8 f. I had stood there but a (little) while,
indeed, not as long as it would take to go a mile   10 renning: run-
ning   without . . .: truly

250

My Twelve Oxen

WITH hay, with how, with hoy!
  Sawest thou not myn oxen, thou litel pretty boy?

I have twelve oxen that be fair and brown,
And they go a-grasing down by the town.

I have twelve oxen, and they be fair and white,   5
And they go a-grasing down by the dike.

I have twelve oxen, and they be fair and blake,
And they go a-grasing down by the lake.

I have twelve oxen, and they be fair and rede,
And they go a-grasing down by the mede.   10

251

Now is the Time of Christmas

MAKE we mery, both more and lass,
  For now is the time of Cristymas.

Let no man cum into this hall,
  Grome, page, nor yet marshàll,
  But that some sport he bring withall,   5
    For now is the time of Cristmas.

250. 4 town: village
251. 1 both . . .: everyone   4 grome: man-servant

If that he say he can not sing,
Some other sport then let him bring
That it may please at this festing,
    For now is the time of Cristmas.   10

If he say he can nought do,
Then for my love ask him no mo,
But to the stokkes then let him go,
    For now is the time of Cristmas.

252   *The Jolly Shepherd Wat*

    C AN I not sing but 'hoy!'
      When the joly sheperd made so much joy.

The sheperd upon a hill he sat;
He had on him his tabard and his hat,
His tar-box, his pipe, and his flagàt;   5
His name was called Joly, Joly Wat,
    For he was a good herdes-boy.
      With hoy!
    For in his pipe he made so much joy.

The sheperd upon a hill was laid;   10
His dog to his girdel was taid.
He had not slept but a litel braid
But '*Gloria in excelsis*' was to him said.
      With hoy!
    For in his pipe he made so much joy.   15

251. 9 That it: which   12 love: sake   mo: more
252. 5 flagat: flask   11 taid: tied   12 braid: moment

The sheperd on a hill he stood;
Round about him his shepe they yood;
He put his hand under his hood;
He saw a star as red as blood.
    With hoy!   20
  For in his pipe he made so much joy.

'Now farewell Mall, and also Will;
For my love go ye all still
Unto I cum again you till;
And evermore, Will, ring well thy bell.'   25
    With hoy!
  For in his pipe he made so much joy.

'Now must I go ther Crist was born;
Farewell, I cum again to-morn.
Dog, kepe well my shepe fro the corn,   30
And warn wel Warrok when I blow my horn.'
    With hoy!
  For in his pipe he made so much joy.

The sheperd said anon-right:
'I will go see yon ferly sight,   35
Wheras the angel singeth on hight,
And the star that shineth so bright.'
    With hoy!
  For in his pipe he made so much joy.

---

17 yood: went   22 Mall, Will: names of sheep   23 still: quietly   24 until I come back to you   28 ther: where   29 to-morn: tomorrow   31 warn: summon Warrok: *obscure*   34 anon-right: straightaway   35 ferly: marvellous   36 Wheras: where   on hight: loudly

When Wat to Bedleëm cum was,   40
He swet: he had gon faster than a pace.
He found Jesu in a simpel place
Between an ox and an ass.
    With hoy!
    For in his pipe he made so much joy.   45

'Jesu, I offer to thee here my pipe,
My skirt, my tar-box, and my scripe;
Home to my fellowes now will I skipe,
And also looke unto my shepe.'
    With hoy!   50
    For in his pipe he made so much joy.

'Now farewell, mine own herdesman Wat.'
'Yea, for God, Lady, even so I hat.
Lull well Jesu in thy lap,
And farewell, Joseph, with thy round cap.'   55
    With hoy!
    For in his pipe he made so much joy.

'Now may I well both hop and sing,
For I have been at Cristes bering.
Home to my fellowes now will I fling.   60
Crist of heven to His blis us bring!'
    With hoy!
    For in his pipe he made so much joy.

---

41 pace: walking-pace   **47 skirt:** kilt   **scripe:** bag   **53 for:**
before   **hat:** am called   **58 hop:** dance   **59 bering:** birth
60 fling: dash

253   *I am Christmas*

NOW have good day, now have good day!
I am Cristmas, and now I go my way.

Here have I dwelled with more and lass
From Halowtide till Candelmas,
And now must I from you hens pass;   5
    Now have good day!

I take my leve of king and knight,
And erl, baròn, and lady bright;
To wilderness I must me dight;
    Now have good day!   10

And at the good lord of this hall
I take my leve, and of gestes all;
Me think I herė Lent doth call;
    Now have good day!

And at every worthy officère,   15
Marshall, panter, and butlère,
I take my leve as for this yere;
    Now have good day!

Another yere I trust I shall
Makė mery in this hall,   20
If rest and peace in England fall;
    Now have good day!

1 have good day: goodbye   3 more . . .: everyone   4 *i.e.*
from 1 Nov. to 2 Feb.   9 me dight: go   15 officere: servant
16 panter: pantry-man

But oftentimes I have herd say
That he is loth to part away
That often biddeth 'Have good day!';   25
   Now have good day!

Now fare ye well, all in fere,
Now fare ye well for all this yere;
Yet for my sake make ye good chere;
   Now have good day!   30

254   *The Boar's Head*

   *C*APUT *apri refero,*
    Resonans laudes Domino.

The borės hed in hands I bring,
With garlands gay and birds singing.
I pray you all, help me to sing,   5
   Qui estis in convivio.

The borės hed, I understand,
Is chef servìce in all this land;
Whersoever it may be fand,
   Servitur cum sinapio.   10

The borės hed, I dare well say,
Anon after the Twelfthė Day
He taketh his leve and goth away,
   Exibit tunc de patria.

253. 27 in fere: together

254. 8 chef service: the best dish   9 fand: found   10 it is served
with mustard   12 Anon: immediately

255   *My Heart is Woe*

'O MY hart is wo!', Mary she said so,
   'For to see my dere Son dy, and sones have I no
   mo.'

'When that my swete Son was thirty winter old,
Then the traitor Judas wexèd very bold:
For thirty plates of money his master he had sold.   5
But when I it wistè, Lord, my hart was cold!

'Upon Sherè Thursday then truly it was
On my Sonès deth that Judas did compàss.
Many were the fals Jewes that folowed him by trace;
And there before them all he kissed my Sonès face.   10

'My Son before Pilat brought was He,
And Peter said three times he knew Him not, pardee.
Pilat said unto the Jewes: "What say ye?"
Then they cryed with one vois: "*Crucifige!*"

'On Good Friday, at the mount of Calvary,   15
My Son was don on the crosse, nailed with nailès three.
Of all the frendes that He had, never one could He see
But jentil John the Evangelist, that still stood Him by.

'Though I were sorowfull, no man have at it wonder;
For huge was the erth-quak, horìble was the thonder.   20
I loked on my swete Son on the cross that I stood under;
Then came Longeus with a spere and cleft His hart in sonder.'

2 mo: more	4 wexed: grew	5 plates: pieces
6 wiste: knew	7 Shere: Maundy	8 compass (on): plot
9 him . . .: in his path	12 pardee: by God	18 still: silently

256 *Assay a Friend*

MAN, be ware and wise in dede,
And assay a frend or thou have nede.

Through a forest that was so long
As I rode with mikel drede,
I herd a bird singing a song: 5
'Assay a frend or thou have nede.'

As I stood and hovèd still
And to a tree I tied my stede,
Ever the bird sat singing still:
'Assay a frend or thou have nede.' 10

Me thought it was a wonder noise,
And nerè-hand the bird I yede;
Y-wis she sang with a loud voise:
'Assay a frend or thou have nede.'

The bird sat high upon a tree; 15
Of feders gray then was her wede.
She said: 'Do as I bid thee,
Assay a frend or thou have nede.'

I beheld her wonder long;
She said: 'Do as I bid thee, in dede, 20
Whether thou do right or wrong,
Assay a frend or thou have nede.'

2 assay: test   or: before   7 hoved still: paused   11 wonder:
amazing   12 nere-hand: closer to   yede: went   13 Y-wis:
indeed   16 wede: garb

I trow of me she was agast;
   She took her flight; away she yede.
Thus she said, when she sang last: 25
   'Assay a frend or thou have nede.'

257   *The Juggler and the Baron's Daughter*

D RAW me nere, draw me nere,
   Draw me nere, the joly juggelère.

Here-beside dwelleth a rich barons doughter;
She wold have no man that for her love had sought her,
   So nice she was;   5
She wold have no man that was made of mold,
But if he had a mouth of gold to kiss her when she wold,
   So dangerous she was.

Therof herd a joly juggeler that laid was on the green,
And at this ladys wordes y-wis he had grete teen—   10
   An-angred he was.
He juggeled to him a well good steede of an old hors-bone,
A sadel and a bridel both, and set himself theron—
   A juggler he was.

He priked and pransed both before that ladys gate;   15
She wend he had been an angel was com for her sake—
   A prikker he was;
He priked and pransed before that ladys bowr;
She wend he had been an angel comen from heven-towr—
   A pranser he was.   20

257. 1 me nere: nearer me   5 nice: fastidious   6 mold: earth
7 But if: unless   8 dangerous: hard to please   10 y-wis: indeed
teen: fury   12 of: out of   15 priked: rode   16 wend: sup-
posed   was: (who) had

Four and twenty knightes led him into the hall,
And as many squires his hors to the stall
   And gave him mete;
They gave him otes and also hay;
He was an old shrew and held his hed away,   25
   He wold not ete.

The day began to passe, the night began to com;
To bedde was brought the faire gentilwomàn
   And the juggler alsò.
The night began to passe, the day began to spring;   30
All the birdes of her bowr they began to sing,
   And the cukoo alsò.

'Wher be ye, my mery maidens, that ye cum not me to?
The joly windows of my bowr look that you undo,
   That I may see;   35
For I have in myn armes a duk or els an erle.'
But when she looked him upon, he was a blere-eyed cherle.
   'Alas!', said she.

She led him to an hill, and hanged shuld he be;
He juggeled himself to a mele-poke, the dust fell in her ee;
   Begiled she was.   41
God and our Lady and swete Saint Johàn
Send every giglot of this town such another lemmàn
   Even as he was.

---

25 shrew: rascal   40 mele-poke: meal-bag   ee: eye   43
giglot: strumpet   lemman: lover

Good Gossips Mine

HOW! gossip mine, gossip mine,
  When will we go to the wine,
   Good gossipes mine?

I shall you tell a full good sport,
How gossipes gader them on a sort,   5
Their seke bodies to comfòrt
  When they meet
  In lane or street,
   Good gossipes mine. . . . .

'Good gossip mine, wher have ye be?   10
It is so long sith I you see;
Wher is the best wine? Tell you me.
  Can ye aught tell?'
  'Yea, full well,
   Good gossipes mine.   15

'I know a draught of mery-go-down;
The best it is in all this town;
But yet I wold not, for my gown,
  My husband wist.'
  'Ye may me trist,   20
   Good gossipes mine.'

'Call forth our gossipes by and by,
Elinore, Joan, and Margery,
Margret, Alis, and Cecely,

---

5 how gossips gather in a party   6 seke: sick   11 sith: since
16 mery-go-down: strong ale   19 wist: knew   20 trist: trust
22 by and by: one by one

For they will cum,   25
Both all and sum,
   Good gossipes mine-a.

'And eche of them will sumwhat bring,
Goose or pigg, or capons wing,
Pastés of pigenes, or sum other thing;   30
   For we must ete
   Sum maner mete,
      Good gossipes mine-a.' . . .

'Now be we in the tavern set,
A draught of the best let him fet,
To bring our husbands out of det;   35
   For we will spend
   Till God more send,
      Good gossipes mine-a.' . . .

'How looke ye, gossip, at the bordes end?   40
Not mery, gossip? God it amend!
All shall be well, els God defend!
   Be mery and glad
   And sit not so sad,
      Good gossipes mine-a.'   45

'Wold God I had done after your counsèll!
For my husband is so fell
He beteth me like the devil of hell,
   And the more I cry,
   The less mercỳ,   50
      Good gossipes mine-a.' . . .

26 one and all   32 some kind of food   35 fet: fetch
40 bordes: table's   42 els . . .: God forbid that it be otherwise
46 done after: acted on   47 fell: savage

Margret Meke said: 'So mot I thrive,
I know no man that is alive
That giveth me two strokes, but he have five:
  I am not afèrd,   55
    Though he have a berd,
      Good gossipes mine-a.'

One cast down her shot and went away.
'Gossip', quod Elinore, 'what dide she pay?
Not but a peny? Lo! therfor I say   60
  She shall no more
  Be of our lore,
    Good gossipes mine-a.

'Such gestes we may have ynow
That will not for their shot alow;   65
With whom com she, gossip? With you?'
  'Nay', quod Joan,
  'I com alone,
    Good gossipes mine-a.'

'Now reken our shot, and go we hens;   70
What cometh to eche of us? But three pens?
Pardé, this is but a small expens
  For such a sort,
  And all but sport,
    Good gossipes mine-a.'   75

'Turn down the street, when ye cum out,
And we will cumpas round about.'
'Gossip', quod Anne, 'what nedeth that dout?

52 mot: may   54 but . . .: without getting five   55 aferd: afraid   58 shot: contribution   59 quod: said   62 lore: party   65 who refuse to pay their share   66 com: came   72 Pardé: by God   73 sort: party   74 but: sheer   77 cumpas . . .: go a roundabout way   78 what . . .: why worry about that

Your husband is pleased,
When ye be eased,   80
  Good gossipes mine-a.' . . .

This is the thought that gossipes take:
Ons in the week mery will they make,
And all small drinkes they will forsake;
  But wine of the best   85
  Shall have no rest,
    Good gossipes mine-a. . . .

259   *A Call for a Song*

B ON *jour, bon jour a vous!*
  I am cum unto this hous
  With *par la pompe*, I say.

Is there any good man here
That will make me any chere?   5
And if there were, I wold cum nere
  To wit what he wold say.
    A! will ye be wild?
    By Mary mild
    And her swete child,   10
  I trow ye will sing gay.

258. 80 eased: refreshed   83 ons: once   84 small: weak
259. 3 *par la pompe*: ?ceremony   5 make . . .: entertain me in any
way   8 wild: ?refractory

Be gladly, masters everichone;
I am cum myself alone
To appose you one by one;
    Let see who dare say nay.   15
        Sir, what say ye?
        Sing on; let us see.
        Now will it be
    This or another day?

Lo, this is he that will do the dede;   20
He tempereth his mouth; therfore take hede.
Singe softe, I say, lest your nose blede,
    For hurt yourself ye may.
        But, by God that me bought,
        Your brest is so tought,   25
        Till ye have well cought
    Ye may not therwith away.

Sir, what say ye with your face so lene?
Ye sing neither good tenour, treble, ne mene.
Utter not your voice without your brest be
    clene,   30
    Hartely I you pray.
        I hold you excused;
        Ye shall be refused,
        For ye have not be used
    To no good sport nor play.   35

12 be merry, sirs, every one of you   14 appose: interrogate
15 Let see: let (us) see   21 tempereth: tunes up   25 tought:
congested   26 cought: coughed   27 you cannot get rid of it
29 mene: middle part   30 without: unless   31 Hartely:
earnestly

Sir, what say ye with your fat face?
Me thinketh ye shuld bere a very good bace
To a pot of good ale or ipocrace,
   Truly, as I you say.
     Hold up your hed;   40
     Ye looke like led!
     Ye waste much bred
   Evermore from day to day.

Now will ye see wher he standeth behind?
Y-wis, brother, ye be unkind.   45
Stand forth and waste with me some wind,
   For ye have been called a singer ay.
     Nay, be not ashamed;
     Ye shall not be blamed,
     For ye have been famed   50
   The worst in this contray!

260   *Fill the Bowl, Butler*

H OW, butler, how! *Bevis a tout!*
  Fill the boll, gentil butler, and let the cup rout.

Gentil butler, bell amy,
Fill the boll by the eye,
That we may drink by and by.   5
   With how, butler, how! *Bevis a tout!*
   Fill the boll, butler, and let the cup rout.

259. 38 ipocrace: spiced wine   **45** Y-wis: indeed   **46** waste . . .:
i.e. speak (?sing) with me

260. 1 *Bevis a tout* (= *beuvez a tout*): drink to all   **2** boll: bowl
rout: go round   **3** bell amy: good friend   **4** by the eye: to the
brim   **5** by and by: one and all

FILL THE BOWL, BUTLER

Here is mete for us all,
Both for grete and for small;
I trow we must the butler call.   10
   With how, butler, how! *Bevis a tout!*
   Fill the boll, butler, and let the cup rout.

I am so dry I can not speke;
I am nigh chokèd with my mete;
I trow the butler be aslepe.   15
   With how, butler, how! *Bevis a tout!*
   Fill the boll, butler, and let the cup rout.

Butler, butler, fill the boll,
Or ellès I beshrew thy noll!
I trow we must the bell toll.   20
   With how, butler, how! *Bevis a tout!*
   Fill the boll, butler, and let the cup rout.

If the butlers name be Water,
I wold he were a galow-claper,
But if he bring us drink the rather.   25
   With how, butler, how! *Bevis a tout!*
   Fill the boll, butler, and let the cup rout.

8 mete: food   19 or else I curse your head   23 Water: pun on
'water' and 'Walter' (pronounced 'Water')   24 galow-claper: gallows-
bird   25 But if: unless   rather: quicker.

261 *A Schoolboy's Complaint*

HAY, hay, by this day,
What availeth it me though I say nay?

I wold fain be a clerk,
But yet it is a stronge werk;
The birchen twigges be so sharp   5
It maketh me have a faint hert.
    What availeth it me though I say nay?

On Monday in the morning when I shall rise,
At six of the clok, it is the gise
To go to scole without avise—   10
I had lever go twenty mile twise.
    What availeth it me though I say nay?

My master looketh as he were mad:
'Where hast thou be, thou sory lad?'
'Milke dukkes my moder bad'—   15
It was no mervaile though I were sad.
    What availeth it me though I say nay?

My master pepered my ars with well good spede;
It was worse than finkell sede;
He wold not leve till it did blede—   20
Mich sorow have he for his dede!
    What availeth it me though I say nay?

---

1 by . . . : indeed   3 clerk: scholar   4 stronge werk: painful labour
9 gise: custom   10 without avise: without question   11 lever:
rather   15 My mother told (me) to milk ducks   18 with . . .:
very effectively   19 finkell sede: fennel seed   21 Mich: much

I wold my master were a watt,
And my book a wild catt,
And a brace of grehoundes in his topp: 25
I wold be glad for to see that!
   What availeth it me though I say nay?

I wold my master were an hare,
And all his bookes houndes were,
And I myself a joly huntère;   30
To blow my horn I wold not spare,
For if he were dede I wold not care.
   What availeth me though I say nay?

262   *Farewell this World!*

FAREWELL this world! I take my leve for ever;
   I am arrested to appere afore Godes face.
O merciful God, thou knowest that I had lever
  Than all this world to have an hourè space
  For to make asseth for my gret trespàce.   5
   My harte, alas, is broken for that sorow:
   Some be this day that shall not be to-morow.

This world, I see, is but a chery-fair;
  All thingès passeth, and so moste I algate.
This day I sat full royally in a chair,   10
  Till sutil deth knokkèd at my gate,

---

261. 23 watt: hare   25 in his toppe: *i.e.* harrying him

262. 3 lever: rather   5 asseth: amends   8 chery-fair: cherry-fair
(*i.e* short-lasting)   9 moste . . .: must I in any event   11 sutil:
insidious

And unavised he said to me 'chekmate!'
  Lo! how sudeinly he maketh a devorce!
And, wormes to fede, here he hath laid my corse.

Speke softe, ye folkes, for I am laid aslepe;   15
  I have my dreme; in trust is muchè treason.
From dethès hold fain wold I make a lepe;
  But my wisdom is turned into feble reason.
I see this worldes joy lasteth but a season;
  Wold God I had remembred this beforne!   20
  I say no more, but beware of an horne!

This fikel world, so false and so unstable,
  Promoteth his lovers but for a litel while;
But at the last he giveth them a bable,
  When his painted trowth is turned into gile.   25
  Experience causeth me the trowth to compile,
  Thinking this—too late, alas, that I began!
  For foly and hope disseiveth many a man.

Farewell, my frendes! the tide abideth no man;
  I moste departè hens, and so shall ye.   30
But in this passage, the best song that I can
  Is 'Requiem Eternam': I pray God grant it me.
When I have ended all myn adversité,
  Grante me in Paradise to have a mansion
  That shede His blode for my redempcion!   35

12 unavised: without warning   13 maketh . . : *i.e.* parts soul and body   21 horne: *i.e.* Death's summoning trumpet   24 bable: bauble   25 painted: feigned   26 compile: formulate   31 passage: voyage   can: know   34 f. may He grant me a dwelling in Paradise who shed His blood for my redemption

263   *Roses*

A song for three voices

'I LOVE, I love, and whom love ye?'
  'I love a flowr of fresh beauté.'
'I love another as well as ye.'
   'Then shal be provèd here anon
   If we three can agree in on.'   5

'I love a flowr of swete odòur.'
'Magèrome gentil, or lavendòur?'
'Columbine, goldès of swete flavòur?'
   'Nay, nay, let be!
   Is none of them   10
   That liketh me.' *I love, I love, etc.*

'There is a flowr, where so he be,
And shall not yet be named for me.'
'Primèros, violet, or fresh daisỳ?'
    'He pass them all   15
    In his degré
    That best liketh me.' *I love, I love, etc.*

'One that I love most enterly.'
'Gelofer gentil, or rosemary?'
'Camamil, borage, or savery?'   20
   'Nay, certenly,
   Here is not he
   That pleseth me.' *I love, I love, etc.*

4 proved: found out   5 in on: together   7 Magerome:
marjoram   8 goldes: marigolds   11 liketh: pleases   13 for
me: for my part   15 pass: excels   16 degré: quality
18 (There is) one whom I love most whole-heartedly   19 Gelofer:
gillyflower   20 savery: savory

'I chese a flowr freshest of face.'
'What is his name that thou chosen has?'   25
'The rose, I suppose. Thyn hart unbrace!'
  'That same is he,
  In hart so free,
  That best liketh me.' *Now have I loved, etc.*

'The rose it is a ryal flowr.'   30
'The red or the white? Shew his colòur.'
'Both be full swete and of like savòur.'
  'All one they be;
  That day to see
  It liketh well me.' *Now have I loved, etc.*   35

'I love the rose both red and white.'
'Is that your pure perfite appetite?'
'To here talke of them is my delite.'
  'Joyed may we be
  Our prince to see   40
  And roses three!'

  'Now have we loved and love will we
  This fair fresh flowr, full of beauté;
  Most worthy it is, as thinketh me.
    Then may be provèd here anon   45
    That we three be agreed in on.'

---

24 chese: choose   26 unbrace: lay open   28 free: noble
30 ryal: royal   31 Shew: declare   37 Is that the single and
whole object of your love   44 thinketh me: it seems to me

SNATCHES

264
MERIÈ sungen the munèchès binnen Ely
Tha Knut king rew ther-by.
'Roweth, knightès, neer the land
And herè we thes munèchès sang.'

265
SAINTE Marìè virginè,
Moder Jesu Cristès Nazarenè,
Onfo, shild, help thyn Godrich,
Onfang, bring heghilich with thee in Godès riche.

Saintè Marìè, Cristès bur,   5
Maidenès clenhad, moderès flur,
Dilìè myn sinnè, rixe in myn mod,
Bring me to winnè with the selfè God.

266
FOWELES in the frith,
The fishes in the flod,
And I mun waxè wod.
Much sorwe I walkè with
For best of bon and blod.   5

---

264. Sweetly sang the monks in Ely when King Canute rowed by.
'Row, men, nearer the land and let us hear this song of the monks.'
265. 3 Onfo: receive shild: protect   4 Receive, bring him gloriously with
you into God's kingdom   5 bur: chamber   6–8 virgin's purity,
mother's flower, wipe out my sin, reign in my heart, bring me to bliss with
the very God   **266.** 1 Birds in the wood   3 and I must go mad
4 walke: toss about restlessly   5 for the best lady of flesh and blood

267

(i) SO longe ich havė, lavėdy,
  Y-hovėd at thy gate,
  That my fot is y-frore, faire lavedy,
  For thy love faste to the stake.

(ii) WERE that that is y-don   5
  Yet for to done,
  N'olde it nevere been y-don
  For nonės mannės bone.

(iii) HER is y-cumė to this tune
  Godith and Godrun.   10
  Raine hu the raine, forth I mot,
  Mantel-les other barefot.

(iv) 'RECHE me my rocke', queth Alfled,
  'The while ich thrille me a thred,
  Nu ich have ned.'   15

268

LOVERD, thy passion—
Who the thencheth aright theron—
Terės it tolleth,
And eyėn it bolleth,
Nebbės it weteth,   5
And hertės it sweteth.

---

267. 1 ich: I   lavedy: lady   2 y-hoved: waited   3 y-frore: frozen
4 stake: gate-post   6–8 still to be done, it would never be done (again)
for any man's entreaty   9 tune: village   10 women's names   11 rain
how it may, I must go forth   12 other: or   13–15 'Hand me my
distaff', said Alfled, 'while I spin myself a thread, now that I have need.'
268. 1 Loverd: Lord   2 whoever thinks about it rightly   3 tolleth:
draws   4 bolleth: swells   5 Nebbes: faces   6 sweteth: sweetens

269   NOW goth sunne under wode—
Me reweth, Marie, thy fairė rode.
Now goth sunne under tree—
Me reweth, Marie, thy Sone and thee.

270   A SHELD of red, a crosse of grene,
A crowne y-writhe with thornės kene,
A sper, a sponge, with nailės three,
A body y-boundė to a tree—
Who this sheld in herte wil take,   5
Amonge his enimés thar he nought quake.

271   WHENNE I thenkė thingės three,
Ne may I nevrė blithė be:
The ton is that I shal away;
The tother is, I ne wot whilk day;
The thriddė is my mostė care—   5
I ne wot whider I shal fare.

272   I MAY come to my lef bute by the watere;
Whenne me lust slepen thenne mot I wakie—
Wonder is that I livie!

273   (i) NE shalt thou never, levedy,
        Twinklen with thyn eyen.

---

269. 2 Me reweth: I grieve for   rode: face   **270.** 1 sheld: shield
2 y-writhe: twisted   5 Who: whoever   6 thar: need   **271.** 1
thenke: consider   3 f. the first is that I must depart, the second is, I do
not know which day   5 moste: greatest   6 whider . . .: where I shall
have to go   **272.** 1 lef: sweetheart   bute: only   2 when I want
to sleep I must lie awake   **273.** 1 levedy: lady   2 Twinklen: wink

(ii) ICH habbe y-don al myn youth:
    Ofte, ofte, and ofte,
    Long y-loved and yerne y-beden—
    Ful dere it is a-boght!   5

(iii) DORE, go thou stille,
    Go thou stillė, stille,
    That ich habbe in the bowre
    Y-don al myn willė, wille.   10

274   (i) AT the wrastlinge my lemman I ches,
    And at the ston-casting I him for-les.

    (ii) AT the ston-castings my lemman I ches,
    And at the wrastlings sone I him les;
    Allas that he so sonė fel!   5
    Why n'adde he stondė, vile gorel?

275   ICH wille bere to washen doun i the toun
    That was blac and that was broun.

276   WELA! qwa sal thir hornės blau,
    Haly Rod, thy day?
    Now is he dede and liės law
    Was wont to blaw thaim ay.

273. 3 I have spent all my youth   5 yerne . . .: eagerly entreated   6 a-boght: paid for   7 stille: silently   9 That: till   **274.** 1 lemman: sweetheart ches: chose   2 for-les: abandoned   4 les: lost   6 why didn't he stand up, the disgusting pig?   **275.** 1 Ich: I bere: carry toun: village   2 That: what   **276.** Alas! who shall blow these horns, Holy Rood, on thy day (14 Sept.)? Now he (Robert de Neville) is dead and lies low who always used to blow them.

277   AN apĕ may on book beholde
And levĕs wende and eft folde;
Ac he ne con the bet therfore
Of clerkĕs lorĕ top ne more.

278   THEI thou the wulf hore hodĕ to preste,
Thei thou him to scole sette salmĕs to lerne,
Evere beeth his gerĕs to the grove grene.

279   LEVERE is the wrenne
Abouten the shawe renne
Than the fithel draft
Other the flutĕ craft.

280   LET take a cat, and fostre him wel with milk
And tendre flesh, and make his couch of silk,
And let him seen a mous go by the wall,
Anon he weiveth milk and flesh and all,
And every deintee that is in that hous,   5
Swich appetit hath he to ete a mous.

277. An ape can gaze at a book and turn the leaves and close it again; but he is none the better able for that to make head or tail of the learning of scholars.   **278.** 1 though you ordain the grey wolf as a priest 3 geres: inclinations   **279.** The wren likes fluttering about the wood better than fiddle-playing or skill on the flute   **280.** 4 Anon he weiveth: immediately he abandons   6 Swich: such

281 A MAN may a while
   Nature begile
    By doctrine and lore,
   And yet at the end
   Wil Nature home wend   5
    There she was before.

282 MAIDENES of Engelande, sare may ye morne,
   For tint ye have youre lemmans at Bannokèsborne,
    With hevalogh.
   What! wende the King of Engeland
   Have y-gete Scotlande?   5
    With rombylogh.

283 BISHOP lorless,
   King redeless,
   Yung man rechless,
   Old man witless,
   Womman shameless—   5
   I swer by Heven-King
   Thos beeth five lither thing!

284 ERTHĖ tok of erthe erthė with wogh;
   Erthe other erthė to the erthė drogh;
   Erthė laide erthe in erthenė throgh:
   Tho havėde erthe of erthe erthe ynogh.

---

281. 6 There: where **282.** 2 tint: lost lemmans: sweethearts 4 f.
What! did the King of England suppose he would have won Scotland?
283. 1 lorless: ignorant 2 redeless: without wisdom to govern 3 rech-
less: heedless 7 lither . . .: evil things **284.** Earth took from earth
earth wrongfully; earth drew other earth to the earth; earth laid earth in
an earthen tomb: then earth of earth had earth enough.

285   WAKE wel, Annot,
        Thy maiden boure,
    And get thee fra Walterot,
        For he is lechòure.

286   ALAS! how shold I singe? Y-loren is my playinge.
    How shold I with that oldė man
    To liven, and let my lemàn,
        Swetest of allė thinge?

287   ICH have a love untrewe—
        That is myn hertė wo;
    That makės me of reuful hewe
        Late to beddė go.
    Sorė me may rewe   5
        That evere I lovede hir so!

288   THE levedy Fortune is bothe frend and fo;
    Of pore she maketh riche, of richė pore alsò;
    She turnės wo al into wele, and wele al into wo:
    No tristė no man to his wele, the wheel it turneth so.

289   THE formest of these bestės three
    Is worst of alle, as thou might see:

---

285. 1 Wake: watch   3 get: guard   **286.** 1 Y-loren: lost   playinge: happiness   3 live, and give up my lover   4 thinge: creatures
287. 1 Ich: I   5 Bitterly may I regret   **288.** 1 levedy: lady   4 No . . . man: let no man trust   **289.** 1 formest: first

(i) THE Lion is wonderliche strong
    And ful of wiles of wo,
    And whether he pleye   5
    Other take his preye,
    He can not do but slo.

(ii) WARE thee from the Bere play
     Ananter lest he bite;
     For selde he stinteth of his play   10
     But if he bite or smite.

(iii) 'I WILLE you alle swalewe withouten any bot;
      But some wille I save, and some wille I not.'

290   ME thinketh thou art so lovely,
             So fair and so swete,
           That sikerly it were my deth
             Thy companie to lete.

291   WHIL that I was sobre
             Sinne ne dide I nought;
           But in drunkeshipe I dide
             The werste that mighten been thought.

289. 3 wonderliche: wonderfully   4 of wo: wretched   6 Other: or
7 he can do nothing but slay   8 f. Beware of the Bear's play lest he bite
10 selde: seldom   stinteth of: desists from   11 But if: unless   12 I:
i.e. the Dragon   bot: deliverance   **290.** 1 Me thinketh: it seems to
me   3 sikerly: certainly   4 lete: quit   **291.** 4 the worst (crimes)
that could be conceived

292   HOPE is hard ther hap is fo;
    Hap wille helpen ther hope is fro.
    Unhap at nede is worldés wo:
    God sende him hap that wolde wel do!

293   MARIE, thou queen, thou moder, thou maiden
        bright!
    Thou wilt, thou canst, thou art of might!
    Thou lif, thou love, thou hope of blisse!
    In sinne, in sorwe, in nede us wisse.

294   HAVE good day now, Mergerète,
    With grete love I thee grete.
    I wolde we mighten us ofte mete
    In halle, in chaumbre, and in the strete,
    Withouté blame of the contré—   5
    God yivé that so mighte it be!

295   WHEN ye see the sunne amis and two monkes hedes,
    And a maide have the maistrie, and multiplied by eight,
    Thenne shal Deth withdrawe, and Derthe be justice,
    And Dawe the diker deye for hunger,
    But if God of his goodnesse graunt us a trewe.   5

292. 1 ther: where   hap: fortune   2 fro: gone   3 Unhap at nede:
misfortune in time of trouble   **293.** 4 wisse: guide   **294.** 1 Have
good day: goodbye   5 without the censure of the community
6 yive: grant   **295.** 2 maistrie: mastery   3 Deth: Plague   Derthe:
Famine   4 Davy the ditcher   5 But if: unless   trewe: respite

296   SPENDE, and God shal sende;
Spare, and ermor care;
Non peny, non ware;
Non catel, non care.
Go, peny, go!   5

297   TAX has teened us alle,
Probat hoc mors tot validorum;
The King therof had smalle,
Fuit in manibus cupidorum.

298   JOHAN the Millere hath y-grounde smal, smal, smal;
The Kinges Sone of hevene shal paye for al;
Be ware or ye be wo;
Knoweth your frend fro your fo;
Haveth ynow and saith 'Ho!';   5
And do wel and bettre, and fleeth sinne,
And seketh pees, and hold you therinne;
and so biddeth Johan Trewman and alle his felawes.

299   THE ax was sharpe, the stokke was harde,
In the fourthè yere of King Richàrde.

300   WHEN Adam dalf and Evè span
Who was tho a gentelman?

296. 2 ermor: evermore   3 ware: anxiety   4 catel: possessions
297. 1 teened: ruined   3 smalle: little   **298.** 3 or: before   4 Know-
eth: know   5 ynow: enough Ho: *i.e.* stop   6 fleeth: shun   **299.** 1
stokke: block   **300.** 1 dalf: dug   2 tho: then

301
WHENNE bloweth the brom
Thenne woweth the grom;
Whenne bloweth the furs
Thenne woweth he wurs.

302
WEL were him that wiste
To whom he mightė triste;
Bet were him that knewe
The falsė fro the trewe.

303
(i) TEL thou never thy fomon
Shame ne teene that thee is on,
   Thy carė ne thy wo;
For he wil fonde, if he may,
Bothe by nightės and by day,   5
   Of one to makė two.
'Tel thou never thy fo that thy fot aketh',
   Quoth Hending.

(ii) MANY man singeth
When he hom bringeth   10
   His yongė wif:
Wistė what he broghte,
Wepen he moghte,
   Er sith his lif,
      Quoth Hending.   15

---

301. 1 brom: broom   2 woweth: woos   grom: lad   3 furs: gorse
4 wurs: worse   **302.** 1 It would be well for him who knew   2 triste:
trust   3 Bet: better   **303.** 1 fomon: foe   2 teene . . .: trouble
that is upon you   4 fonde: attempt   12 Wistė: if he knew   13 f. he
might weep ever afterwards all his life

304   (i) WHAT shul these clothes thus manifold,
           Lo! this hot somers day?
           After grete hetè cometh cold:
           No man caste his pilch away.

       (ii) OF al this world the large compàs   5
            It wil not in myn armès twaine:
            Whoso muchel wil embrace,
            Litel therof he shal distraine.

305   FOR ye be like the sweintè cat
       That wolde have fish; but wost thou what?
       He woldè nothing wete his clawes.

306   (i) JON, Jon pike-a-bone
           To-morrow thou shall pikè none.

       (ii) BE it beter, be it wurse,
            Folow him that bereth the purse.

       (iii) IT is mery in hall
             When berdes waggeth all.

307   (i) WINTER alle etes
           That summer begetes.

       (ii) IT is no wise mannes lore
            To take the less and leve the more.

304. 1 What shul: why must (we have)   4 let no man cast his coat away
6 wil not in: will not (be contained) in   8 distraine: grasp   305. 1
sweinte: hungry   2 wost thou: do you know   3 nothing: not at all
307. 2 begetes: produces   3 lore: precept

(iii) ALL it is for wo   5
    That the hen singes in the snow.

(iv) O BEGGER is wo
    That another in the town go.

 (v) DERE is that hony bought
    That on the thorn is y-sought.   10

(vi) THE smallere peses, the mo to potte;
    The fairer woman, the more giglotte.

(vii) THOUGH peper be blak
    It hath a good smak.

(viii) WIST ever any man how brechel were his shinne-
        bon,   15
    Wold he never lepen there that he mighte gon.

 (ix) TWO freres and a fox maken three shrewes,
    And ever bereth the fox the box of all good
        thewes.

308   GRET hunting by rivers and wood
        Maketh a mannes here to grow through his hood.

307. 7 O: one   11 peses: peas mo: more   12 giglotte: wanton   15 f.
If anyone ever knew how brittle his shin-bone was, he would never run
where he could walk   17 freres: friars shrewes: rascals   18 good
thewes: virtuous habits   **308.** 1 rivers: river-sides   2 here: hair (*i.e.*
makes a man poor)

309
TWO wimen in one house,
Two cattes and one mouse,
Two dogges and one bone
May never accorde in one.

310
THERE is none so wise a man
But he may wisdom leere;
And there is none so strong a man
But he may find his peere;
Nor there is none so false a man   5
But some man wil him leeve;
And there is none so meke a man
But some man may him greeve.

311   (i) WHO so cometh to any hous,
Ne be he nought dangerous—
    Take that he findeth;
And but a wil do so,
Resone wolde accorde therto   5
    To take that he bringeth.

(ii) WHO so wil his worship save,
Honest maners he most have.
It falleth to a gentilman
To say the best that he can   10
Of every man in his absènce
And say him sooth in his presènce.

309. 4 in one: together   **310.** 2 leere: learn   6 leeve: believe   8 greeve:
anger   **311.** 2 dangerous: hard to please   3 that: what   4 ff. and
unless he is willing to do so, it stands to reason that he must take what he
brings   7 Whoever wishes to preserve his good name   8 Honest: good
most: must   9 falleth to: befits

312   IN whom is trauth, petee, fredome, and hardinesse,
        He is a man inherite to gentilnesse.
        Of these virtues four who lakketh three,
        He aught never gentilman called to be.

313   'ICH'ILL pray for his soule that God gif him rest.'
        'And ich'ill hope for his soule, for that can I best.'
        'He n'old nought do for himself whiles he was on live,
        And if I do for his soule, smal mote I thrive!'

314   HERE lieth under this marbel ston
        Riche Alàne, the ballèd man.
        Whether he be safe or nought
        I recke never, for he ne rought.

315   JOLY sheperde of Aschell Down
        Can more on love than al this town. . . .

316   WALTERIUS Pollard *non est* but a dullard;
        I say that Pollard is none mery gollard.

317 (i) THIS book is one
           And Godes curs is another;
           They that takes the tone
           God give them the tother!

312. 1 trauth . . .: integrity, piety, generosity, and courage   2 inherite: born   **313.** 1 Ich'ill: I will   3 n'old: would not   4 smal . . .: I am little likely to succeed   **314.** 2 balled: bald   3 safe: saved   4 rought: cared   **315.** 2 Can more on: knows more about   **316.** 2 gollard: jester   **317.** 3 the tone: the one

  (ii) *This book is mine, Eleanour Worcestar:*
> AND I it lose and you it find,   5
> I pray you hartely to be so kind
> That you wil take a litel pain
> To see my book brought home again.

318
> WHO that lust for to looke
> Or for to rede on this booke,
> Be he of cité, town, or thrope,
> Pray he for my Lady Scrope.
>
> And thinke ye never to don amis,   5
> But thinke on him that gave you this;
> For Jesu love have him in minde
> That this sette on youre booke behinde.

319
> HERE I was and here I drank;
> Farewell Dam, and mikel thank.
> Here I was and had good cheer.
> And here I drank well good beer.

320
> THERE was a man that hadde nought;
> There come theves and robbed him and tooke
>   nought;
> He ran out and cryde nought.
> Why shoulde he cry? He loste nought.
> Here is a tale of right nought.   5

317. 5 And: if   6 hartely: earnestly   7 pain: trouble   **318.** 1 lust:
desires   3 thrope: village   5 thinke: resolve   7 f. for the love of Jesus
remember him who inscribed this at the back of your book   **319.** 2
Dam: hostess   mikel . . .: many thanks   **320.** 2 come: came

321 AN old wif and an empty cup,
   Ther is no merth in nother;
  A man that hath y-teyd him up
   May nought chese another.

  A yong wif and an harvest gos,   5
   Muche gagil with bothe:
  A man that hath hem in his clos,
   Reste shal he wrothe.

322 KNOW or thou knitte; prove or thou praise it.
  If thou know or thou knit, then mayst thou abate;
  And if thou knit er thou knowe, then it is to late.
  Therefore avise thee er thou the knot knitte;
  For 'had I wist' cometh to late for to louse it. 5

323 WHAT! why didest thou wink when thou a wife
   tooke?
  Thou haddest never mor need brodĕ to looke!
  A man that weddeth a wife when he winketh,
  But he stare afterward, wonder me thinketh.

321. 2 nother: neither 3 y-teyd him: tied himself 4 chese: choose 7
hem: them clos: homestead 8 wrothe: ill **322.** 1 or: before knitte:
tie (in marriage) prove: test praise: appraise 2 abate: break off
4 avise thee: reflect 5 wist: known louse: untie **323.** 1 wink:
shut your eyes 2 brode to looke: to keep eyes wide open 4 But he:
if he does not wonder . . .: it seems to me surprising

324   IN soothe to say, though all the erthe so wanne
     Were parchêmine smoothe, white, and scribàble;
  And the gret see that called is the ociànne
     Were turnèd into inke blakker than sable;
    Every stik a penne, eche man a scrivener able: 5
     Not coude they then write womans trechery.
    Be ware therfore—the blinde eteth many a fly.

325   IF that a yong man wold atain
    Unto worship, must him refrain
    From swering, from lyeing,
    From scorning, from vanting,
    From brawling, from desimeling   5
     And from dicing.

326   FAR from thy kin kest thee,
    Wreth not thy neighber nest thee,
    In a good corn contrey rest thee,
    And sit down, Robyn, and rest thee.

327   KEPE well ten and flee from seven;
    Rule well five and come to heven.

328   WIT hath wonder and kind ne can
    How maiden is moder and God is man.
    Leve thy asking and beleve that wonder,
    For might hath maistry and skill goth under.

324. 1 wanne: dark   2 parchemine: parchment scribable: suitable for
writing   5 able: capable   **325.** 2 worship: respect   5 desimeling:
dissembling   **326.** 1 kest: betake   2 Wreth: annoy nest: nearest
3 rest thee: settle   **328.** 1 kind ne can: nature does not explain   3
Leve: stop   4 maistry: the upper hand skill: reason

329
THE Cat, the Rat, and Lovel our dog
Ruleth all England under a Hog.

330
BRISSIT brawnis and brokin banis,
Strif, discord, and wastie wanis,
Crukit in eld, sin halt withall:
Thir are the bewteis of the fut-ball.

331
PEES maketh plenté,
Plenté maketh pride,
Pride maketh plee,
Plee maketh povert,
Povert maketh pees.   5

332
(i) GARDEN wayes and comfort of flowres,
So hight my trew love, How hight yowres?
[Aleysun]

(ii) WATER frosen and Caines brother,
So hight my trew love and non other.
[Isabel]

333
THE nightingale singes
That all the wood ringes;
She singeth in hir song
That the night is to long.

330. 1 Bruised muscles and broken bones   2 wastie . . .: desolate homes
3 crooked in old age, than lame too   4 Thir: these   **331.** 3 plee:
litigation   **332.** 2 hight: is called   4 non other: nothing else

THE TEXTUAL NOTES

THE Textual Notes give for each piece: (i) The manuscript used, its approximate date, and the folio or page on which the piece begins; when successive pieces are from the same manuscript, the date and often the full manuscript reference are not repeated. Where no manuscript survives, an early printed source is given. (ii) A reference to one or more modern standard editions; when several pieces are from the same edition, the full reference is not repeated; works regularly referred to by short titles are listed below. Editions are generally preferred which do not normalize the spelling; where possible, an edition with a commentary is given. (iii) A reference to *The Index of Middle English Verse* by C. Brown and R. H. Robbins, or to its *Supplement* by R. H. Robbins and J. L. Cutler; these give a full list of the manuscripts in which any piece occurs, and of the places where they are printed.

The following abbreviations are used:

ABBREVIATIONS

B.M.	British Museum.
Bodl.	Bodleian Library, Oxford.
Böddeker	*Altenglische Dichtungen des MS. Harl. 2253*, ed. K. Böddeker, Berlin, 1878.
Brook	*The Harley Lyrics*, ed. G. L. Brook, Manchester, 1948, 4th ed., 1968.
C.T.	*Canterbury Tales.*
D.N.B.	*Dictionary of National Biography.*
Dickins and Wilson	*Early Middle English Texts*, ed. B. Dickins and R. M. Wilson, Cambridge, 1951.
Dobson and Harrison	*Medieval English Songs*, ed. E. J. Dobson and F. Ll. Harrison, London, forthcoming.

ABBREVIATIONS

Dyboski	*Songs, Carols, and other Miscellaneous Poems from the Balliol MS. 354*, ed. R. Dyboski, E.E.T.S. E.S. 101, 1908.
Early Bodl. Music	*Early Bodleian Music*, ed. J. Stainer, London, 1901.
E.E.T.S.	Early English Text Society: O.S. = Original Series; E.S. = Extra Series.
E.M.E. Verse and Prose	*Early Middle English Verse and Prose*, ed. J. A. W. Bennett and G. V. Smithers, with a Glossary by N. Davis, Oxford, 1966, 2nd ed., 1968.
Greene, *Carols*	*The Early English Carols*, ed. R. L. Greene, Oxford, 1935.
Greene, *Selection*	*A Selection of English Carols*, ed. R. L. Greene, Oxford, 1962.
Index	C. Brown and R. H. Robbins, *The Index of Middle English Verse*, New York, 1943.
Index Suppl.	R. H. Robbins and J. L. Cutler, *Supplement to the Index of Middle English Verse*, Lexington, 1965.
J.E.G.P.	*Journal of English and Germanic Philology.*
Lyrics XIII C.	*English Lyrics of the XIIIth Century*, ed. C. Brown, Oxford, 1932.
M.L.N.	*Modern Language Notes.*
M.P.	*Modern Philology.*
MS.	Manuscript.
N. & Q.	*Notes and Queries.*
R.E.S.	*Review of English Studies.*
Rel. Ant.	*Reliquiæ Antiquæ*, ed. T. Wright and J. O. Halliwell, 2 vols., London, 1841–3.
Rel. Lyr. XIV C.	*Religious Lyrics of the XIVth Century*, ed. C. Brown, Oxford, 1924; revd. G. V. Smithers, 1957.
Rel. Lyr. XV C.	*Religious Lyrics of the XVth Century*, ed. C. Brown, Oxford, 1939.
Robbins, *Hist. Poems*	*Historical Poems of the XIVth and XVth Centuries*, ed. R. H. Robbins, New York, 1959.

Robbins, *Sec. Lyr.*   *Secular Lyrics of the XIVth and XVth Centuries*, ed. R. H. Robbins, Oxford, 1952, 2nd ed. 1955.

Robinson   *The Works of Geoffrey Chaucer*, ed. F. N. Robinson, 2nd ed., Boston, 1957.

S.T.S.   Scottish Text Society.

U.L.   University Library.

XIV C. Verse and Prose   *Fourteenth Century Verse and Prose*, ed. K. Sisam, Oxford, 1921.

1. B.M. MS. Cotton Caligula A. ix, f. 171a, col. i (*c.* 1275); another version in MS. Cotton Otho C. xiii (*c.* 1275). Layamon (a form of *Lawman* 'a man appointed to declare the law') describes himself as a priest at 'Ernleȝe' (Areley Kings, Worcs.) on the bank of the Severn. From *The Brut*; ed. F. Madden (London, 1847), iii. 138 ff., ll. 28486–651; G. L. Brook, *Selections from Laȝamon's Brut* (Oxford, 1963), ll. 4010–90; *E.M.E. Verse and Prose*, pp. 154 ff., ll. 247 ff. *Index* 295.

Emendations supported by MS. Otho are: 18 *rein*, MS. *rim* or *run*; 39 *And . . . y-slawe* not in MS.; 41 *and lowe* not in MS. MS. Otho differs at 71 *heo gunnen*, MS. *gunnen hine*.

2. B.M. MS. Royal 4 A. xiv, f. 106b (*c.* 1150). Ed. E. Van K. Dobbie, *The Anglo-Saxon Minor Poems* (New York and London, 1942), p. 128; G. Storms, *Anglo-Saxon Magic* (The Hague, 1948), p. 154. *Index* 3896.

9 *scerne*: MS. *scesne*.

3. Bodl. MS. Rawlinson G. 22, f. 1b (*c.* 1225), with music. Ed. *Early Bodl. Music*, ii. 5; *Lyrics XIII C.*, no. 7; *E.M.E. Verse and Prose*, p. 111; Dobson and Harrison, i, no. 5. *Index* 2163.

5 *is*, 7 *fast* not in MS., because of damage to the leaf.

4. Durham Cathedral MS. A. III. 12, f. 49a (*c.* 1225–50). Ed. F. J. Furnivall, *Political, Religious, and Love Poems*, E.E.T.S. o.s. 15 (1903), p. 243; *Rel. Lyr. XIV C.*, no. 1A. *Index* 4088.

5. Jesus Coll., Oxford, MS. 29, f. 156a, col. i (*c.* 1275). From *The Owl and the Nightingale*, 1–94; ed. J. W. H. Atkins (Cambridge, 1922); E. G. Stanley, from B.M. MS. Cotton Caligula A. ix (London and Edinburgh, 1960); *E.M.E. Verse and Prose*, pp. 2 ff. Both MSS. ed. in facsimile by N. R. Ker, E.E.T.S. 251 (1963). *Index* 1384.

Readings from Cotton MS. are: 10 *wuste*, MS. *ywuste*; 14 *breche*, MS. *beche*; 30 *biheld*, MS. *biholdeþ*; 34 *see*, MS. *iseo*; 40 *yowelinge*, MS. *howelynge*; 41 *fort*, MS. *for*; 48 *Thei*, MS. *þe*.

6. Jesus Coll., Oxford, MS. 29, f. 189b. From *The Proverbs of Alfred*; ed. R. Morris, *An Old English Miscellany*, E.E.T.S. O.S. 49 (1872), pp. 108 ff.; O. Arngart, *The Proverbs of Alfred* (Lund, 1955), ii. 83; Dickins and Wilson, pp. 78 f. *Index* 433.

11 *wurthere*: MS. *furþer*.

7. Jesus Coll., Oxford, MS. 29, f. 185a. From 'A Lutel Soth Sermun', 25–92; ed. Morris, E.E.T.S. O.S. 49, pp. 187 ff. *Index* 1091.

8. Jesus Coll., Oxford, MS. 29, f. 187b. From 'A Luve Ron', 65–80; ed. Morris, E.E.T.S. O.S. 49, pp. 93 ff.; *Lyrics XIII C.*, no. 43; Dickins and Wilson, pp. 103 ff. *Index* 66.

9. Guildhall, London, Liber de Antiquis Legibus, f. 160b (*c.* 1225–50), with music. Ed. A. J. Ellis, *On Early English Pronunciation*, ii, E.E.T.S. E.S. 7 (1869), pp. 428 ff.; *Lyrics XIII C.*, no. 5; Dobson and Harrison, i, no. 4 (ii). *Index* 322.

A French version, from which the English seems to be derived, precedes the English verses in the MS.

10. B.M. MS. Harley 978, f. 11b (*c.* 1260), with music. Ed. A. J. Ellis, E.E.T.S. E.S. 7, pp. 426 ff.; J. B. Hurry, *Sumer is icumen in* (Reading, 1913); *Lyrics XIII C.*, no. 6; *E.M.E. Verse and Prose*, p. 110; Dobson and Harrison, i, no. 9. *Index* 3223.

11. B.M. MS. Cotton Cleopatra B. vi, f. 204b (*c.* 1250). Ed. *Lyrics XIII C.*, no. 67. *Index* 519.

12. B.M. MS. Egerton 613, f. 1b (*c.* 1250). Ed. Morris, E.E.T.S. O.S. 49, pp. 197 ff.; *Lyrics XIII C.*, no. 54. *Index* 3221.

6 *me fint*: MS. *is funde*; 21 *milde and hold*: MS. *wilde and wlong*; 44 *falle*: MS. *walle*. After l. 50 one stanza omitted.

13. MS. Egerton 613, f. 2a. Ed. *Lyrics XIII C.*, no. 17B; Greene, *Carols*, no. 191Ba; Dickins and Wilson, pp. 125 f.; *E.M.E. Verse and Prose*, pp. 129 f. *Index* 2645.

The verses are in the corrected order marked in the MS.

30 *Loverd*: MS. *lord*.

14. Bodl. MS. Digby 86, f. 126b, col. i (*c.* 1275). Ed. F. J. Furnivall, *The Minor Poems of the Vernon MS.* ii, E.E.T.S. O.S. 117 (1901), pp.

761 ff.; *Lyrics XIII C.*, no. 48; Dickins and Wilson, pp. 127 f. *Index* 3310.

   33 *Nethere*: MS. þere neþere. After l. 42, two stanzas omitted.

15. MS. Digby 86, f. 134b, col. i. Ed. *Lyrics XIII C.*, no. 50; *E.M.E. Verse and Prose*, p. 131. *Index* 3236.

16. MS. Digby 86, f. 138a, col. ii. Ed. Dickins and Wilson, pp. 62 ff.; *E.M.E. Verse and Prose*, pp. 65 ff. *Index* 35.
   199 *y-faye*: MS. *I fare*.

17. MS. Digby 86, f. 200a. Ed. *Lyrics XIII C.*, no. 53. *Index* 2009.
   13 *hath*: MS. *had*;   16 *ansete*: MS. *an wede*;   22 *gladhede*: MS. *geddede*.

18. Bodl. MS. Digby 2, f. 6a (*c.* 1275). Ed. Furnivall, E.E.T.S. o.s. 117, pp. 753 ff.; *Lyrics XIII C.*, no. 64. Another version in MS. Harley 2253, f. 80a, col. i, ed. Brook, no. 22. *Index* 1365.
   16 *weren*: MS. *werin al*; 20 *way-la-way*: MS. *way* (*la way* lost from right margin); 22 *bo*: MS. *boþe*; 25 *hangeth*: MS. *honge*; 40 *thurgh*: MS. *þorit* (=*þorþ, þorh*); 41 *stronge* (so MS. Harl.): MS. *longe*; 52 *thurgh-*: MS. *þoit* (MS. Harl. *þourhsoht*); 53 *I wepe*: MS. *and wende*.

19. MS. Digby 2, f. 6b. Ed. Furnivall, E.E.T.S. o.s. 117, pp. 755 f.; *Lyrics XIII C.*, no. 65. *Index* 1066.
   20 *For to*: MS. *fort*.

20. Lambeth Palace MS. 557, f. 156b (*c.* 1275). Printed by M. R. James, *A Descriptive Catalogue of the Manuscripts in the Library of Lambeth Palace* (Cambridge, 1932), p. 760. *Index* 143.
   8 *I* not in MS.

21. New College, Oxford, MS. F. 88, f. 181b (*c.* 1275–1300). Ed. *Rel. Lyr. XIV C.*, no. 5. *Index* 1978.

22. Corpus Christi Coll., Oxford, MS. E. 59, f. 113b (*c.* 1275–1300), with music. Ed. *Lyrics XIII C.*, no. 60; Dobson and Harrison, i, no. 13. *Index* 708.
   6 *the*: MS. *þet* (emended Dobson). After l. 40, three stanzas, probably not part of the original poem (see Dobson and Harrison) are omitted.

23. B.M. MS. Royal 2 F. viii, f. 1b (*c.* 1275–1300). Ed. *Lyrics XIII C.*, no. 63; *E.M.E. Verse and Prose*, pp. 132 ff. Another version is found in MS. Harley 2253, f. 76a; ed. Brook, no. 18. *Index* 3963.

41 softe: MS. *suete*; *45 And leve me*: MS. *a* (? orig. *an*) *leue* (or *lene*); *48–50* not in MS., supplied from MS. Harley.

24. Trinity Coll., Cambridge, MS. B. 1. 45, f. 73b (*c.* 1275–1300). Ed. *Lyrics XIII C.*, no. 71. *Index* 3998.

25. B.M. MS. Arundel 292, f. 3b (*c.* 1275–1300). Ed. *Lyrics XIII C.*, no. 13. *Index* 1422.

26. MS. Arundel 292, f. 7b. From 'The Bestiary'; ed. Morris, E.E.T.S. o.s. 49, pp. 16 ff., ll. 499–554; Dickins and Wilson, pp. 60 f.; *E.M.E. Verse and Prose*, pp. 171 ff. *Index* 3413.
28 *that*: MS. *ðar*; 38 *Bel* (see N. Davis, *Medium Ævum*, xix (1950), 58 f.): MS. *pel.*

27. B.M. MS. Add. 23986 (roll) verso (*c.* 1275–1300). Ed. E. K. Chambers, *The Mediaeval Stage* (Oxford, 1903), ii. 324 ff.; Dickins and Wilson, pp. 132 ff.; *E.M.E. Verse and Prose*, pp. 196 ff. *Index* 668.
4 *nother*: MS. *nouer* or *noner*; 12 *hire*: MS. *wile*; 14 *wist*: MS. *wis*; 18 *ay*: MS. *hay*; 67 f. rhyme corrupt; 83 *me on*: MS. *onne me*. The end of the text is lost.

28. Trinity Coll., Cambridge, MS. B. 14. 39, f. 28a (*c.* 1275–1300). Ed. *Lyrics XIII C.*, no. 21A; Dickins and Wilson, p. 119. *Index* 3078.

29. Trinity Coll., Cambridge, MS. B. 14. 39, f. 42b. Ed. *Lyrics XIII C.*, no. 27. *Index* 1836.
11 *erndie*: MS. *herdie.*

30. Trinity Coll., Cambridge, MS. B. 14. 39, f. 34a. Ed. F. J. Child, *The English and Scottish Popular Ballads* (Boston and New York, 1883–98), no. 23; *XIV C. Verse and Prose*, pp. 168 f.; *Lyrics XIII C.*, no. 25. *Index* 1649.

31. B.M. MS. Sloane 2593, f. 22b (*c.* 1450). Ed. Child, op. cit., no. 22; J. Kinsley, *The Oxford Book of Ballads* (1969), pp. 3 f. *Index* 3058.

32. (*a*) Bodl. MS. Rawlinson B. 171, f. 107a (*c.* 1400). Ed. F. W. D. Brie, *The Brut*, E.E.T.S. o.s. 131 (1906), i. 189. *Index Suppl.* 3918.5.
(*b*) B.M. MS. Royal 20 A. xi, f. 107b (*c.* 1325–50). Ed. T. Wright, *The Political Songs of England* (Camden Soc., 1839), p. 286. *Index* 2754.

33. B.M. MS. Cotton Julius A. v, ff. 147b, 148a (*c.* 1325). Ed. T. Wright, *The Chronicle of Pierre de Langtoft* (Rolls Series, 1868), ii. 248, 252. *Index* 3352, 841. Between ll. 12 and 13 a passage of Langtoft's Chronicle intervenes.

34. Bodl. MS. Laud misc. 108, f. 208a, col. i (*c.* 1300–25). From *The Lay of Havelok the Dane*, 749–958; ed. W. W. Skeat, revised K. Sisam (Oxford, 1915). *Index* 1114.

On the death of King Birkabeyn of Denmark, Earl Godard, guardian of the King's young son Havelok, usurped the throne, and after murdering Havelok's two sisters, ordered Grim, a fisherman, to drown the boy. Grim, recognizing the prince by a miraculous light from his mouth, secretly saved him and emigrated with him to Grimsby, so called after him. This passage tells how Grim and his sons, helped later by Havelok, prospered there as fishermen, until a great dearth forced Grim to send Havelok to seek work in Lincoln. Eventually Havelok became king of Denmark and England.

Careless manuscript spellings (e.g. *bigge* for *brigge* 133, 190) have been emended without notice. More important departures from the MS. are: 7 *el*: MS. *hwel*; 15 *change*: MS. *fonge*; 27 *al*: MS. *wol*; lines 121, 126 not in MS.; 143 *until*: MS. *til*; 183 *When*: MS. *Han, an* crossed out; perhaps *þan* (=MS. *þanne* 'when') was intended.

For '36 *see-weres* (MS. *se were*), see *E.M.E. Verse and Prose*, 2nd ed. (1968), no. iv, 52 and n.

35. Edinburgh, National Library of Scotland, Adv. MS. 19. 2. 1 (Auchinleck MS.), f. 102a, col. ii (*c.*1330). From *Floris and Blauncheflour*; ed. A. B. Taylor (Oxford, 1927), 849–960, 979–1018. *Index* *45, *Index Suppl.* *2288.8.

Blauncheflour, whom Floris has loved since childhood, has been sold to an Emir (Amiral) by Floris's parents to prevent the match. Floris seeks her out, bribes the Emir's porter to help him, and so gains admittance, hidden in a basket of flowers.

5 *thought*: MS. *þou3t he þout*; 14 *anond*: MS. *an hond*; 25 *maiden*: MS. *maide*; 27 *he*: MS. *3he*; *hié*: MS. *he*; 36 *Blauncheflours*: MS. *Blauncheflour þat*; 47 *so* not in MS.; 57 *Avoy*: MS. *auoþ*; 58–60 supplied from Cambridge U.L. MS. Gg. 4. 27, II: MS. *To scorne me is litel honour*; 82 *They clipte*: MS. *þat clepte*; 108 *roun*: MS. *roum*; 110 *every*: MS. *euer*; 111 *Two*: MS. *þre*; 113 MS. *Wi3 water and cloþ and bacyn*; 115 *That other*: MS. *þe þridde*; 136 *hath*: MS. *had*; 145 *Certes*: MS. *Certe*.

36. MS. as no. 35, f. 105a, col. i. Ed. Robbins, *Hist. Poems*, no. 54. *Index* 1857.

12 MS. *liht is niht*; 24 *Wele*: MS. *Anoþer*; 26 *the*: MS. *that*. Sixteen lines omitted at the beginning, thirty at the end.

37. MS. as no. 35, f. 300a, col. i. The leaf containing ll. 1–24 is missing; ll. 33–46 are omitted in this MS. These gaps are supplied from B.M. MS. Harley 3810, f. 1a and b (*c.* 1425–50). Ed. *XIV C. Verse and Prose*, pp. 13 ff.; A. J. Bliss, *Sir Orfeo* (2nd ed., Oxford, 1966). *Index* 3868.

19 *her harpes toke*: MS. *toke her harpys*; 82 *reveysed*: MS. *reueyd* or *reneyd*; 140 *I no*: MS. *Yn*; 230 *no* not in MS.; 363 *anowrned*: MS. *anowed* or *auowed*; 388 *liggeand*: MS. *ful liggeand*; 406 *leef*: MS. *liif*; 521 *trumpours*: MS. *trompour*; 527 *blissfulest*: MS. *blifulest*; 531 *also*: MS. *als*.

38. Lincoln's Inn MS. Hale 135, f. 137b (*c.* 1300). Ed. *XIV C. Verse and Prose*, p. 163; *Lyrics XIII C.*, no. 62. *Index* 360.

This fly-leaf is badly faded: *Now springes* (1), *playinge* (5), *in* (14) are not legible. 4 MS. *þis endre dai als i me rode*; 8 MS. *clingges*.

39. B.M. MS. Arundel 248, f. 154a (*c.* 1300), with music. Ed. *Lyrics XIII C.*, no. 44; Dobson and Harrison, i, no. 15 (ii). *Index* 888.

40. Corpus Christi Coll., Cambridge, MS. 8, end fly-leaf recto (*c.* 1300), with music. Ed *Lyrics XIII C.*, no. 58; Dobson and Harrison, i, no. 17. *Index* 4221.

5 *shed He*: MS. *ssadde*; 7 *y-tent*: MS. *y tend*; 21 *herte myn*: MS. *min herte*.

41. B.M. MS. Harley 2253, f. 58b (*c.* 1340), ed. in facsimile by N. R. Ker, E.E.T.S. 255 (1965). Ed. Böddeker, pp. 95 ff.; *Lyrics XIII C.*, no. 72; Dickins and Wilson, pp. 10 ff. *Index* 3155.

Richard, Earl of Cornwall and Emperor elect of Germany (Alemaigne), helped his brother, King Henry III (here represented by Windsor, his castle) and Prince Edward against the rebel barons under Simon de Montfort at the battle of Lewes, 14 May 1264. When Richard saw that the King's army was beaten, he took refuge in a windmill. He was taken prisoner and confined in his own castle at Wallingford. Prince Edward was imprisoned at Wallingford, and was moved to Dover castle in January 1265. The Royalists Hugh Bigod and the Earl of Warenne escaped to France.

42. MS. Harley 2253, f. 63a. Ed. Böddeker, pp. 144 ff.; *Lyrics XIII C.*, no. 76; Brook, no. 3. *Index* 1394.

22 *The*: MS. *to*; 23 *and*: MS. *in*; 24 *on wolkne*: MS. *ant wolc*. The last two stanzas omitted.

43. MS. Harley 2253, f. 63b. Ed. Böddeker, pp. 147 f.; *XIV C. Verse and Prose*, pp. 165 f. *Lyrics XIII C.*, no. 77; Brook, no. 4. *Index* 515.

44. MS. Harley 2253, f. 63b. Ed. Böddeker, pp. 149 f.; *Lyrics XIII C.*, no. 78; Brook, no. 5; *E.M.E. Verse and Prose*, pp. 111 f. *Index* 4194.

45. MS. Harley 2253, f. 64a. Ed. Böddeker, pp. 100 ff.; Robbins, *Hist. Poems*, no. 2. *Index* 696, *Index Suppl.* 1320.5.

26 *men*: MS. *me*; 29 *Men*: MS. *meni*; 43 *no*: MS. *ne*; 50 *come*: MS. *comeþ*.

46. MS. Harley 2253, f. 66b. Ed. Böddeker, pp. 158 ff.; Brook, no. 8; *E.M.E. Verse and Prose*, pp. 116 f. *Index* 1449.

18 *beth*: MS. *be*; 31 *sechen*: MS. *vachen* (=*fechen*).

47. MS. Harley 2253, f. 67a. Ed. Böddeker, pp. 161 ff.; Brook, no. 9; *E.M.E. Verse and Prose*, pp. 117 ff. *Index* 105.

4 MS. *tounes*; 19 *of* not in MS.; 32 *wurdes*: MS. *wurþes*; 42 *As*: MS. *al*; 48 *site*: MS. *syke*.

48. MS. Harley 2253, f. 71b, col. i. Ed. Böddeker, pp. 163 ff.; *XIV C. Verse and Prose*, pp. 164 f.; *Lyrics XIII C.*, no. 81; Brook, no. 11. *Index* 1861.

11 *winne*: MS. *wynter*.

49. MS. Harley 2253, f. 72b, col. i. Ed. Böddeker, pp. 167 ff.; *Lyrics XIII C.*, no. 83; Greene, *Carols*, no. 440; Brook, no. 14; Greene, *Selection*, no. 92; *E.M.E. Verse and Prose*, pp. 121 ff. *Index* 1395.

72 *swore*: MS. *sore*; 77 *Love*: MS. *Hire loue*; 81 *biseche*: MS. *bisecheþ*.

50. MS. Harley 2253, f. 75b, col. ii. Ed. Böddeker, p. 195; *Rel. Lyr. XIV C.*, no. 9; Brook, no. 17. *Index* 4177.

11 *greve*: MS. *greu me*.

51. MS. Harley 2253, f. 80a, col. ii. Ed. Böddeker, pp. 212 ff.; *Rel. Lyr. XIV C.*, no. 10; Brook, no. 23. *Index* 2359.

41 *hir*: MS. *his*; 58 *me*: MS. *vs*.

52. MS. Harley 2253, f. 80b. Ed. Böddeker, pp. 171 ff.; *Lyrics XIII C.*, no. 85; Brook, no. 24; *E.M.E. Verse and Prose*, pp. 124 ff.; *Index* 2236.

31 *thee* not in MS.

53. MS. Harley 2253, f. 80b. Ed. Böddeker, pp. 173 f.; *Lyrics XIII C.*, no. 86; Brook, no. 25; *E.M.E. Verse and Prose*, p. 126. *Index* 4037.

54. MS. Harley 2253, f. 114b. Ed. Böddeker, pp. 175 ff.; *Lyrics XIII C.*, no. 89; Brook, no. 30; *E.M.E. Verse and Prose*, pp. 127 f. *Index* 2066. See R. J. Menner, *J.E.G.P.* xlviii (1949), 1 ff.

The man in the moon was supposed to be a peasant banished to the moon for stealing thorns from the hedges and still carrying the stolen bundle on his fork.

9 *we* not in MS.; 35 *he* not in MS.

55. MS. Harley 2253, f. 128a. Ed. Böddeker, pp. 177 ff.; *Lyrics XIII C.*, no. 91; Brook, no. 32. *Index* 1921.

17 *cried*: MS. *crie*; 24 *hewe*: MS. *heowes*; 26 *glewe*: MS. *gleowes*.

56. B.M. MS. Royal 12 E. i, f. 193a (*c.* 1300), with music. Ed. *Lyrics XIII C.*, no. 49B; Dobson and Harrison, i, no. 11. *Index* 3211.

Gaps in ll. 39–48, caused by a cut across the bottom corner of f. 194a, are filled from MS. Harley 2253, f. 79b: viz. 39 *maidenm[an]*; 42 *M[ai]den*; 43 *[lenger]*; 45 *[thridde day]*; 47 *[dye y-wis]*; 48 *neve[r non]*. Other readings from MS. Harley are: 4 *I*, not in MS.; 29 *pineth*, MS. *pined*; 40 *at alle*, MS. *alle at*. One stanza omitted after l. 18, two after l. 48.

57. B.M. MS. Royal 12 E. i, f. 194b. Ed. *Lyrics XIII C.*, no. 35B. *Index* 3964.

58. B.M. MS. Cotton Vespasian A. iii, f. 120b, col. i (*c.* 1350). From *Cursor Mundi*, 21407–500; ed. R. Morris, E.E.T.S. O.S. 66 (1877), pp. 1226 ff. *Index* 2153.

20 *slik* not in MS.; 88 *for* not in MS.

59. B.M. MS. Cotton Caligula A. xi, f. 157b (*c.* 1325). From *The Metrical Chronicle of Robert of Gloucester*, 11,186 ff.; ed. W. A. Wright (Rolls Series, 1887), ii. 741 ff.; *E.M.E. Verse and Prose*, pp. 163 f., ll. 127 ff. *Index* 727. See A. Hudson, *N. & Q.* (1969), 322 ff.

4 *faste* not in MS.; 11 *bailifs*: MS. *bailif*; 15 *dashte*: MS. *dasse*.

60. B.M. MS. Harley 1701, f. 60a, col. i (*c.* 1375). From *Handlyng Synne,* 9015–9242; ed. F. J. Furnivall, E.E.T.S. o.s. 123 (1903); *XIV C. Verse and Prose,* pp. 4 ff. *Index* 778.

66 *they,* 78 *he* not in MS.; 112 *it*: MS. *on*; 143 *ne*: MS. *hyt ne*; 160 *band*: MS. *banned*; 161 *wand*: MS. *woned*; 206 MS. *Wyth sundyr lepys*; 213 MS. *Seynt Teodryght.*

61. B.M. MS. Harley 913, f. 32a (*c.* 1300–25). Ed. W. Heuser, *Die Kildare-Gedichte (Bonner Beiträge zur Anglistik,* xiv, Bonn, 1904), pp. 172 ff.; *Rel. Lyr. XIV C.,* no. 28. *Index* 2025.

`3 *evermore*: MS. *euer*; 13 *it* not in MS.; 23 *thy*: MS. *þe*; 25–8 the rhyme words in the MS. are *ibor, bifor, horre, befor.*

62. MS. Harley 913, f. 7a. Ed. Heuser, op. cit., pp. 150 ff. *Index* 1078.

1 *thy longe*: MS. *þe large*; 37 *bouchers*: MS. *potters*. One stanza omitted after ll. 12, 48, 54, four stanzas after l. 30, three stanzas after l. 36.

63. MS. Harley 913, f. 3a. Ed. Heuser, op. cit., pp. 145 ff.; *E.M.E. Verse and Prose,* pp. 136 ff. *Index* 762.

49 *many* not in MS.; 53 *cloisters* not in MS.; 69 *bas*: MS. *las*. After l. 110, 80 lines omitted.

64. King's Coll., Cambridge, Muniment Roll 2 W. 32, verso (*c.* 1300–25), with music. Ed., with facsimile, J. Saltmarsh, 'Two Medieval Love-songs set to Music', *The Antiquaries Journal,* xv (1935), 1–12; Robbins, *Sec. Lyr.,* no. 147; Dobson and Harrison, i, no. 16a. *Index* 521.

The following words have been repeated to regularize the metre: 3 *on me,* 6 *hende,* 8 *and flowr,* 9 *wille,* 11 *hie may,* 12 *were ere.*

65. B.M. MS. Add. 17376, f. 204b (*c.* 1350). Ed. M. Konrath, *The Poems of William of Shoreham,* E.E.T.S. e.s. 86 (1902), pp. 127 ff.; *Rel. Lyr. XIV C.,* no. 32. *Index* 2107.

33 *Thee*: MS. *þey*; 51 *moone*: MS. *mowe*. Two stanzas omitted after l. 30, one stanza after l. 36.

66. Bodl. MS. Rawlinson D. 913, f. 1a (*c.* 1325–50). Ed. Robbins, *Sec. Lyr.,* no. 16; see also P. Dronke, *N. & Q.* (1961), 245. *Index* 2622.

5 *her kinne*: MS. *er inne.*

67. MS. Rawlinson D. 913, f. 1b. Ed. *XIV C. Verse and Prose*, p. 166; Greene, *Carols*, p. xxxvi; Robbins, *Sec. Lyr.*, no. 15. *Index* 1008.
   4 *thee*: MS. *ȝe*; 5 *Of*: MS. *for of*.

68. MS. Rawlinson D. 913, f. 1b. Ed. *XIV C. Verse and Prose*, p. 167; Robbins, *Sec. Lyr.*, no. 18; Dobson and Harrison, i, no. 16b(i). *Index* 3891; *Index Suppl.* 2037.5.
   7 *Sevenighte*: MS. *seuenistes*; 8 *was*: MS. *wat*.

69. MS. Rawlinson D. 913, f. 1b. Ed. Robbins, *Sec. Lyr.*, no. 9. *Index* 3898.
   5 *that* not in MS.; 15 *I ne*: MS. *ine* or *me*.

70. MS. Rawlinson D. 913, f. 1b. Ed. Robbins, *Sec. Lyr.*, no. 117. *Index* *24; *Index Suppl.* 4256.8.
   P. Dronke's readings (*N. & Q.* (1961), 246) are not accepted. The beginning is illegible. 8 *Ye*: MS. *þe*.

71. B.M. MS. Cotton Galba E. ix, f. 52 b, col. i (*c.* 1400–25). Ed. *XIV C. Verse and Prose*, pp. 152 f.; Robbins, *Hist. Poems*, no. 9. *Index* 3080.
   25 *Scot*: MS. *Skottes*.

72. MS. Cotton Galba E. ix, f. 78a, col. ii. From *The Pricke of Conscience* i. 468–509; ed. R. Morris, Philological Soc. (1863). *Index* 3428.

73. B.M. MS. Add. 46919 (formerly Phillipps 8336), f. 206a (*c.* 1330); probably the autograph of William Herebert (d. 1333); see H. Gneuss, *Anglia*, lxxviii (1960), 169 ff. Ed. *Rel. Lyr. XIV C.*, no. 15. *Index* 2241.

74. B.M. MS. Add. 46919, f. 210a. Ed. *Rel. Lyr. XIV C.*, no. 25. *Index* 3906. A paraphrase of Isaiah 63: 1–7.

75. Merton Coll., Oxford, MS. 248, f. 139b (*c.* 1350). Ed. *Rel. Lyr. XIV C.*, no. 36. *Index* 1353.
   6 *as*: MS. *a*.

76. Merton Coll., MS. 248, f. 167a, col. ii. Ed. *Rel. Lyr. XIV C.*, no. 40. *Index* 3212.

77. Longleat MS. 29, f. 51b (*c.* 1400–25). Ed. S. Wilson, *R.E.S.* N.S. x (1959), 337 ff. Ed. from Cambridge U.L. MS. Dd. 5. 64, III, *XIV C. Verse and Prose*, pp. 37 ff.; *Rel. Lyr XIV C.*, no. 84; from

Lambeth Palace MS. 853, F. J. Furnivall, *Hymns to the Virgin and Christ*, E.E.T.S. o.s. 24 (1867), pp. 22 ff. *Index* 2007. The poem is based on Rolle's *Incendium Amoris*, chaps. 40 and 41, ed. M. Deanesly (Manchester, 1915), pp. 267 ff.

The following emendations are supported by the Cambridge and Lambeth MSS.: 12 *coupleth*, MS. *compileth*; 14 first *it* not in MS.; 28 *heldand*, MS. *holdynge*.

78. Eton Coll. MS. 36, Part II, f. 103a (*c.* 1350). Ed. *Rel. Lyr. XIV C.*, no. 49. *Index* 196.

9 *fresh* not in MS. Three verses omitted after l. 16.

79. MS. Bodley 26, f. 202b (*c.* 1350). Ed. *Rel. Lyr. XIV C.*, no. 88; Greene, *Carols*, no. 12; *Selection*, no. 6. *Index* 29.

21 *he*: MS. *3e*.

80. B.M. MS. Arundel 292, f. 70b (*c.* 1350). Ed. *Rel. Ant.* i. 291 f.; F. L. Utley, *Speculum* xxi (1946), 194 ff. *Index* 3819. For the musical terms, see Grove's *Dictionary of Music and Musicians*.

6 *I*: MS. *it*; 13 *to* not in MS.

81. MS. Bodley 264, f. 209a, col. ii (*c.* 1425). From *Alexander Fragment B* (*Alexander and Dindimus*), 65–110; ed. W. W. Skeat, E.E.T.S. E.S. 31 (1878), pp. 3 ff.; F. P. Magoun, *The Gests of King Alexander of Macedon* (Cambridge, Mass., 1929), pp. 173 ff. *Index* 4262.

31 *goddes*: MS. *goodus*.

82. Göttingen Univ. MS. theol. 107r, f. 169a, col. i (*c.* 1375). Ed. R. Morris, *Cursor Mundi*, E.E.T.S. o.s. 68 (1878), v. 1468 f.; *Rel. Lyr. XIV C.*, no. 31. *Index* 1029.

13 *hevene-towre*: MS. *heue*; 61 *thee* not in MS.; 65 *levedy*: MS. *fair leuedi*.

83. Edinburgh, National Library of Scotland, Adv. MS. 19.2.2, f. 23a, col. i, copied by John Ramsay in 1489. From *The Bruce* (1375), vii. 105–224; ed. W. W. Skeat, E.E.T.S. E.S. 11 (1870), from St. John's Coll., Cambridge, MS. G. 23, copied in 1487. *Index* 3217.

Departures from the (Edinburgh) MS. follow the Cambridge MS.: 12 *halsit*, MS. *halist*; 35, 41 *forouth*, MS. *furth, fourth*; 37 *you* not in MS.; 39 *intill*, MS. *in*; 86 *a* not in MS.; 97 *he slepit*, MS. *him sleip*.

84. Edinburgh, National Library of Scotland, Adv. MS. 18. 7. 21, f. 121a, col. i, copied by John de Grimestone, a Franciscan friar, in 1372. Ed. *Rel. Lyr. XIV C.*, no. 66. *Index* 2012.

85. MS. as no. 84, f. 124b, col. i. Ed. *Rel. Lyr. XIV C.*, no. 69; Greene, *Carols*, no. 271. *Index* 3691.
   One stanza omitted after l. 16.

86. B.M. MS. Harley 7322, f. 79a (*c.* 1375). Ed. Furnivall, *Political, Religious, and Love Poems*, E.E.T.S. o.s. 15 (1903), p. 251. *Index* 1822.

87. MS. Harley 7322, f. 135b. Ed. Furnivall, E.E.T.S. o.s. 15, p. 255; *XIV C. Verse and Prose*, pp. 167 f.; a longer version ed. *Rel. Lyr. XIV C.*, no. 75. *Index* 1847.

88. MS. Harley 7322, f. 136b. Ed. Furnivall, E.E.T.S. o.s. 15, pp. 255 f. *Index* 3411.
   3 *drede*: MS. *derknesse*.

89. MS. Harley 7322, f. 163a. Ed. Furnivall, E.E.T.S. o.s. 15, p. 266. *Index* 1269.

90. B.M. MS. Add. 31042, f. 169a (*c.* 1450). From *The Parlement of the Thre Ages*, 1–53; ed. M. Y. Offord, E.E.T.S. 246 (1959), pp. 1 f. *Index* 1556.
   1 *monethe*: MS. *monethes*; 8 *was*: MS. *wat*; 17 MS. *gouen* or *gonen* (? for *gongen* 'go'); 48 *minted*: MS. *mytid*.

91. B.M. MS. Cotton Nero A. x, f. 39a (*c.* 1400); reproduced in facsimile, with introd. by I. Gollancz, E.E.T.S. 162 (1923). From *Pearl*, 1–180; ed. R. Morris, *Early English Alliterative Poems*, E.E.T.S. o.s. 1 (2nd ed., 1869), pp. 1 ff.; E. V. Gordon, *Pearl* (Oxford, 1953), pp. 1 ff. *Index* 2744.
   The poet, grieving for his lost Pearl, an infant daughter, falls asleep over her grave and dreams that he sees her, a heavenly virgin in beautiful surroundings, on the far side of a stream he cannot cross. Through his vision and the maiden's teaching he is finally reconciled to his loss.
   8 *synglere*: MS. *synglure*; 54 *fyrce*: MS. *fyrte*; 115 *As*: MS. *a*; *strothe*: meaning obscure; 138 *over*: MS. *oþer*; 142 *hoped*: MS. *hope*; 144 *ay*: MS. *a*; 154 *wo*: ? read *woþe* 'danger'.

92. MS. Cotton Nero A. x, f. 84b. From *Patience*, 137–240; ed. Morris, E.E.T.S. o.s. 1, pp. 93 ff.; I. Gollancz, *Patience* (London, 1913); J. J. Anderson (Manchester, 1969). *Index* 2739.

50 *slomberande*: MS. *sloberande*; 53 *here* not in MS.; 83 *haled*: MS. *hale*; 104 *on*: MS. *vn*.

93. MS. Cotton Nero A. x, f. 106b. From *Sir Gawain and the Green Knight*, 1178–1318, 1372–1401; ed. J. R. R. Tolkien and E. V. Gordon, 2nd ed. revised N. Davis (Oxford, 1967). *Index* 3144.

At a New Year's feast in King Arthur's hall Sir Gawain takes up a challenge from an unknown Green Knight: Gawain is to strike a single blow with a battle-axe at the Green Knight's neck, on condition that he offers himself to the Green Knight for a return blow in a year and a day. Gawain strikes off his head; but, to the astonishment of the court, the Green Knight picks it up, requires Gawain to receive the return blow at the Green Chapel, and rides off. On his journey to find the Green Chapel, Gawain is entertained over Christmas at a castle. Since the castle is near the Green Chapel, his host persuades him to stay for the last three days of December, to rest and enjoy the ladies' company while the host hunts; he and Gawain agree to exchange their winnings each day. Here the host's wife visits Gawain on the first of the three days.

6 *dernly*: MS. *derfly*; 29 *ho*: MS. *he*; 31 *gay*: MS. *fayr*; 39 *be*: MS. *he*; 88–9 meaning obscure; 104 *as ho*: MS. *a*; 127 first *no* not in MS. *so*: MS. *fo*; 138 *Was*: MS. *wᵗ*; 156 *That*: MS. *&*; *wonnen* not in MS.; 159 *he*: MS. *ho*; 164 *yorselven*: MS. *hor-*.

94. Chetham's Library, Manchester, MS. 8009, f. 292b (*c.* 1475). From *Ipomadon*, 6226–6429; ed. E. Kölbing (Breslau, 1889), pp. 178 ff. *Index* 2635.

Ipomadon, son of the King of Apulia, loved 'the fair one', ruler in her own right of Calabria and niece of King Mellengere of Sicily; entered her service incognito, later won her hand at a tournament, but disappeared without revealing his identity to seek further adventures before marrying her. In this passage Ipomadon, hearing that a terrifying knight, Sir Lyolyne, is about to marry 'the fair one' by force, goes, disguised as a fool, with his tutor and servant Thalamewe to Mellengere's court (to which 'the fair one' sends in vain for help) and insists on going to rescue her. His apparently jesting boasts are all true; they refer to the time when he used to kiss Mellengere's queen as her favourite servant, and, in disguise, won the tournament.

Finally he defeats Sir Lyolyne, discovers that Cabanus, Mellengere's heir, is his own lost brother, and marries 'the fair one'.

9 *briny*: MS. *brande*; 37 *lere*: MS. *sere*; 56 *folie*: MS. *fowle*; 82 *I* not in MS.; 91 *love*: MS. *louythe*; 102 *Turne*: MS. *But turne*; 109 *ynough*: MS. *i nowthe*; 124 *is* not in MS.; 127 *is*: MS. *ben*; 130 *sore*: MS. *so*; 134 *ye*: MS. *he*; 141 *In* not in MS.; 142 *They*: MS. *The*; 157 *him*: MS. *hym onys*; 164 *bus*: MS. *mvste*; 166 *you*: MS. *youre*; 185 *afar fro thee*: MS. *a frome* (*ro* altered from *ar*); 186 *afraid*: MS. *aferde*; 190 *I moste*: MS. *nedes I mvste*; 199 *arme*: MS. *myghte*.

95. B.M. MS. Harley 2316, f. 25a (*c.* 1375–1400). Ed. *Rel. Lyr. XIV C.*, no. 52. *Index* 1684.

   5 *into* corrected to *in* in MS.

96. MS. Harley 2316, f. 25b. Ed. *Rel. Ant.* ii. 120. *Index* 2158.
   3 *loketh*: MS. *loke*.

97. Trinity Coll., Cambridge, MS. B. 15. 17, f. 147a, col. ii (*c.* 1375–1400). Ed. *Rel. Ant.* i. 166 f. *Index* 611.

   The following readings are from Glasgow University Library, Hunterian MS. V. 8. 15, f. 34a (*c.* 1375–1400), ed. *Rel. Lyr. XIV C.*, no. 90: 3 *lent*, MS. *sent*; 15 *bent*, MS. *blent*; 19 *thee*, 29 *herte* not in MS.; 34 *of day*, MS. *day of.* 40 *hath* (so Huntington Library MS. HM 127): MS. *is*.

98. Trinity Coll., Cambridge, MS. R. 3. 19, f. 154a (*c.* 1500). Ed. Robbins, *Sec. Lyr.*, no. 160. The first line is quoted by Chaucer, *The Nun's Priest's Tale*, B 4069. *Index* 2254.

   1 *londe* (so Chaucer): MS. *a lond*; 3 *in bonde*: MS. *bound*.

99. Trinity Coll., Cambridge, MS. R. 3. 14, f. 2a (*c.* 1400). From *Piers Plowman*, A-Text Prologue, 1–109; ed. G. Kane, *Piers Plowman: The A Version* (London, 1960), pp. 175 ff.; W. W. Skeat, from another MS., (Oxford, 1886), i. 2 ff. *Index* 1459.

   22 *Wonne*: MS. *Whom*; 27 *for* not in MS.; 57 *hem*; MS. *him*; 63 *hy*: MS. *þei*; 73 *given*: MS. *ȝouen*; 86 *poundes*: MS. *poynteþ*; 88 *Thou*: MS. *Tho*; 96 first *and* not in MS.; 107 *Whit*: MS. *Wiþ*.

100. Huntington Library, San Marino, California, MS. HM 143, f. 3a (*c.* 1400–25); reproduced in Photostat, with an Introduction by R. W. Chambers and Technical Examination by R. B. Haselden and H. C. Schulz (Henry E. Huntington Library and Art Gallery, San Marino, California, 1936). From *Piers Plowman*, *C-Text* i. 165–215;

ed. W. W. Skeat, from another MS., (Oxford, 1886), i. 15 ff. *Index* 1459.

15 *knightes*: MS. *knyghte*; 17 *way roume*: MS. *ben war bryghte syluer* (*bryghte syluer* caught up from 19): 18–19 omitted in MS. and supplied from Bodl. MS. Laud misc. 656; 22 *rit*: MS. *riht*; 23 *him*: MS. *us*; 52 *reed* altered to *ryot* in MS.

101. MS. as no. 100, f. 20b. From *Piers Plowman*, C-Text vi. 1–104; ed. W. W. Skeat, from another MS., i. 118 ff. *Index* 1459.

21 supplied from MS. Laud misc. 656: MS. *That þou betre* (orig. *They y betered*) *the by þat byleue the fynden* (*and þe the fayrer* added in margin after *byleue*); 29 *mennes*: MS. *men*; 30 MS. *feste day*; 36 *quod ich* (so Laud misc. 656) not in MS.; 45 *qua*: MS. *quia*; 60 *vaune-warde*: MS. *faumewarde*; 66 *knaves*: MS. *knaue*; 80 *mendenants*: MS. *mendenant*; 85 *or* not in MS.; 88 *discrete*: MS. *desirede*; 94 *begge*: MS. *bigge*; 100 *He boughte*: MS. *Aboute*; 102 *werdes*: MS. *wordes*; 104 *que*: MS. *qui*.

102. MS. as no. 100, f. 28a. From *Piers Plowman*, C-Text vii. 350–97; ed. W. W. Skeat, from another MS., (Oxford, 1886), i. 159 ff. *Index* 1459.

18 *Peres* erased; 32 *not have*: the A and B reading *have amendes of* gives better sense.

103. MS. as no. 100, f. 40a. From *Piers Plowman*, C-Text x. 71–95; ed. W. W. Skeat, from another MS., (Oxford, 1886), i. 234. *Index* 1459.

18 *I*: MS. *he* (added above line).

104. MS. as no. 100, f. 85a. From *Piers Plowman*, C-Text xx. 168–215; ed. W. W. Skeat, from another MS., (Oxford, 1886), i. 511 ff. *Index* 1459.

6 *see* not in MS.; 32 *derknesse*: MS. *derkenesses*.

105. Bodl. MS. Fairfax 16, f. 161a (*c.* 1425–50). From *The House of Fame*, 529–668 (Book ii. 21–160); ed. Robinson, pp. 287 f. *Index* 991.

Departures from the readings of the MS. are: 7 *thing*: MS. *kynge*; 8 *to*: MS. *of*; 9 *brende*: MS. *beende*; 17 *carying*: MS. *cryinge*; 24 *That*: MS. *And*; 30 *tho* not in MS.; 38 *n'as*: MS. *was*; 47 *it* not in MS.; 93 *lit*: MS. *lytel*; 94 MS. *songes dytees bookys*; 119 *fer*: MS. *frerre*; 123 *ne*: MS. *ner*; 125 *made alle thy*: MS. *ymade*.

106. MS. Fairfax 16, f. 166a. From *The House of Fame*, 887–1045 (Book ii. 379–537); ed. Robinson, pp. 290 ff. *Index* 991.

25–7 *And . . . saide* not in MS., supplied from MS. Pepys 2006, which reads *token* for *town* (25); 36 *fel*: MS. *ful*; 40 *space*: MS. *place*; 45 *speketh*: MS. *seketh*; 46 *th'* not in MS.; 60 *gunne*: MS. *gan*; 70 *fro*: MS. *fer fro*; 71 *grete*: MS. *mochil*; 78 *loken*: MS. *to loken*; 87 *A*: MS. *of*; 92 *Cloude*: MS. *Cloude and erthe*; 98 *me* not in MS.; 105 *gan*: MS. *began*; *wold I*: MS. *I wold*; 113 *No*: MS. *and no*; 117 *Brid*: MS. *Briddes*; 128 *As*: MS. *Alle*; 129 *they shinen*: MS. *thy seluen*; 143 *sooth*: MS. *that soth*; 148 *like* not in MS.; 158 *biten*: MS. *beten*.

107. MS. Fairfax 16, f. 83a. From the Prologue to *The Legend of Good Women*, version F (B), 1–39; ed. Robinson, pp. 482 f. *Index* 100.

Departures from the readings of the MS. follow Magdalene Coll., Cambridge, MS. Pepys 2006 [P], p. 53 (*c.* 1475), or Trinity Coll., Cambridge, MS. R. 3. 19 [T], f. 114a (*c.* 1500): 1 *have I herd men* (T): MS. *I haue herd*; 2 *That* (PT) not in MS.; 5 *n'is* (P): MS. *is*; 6 *hell or heven be* (T): MS. *heuene or in helle ybe*; 29 *can* (P): MS. *konne*.

108. Corpus Christi Coll., Cambridge, MS. 61, f. 39a (*c.* 1400–15). From *Troilus and Criseyde*, ii. 610–51; ed. Robinson, pp. 408 f. *Index* 3327.

8 *fro*: MS. *to*; 12 *day*, 41 *it* not in MS.

109. Corpus MS. 61, f. 129a. From *Troilus and Criseyde*, v. 533–53; ed. Robinson, p. 465. *Index* 3327.

15 *houses*: MS. *paleis*.

110. Corpus MS. 61, f. 149a. From *Troilus and Criseyde*, v. 1786–92; ed. Robinson, p. 479. *Index* 3327.

6 *pace*: MS. *space*.

111. Corpus MS. 61, f. 149b. *From Troilus and Criseyde*, v. 1835–69; ed. Robinson, p. 479. *Index* 3327.

23 Second *thee* not in MS.

112. Huntington Library, San Marino, California, MS. EL 26 C. 9 (Ellesmere), f. 2a (*c.* 1410). Reproduced in Facsimile, *The Ellesmere Chaucer*, 2 vols. (Manchester, 1911). From *The Prologue, The Canterbury Tales*, I(A), 118–62; ed. Robinson, p. 18. *Index* 4019.

23 *been*: MS. *to been*; 31 *oon*: MS. *any*.

113. MS. as no. 112, f. 3b. From *The Prologue, C.T.* I(A), 285–308; ed. Robinson, p. 20. *Index* 4019.

3 *As*: MS. *And.*

114. MS. as no. 112, f. 5b. From *The Prologue, C.T.* I(A), 445–76; ed. Robinson, p. 21. *Index* 4019.

115. MS. as no. 112, f. 69b. From 'The Wife of Bath's Prologue', *C.T.* III(D), 627–856; ed. Robinson, pp. 82 ff. *Index* 4019.

34 *sawe*: MS. *lawe*; 65 *of*, 91 *that Jesu* not in MS.; 93 *wimmen*: MS. *womman*; 101 *the wo*: MS. *wo*; 124 *on*: MS. *vpon*; 131 *how*: MS. *how þat*; 160 *wene*: MS. *leeue*; 189 second *of* not in MS.; 194 *the*: MS. *to*; 210 second *eke* not in MS.; 226 *been*: MS. *were.*

116. MS. as no. 112, f. 7a. From *The Prologue, C.T.* I(A), 587–622; ed. Robinson, pp. 22 f. *Index* 4019.

18 *ne* not in MS.; 26 *cote*: MS. *gowne.*

117. MS. as no. 112, f. 42a. From *The Reeve's Tale, C.T.* I(A), 3921–4148; ed. Robinson, pp. 56 ff. *Index* 4019.

19 MS. *A theef he was of corn and eek of mele*; 28 *But*: MS. *But if*; 45 *And*: MS. *As*; 99 *with* not in MS.; 117 *howgates*: MS. *how that*; 120 *and*, 136 *ne* not in MS.; 153 *lost*: MS. *lorn*; 154 *off*: MS. *out*; 158 *gaan*: MS. *geen*; 164 *John* not in MS.; 167 *Goddes*: MS. *god*; 174 *a* not in MS.

The students speak Northern dialect.

118. MS. as no. 112, f. 140a. From *The Pardoner's Tale, C.T.* VI(C), 661–888; ed. Robinson, pp. 152 ff. *Index* 4019.

40 *he*: MS. *which*; 45 *al*: MS. *and*; 100 *you*: MS. *ye*; 117 *that*, 136 *the* not in MS.; 143 *hem*: MS. *hym*; 146 *a-gon*: MS. *gon*; 147 *of hem* not in MS.; 157 *wel*: MS. *how*; 158 first *What shal*: MS. *Whal*; 163 *wil*: MS. *shal*; 177 *to*: MS. *vnto*; 188 *him*: MS. *hem*; 211 *of* not in MS.; 213 *his*: MS. *his owene*; 220 *as*: MS. *so as.*

119. Cambridge, U.L. MS. Ii. 3. 21, f. 52b (*c.* 1425). Ed. Robinson, p. 534. *Index* 28.

3 *fruites*: MS. *the fructes*; 11 *gniden*: MS. *gnodded*; 20 *was*: MS. *is*; 23 *No*: MS. *no batails*; 34 *No*: MS. *no places*; 39 and 40 transposed in MS.; 41 *were*: MS. *was*; 42 *in* not in MS.; 44 MS. *Or gras or leues in parfyt Ioye reste & quiete*; 50 *void*: MS. *voyded*; after l. 55 a line is missing; 60 *men* not in MS.; 63 *Poisoun*: MS. *poyson &.*

120. Cambridge, U.L. MS. Gg. 4. 27, I, f. 490b. From *The Parlia-ment of Fowls*, 680–92; ed. Robinson, p. 318. *Index* 2375.

This song has been crowded into the space of a seven-line stanza left for it by the scribe (*c.* 1425–50), in a later hand (*c.* 1475–1500). Departures from the MS. follow Bodl. MS. Digby 181, f. 51b (*c.* 1475): 1 *thy* not in MS.; 3 *longe*: MS. *large*; 10 *singe*: MS. *ben.*

121. Trinity Coll., Cambridge, MS. R. 3. 20. p. 367 (copied by John Shirley, *c.* 1425). Ed. Robinson, p. 534. *Index* 120.

122. B.M. MS. Cotton Cleopatra D. vii, f. 189a (*c.* 1425–50). Ed. Robinson, p. 536. *Index* 809.

4 *blent* MS. *blindeth*; 12 first *the*: MS. *to*; 17 *n'is*: MS. *is*; *wilder-nesse*: MS. *wildnesse*. ll. 22–8, found only in B.M. MS. Add. 10340, are not here printed.

123. Bodl. MS. Arch. Selden B. 24, f. 156a (*c.* 1500). From the Pro-logue to *The Legend of Good Women*, version F(B), 249–69; ed. Robinson, p. 488. *Index* 100.

5 *wifhood*: MS. *wyfhede*; 11 *al* not in MS.

124. Bodl. MS. Fairfax 16, f. 193a (*c.* 1425–50). Ed. Robinson, pp. 539 f. *Index* 3787.

Readings from B.M. MS. Add. 22139, f. 138a, col. i (*c.* 1432) are: 4 *That*, MS. *For*; *but*, MS. *but yf*; 19 *any*, MS. *is a*. From Cam-bridge U.L. MS. Ff. 1. 6, f. 59a (*c.* 1475–1500) is 25 *oure harmes*, MS. *myn harme.*

125. Magdalene Coll. Cambridge, MS. Pepys 2006, p. 390 (*c.* 1475). Ed. Robinson, p. 542. *Index* 4282.

1 *eyen two*: MS. *two yen*; 28 *his*: MS. *in his*; 36 *ther*: MS. *this.*

126. Bodl. MS. Fairfax 3, f. 78a, col. ii (*c.* 1400). From *Confessio Amantis*, iv. 2927–3123 (based on Ovid, *Metamorphoses*, xi. 410 ff.); ed. G. C. Macaulay, *The Complete Works of John Gower* (Oxford, 1899–1902), ii. 380 ff. *Index* 2662.

127. MS. Fairfax 3, f. 104a, col. ii. From *Confessio Amantis*, v. 3957–4174 (based on Ovid, *Metamorphoses*, vii. 179 ff.); ed. Macaulay, op. cit., iii. 54 ff.; J. A. W. Bennett, *Selections from John Gower* (Oxford, 1968), pp. 74 ff. *Index* 2662.

On 38 *Crete*, 55 *Rede*, see Macaulay's and Bennett's notes. 83 Misunderstanding of Ovid's *verbenis silvaque incinxit agresti* (242) 'and wreathed them with boughs from the wild wood'; 171-3 misunderstanding of Ovid's *Nec defuit illis/Squamea Cinyphii tenuis membrana chelydri* (271 f.) 'nor was the thin scaly skin of a Cinyphian water-snake lacking'.

128. MS. Fairfax 3, f. 109b, col. i. From *Confessio Amantis*, v. 4937–5162; ed. Macaulay, op. cit. iii. 81 ff. *Index* 2662.

129. B.M. MS. Add. 27944, f. 8a (*c.* 1400-25). Other versions printed by A. J. Perry, *Dialogus inter Militem et Clericum*, E.E.T.S. o.s. 167 (1925), p. cxxix; Robbins, *Sec. Lyr.*, no. 101. Prologue to Trevisa's translation of Bartholomew de Glanville's *De Proprietatibus Rerum*. *Index* 33.

9 *meedes*: MS. *in medes*; 11 *prayede*: MS. *preye*; *deedes*: MS. *wise*; 17 *Bothe* not in MS.

130. Bodl. MS. English poet. a. 1 (Vernon), f. 410b, col. iii (*c.* 1400). Ed. F. J. Furnivall, *The Minor Poems of the Vernon MS.*, E.E.T.S. o.s. 117 (1901), ii. 715 ff.; *XIV C. Verse and Prose*, pp. 157 ff.; Robbins, *Hist. Poems*, no. 39. *Index* 5.

106 *dyede*: MS. *dyʒedē*.

131. MS. as no. 130, f. 411a, col. ii. Ed. Furnivall, E.E.T.S. o.s. 117, pp. 719 ff.; *Rel. Lyr. XIV C.*, no. 113; Robbins, *Hist. Poems*, no. 20. *Index* 4268. The earthquake (17 ff.) was on 21 May, 1382.

After ll. 8 and 16 one stanza omitted, after l. 46 two stanzas.

132. MS. as no. 130, f. 407a, col. iii. Ed. Furnivall, E.E.T.S. o.s. 117, pp. 664 ff.; *Rel. Lyr. XIV C.*, no. 96. *Index* 1448.

After l. 48, five stanzas omitted.

133. MS. as no. 130, f. 408a, col. i. Ed. Furnivall, E.E.T.S. o.s. 117, pp. 675 ff.; *Rel. Lyr. XIV C.*, no. 101. *Index* 3996.

Five stanzas omitted after l. 12, three stanzas after ll. 24, 36.

134. MS. as no. 130, f. 409a, col. iii. Ed. Furnivall, E.E.T.S. o.s. 117, pp. 692 ff.; *Rel. Lyr. XIV C.*, no. 106. *Index* 1402.

15 *bos*: MS. *hos*; 35 *is* not in MS. First three and last five stanzas omitted.

135. B.M. MS. Add. 11307, f. 15a (*c.* 1425). From *Meditations on the Life and Passion of Christ* (*c.* 1375), 218–50; ed. C. D'Evelyn, E.E.T.S. o.s. 158 (1921). *Index* 1034.

136. Cambridge, U.L. MS. Hh. 4. 12, f. 41b (*c.* 1475); also in Lambeth Palace MS. 853, p. 7 (c. 1400). Ed. F. J. Furnivall, *Political, Religious, and Love Poems*, E.E.T.S. o.s. 15 (1903), pp. 180 ff. *Index* 1463.

The following departures from the Cambridge MS. are supported by MS. Lambeth: 31 *ever*, MS. *ouer*; 40 *Quia*, MS. *but Quia*; 66 *her sue if*, MS. *to hyr send or*; 70 *me* not in MS.; 89 *make thee*, MS. *make*, MS. L *þee make*; 101 *blisse*, MS. *in blysse*; 111 *preve thy*, MS. *pray the*; 124 *often-*, MS. *ofter-*. 128 *Quia*: MS. *in blysse. Quia.*

137. Cambridge, U.L. MS. Dd. 5. 64 III, f. 34b (*c.* 1400). Ed. *Rel. Lyr. XIV C.*, no. 78. *Index* 1930.

138. Bodl. MS. Rawlinson poet. 175, f. 80a, col. ii (*c.* 1400). Ed. *Rel. Lyr. XIV C.*, no. 46. *Index* 110.
14 *thy*: MS. *m.*

139. Lambeth Palace MS. 853, p. 61 (*c.* 1400). Ed. F. J. Furnivall, *Hymns to the Virgin and Christ*, E.E.T.S. o.s. 24 (1867), p. 91. *Index* 1454.
ll. 33–120 omitted.

140. B.M. MS. Cotton Cleopatra B. ii, f. 63b (*c.* 1400). Ed. T. Wright, *Political Poems and Songs* (Rolls Series, 1859), i. 263 ff.; Robbins, *Hist. Poems*, no. 65. *Index* 2777.
Two stanzas omitted after l. 72, three stanzas after l. 96.

141. B.M. MS. Add. 41666, f. 10a (*c.* 1450). From *Mum and the Sothsegger*, fragment M, 876–943; ed. M. Day and R. Steele, E.E.T.S. o.s. 199 (1936), pp. 52 ff. *Index* *6, *Index Suppl.* *296.3.
9 *of*, 60 *sounes* not in MS.; 64 *cheerly*: MS. *cleerly.*

142. B.M. MS. Arundel 292, f. 71b (*c.* 1400–25). Ed. *XIV C. Verse and Prose*, pp. 169 f.; Robbins, *Sec. Lyr.*, no. 118. *Index* 3227.

143. Bodl. MS. Gough Eccl. Top. 4, f. 128b (*c.* 1425). Quoted by John Mirk (*fl. c.* 1400), in his sermon '*De Assumpcione Beate Marie*'; ed. T. Erbe, *Mirk's Festial*, E.E.T.S. e.s. 96 (1905), p. 224; noted by R. Woolf, *The English Religious Lyric in the Middle Ages* (Oxford, 1968), p. 299.

144. Cambridge, U.L. MS. Add. 5943, f. 164b (*c.* 1400), with music. The MS. belonged to Thomas Turk, Fellow of Winchester College

1395–8, 1400–1. Ed. E. K. Chambers and F. L. Sidgwick, *Early English Lyrics* (London, 1907), p. 256; Dobson and Harrison, i, no. 29. *Index* 2138.

145. MS. as no. 144, f. 145b, but in a later hand (*c.* 1425–50). Ed. Greene, *Carols*, no. 349; *Rel. Lyr. XV C.*, no. 185; Greene, *Selection*, no. 72. *Index* 1415.

  6 *fon*: MS. *fow*.

146. MS. as no. 144, f. 178b, in the same hand as no. 145 (*c.* 1425–50). Ed. Greene, *Carols*, no. 451; Robbins, *Sec. Lyr.*, no. 22. *Index* 3418.

  8 Line missing: MS. *He wold noght sey onys farewelle* caught from l. 9.

147. B.M. MS. Royal 18 A. xiii, f. 61a (*c.* 1425). From *Boethius: De Consolatione Philosophiae, translated by John Walton*, iii, Metre x; ed. M. Science, E.E.T.S. o.s. 170 (1927), p. 185. *Index* and *Suppl.* 1254, 1597. Walton, an Augustinian Canon of Osney Abbey, made his translation in 1410.

148. B.M. MS. Royal 17 D. vi, f. 4a (*c.* 1400–25). From *The Regement of Princes* (1411–12), 1–112; ed. F. J. Furnivall, E.E.T.S. e.s. 72 (1897), pp. 1 ff. *Index* 2229.

  30 *it* not in MS.; 38 *firy-hot*: MS. *his firy*; 40 *han*: MS. *hath*. Nine stanzas omitted after l. 14, one stanza after l. 28.

149. B.M. MS. Harley 4866, f. 36a (*c.* 1400–25). From *The Regement of Princes*, 1961–81; ed. Furnivall, E.E.T.S. e.s. 72, pp. 71 f. *Index* 2229.

  18 *y-ment*: MS. *ment*.

150. Bodl. MS. Douce 381, f. 20a (*c.* 1400–25), with music. Ed. *Early Bodl. Music*, ii. 51 f.; *Rel. Lyr XIV C.*, no. 129; Dobson and Harrison, i, no. 23. *Index* 1311.

  3 *drye*: MS. *dryue*.

151. Bodl. MS. Arch Selden B.26, f. 17b (*c.* 1450), with music. Ed. *Early Bodl. Music*, ii. 128 ff.; Greene, *Carols*, no. 426; Robbins, *Hist. Poems*, no. 32; Greene, *Selection*, no. 90. *Index* 2716.

152. Bodl. MS. Arch. Selden B.26, f. 19a, with music. Ed. *Early Bodl. Music*, ii. 132 f.; Robbins, *Hist. Poems*, no. 37. *Index* 3434.

153. Bodl. MS. Arch. Selden B. 26, f. 32b. Ed. *Early Bodl. Music*, ii.
177 f.; Robbins, *Sec. Lyr.*, no. 11. *Index* 3259.
The text, with music, is written for three parts, some words
being omitted from each. This is the tenor part, with *Anon* (l. 2)
added from the counter-tenor.

154. Bodl. MS. Rawlinson C. 506, f. 297a (*c.* 1425–50). Ed. Robbins,
Sec. Lyr., no. 66. *Index* 2903.
10 Third *George* not in MS.

155. Bodl. MS. Rawlinson C. 288, f. 113b (*c.* 1475–1500). Ed. F. J.
Furnivall, *Political, Religious, and Love Poems*, E.E.T.S. o.s. 15
(1903), p. 43; *XIV C. Verse and Prose*, p. 170. *Index* 1290.
9 *none* not in MS.

156. Bodl. MS. Fairfax 16, f. 195a (*c.* 1425–50). Ed. *Rel. Lyr. XV C.*,
no. 171. *Index* 3504, 3437. Attributed to Squire Halsham (possibly
John Halsham, d. 1415); but Lydgate, who used these verses, may
have been their author (see C. F. Bühler, *M.L.N.* lv (1940), pp.
567 ff.).
3 *of*: MS. *and*.

157. Bodl. MS. Douce 302, f. 29a, col. i (*c.* 1430). Ed. E. K. Whiting,
The Poems of John Audelay, E.E.T.S. o.s. 184 (1931), no. 38; Greene,
Carols, no. 117; *Selection*, no. 25. *Index* 21.

158. MS. Douce 302, f. 31b, col. i. Ed. Whiting, E.E.T.S. o.s. 184,
no. 44; Greene, *Carols*, no. 172. *Index* 3603.
20 *shulde*: MS. *schul*; 24 *his*: MS. *his his*; *forth* not in MS.

159. MS. Douce 302, f. 30b, col. i. Ed. Whiting, E.E.T.S. o.s. 184,
no. 50; Greene, *Carols*, no. 272. *Index* 831.
15 *blin*: MS. *bly*; 26 *Without*: MS. *w^t* (= with).

160. MS. Douce 302, f. 30b, col. ii. Ed. Whiting, E.E.T.S. o.s. 184,
no. 51; Greene, *Carols*, no. 369. *Index* 693. Audelay was blind and deaf.

161. B.M. MS. Harley 2255, f. 3b (*c.* 1425–50). Ed. H. N.
MacCracken, *The Minor Poems of John Lydgate*, ii, E.E.T.S. o.s. 192
(1934), 780 ff. *Index* 1865.
4 MS. *and prudence*; 15 *atwixen*: MS. *atwix*; 18 *they*: MS. *day*;
28 *Jove*: MS. *Imo* (see J. Norton-Smith, *John Lydgate: Poems*, Oxford,
1966, p. 137); 44 *al* not in MS.; 76 *splayed*: MS. *splayned*. Four
stanzas omitted after l. 16, one stanza after l. 64.

162. Bodl. MS. Laud misc. 683, f. 54b (*c.* 1475). Ed. MacCracken, E.E.T.S. o.s. 192, 445 ff.; J. Norton-Smith, *John Lydgate: Poems,* pp. 12 f. *Index* 36.

21 *He*: MS. *And he*; 35 *take*: MS. *shake.*

163. B.M. MS. Harley 1766, f. 261b (*c.* 1450). From *The Fall of Princes,* ix. 3387–3442; ed. H. Bergen, E.E.T.S. e.s. 123 (1924), pp. 1015 f. *Index* 1168.

16 *the* not in MS.

164. York Minster MS. xvi. K. 6, f. 98b (*c.* 1425). Ed. T. F. Simmons, *The Lay Folks Mass Book,* E.E.T.S. o.s. 71 (1879), p. 350; F. A. Patterson, *The Middle English Penitential Lyric* (New York, 1911), p. 72. *Index* 2892.

165. B.M. MS. Add. 37049, f. 20a (*c.* 1425–50). Ed. *Rel. Lyr. XV C.,* no. 108. *Index* 2504.

Last three verses, man's reply, omitted.

166. B.M. MS. Add. 37049, f. 36a. Ed. *Rel. Lyr. XV C.,* no. 158b. *Index* 1387.

12 *I wende . . . you* cut off at foot of page; supplied from B.M. MS. Stowe 39.

167. Lincoln Cathedral MS. 91 (Thornton MS)., f. 148a, col. ii (*c.* 1425–50). Ed. *Rel. Ant.* ii. 280. *Index* 2026.

ll. 13 ff. omitted.

168. Lincoln Cathedral MS. 91, f. 213a. Ed. G. G. Perry, *Religious Pieces in Prose and Verse,* E.E.T.S. o.s. 26 (1914), pp. 88 ff. *Index* 3921.

169. Trinity Coll., Cambridge, MS. O. 3. 58 (roll) recto (*c.* 1425–50), with music. Ed. Greene, *Carols,* no. 173; J. Stevens, *Mediaeval Carols, Musica Britannica,* iv (2nd ed., London, 1958), pp. 10 f.; Greene, *Selection,* no. 46. *Index* 3536.

This part of the roll is badly worn; some letters are illegible. The first two lines are also the refrain.

170. Bodl. MS. Arch. Selden B. 24, f. 195a (*c.* 1500). From *The Kingis Quair,* stanzas 31–35; ed. W. W. Skeat, S.T.S. n.s. 1 (1911), pp. 10 f.; A. Lawson (London, 1910), pp. 16 ff.; W. M. Mackenzie (London, 1939), pp. 53 ff. *Index* 1215.

20 Second *of*: MS. *on.*

171. St. John's Coll., Cambridge, MS. G. 28, f. ib (*c.* 1425). Ed. H. A. Person, *Cambridge Middle English Lyrics* (Seattle, 1953, revd. 1962), no. 51; Robbins, *Hist. Poems*, no. 68. *Index* 3697.

172. MS. as no. 171, f. 1b. Ed. Person, op. cit., no. 51; Robbins, *Hist. Poems*, no. 69. *Index* 161.
   25 *bidde* not in MS.

173. Bodl. MS. Laud misc. 704, ff. 17b, 18a (*c.* 1450). From *The Libelle of Englyshe Polycye* (1436), 1064–75, 1092–1107; ed. Sir George Warner (Oxford, 1926). *Index* 3491.
   13 *Kepe*: MS. *kepte*.

174. Bodl. MS. Ashmole 191, f. 191a (*c.* 1445), with music. Ed. *Early Bodl. Music*, ii. 66; Robbins, *Sec. Lyr.*, no. 171. *Index* 2381.
   6 *far*: MS. *for*; 8 *And*: MS. *a*; 9 first *I* not in MS.; 14 *her* not in MS.; 20 *no*: MS. *& no*.

175. MS. Ashmole 191, f. 192b, with music. Ed. *Early Bodl. Music*, ii. 68 ff.; Robbins, *Sec. Lyr.*, no. 155. *Index* 925.

176. B.M. MS. Egerton 3307, f. 66b (*c.* 1450), with music. Ed. J. Stevens, *Mediaeval Carols, Musica Britannica*, iv (2nd ed., London, 1958), p. 53; Greene, *Selection*, no. 69. *Index* 1234.

177. Cambridge, U.L. MS. Ff. 5. 48, f. 43b (*c.* 1450). Ed. H. A. Person, *Cambridge Middle English Lyrics*, (revd. ed., Seattle, 1962), no. 8. *Index* 4185. Another version in MS. Harley 2339, ed. *Rel. Lyr. XIV C.*, no. 127.
   7 *it* not in MS.; 13 *unlust*: MS. *luste*; 16 *theron*: MS. *on*; 17 *left*: MS. *right*; 20 so MS. Harley: MS. *þat at þi deyng heuen may be þi mede*.

178. MS. Porkington 10, f. 81b (*c.* 1450). The MS., owned by Lord Harlech, Brogyntyn, Oswestry, is deposited in the National Library of Wales, Aberystwyth. Ed. Robbins, *Sec. Lyr.*, no. 119. *Index* 559.
   4 *made*: MS. *mad he*; 22 MS. *I loke alowe and syt ful style and love*; 30 *seche* (? read *serche*): MS. *sche*; 36 *fleche*: MS. *flece*; 65 *leve*: MS. *le*.

179. MS. as no. 178, f. 152a. Ed. *Rel. Ant.* i. 85 f. *Index* 1116.
   23 *mass*: *ass* lost at edge of leaf; 26 *Mid-summer-day*: MS. *mydesōday*. After l. 26, 34 lines omitted.

180. MS. as no. 178, f. 198a. Ed. Greene, *Carols*, no. 323; *Rel. Lyr. XV C.*, no. 116; Greene, *Selection*, no. 68. *Index* 298.
  4 *with*: MS. *wyhte.*

181. B.M. MS. Harley 682, f. 88b (*c.* 1440). Ed. R. Steele, *The English Poems of Charles of Orleans*, E.E.T.S. o.s. 215 (1941), p. 133, o.s. 220 (1946); Robbins, *Sec. Lyr.*, no. 185. *Index* 2243.
  11 *to* not in MS.

182. MS. Harley 682, f. 46b. Ed. Steele, E.E.T.S. o.s. 215, p. 81, o.s. 220. *Index* 1549.

183. B.M. MS. Sloane 2593, f. 2a (*c.* 1450). Ed. Greene, *Carols*, no. 336. *Index* 1568.

184. MS. Sloane 2593, f. 6a. Ed. Greene, *Carols*, no. 390; *Selection*, no. 79. *Index* 3959.

185. MS. Sloane 2593, f. 6b. Ed. Dyboski, p. 170; Greene, *Carols*, no. 175C. *Index* 1893.

186. MS. Sloane 2593, f. 7a. Ed. Greene, *Carols*, no. 385; *Selection*, no. 77; Robbins, *Hist. Poems*, no. 59. *Index* 72.
  24 *him,* 26 *pardee* not in MS.

187. MS. Sloane 2593, f. 8a. Ed. Greene, *Carols*, no. 381; *Selection*, no. 76. *Index* 1433.

188. MS. Sloane 2593, f. 10b. Ed. *Rel. Lyr. XV C.*, no. 81. *Index* 1367.

189. MS. Sloane 2593, f. 10b. Ed. Robbins, *Sec. Lyr.*, no. 46. *Index* 1299.

190. MS. Sloane 2593, f. 10b. Ed. Robbins, *Sec. Lyr.*, no. 5. *Index* 2675.
  9 *it*: MS. *is.*

191. MS. Sloane 2593, f. 11a. Ed. *Rel. Lyr. XV C.*, no. 83. *Index* 117.

192. MS. Sloane 2593, f. 11a. Ed. Robbins, *Sec. Lyr.*, no. 45. *Index* 1303.
  2 *see*: MS. *þe se*; 7 *the* not in MS.; 15 *any*: MS. *only.*

193. MS. Sloane 2593, f. 11b. Ed. Greene, *Carols*, no. 25. *Index* 3472.

4 *On a*: MS. *In on*; the last two letters of *morwe* (4), *undern* (16) lost at edge of leaf.

194. MS. Sloane 2593, f. 14b. Ed. F. J. Child, *The English and Scottish Popular Ballads* (Boston and New York, 1883–98), no. 115; J. Kinsley, *The Oxford Book of Ballads* (1969), pp. 374 ff. *Index* 1317.

17 *Robin* not in MS.; 19 *bent*: MS. *went*; 33 *west*: MS. *loked west*; 61 *the*: MS. *þou*.

195. MS. Sloane 2593, f. 24b. Ed. Greene, *Carols*, no. 405; Robbins, *Sec. Lyr.*, no. 43; Greene, *Selection*, no. 82. *Index* 4279.

196. MS. Sloane 2593, f. 26b. Ed. Greene, *Carols*, no. 392; Robbins, *Sec. Lyr.*, no. 57. *Index* 2747.

197. MS. Sloane 2593, f. 29a. Ed. Greene, *Carols*, no. 417. *Index* 1896.

198. MS. Sloane 2593, f. 30a. Ed. Greene, *Carols*, no. 341; *Selection*, no. 70. *Index* 3537.

6 *and* lost in MS. margin; 19 *sitten*: MS. *stondyn & syttyn*.

199. MS. Sloane 2593, f. 34a. Ed. Greene, *Carols*, no. 457; Robbins, *Sec. Lyr.*, no. 27; Greene, *Selection*, no. 98. *Index* 377.

Kyrieleyson not in MS. at ll. 8, 18, 23, 33.

200. B.M. MS. Harley 367, f. 127a (*c.* 1600–25). Ed. Robbins, *Hist. Poems*, no. 50. *Index* 3759. This version, wrongly attributed to Lydgate, has been 'newly ouersene and amended', presumably in the sixteenth century.

One stanza omitted after ll. 14, 21, 35.

201. Corpus Christi Coll., Oxford, MS. C. 237, f. 243b (*c.* 1475–1500). Ed. T. Wright, *Political Poems and Songs* (Rolls Series, 1861), ii. 252 f. *Index* 2335.

202. B.M. MS. Harley 5396, f. 275b (*c.* 1455). Ed. Greene, *Carols*, no. 136A; *Selection*, no. 34A. *Index* 1226.

203. Bodl. MS. Ashmole 1378, p. 60 (*c.* 1475). Ed. Robbins, *Sec. Lyr.*, no. 64. *Index* 1199.

5 Second *me*: MS. *the*.

204. Gonville and Caius Coll., Cambridge, MS. 383, p. 41 (*c.* 1475). Ed. Greene, *Carols*, no. 452; Robbins, *Sec. Lyr.*, no. 29; Greene, *Selection*, no. 95. *Index* 225.

20 MS. *Outh me bred al þis schayl*; 29 *throt*: MS. *wroth*; 40 *Also*: MS. *a.*

205. MS. as no. 204, p. 68, col. ii. Ed. Greene, *Carols*, no. 470; Robbins, *Sec. Lyr.*, no. 37; Greene, *Selection*, no. 99. *Index* 1280.

206. MS. as no. 204, p. 190. Ed. Robbins, *Sec. Lyr.*, no. 33. *Index* 3174.

207. MS. as no. 204, p. 210. Ed. Greene, *Carols*, no. 455; Robbins, *Sec. Lyr.*, no. 23; Greene, *Selection*, no. 97. *Index* 1330.

A different refrain, *Bryd on brere, y telle yt to non oþur, y ne dar*, precedes l. 1, and perhaps indicated the tune; it is repeated after l. 6, and corrected to *Wer it undo* etc.

208. B.M., *The Morall Fabillis of Esope the Phrygian* etc. (Charteris Print, Edinburgh, 1570). Ed. G. Gregory Smith, *The Poems of Robert Henryson*, S.T.S. 55 (1906), ii. 14 ff.; C. Elliott, *Robert Henryson: Poems* (Oxford, 1963), pp. 6 ff., edits from the Bassandyne Print (Edinburgh, 1571) in the National Library of Scotland. *Index* 3703.

The following readings, not in the Charteris Print[C], are from the Bassandyne Print: 23 *busk*, C *blak*; 24 *Sho ran cryand quhill sho come to a balk*, C *Scho ranne with mony ane hiddeous quaik*; 26 *culd*, C *cryit*; 74 *seith*, C *seik*; 77 *vult*, C *will*; 154 *hunny-sweit*, C *humbill & sweit*; 188 *yone*, C *ane*; 191 *I* not in C; 198 *woll*, C *weill*.

209. Bodl. MS. Eng. poet. e. 1, f. 13a (*c.* 1475–1500). Ed. T. Wright, *Songs and Carols*, Percy Soc. xxiii (1847), pp. 4 f. *Index* 3552.

210. MS. Eng. poet. e. 1, f. 17b. Ed. Greene, *Carols*, no. 150B. *Index* 3627.

8 *can say*: MS. *sayd*; 19 *be kidde for* later altered in MS. to *be kyndde ame*; *Heven-King* (so MS. Adv. 19. 3. 1): MS. *a kyng*; 29 MS. *nere* later altered to *ne þou*; 49 *I* and *thy* added by corrector; 59 *right* (so MS. Adv. 19. 3. 1) not in MS.; 63 *me* not in MS.; 72 *wil*: MS. *wyl be*, later corrected to *wyl*.

211. MS. Eng. poet. e. 1, f. 18b. Ed. Greene, *Carols*, no. 37. *Index* 34.

42 *thar* later altered in MS. to *dede*; 52 *him* (MS. *hyme*) added later; 56 *fro*: MS. *for fro*.

212. MS. Eng. poet. e. 1, f. 20a. Ed. Greene, *Carols*, no. 151A. *Index* 3596.

45 *Whether*: MS. *Wher*. After lines 34, 46, one stanza omitted.

213. MS. Eng. poet. e. 1, f. 21b. Ed. Robbins, *Sec. Lyr.*, no. 113. *Index* 813.

214. MS. Eng. poet. e. 1, f. 22a. Ed. Greene, *Carols*, no. 344. *Index* 543.

20 *Stop*: MS. *& stop*.

215. MS. Eng. poet. e. 1, f. 23a. Ed. Greene, *Carols*, no. 406; Robbins, *Sec. Lyr.*, no. 44. *Index* 210.

216. MS. Eng. poet. e. 1, f. 23b. Ed. Greene, *Carols*, no. 414; Robbins, *Sec. Lyr.*, no. 8. *Index* 1468.

3 *n'is*: MS. *is*.

217. MS. Eng. poet. e. 1, f. 24b. Ed. Greene, *Carols*, no. 334. *Index* 4000.

218. MS. Eng. poet. e. 1, f. 25a. Ed. Greene, *Carols*, no. 180A; *Selection*, no. 48. *Index* 1650.

219. MS. Eng. poet. e. 1, f. 30a. Ed. Greene, *Carols*, p. xcix; Robbins, *Sec. Lyr.*, no. 50. *Index* 1225.

4 *joly*: MS. *jo*, end obliterated by hole; 6, 9 *we*: MS. *þei*; 10 *on*: MS. *downe on*.

220. MS. Eng. poet. e. 1, f. 54a. Ed. Greene, *Carols*, no. 138; Robbins, *Sec. Lyr.*, no. 52; Greene, *Selection*, no. 35. *Index* 3438.

4 *doth*: MS. *do*.

221. MS. Eng. poet. e. 1, f. 34b. Ed. Greene, *Carols*, no. 409. *Index* 3593.

222. MS. Eng. poet. e. 1, f. 41b. Ed. *Early Bodl. Music*, ii. 184; Greene, *Carols*, no. 422A; Robbins, *Sec. Lyr.*, no. 13; Greene, *Selection*, no. 88. *Index* 549. Greene notes that the tune preceding this carol in the MS. does not apply to it.

After l. 20, three (corrupt) lines omitted.

223. MS. Eng. poet. e. 1, f. 52a. Ed. Greene, *Carols*, no. 423; *Selection*, no. 89. *Index* 163.

224. Bodl. MS. Douce 104, f. 112b (*c.* 1475–1500). Ed. *Rel. Lyr. XV C.*, no. 179. *Index* 3812.

  12 *multum*: MS. faded; other eds. *autem.*

225. Bodl. MS. Digby 88, f. 97b (*c.* 1475–1500). Ed. Robbins, *Sec. Lyr.*, no. 67. *Index* 579.

226. B.M. MS. Harley 541, f. 228b (*c.* 1475–1500). Ed. *Rel. Lyr. XV C.*, no. 127. *Index* 3844.

227. Manchester, John Rylands Library, Lat. MS. 395, f. 120a (*c.* 1475–1500). Ed. Greene, *Carols*, no. 161; *Rel. Lyr. XV C.*, no. 9. *Index* 4189.

  13 *shortly with wordes* (so Trinity Coll., Cambridge, MS. O.9.38): MS. *with wordys shortly*; 20 *me* (so Trinity MS.): MS. *þe.*

228. Lincoln Cathedral MS. 133, f. 122b (*c.* 1475–1500). Ed. Robbins, *Sec. Lyr.*, no. 148. *Index* 1305.

  12 *nought* not in MS.; 15 *brought*: MS. *boght*. The text is incomplete, because the MS. leaf is damaged.

229. Lincoln Cathedral MS. 132, f. 100a (*c.* 1475–1500). Ed. Robbins, *Sec. Lyr.*, no. 116. *Index* 3895.

  10 *thee* not in MS.; 22 *thou are*: MS. ? *tire af.*

230. Cambridge, U.L. MS. Ff. 1. 6, f. 139b (*c.* 1475–1500). Ed. Greene, *Carols*, no. 469. *Index* 3180.

  15 *God* not in MS.

231. Aberystwyth, National Library of Wales, MS. Peniarth 356, p. 44 (*c.* 1475–1500), with Latin renderings. Ed. Robbins, *Sec. Lyr.*, no. 115. *Index* 3324.

  1 *hem*: MS. *her*; 6 *knappes which*: MS. *knapp w^t*; 9 *sete*: MS. *sedet.*

232. Bodl. MS. Lat. misc. c. 66 (formerly Capesthorne), f. 93b, col. ii (*c.* 1500). Ed. Robbins, *Sec. Lyr.*, no. 193. *Index* 1344.

  18 *There*: MS. *the*; 24 *ne* not in MS.

233. Bodl. MS. Ashmole 1379, p. 32 (*c.* 1500). Ed. Greene, *Carols*, no. 170; *Selection*, no. 45. *Index* 3525.

  30 *may*: MS. *mayde*. After l. 32, twelve lines omitted.

234. From *The Squyer of Lowe Degré*, 739–854, printed by Wyllyam Copland, *c.* 1560; ed. Joseph Ritson, revised Goldsmid, *Ancient*

English Metrical Romances (Edinburgh, 1886), iii. 160 ff.; W. H. French and C. B. Hale, *Middle English Metrical Romances* (New York, 1930), pp. 744 ff. *Index* 1644.

26 *grehound*: Print *Hrehound*; 51 *non*: Print *nor*.

235. B.M. MS. Harley 7371, f. 80b (*c.* 1500). Ed. *Rel. Ant.* i. 269 f. *Index* 3449.

236. Trinity Coll., Cambridge, MS. R.3.19, f. 208a (*c.* 1500). Ed. *Rel. Ant.* i. 2 f.; F. J. Furnivall, *The Stacions of Rome, &c.*, E.E.T.S. O.S. 25 (1867), pp. 37 ff.; A. S. Cook, *A Literary Middle English Reader* (Boston, 1915), pp. 261 ff. *Index* 2148.

237. Cambridge, U.L. MS. Ee. 1. 12, f. 58b (*c.* 1500). Ed. Greene, *Carols*, no. 3; *Selection*, no. 1. *Index* 4197. A colophon on f. 80a notes the end of the book of hymns and songs compiled by James Ryman, a Franciscan, in 1492.

238. MS. as no. 237, f. 102b. Ed. Greene, *Carols*, no. 154. *Index* 3284.

51 *thought*: MS. *nought*.

239. MS. as no. 237, f. 80b. Ed. Robbins, *Sec. Lyr.*, no. 49. *Index* 3328.

38 Line added in later hand.

240. B.M. MS. Royal 19 B. iv, f. 97b, col. ii (*c.* 1500). Ed. Robbins, *Sec. Lyr.*, no. 48. *Index* 1622.

8 *all*: MS. *ill*.

241. B.M. MS. Add. 14997, f. 39b (*c.* 1500, Welsh). Ed. Robbins, *Sec. Lyr.*, no. 6. *Index* 1608.

The first quatrain is an example of the Welsh *englyn unodl union*, consisting of 30 syllables, distributed 10, 6, 7, 7 over the lines. The rhyme falls not at, but near, the end of the first line: so *Tayliur: plesur*, etc. The word or words following the first rhyme form a metrical phrase with the beginning of line 2, the metre requiring a complex use of alliteration and assonance: e.g. *Dame, deme*. The second quatrain is an example of another Welsh metrical form, *englyn proest*.

242. B.M. MS. Add. 14997, f. 44b (dated in MS. 4 October 1500). Ed. Greene, *Carols*, no. 10; Robbins, *Sec. Lyr.*, no. 3; Greene, *Selection*, no 4. *Index* 2343.

243. Cambridge, U.L., *Here begynneth a lytell geste how the plowman lerned his pater noster*, printed by Wynkyn de Worde, no date. Ed. *Rel. Ant.* i. 43 ff. *Index* 3182.

12 *no*: Print *not*; 15 *Strip*: Print *Srtype*; 17 and 18 transposed in Print; 40 *elders*: Print *olders*; 57 *ten yere*: Print *yeres ten*; 58 *lere*: Print *leren*; 84 *So*: Print *Se*; 96 *more*: Print *mere*.

244. B.M. MS. Harley 4294, f. 81a (*c.* 1500–25). Ed. Greene, *Carols*, no. 396; Robbins, *Sec. Lyr.*, no. 34. *Index* 3782.

245. Canterbury Cathedral, Christ Church Letters, ii. 173 (*c.* 1525). Ed. Greene, *Carols*, no. 443; Robbins, *Sec. Lyr.*, no. 32. *Index* 150.
The MS. leaf is faded and holed, and in places hard to read.
11 *Wherefore*: MS. *where*; 22 MS. *let me loke let me kyss yore karches nocke.*

246. B.M. MS. Add. 5665, f. 53b (*c.* 1500–25), with music. Ed. Greene, *Carols*, p. 451. *Index Suppl.* 1303.3.

247. Balliol Coll., Oxford, MS. 354, f. clxvb (*c.* 1530). Ed. Dyboski, no. 86; Greene, *Carols*, no. 322A; *Selection*, no. 67A. *Index* 1132.

248. Balliol MS. 354, f. clxxvib. Ed. Dyboski, no. 4. Another version, from Bodl. MS. Eng. poet. e. 1, ed. Greene, *Carols*, no. 370; *Selection*, no. 75. *Index* 375.
ll. 16 and 17 transposed in MS.

249. Balliol MS. 354, f. clxxvib. Ed. Dyboski, no. 87; Greene, *Carols*, no. 424A. *Index* 418.

250. Balliol MS. 354, f. clxxviiib. Ed. Dyboski, no. 88; Robbins *Sec. Lyr.*, no. 47. *Index* 1314.
1 *hoy*: MS. *hay.*

251. Balliol MS. 354, f. 223b. Ed. Dyboski, no. 27; Greene, *Carols*, no. 11; Robbins, *Sec. Lyr.*, no. 2; Greene, *Selection*, no. 5. *Index* 1866.

252. Balliol MS. 354, f. 224a. Ed. Dyboski, no. 30; Greene, *Carols*, no. 78; *Selection*, no. 16. *Index* 3460.
47 MS. transposes *skyrte* and *scrype.*

253. Balliol MS. 354, f. 224b. Ed. Dyboski, no. 31; Greene, *Carols*, no. 141; *Selection*, no. 38. *Index* 1198.
21 *fall*: MS. *may fall.*

254. Balliol MS. 354, f. 228a. Ed. Dyboski, no. 42; Greene, *Carols*, no. 132A; Robbins, *Sec. Lyr.*, no. 55; Greene, *Selection*, no. 32. *Index* 3313.

2 MS. *Resonens*; 14 MS. *Exiuit*.

255. Balliol MS. 354, f. 230a. Ed. Dyboski, no. 50; Greene, *Carols*, no. 163. *Index* 4023.

8 *compass*: MS. *on passe*; 18 *John* not in MS.

256. Balliol MS. 354, f. 231a. Ed. Dyboski, no. 57; Greene, *Carols*, no. 389b. *Index* 3820.

21 *or*: MS. *&*.

257. Balliol MS. 354, f. 251a. Ed. Dyboski, no. 98. *Index Suppl.* 1194.5.

2 *juggelere*: MS. *Iuggelege*; 3 *a*: MS. *as*; 16 *had* not in MS.; 18 *bowr*: MS. *towr*; 38 *said she*: MS. *she sai[d]*.

258. Balliol MS. 354, f. 206b. Ed. Dyboski, no. 90; Greene, *Carols*, no. 419A; *Selection*, no. 86. *Index* 1362.

79 *husband is*: MS. *husbondes*. One verse omitted after l. 9, two verses after l. 33, three verses after l. 39, one verse after ll. 51, 81, 87.

259. Balliol MS. 354, f. 251b. Ed. Dyboski, no. 100; Greene, *Carols*, no. 420; Robbins, *Sec. Lyr.*, no. 1. *Index* 1609.

10 not in MS.

260. Balliol MS. 354, f. 251b. Ed. Dyboski, no. 101; Greene, *Carols*, no. 421; Robbins, *Sec. Lyr.*, no. 14; Greene, *Selection*, no. 87. *Index* 903.

261. Balliol MS. 354, f. 252a. Ed. Greene, *Carols*, no. 413; *Selection*, no. 83. *Index* 1399.

4 *stronge*: MS. *strange*; 15 *Milke*: MS. *Milked*.

262. Balliol MS. 354, f. 199a. Ed. Dyboski, no. 78. Also in Trinity Coll., Cambridge, MS. O. 2. 53 [T], f. 67a (*c.* 1500), ed. *Rel. Lyr. XV C.*, no. 149. *Index* 769.

4 *world* (so T): MS. *worldes good*; 24 *the last* (so T): MS. *last*.

263. B.M. MS. Add. 5465, f. 40b (*c.* 1500–25), with music for three voices. Ed. Greene, *Carols*, no. 433; Robbins, *Hist. Poems*, no. 35. *Index* 1327.

The poem refers (l. 33) to Henry VII's marriage to Elizabeth of York (1486); *Our prince* (l. 40) is probably Prince Arthur (d. 1502).

264. Trinity Coll., Cambridge, MS. O. 2. 1, f. 87b (*Liber Eliensis, c.* 1175–1200). Printed N. R. Ker, *Catalogue of MSS. containing Anglo-Saxon* (Oxford, 1957), no. 93. *Index* 2164.

265. B.M. MS. Royal 5 F. vii, f. 85a (*c.* 1200–25), with music. For the author, St. Godrich of Finchale (d. 1170), see *D.N.B.* Ed. J. Zupitza, *Englische Studien*, xi (1888), 401 ff.; Dobson and Harrison, i, no. 1. *Index* 2988.

266. Bodl. MS. Douce 139, f. 5a (*c.* 1250), with music. Ed. *Early Bodl. Music*, ii. 10 f.; *Lyrics XIII C.*, no. 8; Dickins and Wilson, p. 119; *E.M.E. Verse and Prose*, p. 111; Dobson and Harrison, i, no. 8. *Index* 864.

267. Stiftung Preussischer Kulturbesitz, Staatsbibliothek, Berlin-Dahlem, MS. theol. lat. fol. 249 (*c.* 1275): (i) f. 131a, col. ii; (ii) f. 13rb, col. i; (iii) f. 134a, col. i; (iv) f. 134a, col. ii. (i) published by R. H. Robbins, *Anglia*, lxxxiii (1965), 46. *Index Suppl.* 3167.3; 3897.5; 1631.3; 2794.6. Professor H. Gneuss kindly drew our attention to these fragments.

268. St. John's Coll., Cambridge, MS. C. 12, f. 126b, col. ii (*c.* 1250–75). Ed. *Lyrics XIII C.*, no. 56B. *Index* 1977.

269. Bodl. MS. Selden Supra 74, f. 55b, col. ii (*c.* 1275–1300). Ed. *Lyrics XIII C.*, no. 1; *E.M.E. Verse and Prose*, p. 129. *Index* 2320.

270. MS. Bodley 622, f. 116a (*c.* 1325). Ed. *Rel. Ant.* ii. 18. *Index* 91.

271. B.M. MS. Arundel 292, f. 3b (*c.* 1275–1300). Ed. *Lyrics XIII C.*, no. 12B. *Index* 3969.

272. Worcester Cathedral MS. F. 64, f. 8a, col. ii (*c.* 1275–1300). Ed. B. Dickins, *Leeds Studies in English*, iv (1935), 44; *E.M.E. Verse and Prose*, p. 128. *Index* 1142.
    1 *I*: MS. *He.*

273. Worcester Cathedral MS. Q. 50, f. 46a, col. ii (*c.* 1275–1300). Ed. B. Dickins, *Leeds Studies in English*, iv (1935), 44 ff.; *E.M.E. Verse and Prose*, pp. 128 f.; see C. Sisam, *N. & Q.* (1965), 245 f. *Index* 2288.
    10 *wille, wille*: MS. *uyllee.*

274. (i) Trinity Coll., Cambridge, MS. B. 1. 45, f. 41b (*c.* 1275–1300); (ii) Cambridge, U.L. MS. Ii. 3. 8, f. 87a (*c.* 1350). Printed Robbins, *Sec. Lyr.*, p. xxxix. *Index* 445.

(ii) ll. 5 f. are written twice in the MS.; the second, more correct, version is here printed.

275. Trinity Coll., Cambridge, MS. B. 14.39, f. 27b (*c.* 1275–1300). Printed M. R. James, *The Western Manuscripts in the Library of Trinity College, Cambridge* (Cambridge, 1900), i. 441. *Index Suppl.* 1389.5.

276. York Minster MS. xvi. I. 12, f. 219b, col. ii (*c.* 1350), quoted in a law-suit in 1331, reported by Robert de Graystanes, *Historia*, chap. xliv. Ed. J. Raine, *Historiæ Dunelmensis Scriptores Tres*, Surtees Soc. ix (1839), p. 112; Dickins and Wilson, p. 118. *Index Suppl.* 3857.5. Robert de Neville died 1282.

1 *Wela*: MS. *Wel.*

277. Jesus Coll., Oxford, MS. 29, f. 165b, col. i (*c.* 1275). From *The Owl and the Nightingale*, 1325 ff.; ed. J. W. H. Atkins (Cambridge, 1922). *Index* 1384.

278. B.M. MS. Add. 11579, f. 102b (*c.* 1300–25). Printed by J. A. Herbert, *Catalogue of Romances in the Department of Manuscripts in the British Museum* (1910), iii. 39; R. M. Wilson, *Leeds Studies in English*, vi (1937), 44. *Index* 3513.

279. B.M. Arundel 220, f. 303b (*c.* 1300–25). Ed. *Rel. Ant.* ii. 107. *Index* 1851.

280. Huntington Library, San Marino, California, MS. EL 26 C. 9 (Ellesmere), f. 204a (*c.* 1410). From Chaucer, *The Manciple's Tale*, 175–80; ed. Robinson, p. 226. *Index* 4019.

6 *hath he*: MS. *he hath.*

281. B.M. MS. Harley 116, f. 170b (*c.* 1475). *Index* 68.

282. Bodl. MS. Rawlinson B. 171, f. 119a (*c.* 1400). Ed. F. W. D. Brie, *The Brut*, E.E.T.S. o.s. 131 (1906), i. 208. *Index Suppl.* 2039. 3.

283. B.M. MS. Harley 913, f. 6b (*c.* 1300–25). Ed. Heuser (op. cit., no. 61, textual note), pp. 183 f.; Robbins, *Hist. Poems*, no. 56. *Index* 1820.

284. B.M. MS. Harley 2253, f. 59b (*c.* 1340). Ed. H. M. R. Murray, *Erthe upon Erthe*, E.E.T.S. o.s. 141 (1911), no. 1; *Lyrics XIII C.*, no. 73; Brook, no. 1. *Index* 3939.

285. B.M. MS. Cotton Faustina A. v, f. 9a (*c.* 1325). Printed Robbins, *Sec. Lyr.*, p. xxxix. *Index Suppl.* 3859.5.

286. Kilkenny, Episcopal Palace, the Red Book of Ossory, f. 71b (*c.* 1350). Printed Greene, *Carols*, p. xci; Robbins, *Sec. Lyr.*, p. xxxvi. *Index* 1265.

287. Cambridge, U.L. MS. Ii. 3. 8, f. 84a (*c.* 1350). Printed by R. Woolf, *R.E.S.*, n.s. xiii (1962), 4 f. *Index* 1301.
  2 *is* not in MS.

288. Cambridge, U.L. MS. Oo. 7. 32, (roll) recto (*c.* 1325). Ed. *Rel. Lyr. XIV C.*, no. 42. *Index* 3408.
  4 *his*: MS. *þis.*

289. B.M. MS. Harley 7322, f. 163a (*c.* 1375). Ed. F. J. Furnivall, *Political, Religious, and Love Poems*, E.E.T.S. o.s. 15 (1903), pp. 265 f. *Index* 3353. The three beasts are part of a description, in Latin, of Fortune's Wheel.
  13 *But*: MS. *dot.*

290. MS. Harley 7322, f. 162b. Ed. Furnivall, E.E.T.S. o.s. 15, p. 265; Robbins, *Sec. Lyr.*, no. 142. *Index* 2141.

291. B.M. MS. Harley 2316, f. 15a (*c.* 1375–1400). Ed. T. Wright, *Latin Stories*, Percy Soc. viii (1842), p. 84; C. Brown, *A Register of Middle English Religious and Didactic Verse* (1916), i. 329. *Index* 4079.

292. MS. Harley 2316, f. 26a. Ed. *Rel. Ant.* ii. 120. *Index* 1251.
  3 *worldes*: MS. *werdes.*

293. MS. Harley 2316, f. 26a. Ed. *Rel. Ant.* ii. 120; F. A. Patterson, *The Middle English Penitential Lyric* (New York, 1911), p. 139. *Index* 2125.

294. Gonville and Caius Coll., Cambridge, MS. 54, f. 155b (*c.* 1375–1400). Ed. Robbins, *Sec. Lyr.*, no. 149. *Index* 1121.

295. Bodl. MS. Laud misc. 581, f. 30a (*c.* 1400). From William Langland, *Piers Plowman*, B-Text vi. 328–32; ed. W. W. Skeat (Oxford, 1886), i. 224. *Index* 1459.

296. Gonville and Caius Coll., Cambridge, MS. 261, f. 234a (*c.* 1375–1400). Ed. Robbins, *Sec. Lyr.*, no. 60. *Index* 3209.

297. Corpus Christi Coll., Cambridge, MS. 369, f. 46b (*c.* 1400). Ed. T. Wright, *Political Poems and Songs* (Rolls Series, 1859), i. 224; ed. (from MS. Digby 196) Robbins, *Hist. Poems*, no. 19. *Index* 3260.

ll. 5–48 omitted.

298. B.M. MS. Royal 13 E. ix, f. 287a, col. ii (*c.* 1400). Ed. *XIV C. Verse and Prose*, p. 161; Robbins, *Hist. Poems*, no. 18. *Index* 1796. Part of John Ball's Letter to the Peasants of Essex, 1381.

299. St. John's Coll., Oxford, MS. 209, f. 57a (*c.* 1465). Ed. *XIV C. Verse and Prose*, p. 161. *Index* 3306.

2 *fourthe*: MS. *xiiii* (*i.e.* 1391), probably miswritten for *iiii* (*i.e.* 1381).

300. Bodl. MS. Rawlinson D. 328, f. 142b (*c.* 1425–45); the MS. belonged to Walter Pollard (see no. 316, textual note). Ed. S. B. Meech, *M.P.* xxxviii (1940–1), 121. *Index* 3922. Traditional couplet used as the text of John Ball's sermon on Blackheath in 1381.

301. Trinity Coll., Cambridge, MS. O. 2. 45, f. 351a (*c.* 1275). Ed. M. Förster, *Englische Studien*, xxxi (1902), 5. *Index Suppl.* 3927.6.

302. B.M. MS. Cotton Vitellius E. xviii, f. 146b (*c.* 1325). *Index* 3893.

303. B.M. MS. Harley 2253, ff. 125b, col. ii; 126a, col. i (*c.* 1340). Ed. Böddeker, pp. 291; 293. From 'Proverbs of Hending', 87 ff.; 133 ff. *Index* 2078.

14 MS. *er his lyf syþ.*

304. Bodl. MS. Fairfax 16, f. 195b (*c.* 1425–50). Attributed to Chaucer. Ed. Robinson, p. 543. *Index* 3914.

305. MS. Bodley 638, f. 184b (*c.* 1475). From Chaucer's *The House of Fame*, 1783 ff. (iii. 693 ff.); ed. Robinson, p. 299. *Index* 991.

306. MS. as no. 300, f. 141a, 141b. Ed. Meech, *M.P.* xxxviii (1940–1), 119 f. *Index Suppl.* 1793.9, 465.5, 1634.5.

307. Manchester, John Rylands Library, Lat. MS. 394 (*c.* 1450); (i) f. 2a, (ii) f. 3b, (iii) f. 8b, (iv) f. 12a, (v) f. 13a, (vi) f. 16b,

(vii) f. 18b, (viii) f. 22a, (ix) f. 25a. Ed. W. A. Pantin, *Bulletin John Rylands Libr.* xiv (1930), 92 ff. *Index Suppl.* 4176.5, 1635.5, 190.3, 2691.5, 672.3, 3464.5, 3706.2, 4180.6, 3815.5.

308. B.M. MS. Egerton 1995, f. 64b (*c.* 1475). *Index Suppl.* 1014.5.

309. B.M. MS. Lansdowne 762, f. 16b (*c.* 1525). Ed. *Rel. Ant.* i. 233. *Index* 3818.

310. B.M. MS. Harley 2251, f. 80b (*c.* 1475). Ed. *Rel. Lyr. XV C.*, no. 184A. *Index* 3538.

311. MS. Bodley 315, f. 268a, col. i (*c.* 1425–50); copied from the wall of Launceston Priory dining-hall, no longer extant. Ed. R. H. Robbins, *Archiv für das Studium der neueren Sprachen und Literaturen*, 200 (1964), 342. *Index Suppl.* 4135.5.

312. B.M. MS. Sloane 775, f. 56b (*c.* 1475–1500). Ed. *Rel. Ant.* i. 252. Also in Mellish MS., deposited in Nottingham U.L., f. 20a (*c.* 1475); printed N. Davis, *R.E.S.*, N.S. xx (1969), 47. *Index* 1589.
 2 *gentilnesse* (Mellish MS. *gentylnes*): MS. *gentylmen*.

313. St. Paul's Cathedral MS. 8, f. 265b (*c.* 1400). Ed. *Rel. Ant.* i. 166. *Index* 1358. The accompanying Latin shows that the three speakers are the dead man's executors, the second being his wife.

314. B.M. MS. Harley 665, f. 295a (*c.* 1500). Ed. *Rel. Ant.* ii. 179; Robbins, *Sec. Lyr.*, no. 124. *Index* 1207.

315. MS. Bodley 692, f. 2b (*c.* 1450). Printed Robbins, *Sec. Lyr.*, p. xl. *Index* 1798.
 The rest of the poem is badly damaged, because the MS. leaf has crumbled.

316. Bodl. MS. Rawlinson D. 328, f. 162a (*c.* 1450). Walter Pollard of Plymouth was given this MS. 1444–5 (see f. 179a).

317. B.M. MS. Harley 1251, ff. 1a, 184b (*c.* 1450). Ed. *Rel. Ant.* ii. 163; (ii) ed. H. Littlehales, *The Prymer or Lay Folks' Prayer Book*, E.E.T.S. O.S. 109 (1897), ii. xlviii. *Index* 3580, 302.

318. Clare Coll., Cambridge, MS. 5, f. 147a (*c.* 1450). Ed. Robbins, *Sec. Lyr.*, no. 93. *Index* 4104.

319. Trinity Coll., Dublin, MS. 214, f. 1a (*c.* 1450). Ed. Robbins, *Sec. Lyr.*, no. 12. *Index* 1201.

320. B.M. MS. Egerton 1995, f. 60a (*c.* 1475). Ed. Furnivall, E.E.T.S. O.S. 15, p. 63. *Index* 3546.

321. Bodl. MS. Douce 257, f. 99b (*c.* 1450). Ed. Robbins, *Sec. Lyr.*, no. 42. *Index* *63; *Index Suppl.* *3533.5.

1 *an empty c* illegible in MS.; 4 f. *oth* of *another* and *ha* of *harvest* lost from MS., which is damaged by hole.

322. Bodl. MS. Digby 196, f. 20a (*c.* 1475–1500). Ed. Robbins, *Sec. Lyr.*, no. 40. *Index* 1829.

323. Bodl. MS. Eng. poet. e. 1, f. 26a (*c.* 1475–1500). Ed. Robbins, *Sec. Lyr.*, no. 39. *Index* 3919.

324. Trinity Coll., Cambridge, MS. R. 3. 19, f. 207b (*c.* 1500). Ed. Robbins, *Sec. Lyr.*, no. 211. *Index* 1944.

6 *they* not in MS. First five stanzas omitted.

325. B.M. MS. Royal 19 B. iv, f. 98a (*c.* 1500).

326. B. M. MS. Lansdowne 762, f. 16b (*c.* 1525). Ed. *Rel. Ant.* i. 233. For Mellish text (312 note), see N. Davis, loc. cit., 50. *Index* 761.

327. Cambridge, U.L. MS. Ee. 4. 37, f. 113b (*c.* 1500). Ed. Robbins, *Sec. Lyr.*, no. 83. *Index* 1817.

328. Balliol Coll., Oxford, MS. 354, f. clixb (*c.* 1530). Ed. Dyboski, no. 67b. *Index* 4181.

329. Said to have been posted on the doors of St. Paul's by Wyllyam Colyngbourne, who was executed for it in 1485. Recorded by R. Fabyan, *The New Chronicles of England and France* (1516), ed. H. Ellis (London, 1811), p. 672, with the explanation: 'The whiche was ment, that Catisby, Ratclyffe, and the lorde Louell, ruled the lande vnder the kynge, which bare the whyte bore for his conysaunce.' *Index Suppl.* 3318. 7.

330. Magdalene Coll., Cambridge, Maitland Folio MS., p. 215 (*c.* 1575). Ed. W. A. Craigie, *The Maitland Folio Manuscript*, i, S.T.S., N.S. 7 (1919), p. 242.

331. Cambridge, U.L. MS. Ff. 1. 6, f. 53b (*c.* 1475–1500). Ed. Robbins, *Sec. Lyr.*, no. 84. *Index* 2742.

332. MS. Bodley 608, f. 417b (*c.* 1450). Printed by R. H. Robbins, *English Language Notes*, i (1963–4), 2 f. *Index Suppl.* 597.5.

333. Aberystwyth, National Library of Wales, MS. Peniarth 356, p. 296 (*c.* 1475–1500). Ed. R. H. Robbins, *Anglia*, lxxxiii (1965), 46. *Index Suppl.* 3439. 5.

INDEX OF FIRST LINES

First lines of Snatches are not included

INDEX OF FIRST LINES

INDEX OF FIRST LINES

INDEX OF FIRST LINES

INDEX OF FIRST LINES

INDEX OF FIRST LINES

INDEX OF FIRST LINES

INDEX OF FIRST LINES